PC Performance Tuning & Upgrading

Tips & Techniques

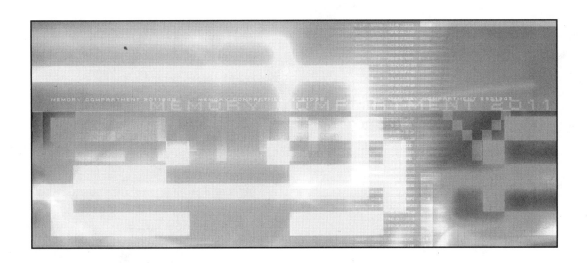

About the Author

Kris Jamsa, Ph.D., MBA, is the author of more than 90 computer books, with cumulative sales of several million copies. Jamsa holds a bachelor's degree in computer science from the United States Air Force Academy; a master's degree in computer science from the University of Nevada, Las Vegas; a Ph.D. in computer science with an emphasis in operating systems from Arizona State University; and an MBA from San Diego State University.

In 1992, Jamsa and his wife, Debbie, founded Jamsa Press, a computer-book publishing company. After expanding the company's presence to 70 countries and 28 languages, Jamsa sold Jamsa Press to a larger publishing house. Today Jamsa is the founder of WirelessLookup.com, a company that puts people and businesses together on the Wireless Web. Jamsa is also very active in analyzing emerging technologies.

Jamsa lives on a ranch in Houston, Texas, with his wife, their three dogs, and six horses. When he is not in front of his PC, Kris is riding and jumping his horse Robin Hood.

PC Performance Tuning & Upgrading

Tips & Techniques

Kris Jamsa

McGraw-Hill/Osborne

New York   Chicago   San Francisco
Lisbon   London   Madrid   Mexico City
Milan   New Delhi   San Juan
Seoul   Singapore   Sydney   Toronto

McGraw-Hill/Osborne
2600 Tenth Street
Berkeley, California 94710
U.S.A.

To arrange bulk purchase discounts for sales promotions, premiums, or fund-raisers, please contact McGraw-Hill/Osborne at the above address. For information on translations or book distributors outside the U.S.A., please see the International Contact Information page immediately following the index of this book.

PC Performance Tuning & Upgrading Tips & Techniques

234567890 CUS CUS 0198765432

ISBN 0-07-219378-6

Publisher	Brandon A. Nordin
Vice President & Associate Publisher	Scott Rogers
Acquisitions Editor	Jim Schachterle
Project Editor	Jennifer Malnick
Acquisitions Coordinator	Timothy Madrid
Technical Editor	Phil Schmauder
Copyeditor	Darren Meiss
Proofreader	Paul Medoff
Indexer	Claire Splan
Computer Designer	Carie Abrew and Jean Butterfield
Illustrator	Richard Coda, Michael Mueller and Lyssa Wald
Series Design	Roberta Steele

This book was composed with Corel VENTURA™ Publisher.

To Mom and Dad, for your constant support, friendship, and love.

Contents at a Glance

Contents

Acknowledgments

I am very proud to be a member of the McGraw-Hill/Osborne team, whose hard work, candor, and selflessness combined to create the new Tips and Techniques series. The result of everyone's efforts is a powerful set of books that puts the reader in a position to instantly solve problems at hand.

In particular, I would like to thank Scott Rogers, Wendy Rinaldi, and Jim Schachterle for the countless hours of discussions and debates over ways we could package strong content in an easy-to-use format that maximized reader productivity. Next, Phil Schmauder, my longtime technical editor and best friend, worked all hours to track down and verify obscure system settings, configure networks and a wide range of operating systems to validate content, and shoot the hundreds of photographs that appear throughout this book.

This book's content benefited from the fact that the copyeditor, Darren Meiss, and the proofer, Paul Medoff, are both "techies." It's pretty cool when a copyeditor or proofer tells you that he fixed a run-on sentence and that his version of Windows supports a hardware switch the user can use to specify a key device setting! Also, I'd like to thank Tim Madrid for his help, support, and sense of humor as we pulled together the nearly one thousand screens, illustrations, and photographs that appear throughout this book.

I want to give special thanks to Jennifer Malnick, the book's project editor, who not only kept the book ahead of schedule, but also made it great fun for everyone involved.

Please take time now to turn to page near the front of the book that lists the Osborne team that brought this book together. As you look through this book's pages, the quality you will encounter is a direct result of everyone's hard work.

Introduction

Users should upgrade their PC for one of two reasons: to add a new capability, such as a CD-ROM or DVD writer, or to improve performance. This book examines the myriad of ways you can upgrade your PC. More importantly, however, this book presents hundreds of operations you can do to improve your system's performance. You will learn ways to determine which PC components are slowing your system down—in other words, you will how to locate the bottlenecks that are stealing your system's processing power.

Each chapter will present ways you can quickly measure your PC's capabilities. You will learn how to determine how much a faster CPU or more RAM would truly impact your system's performance. You will identify behind-the-scenes settings that will fine-tune your modem and network operations. You will learn the role your BIOS and CMOS settings play in your system's operations and ways you can tweak the settings to improve your PC's performance. You will examine disk drive settings, various bus types, video cards, and more. In each case, you will first measure how your device's current settings are impacting performance. Then you will learn hardware and software techniques you can employ to improve the device's operations—for free! Next, you will learn how to determine the impact upgrading the device would have on your system performance and whether or not that upgrade is cost effective. (For example, it does not make sense to spend 50 percent more for a processor that will only improve your system performance by 15 percent.) Finally, if you determine that an upgrade is the correct path to follow, a chapter will provide step-by-step instructions you can follow to quickly and correctly perform the upgrade.

If a faster system is your goal, this book will help you achieve it.

Who Should Read This Book

Across the world, hundreds of millions of computer users work with a PC daily. Despite this, it would be very difficult to find just one user who would not be happier if his or her PC were faster. Most people, for example, want faster Web page downloads or faster printouts. Just about everyone wishes his or her PC did not take so long to start. Regardless of how users work with their PC, faster performance is always welcome.

Unfortunately, by the time users get a new PC home from the store, the PC's hardware is already obsolete. Even if the PC sports a new 2GHz CPU (which will likely make the PC the fastest on the block), the chip manufacturers are already working on new chips with likely double the speed!

Worse yet, as you will learn in later chapters, to maintain compatibility with other devices within the PC, your PC manufacturer has likely reduced the speed at which the new state-of-the-art (and expensive) CPU operates! In other words, your CPU can likely operate faster than the PC manufacturer has configured it to run!

This book will examine hundreds of ways users can improve their PC performance. Best of all, you do not have to be a computer expert or technician to perform the operations. Tips in each chapter present step-by-step instructions every user can perform. Within the books chapters, you will learn:

- How to run benchmark programs to measure the PC's current capabilities

- How to use the PC's CMOS setting and Windows so you can reduce the length of time the PC needs to start

- Whether adding more RAM will improve your system performance—if you normally run multiple programs within Windows

- How your choice of a file system within Windows impacts your system performance and your disk's storage capacity

- Ways you can fine-tune modem and network settings to drive and improve performance

- The differences between various PC buses (such as PCI bus, Universal Serial Bus, and the AGP graphics port) and how your use of each bus impacts your system performance

- Simple operations you can perform within Windows that immediately improve performance

- Ways you can secure your system from hackers and computer viruses

- And much more!

What You Need in Order to Improve Your PC Performance

This book presents a myriad of ways you can improve your PC performance as well as the devices (modems, video cards, networks, and so on) you connect to your PC. Within each chapter, you will find operations you can immediately perform to improve your PC's capabilities. You do not need high-end hardware devices or other electronic equipment to perform the operations. You simply need to spend five to ten minutes performing the tip's step-by-step instructions.

For technicians and power users, this book will examine ways you can use such devices to troubleshoot failed PCs or to better understand the PC's behind-the-scenes operations. If you have not performed such operations before, this book's tips will guide you through the operations.

What This Book Covers

This book contains 18 chapters. Each chapter examines a specific PC device or operating system concept. Within each chapter, you will first learn ways to measure your system performance, followed by operations you can quickly perform to immediately improve your performance, followed by advanced techniques you can use to fine-tune your PC's capabilities.

Chapter 1 — "Measuring PC Performance"   To start, you will learn what PC performance really means, and why upgrading a 100MHz CPU with a 200MHz CPU will not double your system performance. You will also learn how to download a range of benchmark programs that you can run to measure your PC's current capabilities. Later, as you perform the performance tips this book presents, you can use the benchmark programs to measure your performance gains.

Chapter 2 — "Touring the PC System Unit"   You will look inside your PC's chassis and identify the key components you will use in the chapters that follow to upgrade your PC's capabilities. This chapter will also introduce you to various buses on the motherboard and how the PC uses the buses to interact with each device. As you move through the chapter, it will present tips that relate to specific components you can perform in a matter of minutes to improve your system's performance.

Chapter 3 — "Understanding PC Power"   You will take a behind-the-scenes look at electricity and how the PC uses it to power its devices. You will also examine the role surge suppressions and uninterruptible power supplies (UPS) play in protecting your PC assets. In addition, you will examine some powerful capabilities built into most PCs that let you power on your system at a specific time. You might, for example, use the PC's power management capabilities to automatically start your PC each morning at 7:30, so your PC, e-mail, and favorite Web pages are ready waiting for you when you arrive in the office.

Chapter 4 — "The PC Motherboard"   Within the PC system unit, the *motherboard* houses the PC's sensitive electronic chips, such as the CPU, random access memory (RAM), and the BIOS as well as the expansion slots into which users insert cards, such as modems, network interface cards, or high-speed video cards. You will first examine the motherboard's key components, the buses the motherboard uses to let its components interact. Then you will learn how the PC communicates with different hardware devices and how you can resolve electronic conflicts between devices.

Chapter 5 — "Getting the Most from Your Central Processing Unit (CPU)"   The CPU is the PC's workhorse, which executes each of the programs the PC runs. You will take a close look at the operations the CPU performs to run a program and ways chip designers drive higher processing power from new CPUs. Next you will examine the role cache memory plays in improving system performance. Finally, you will learn how you may be able to maximize your CPU's processing capabilities by "overclocking" the CPU or system bus.

Chapter 6 — "Upgrading the PC BIOS"   Each time the PC starts, it uses instructions built in to its Basic Input Output System (BIOS) to run its power on self test (POST) and to load the operating system from disk. The PC also uses the BIOS to help the operating system interact with key hardware devices. In this chapter, you will learn how you may be able to upgrade your BIOS by running a program you can download from your PC manufacturer. You will also examine various BIOS settings you can tweak to fine-tune your system performance.

Chapter 7 — "Getting the Most from Your CMOS Settings"   Within your PC, a special battery-powered memory (which users refer to as the CMOS memory) maintains information about your disk drives and hardware that the BIOS uses later to boot your system. Using a special program that is built in to your PC, called the CMOS setup program, you can view and set various system settings. As you install new hardware, such as a disk drive or RAM, there may be times when you must upgrade the CMOS settings. In addition, most CMOS programs contain several settings you can fine-tune to improve your system's performance.

Chapter 8—"Random Access Memory (RAM)"   Before the CPU can execute a program, the program's instructions and data must reside within the PC's RAM. As programs have become more complex, they have also become larger, which means the programs consume more RAM. If your system has too little RAM, system performance will suffer significantly. In this chapter, you will learn how to monitor your PC's memory use. You will also examine how RAM has evolved (to include such RAM types as fast page mode [FPM], extended data out [EDO] memory, and RAM bus memory) over the years and how that evolution has impacted system performance. Next you will learn how to fine-tune memory settings within Windows to maximize your system's capabilities. Finally, you will learn how to upgrade your PC's RAM and issues you must consider when adding RAM, such as bank size, speed, and socket types.

Chapter 9—"Speeding Up and Troubleshooting System Startup"   If you are like most users, the PC startup process can seem excruciatingly slow. In this chapter you will take a close look at the behind-the-scenes operations your PC performs each time it starts, and steps you can perform to streamline the process. You will also learn how to determine and control which programs your system automatically runs each time it starts. Many users often have programs running they do not need, which needlessly consumes resources (RAM and CPU time) and which prolong the already time-consuming startup process.

Chapter 10—"Operating-System Performance"   To maximize your PC's performance, you must make sure your operating system, which sits between your hardware and the programs you run, is running at its peak performance. Depending on which version of Windows you are running, the steps you can take to "tweak" your operating system's performance will differ. This chapter examines several specific operations—available under most versions of Windows—you can perform to improve your system performance. You will also learn how to use various tools built in to Windows to troubleshoot system conflicts, ensure you are using the most recent device drivers, and resolve potentially conflicting dynamic link library (DLL) files.

Chapter 11—"Understanding Cables and Ports"   When you attach devices to your system, you normally use a cable to connect the device to a port. In this chapter, you will learn how to tell the difference between the hundreds of cable types available for PCs, printers, networks, and other devices. You will also examine characteristics of different cable types (such as twisted-pair, coaxial, and fiber-optic cables) so you can better understand how cable can directly impact your system performance. Finally, this chapter examines serial ports and parallel ports in detail. You will learn that by taking advantage of a ECP or EPP parallel ports, you can reduce the amount of time your PC needs to print a document.

Chapter 12—"PC Buses"   A PC bus is a collection of wires that connect two or more chips or devices. The PC uses several different bus types, such as the system bus that connects the processor, RAM, BIOS, and other key chips in the chipset, as well as the PCI bus that lets the CPU communicate with cards you install into the motherboard's expansion slots. In this chapter, you will examine the PC buses in detail. You will learn how different PC buses operate at different speeds, and the number of wires a bus provides to transfer signals will vary. By the time you finish this chapter, you will understand why you should use one bus type over another to improve performance.

Chapter 13—"Common System Components"   This chapter examines several components that either do not fit well into a different chapter or that do not offer sufficient content to merit chapters of their own. To start, you will examine the keyboard and mouse and operations you can perform to improve keyboard and mouse responsiveness. Next you will examine the PC's sound card and audio capabilities. Then you will examine the steps you must perform to add a video camera or TV receiver to your PC.

Chapter 14—"Modem Operations"   Across the Internet, millions of users (actually, some analysts estimate more than 500 million of them) connect, send, and receive e-mail, "surf" the Web, participate in chat sessions, and more. Most users connect to the Net using a modem, normally using a dial-up account and a 56 Kbs modem. Others connect using a faster cable modem or DSL connection. Still others gain access using a wireless (cellular-based) modem or satellite connection, while the lucky users gain Net access using a high-speed connection, such as a T1 or T3 line. This chapter examines modem operations in detail. You will learn the differences (beyond performance) of each modem connection type. You will also learn how to fine-tune various modem settings to drive faster performance.

Chapter 15—"Network Operations"   Over the past decade, the use of computer networks has exploded. Businesses use networks to let users share resources, such as files, disk space, and printers, to exchange e-mail messages, and more. Further, many home users are finding that using wireless networks lets family members share Internet connections, printers, and more. This chapter examines computer networks in detail. You will learn how network architects design and implement networks and ways in which network administrators improve network performance. You will also learn how to monitor a network's use, down to the packet level, to better understand the processing the network performs. Finally, this chapter examines gigabit Ethernets and how the networks achieve transfer rates of over one billion bits per second.

Chapter 16—"Disk Drives"   The PC stores each of the programs that you run and the documents you create within files that reside on a disk. Disk drives provide you with long-term storage capabilities. Unlike most PC components, a disk drive contains moving parts, which make the drive slower than its electronic components. This chapter examines disk drives in detail. You will learn how the disk stores information as well as the factors that influence a disk's speed and storage capacity. You will also examine steps you can take to improve your disk performance. In addition, you will learn how your choice in file systems can impact your system performance. Finally, you will examine CD-ROM and DVD technologies and how you can use each to retrieve and store large amounts of data.

Chapter 17—"Video Cards and Monitors"   Within the PC, a video card (or, possibly, one or more video chips on the motherboard) produces the images that appear on your monitor's screen. In this chapter, you will examine video cards and monitors in detail. As you will learn, your choice of video cards impacts not only the speed at which your PC can display images, which is critical for multimedia programs and interactive computer games, but it also controls the image resolution (sharpness) and the number of colors the monitor displays. Further, you will understand the role video memory plays in the video-display process. Finally, you will download several video benchmarks to measure your system's current video capabilities.

Chapter 18—"Printer Operations"   Whether you are using a word processor, spreadsheet program, or database application, the last operation you normally perform is to print output. This chapter examines printer operations in detail. You will learn the steps your system performs to print text and graphics and operations you can perform to improve your printer's performance. You will also learn how connecting a printer that supports different ports (such as a parallel port, Universal Serial Bus port, or network interface card) can impact performance. You will also examine ways you can fine-tune the operating system (and your applications) to change printer settings that have a direct impact on speed and quality. Finally, this chapter examines how you can maintain your printer to ensure high-quality output.

How to Read This Book

USE IT   Although this book's chapters build on the information preceding chapters present, I have structured it so that you can turn to any tip and find the information you need. As you scan through a page, watch for the Use It! Icon, which highlights specific steps you can immediately perform to accomplish a task. For example, if you are considering adding more RAM to your PC, you might turn directly to the tip "Monitoring Your System's Memory Use," in Chapter 8, that tells you how to determine whether RAM is currently a bottleneck within your system. Or, if you want to improve the performance of your dial-up modem connection, you might turn to the tip "Tweaking the TCP/IP Max Transfer Unit Setting for a Dial-Up Connection," which appears in Chapter 14. To help you quickly locate the information you need, at the start of each chapter I have included a list of the specific tips that chapter presents. If you need more information on a topic, each chapter provides introductory text that will give you a solid foundation. Throughout this book, you will read about the 80/20 rule, which tells you that you should focus the your upgrading and tuning efforts on the 20 percent of the hardware you use 80 percent of the time. In Chapter 1, you will learn how to use various benchmarks to determine where your PC is performing the major of its work. You will also learn how to identify bottlenecks within your system. After you read Chapter 1, feel free to turn first to the chapters that correspond to hardware you use most, or read your way through the book.

CHAPTER 1

Measuring PC Performance

TIPS IN THIS CHAPTER

If you have used a computer for any length of time, you have quite likely experienced operations that seem to take an unbearably long time, such as downloading files from across the Web, opening an e-mail message that contains a large document attachment, or simply waiting for your system to restart. This book is about ways you can improve your PC's performance—ways you can make those operations you now classify as "unbearably slow" at worst "tolerable." Throughout this book, you will examine hardware and software techniques you can perform to that will improve your system performance. You will also learn techniques that will help you identify the bottlenecks that may be slowing your system down. As you move through this book's chapters, you will examine many behind-the-scenes operations that your hardware and software perform, which will give you a fundamental working knowledge you can use to determine which upgrades will give you the most benefit.

To get you started, this chapter examines performance itself. You will look at ways you can evaluate your system's capabilities and identify your system bottlenecks, and you will run special programs, called *benchmarks*, that evaluate specific aspects of your system, such as your CPU and memory speeds, as well as your system's network bandwidth. This chapter also introduces several key terms you must understand to get the most from the chapters that follow. Throughout this chapter, you will encounter several "rules of thumb" you can apply to determine how much benefit an upgrade will have on your system and whether or not the upgrade is cost-effective.

Understanding Why Computer Systems Keep Getting Faster and Less Expensive

Computer technology (actually any digital technology, for that matter) becomes faster and smaller because of technology improvements (such as smaller and faster chips that emit less heat) and because of human innovation (better hardware and software designs that leverage new technologies). For example, when chip designers created a faster memory chip, the system designers determined that the most cost-effective way to use the new chip was an intermediate cache that sat between the processor (the CPU) and the system's RAM. The designers arrived at their conclusion by running a variety of benchmark programs and then applying their results to economic models that provided the designers with numbers they could use to determine the cost-effective deployment of the new technology. Today, as a result of their efforts, processor performance has increased significantly due to the presence of L1 and L2 caches.

In this chapter, you will perform similar investigations, using your own PC and hardware. You will run benchmarks to determine your system's capabilities (and shortcomings). Then you will examine metrics that may help you determine if an upgrade is cost-effective.

Understanding and, Better Yet, Identifying System Bottlenecks

Computers exist to calculate or retrieve and display data. Within the computer, information flows between the processor and RAM, between RAM and the hard disk, between hardware devices that reside in expansion slots, and so on. Beyond the computer chassis, information flows to devices connected to parallel and serial ports, across modem connections, and across networks.

A *bottleneck* is a location within or outside your computer that slows down the flow of information. Bottlenecks are so named because they eventually force the PC to funnel high-speed data into a slower-speed data stream, as shown in Figure 1-1.

Throughout this book, you will examine ways to identify bottlenecks within your system. In some cases, eliminating a bottleneck is fast, easy, and inexpensive. At other times, you must determine whether eliminating the bottleneck is cost-effective. The tips this book present will provide you with tools to better measure an upgrade's cost-effectiveness.

Where and How to Look for Bottlenecks

This chapter presents several benchmark programs you can run to identify possible bottlenecks within your computer. If you identify a bottleneck, such as your disk drive or RAM, you can then turn to the corresponding chapter in this book to learn how best to eliminate the bottleneck. Each chapter begins with a section that examines a device or topic in detail. Then the chapter presents upgrading and performance solutions specific to that device or topic. If you have never performed a PC upgrade, run a benchmark, or studied the PC's inner workings, relax. Each chapter's text is easy to follow, and each tip gives you the steps you must perform to implement a solution.

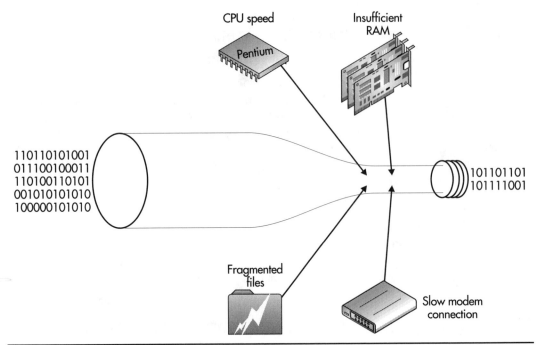

Figure 1.1   Bottlenecks slow the flow of information within or outside of a PC.

Getting a Handle on the Meaning of "Performance"

When users complain about performance, they are normally saying, "My system is slow, why does this take forever?" To computer users, the measure of performance is the speed at which they receive their response.

Likewise, most programmers will state that one program has better performance than another if the computer runs the first program faster than the second.

A network manager, in turn, may measure performance in the amount of data his or her server can receive, process, and send—the network's *throughput*.

Some developers relate performance mathematically to execution time. If you examine the mathematical relationship between performance and execution time, you will find that the two are reciprocals. If you increase performance, for example, you decrease execution time:

```
                          1                                              1
Performance   =   -------------------   Execution Time   =   ----------------
                    Execution Time                              Performance
```

For example, if a program takes 10 seconds to run (the execution time), you calculate the program's performance as follows:

```
                      1
Performance   =   ------------
                      10


              = 0.10
```

If you were to double the system's performance (in this case from 0.10 to 0.20), you would decrease the program's execution time to five seconds, as shown here:

```
                      1
Execution time = -----------
                   Performance


                     1
               = ---------
                     0.2


               = 5
```

Using this simple relationship between performance and execution time, you might think that any time you increase performance, your programs, in turn, will execute faster. Unfortunately, that is not always the case.

▶ **NOTE**

The performance gain from a faster execution of an operation is limited by the fraction of the time the faster execution is in use. —Amdahl's Law

Assume, for example, you purchase a PC with a processor that is 100 percent faster than your current system. From the previous equations, you would estimate that doubling the performance would cut your execution time in half. Unfortunately, you would only experience a 100 percent increase in performance if your CPU is running at 100 percent utilization all the time. Rarely can a user keep his or her CPU active 20 percent of the time. Thus, if you purchase a processor with 100 percent better performance than your existing system, but you only keep that processor active 15 percent of the time, you would only decrease your execution times by 15 percent.

Before you spend 50 percent more money on a processor, you must determine if the processor's benefit is worth the cost. Before you can do that, you must monitor your system's processor use.

You can apply this same concept of measuring your actual use to a disk drive that is 30 percent faster than your current drive or a modem that uses a data compression scheme that increases performance by 25 percent. Before you can measure the effectiveness of a performance increase, you must know how much of the time you will benefit from the increased performance. To start, you would first monitor your disk drive to determine how often your current disk is running at its full capacity. Likewise, to measure the value of a new 25 percent faster modem, you must monitor the amount of data your modem sends and receives on a regular basis before you will know just how much impact increasing performance will make.

Making Sense of Hertz, Megahertz, and Gigahertz

As you examine computer components, you will often encounter speeds expressed in terms of hertz, which corresponds to operations (or cycles) per second. Within the CPU, for example, is a clock that controls all the processor's operations. In general, each time the clock ticks, the CPU performs an instruction. The faster the clock ticks, the more instructions the CPU performs, and hence the faster the CPU. The CPU clock contains a crystal that ticks millions—and in some cases, billions—of times per second. With respect to CPU speed, the term "hertz" corresponds to the number of times the clock ticks per second. A 200 MHz (200 megahertz) CPU, for example, has a clock that ticks 200 million times per second. A 500 MHz CPU has a clock that ticks 500 million times per second. Likewise, a 1 GHz (one gigahertz) CPU has a clock that ticks 1 billion times per second. Someday, systems will have CPUs that execute at terahertz speeds (trillions of times per second).

As you examine other hardware devices throughout this book, you will encounter the term "hertz" used to describe many different operations. For example, to display messages on the screen, a monitor may refresh the screen's colored phosphor elements (which create pixels) 72 times per second (a refresh rate of 72 hertz).

Making Sense of Bytes, Kilobytes, Megabytes, Gigabytes, and Terabytes

Throughout this book, you will examine memory, file, and disk sizes, CD-ROM capacities, and so on. Within the computer, everything operates based on the presence or absence of an electronic signal, which the computer can represent using the values 0 (no signal) and 1 (signal present). The computer, therefore, represents everything using a series of ones and zeros. A Web page you download, for example, that consists of text and graphics, appears as ones and zeros within the computer's memory. When you store a file on disk, the disk stores a sequence of ones and zeros that represent the file's contents. Computer users refer to the ones and zeros as *binary digits*, or *bits*. Depending on the hardware device you are examining, you may find that this book discusses the device in terms of bits, such as a 32- or 64-bit processor, or a 16-, 32-, or 64-bit bus.

To represent a character, such as the letter *A*, for example, the computer must use 8 bits of information. Computer users refer to 8 bits as a *byte*. If a file, for example, contains the contents "Hello, World!" (13 characters), the users would say that the file's size is 13 bytes. Users normally express the size of files and disk drives, as well the amount of memory the PC contains, in terms of bytes.

As an object's size increases, users will typically refer to the device in terms of *kilobytes* (thousands of bytes), *megabytes* (millions of bytes), and *gigabytes* (billions of bytes). Most new disk drives can hold billions of bytes of data (gigabytes of information). As you read through this book's chapters (as well as other PC books and magazines), you will find that they normally use the abbreviation KB for kilobytes, MB for megabytes, and GB for gigabytes. (In the near future, users will purchase hard drives that can store trillions of bytes [terabytes], which users will abbreviate as TB.) Note that the abbreviations capitalize both letters. As you will learn in the next section, a lowercase *b* corresponds to bits (1Mb, for example, means one megabit, not one megabyte [1MB]).

Although for most purposes, thinking of a kilobyte as 1,000 bytes, a megabyte as 1,000,000 bytes, and a gigabyte as 1,000,000,000 bytes works, in actuality, a kilobyte is equal to 1,024 bytes. One megabyte, likewise, is equal to 1,048,576 bytes (1,024×1,024), and one gigabyte is equal to 1,073,741,824 bytes (1,024×1,024×1,024). Normally, you do not need to be this precise. However, knowing this information will sometimes help you understand issues that arise. For example, a few years ago a friend needed to give me a file that contained 1,500,000 bytes. I told him to copy it to a 1.44 MB floppy disk. He said that it would not fit. However, because one megabyte is actually 1,048,576 bytes, a 1.44 MB floppy disk can hold over 1,500,000 bytes.

Pay Attention to Bits Versus Bytes

In the preceding section, you learned that users normally express an object's size in terms of bytes. Throughout this book, you will look at various speeds, such as modem connection speed, network speed, or the transfer rate of a motherboard bus. Normally, users will refer to speeds in terms of bits, not bytes—which often creates a source of confusion. When users refer to network speeds, for example, they will say that a network card supports 10 Mbps (10 megabits per second) or 100 Mbps (100 megabits per second). Within the speeds, note the use of the lowercase *b* to represent bits, as opposed to the uppercase *B* that represents bytes. As you examine device speeds, pay particular attention to whether the speed is expressed in bits or bytes.

Using Benchmarks to Measure Performance

A *benchmark* is a computer program written to measure performance of a specific device. There are benchmarks to measure CPU performance, benchmarks to measure disk drive capabilities, benchmarks to measure video card performance, benchmarks to measure network performance, and more.

The benchmark programs will normally perform a set of operations that are representative of a specific task. For example, one benchmark may measure a system's suitability for business use, another the system's suitability for game development, and another the system's suitability for use as a network server.

After the benchmark runs, it will normally give you values that correspond to your system's capabilities. These values may only become meaningful to you when you compare them to the benchmark results from other systems.

Across the Web, you can find several good sources for benchmark programs. In some cases, the benchmark programs are free, and in others, you must purchase the benchmark (and depending on what you are trying to measure, the benchmarks can become expensive). Remember, benchmarks are programs, and programs that you download from across the Web can contain viruses. As a rule, only download benchmarks from reliable sources and then, only run the benchmark after you have examined it using your virus detection software.

Problems with Benchmarks

Using benchmarks provides you with a way to measure a wide range of system capabilities. Keep in mind that benchmarks are programs that simulate common operations. The operations a benchmark provides and the frequency that the benchmark performs an operation may be much different than how you use your system. Within this chapter's tips, for example, you will learn how to download and run a benchmark that examines your system's video capabilities. The video benchmark will examine many high-end capabilities that you may never perform, unless you are a video game enthusiast or a game developer. Should your system's video capabilities score low, your score may not be a problem, because the benchmark is evaluating operations you don't use. So, as you run the various benchmarks this chapter presents, focus on the operations that better reflect those you perform on a regular basis. Also, as you compare your system's results to others, make sure that you are comparing apples to apples. In other words, make sure that your processor type, installed RAM, operating system version, and so on are the same as the system you are comparing. As you will learn throughout this book, many factors influence system performance. Those same factors influence the results a benchmark may generate.

Using the Windows System Monitor to Identify Bottlenecks and Device Usage

If you are using Windows 9*x*, you should use the Windows System Monitor to look for potential bottlenecks and to measure how much you actually use a device. Using the System Monitor, you can chart usage for memory, disk drives, network connections, and more, as shown in Figure 1-2.

When you feel that your system is running slowly, start the System Monitor to determine potential causes for the slowdown. Also, as you perform different operations throughout the day, you should use the System Monitor to measure your PC's resource use. Should you find, for example, that your PC's RAM is normally 90 percent full, you should consider the benefits of adding more memory.

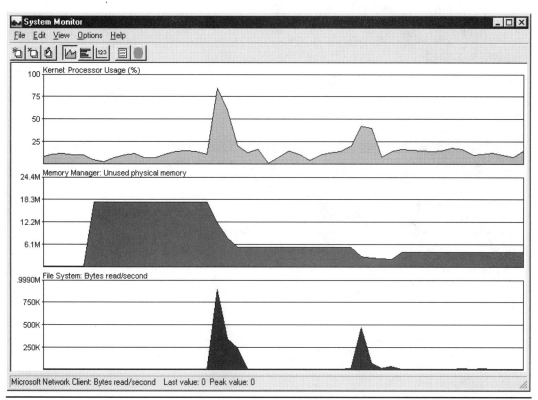

Figure 1.2   Using the System Monitor to examine your system

USE IT To start the System Monitor, perform these steps:

1. Select Start | Programs | Accessories. Windows, in turn, will display the Accessories menu.

2. Within the Accessories menu, select System Tools | System Monitor. Windows will open the System Monitor window.

Within the System Monitor, you can use the Edit menu to add items you want to chart and to stop tracking a specific item. When you select Edit | Add Item, for example, the System Monitor will display the Add Item dialog box, shown in Figure 1-3, that you can use to select the item you want to monitor. When you select an item within the Add Item dialog box, the System Monitor will display a list of subitems you can select. Within the subitem list, you can select one item, or you can select multiple items by holding down the CTRL key as you click each item (you can also hold down the SHIFT key to select a group of successive items). After you select the items you want to track, click OK. Within the System Monitor Add Item dialog box, you can view an explanation of an item by selecting it and then clicking the Explain button.

Using the System Monitor View menu, you can direct the System Monitor to display a line chart, bar chart, or numeric chart. Figure 1-4 illustrates the System Monitor's bar and numeric charts.

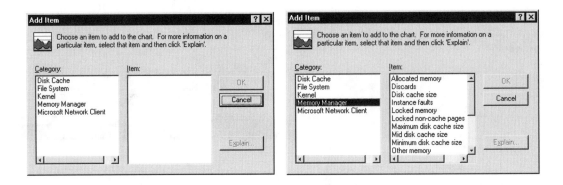

Figure 1.3   Selecting items to track within the System Monitor

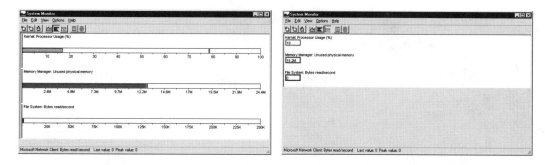

Figure 1.4   Displaying a bar chart and numeric chart of System Monitor data

Using the Windows 2000 Microsoft Management Console to Monitor System Performance

If you are using Windows 2000, you can use the Microsoft Management Console Performance Monitor program to monitor your system performance. The Performance Monitor is an application, which users refer to as a "snap in" that runs within the Microsoft Management Console (MMC). The MMC is a tool you can use, much like a shell, to launch programs that you use to "manage" your system. As you work with Windows 2000, you may encounter many different programs that you can "snap into" the MMC. As it turns out, Windows 2000 includes the Performance Monitor within the MMC. Figure 1-5 illustrates the use of the Performance Monitor within Windows 2000 to measure system performance.

USE IT   To run the Performance Monitor within Windows 2000, perform these steps:

1. Select Start | Settings | Control Panel. Windows 2000 will display the Control Panel window.
2. Within the Control Panel, double-click the Administrative Tools icon. Windows, in turn, will open the Administrative Tools window.
3. Within the Administrative Tools window, double-click the Performance icon. Windows will open the Performance Monitor.
4. Within the Performance Monitor toolbar, click the plus sign (+) icon. Windows will open the Add Counters dialog box.
5. Within the Add Counters dialog box, use the Performance Object pull-down list to select the item you want to monitor and then choose OK.

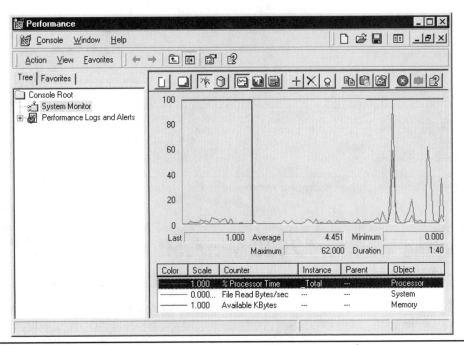

Figure 1.5 Using the MMC Performance Monitor to monitor system performance

Remember that Monitor Programs Skew the Results

When you run programs such as the System Monitor or the MMC, keep in mind that to monitor your system, the monitor programs themselves consume system resources (such as memory and CPU time). As a result, because of their own overhead, the monitor programs may slightly skew the results they display.

USE IT If you are using the Windows System Monitor, you can use the Options menu Chart option to specify the interval (in seconds) for which you want the System Monitor to update your charts. By decreasing the interval, you will increase your system overhead because the System Monitor will run more often. However, if you increase the interval, you may miss the display of key information. When you select Options | Chart, the System Monitor will display the Options dialog box shown in Figure 1-6.

Likewise, within the Windows 2000 Performance Monitor, you can specify the update rate by right-clicking within the monitor chart. Windows, in turn, will display a pop-up menu. Within the menu, select the Properties option. Windows will display the Performance Monitor Properties dialog box General tab, within which you can enter the number of seconds you desire.

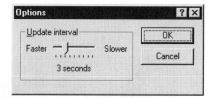

Figure 1.6   Using the Options dialog box to control the System Monitor's charting interval

Monitoring Processor Performance

Within your PC, the CPU is the workhorse that executes the instructions that programs contain. Within the CPU is a clock that controls when the CPU will execute an instruction. As you will learn in Chapter 5, when the CPU executes an instruction, the CPU sends electronic signals to its own integrated circuits, as well as to chips that reside on the motherboard (such as RAM). One set of signals, for example, might direct the memory controller to store a value at a specific location in RAM.

In order for the CPU to successfully complete one instruction, before starting the next instruction (which may send signals to the same locations), the clock within the CPU controls when the CPU ends one instruction and starts the next. In general, the CPU will execute one instruction each time the clock ticks. The clock within a 500 MHz processor, for example, will tick 500,000,000 times per second. The faster the CPU clock, the more instructions the CPU will execute per second.

▶ *FACT*

CPU clock speeds, on average, double nearly every three years.

The CPU clock speed corresponds to the CPU's design and the speed at which signals travel across the CPU's circuitry as well as that of the motherboard. If the clock is too fast, the signals from one instruction might collide with the signals of a previous instruction. If the clock speed is too slow, the system is wasting time that the CPU could be using to execute instructions.

Normally, the CPU will execute one instruction per clock tick. Depending on the instructions, the CPU can sometimes execute two instructions. Some instructions, such as a floating-point operation, might require more than one clock tick.

Although most users consider themselves busy at the computer, most rarely use more than one-tenth of the CPU's processing power—at least for a sustained time. Unfortunately, Windows 9*x* does not provide you with a good way to your to measure your system's CPU use. Within the System Monitor, for example, you can only monitor the amount of time your system spends executing instructions within the operating system's kernel mode.

USE IT   If you are using Windows 9*x*, you may want to download the Active CPU shareware program from www.ntutility.com/freeware.html. As shown in Figure 1-7, the Active CPU program displays your system's current CPU use.

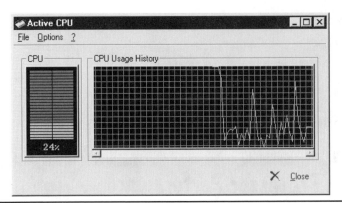

Figure 1.7   Using the Active CPU program to monitor CPU use

If you are using Windows 2000, you can monitor your system's CPU use by performing these steps:

1. Press CTRL-ALT-DEL. Windows 2000 will display the Windows Security dialog box.

2. Within the Windows Security dialog box, select Task Manager. Windows will open the Windows Task Manager dialog box.

3. Within the Windows Task Manager dialog box, select the Performance tab. Windows, in turn, will display your system's current CPU use and physical memory use, as shown in Figure 1-8.

Identifying Memory Bottlenecks

Before the CPU can execute the instructions a program contains, the instructions and the program's data must reside within the computer's *random access memory* (RAM). Windows, as you know, lets you run multiple programs at the same time, each of which must reside in RAM to execute. As you might guess, the more programs you run, the more crowded RAM becomes, eventually to the point that it becomes full.

As you will learn in later chapters, Windows uses a concept known as *virtual memory* to give your system the illusion of having more RAM than it truly does. As RAM becomes crowded, Windows will move one or more programs out of RAM to a special location on your disk (called the *swap file*), in order to free up some RAM. If you later must use one of the "swapped" programs, Windows will move (swap) a different program from RAM to disk and will then move the previously "swapped" program back into RAM so that it can execute.

Although this technique of swapping programs between RAM and the swap file on disk lets you run multiple programs at the same time, the swapping slows down your system performance because you must wait for Windows to move one program out of memory to disk and then to load the second program back into memory from disk. Compared to the fast electronic speed of the computer's RAM, the mechanical hard disk is very slow. By increasing the number of "slow" disk operations your

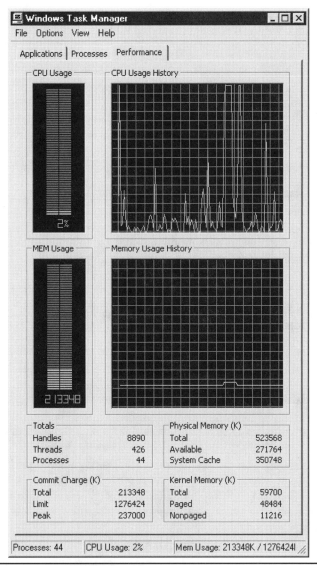

Figure 1.8   Viewing CPU use within the Windows 2000

system must perform, swapping programs to and from RAM slows down your system performance considerably.

When you add RAM to a Windows-based system, you normally reduce the amount of swapping Windows must perform, which, in turn, speeds up your system performance. Most users will tell you that you just cannot have enough RAM—the more RAM, the better your performance. Today, most

PCs ship with 128MB to 256MB of RAM (more RAM storage than large hard disks stored only 10 years ago). Most PCs can hold over 1GB (1 billion bytes) of RAM.

► *FACT*

The density (storage capacity) of RAM chips increases about 60 percent a year—which quadruples chip storage capacity every three years!

USE IT Before you run out and buy more RAM for your system, however, you should use the System Monitor to determine how much physical RAM your system is actually using, as shown in Figure 1-9.

To determine whether RAM is a bottleneck on your system, you should monitor your system's unused physical memory. If your system has very little unused physical memory, Windows will need to swap programs to disk. You might, for example, experiment by loading several additional programs and watching the amount of memory each program consumes. To monitor unused physical memory within the System Monitor, perform these steps:

1. Select Edit | Add Item. Windows, in turn, will display the Add Item dialog box.

2. Within the Add Item dialog box, select Memory Manager. The System Manager will display a list of memory-related items you can chart.

3. Within the memory item list, select Unused Physical Memory and then click OK.

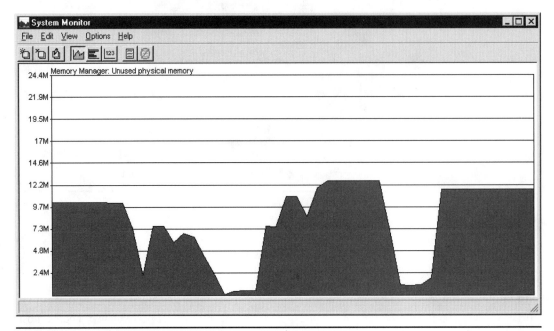

Figure 1.9   Using the System Monitor to measure the system's memory use

If you are using Windows 2000, you can monitor your system's memory use by performing these steps:

1. Press CTRL-ALT-DEL. Windows 2000 will display the Windows Security dialog box.
2. Within the Windows Security dialog box, select Task Manager. Windows will open the Windows Task Manager dialog box.
3. Within the Windows Task Manager dialog box, select the Performance tab. Windows, in turn, will display your system's current CPU use and physical memory use.

In Chapter 8, you will examine several other performance indicators that you can use to determine if memory (or your swap file size) is a system bottleneck.

Measuring Disk Performance

When discussing disks, most users focus on the disk's storage capacity—the amount of information the disk can store. Today, for a few hundred dollars, you can purchase a disk that can store over 100GB.

 FACT

Disk density (the amount of information a disk can store) doubles every three years.

To store information, a disk divides its surface area into circular storage regions called *tracks*. Within each track, the disk further divides the storage area into fixed-sized *sectors*. When a disk drive stores or retrieves data, the disk drive does so one sector at a time.

Unlike the CPU or the computer's random access memory, disk drives are mechanical devices (they have moving parts). As such, disk drives are much slower than the computer's purely electronic components. To read or store information, the disk drive must move its read/write head in and out to the track that contains the desired sector. Within the drive, the disk spins rapidly past the read/write head, normally at 5,400 to 10,000 RPM.

With respect to disk speed, the two factors users consider are *seek time* and *access time*. A disk's seek time measures the speed at which the disk drive can move its read/write head in or out to locate a specific track. A disk's access time specifies the average time it takes the disk to place the information a program requests into RAM. The lower the access time, the faster the disk. Today, common access times range from 3.5 to 12 milliseconds.

Some benchmarks will also provide information about a disk's transfer rate, which specifies the number of bytes the disk can transfer per second.

▶ **FACT**

Because improving upon the mechanical nature of a disk drive's moving parts is difficult, disk access time has increased only about 33 percent over the past 10 years.

As you will learn in Chapter 16, you must consider several different factors in order to determine if your disk is a bottleneck. Sometimes, what will first appear as a disk drive bottleneck is actually a result of *fragmented files* (which are a result of the operating system's file system). If you feel that programs or your data does not load as fast as it used to, the problem may not be your disk speed, but rather, that over time your files have become dispersed across the drive, which means the disk must work harder to read and write the files. The solution for fragmented files is not to replace your disk, but rather, to run a software utility (such as the Windows Defragmenter, which you will learn to do in Chapter 16) that consolidates the file's contents into nearby locations on the disk.

USE IT   Again, before you run out and replace your hard disk, you should monitor your disk's current use. Using the System Monitor, for example, you can view the number of disk read and write operations your system performs per second and the amount of data your system is reading and writing, as shown in Figure 1-10.

To display the disk read and write information within the System Monitor, perform these steps:

1. Select Edit | Add Item. The System Monitor will display the Add Item dialog box.

2. Within the Add Item dialog box, select File System. The System Monitor will display the list of File System options you can monitor.

3. Within the list of options, select the items you want to monitor and then click OK.

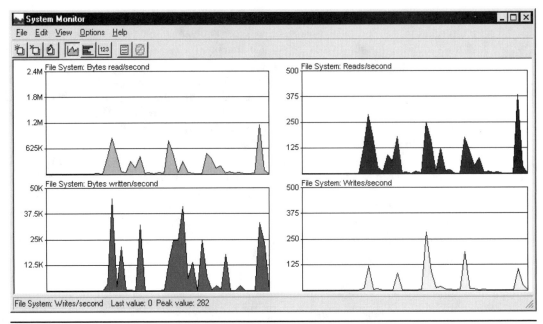

Figure 1.10   Using the System Monitor to view disk read and write information

Within Windows 2000, you can use the Performance Monitor to measure disk performance by performing these steps:

1. Within the Performance Monitor toolbar, click the plus sign (+) icon. Windows will open the Add Counters dialog box.
2. Within the Add Counters dialog box, use the Performance Object pull-down list to select the PhysicalDisk item. The Performance Monitor will display a list of disk properties you can monitor.

To measure your disk's performance, download the WinBench benchmark from the Ziff-Davis testing labs at www.etestinglabs.com/benchmarks/winbench/winbench.asp. The WinBench program provides a wide range of tests, one of which provides you with information regarding your disk.

Keep in mind that throughout this book, you will learn ways to improve your disk performance. Some techniques will require that you adjust file system settings, some may suggest that you change operating system settings, others will modify disk cache attributes, while yet others will examine the disk controller that lets the BIOS interact with the disk drive. So, when you encounter what appears to be a disk bottleneck, the true cause of the problem may lie far beyond the disk itself.

Looking for File System Bottlenecks

As you know, disks store programs and data. To provide a structure (or organization) the disk can use to track information, the operating system provides a *file system*. In general, the file system keeps track of where each file resides on your disk. In Chapter 16, you will examine a variety of file-system issues and steps you can perform to improve the file-system performance, most notably to defragment your disk.

Normally, your first indication of a file-system bottleneck is that your programs or data "seem" to take longer to load than they did in the past. In addition, your disk drive may make more noise than it used to (you can actually hear the disk drive's read/write head moving rapidly in and out between tracks on the disk to locate the file's contents). In such cases, you should immediately defragment your disk. Chapter 16 discusses file fragmentation in detail.

 USE IT   To defragment your disk, perform these steps:

1. Select Start | Programs | Accessories. Windows will display the Accessories submenu.
2. Within the Accessories submenu, select System Tools | Disk Defragmenter. Windows will run the Disk Defragmenter program, which will display the Select Drive dialog box prompting you for the drive you want to defragment.
3. Within the Select Drive dialog box, select the drive you desire and click OK.

Many newer operating systems, such as Windows XP, have an intelligent file system that monitors your programs and data use and then moves the corresponding files on your disk to provide you with faster access. As a rule, if you create, change, and delete many files throughout the day, you should defragment your disk weekly. In Chapter 16, you will learn how to schedule disk defragmentation to run automatically during times when you are not using your PC.

Detecting Network Bottlenecks

Within businesses, schools, and even some homes, users connect PCs within networks to share resources such as files, printers, or a connection to the Internet, or to provide users with access to programs and data that reside on a server.

Network administrators express network performance in terms of *bandwidth* (the amount of data a network can send or receive in a given period of time). Within a small network, several factors influence network performance:

- The number of users and the network data each user requires (which creates the network traffic)
- The speed of the *network interface card* (NIC) that resides within the PC that connects the PC to the network
- The speed at which the cable that connects the PCs within the network can transmit data
- The speed at which the network devices (such as network hubs into which you plug computers that connect to the network) can send and receive data
- The performance of network servers

In general, most NICs and most network cables transmit (and receive) data at 10 Mbps to 100 Mbps (Mbps is an abbreviation for megabits. Do not confuse Mbps with MBps, which would imply mega*bytes* per second, or your network speed calculations will be off by a factor of 8). Newer network cards and cables, however, can now support data rates of 1,000 Mbps (1Gbs, which users refer to as a gigabit Ethernet). Obviously, the faster the network hardware, the greater the network's throughput.

USE IT Again, however, before you decide to upgrade your network, you need to determine that your network is currently a bottleneck. In Chapter 19, you will examine several ways to improve your network performance. If you are a network administrator, you will find that you can use numerous different programs to benchmark your network. If you are interested only in your own computer's network performance, you can use the System Monitor to view a range of network settings, as shown in Figure 1-11.

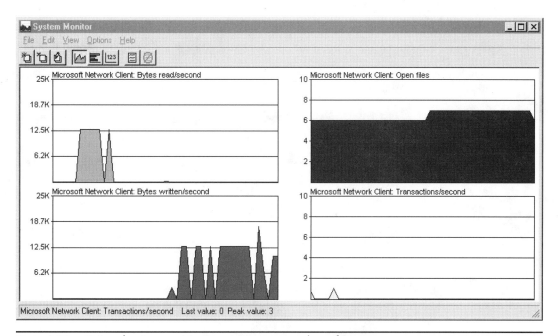

Figure 1.11   Using the System Monitor to view network performance

If you are using Windows 2000, you can use the Performance Monitor to monitor network traffic by performing these steps:

1. Within the Performance Monitor toolbar, click the plus sign (+) icon. Windows will open the Add Counters dialog box.
2. Within the Add Counters dialog box, use the Performance Object pull-down list to select the Network Interface item. The Performance Monitor, in turn, will display a list of network properties you can monitor.

In Chapter 15, you will run the NetBench benchmark, which you can download from www.etestinglabs. com/benchmarks/netbench/netbench.asp. The NetBench benchmark examines your network server capabilities.

If your PC is connected to a network, your system may be configured to let other users access your files or printer. You may, for security reasons, want to disable such file and printer sharing. Further, if you have file and printer sharing enabled, but no one is using it, the software required to support the sharing adds system overhead, which slows your system performance (that's because each time you open a file, Windows must first check if the file is currently open or locked by a network user).

To disable your system's network file sharing support, perform these steps:

1. Select Start | Settings | Control Panel. Windows will open the Control Panel window.

2. Within the Control Panel, double-click the Network icon. Windows will open the Network Properties dialog box, as shown here:

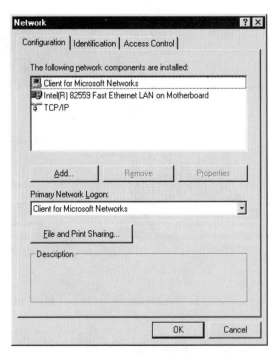

3. Within the Network Properties dialog box, click the File and Print Sharing button. Windows will display the File and Print Sharing dialog box, as shown here:

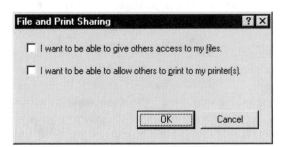

4. Within the File and Print Sharing dialog box, remove the checkmarks (if they are present) from both check boxes and click OK. Within the Network Properties dialog box, click OK to close the dialog box.

Measuring Video Performance

In Chapter 17, you will examine PC video systems in detail. Within that chapter you will learn that with respect to performance, most newer monitors are essentially equal. Monitors differ by their screen size and picture sharpness. The driving factor behind video performance is the video card that resides within your PC.

Depending on the video card type your system uses, the card may contain more *video memory* (a high-speed, dual-ported memory that users refer to as video RAM or VRAM). Before a monitor can display an image, the image must reside in the video card's RAM. Further, the video card may contain a graphics accelerator chip that speeds up various operations.

 To better understand your system's video card capabilities, download and run the 3-D WinBench benchmark, which you can download from www.etestinglabs.com/benchmarks/3dwinbench/3dwinbench.asp. The benchmark will examine a video card's 3-D capabilities, as well as video card capabilities, device driver, and more.

Detecting Printer Bottlenecks

Most printers have a page-per-minute rating that tells you the performance you can expect from the printer. Many high-end laser printers, for example, can print as many as 20 pages per minute. In Chapter 18, you will examine printer operations in detail. You will learn several ways you can improve your printer performance.

When a printer is not performing to its rating, you should first examine how you have connected the printer to your PC. The bottleneck may not be your printer, but rather, the cable you are using to send data to the printer. Normally, if you can connect a printer directly to a network (meaning the printer has its own NIC), you will improve your printer performance. If your printer does not support a network connection, you should try a *universal serial bus* (USB) connection, followed by a parallel connection, and lastly, a serial connection.

As you will learn in Chapter 8, just as adding memory to your PC sometimes increases your system performance, the same is true for printers. Depending on your printer's type, your printer may let you add traditional RAM, which it will use to store incoming print jobs, or your printer may actually have a built-in hard drive to which it stores jobs waiting to print.

 If you are using Windows 2000, you can use the Performance Monitor to monitor some printer operations by performing these steps:

1. Within the Performance Monitor toolbar, click the plus sign (+) icon. Windows will open the Add Counters dialog box.

2. Within the Add Counters dialog box, use the Performance Object pull-down list to select the Printer item. The Performance Monitor, in turn, will display a list of printer properties you can monitor.

One way to improve your printer's performance is to make sure you are using the printer's most recent *device driver*. The device driver is the software that lets Windows communicate with the printer. If your printer is working, you can determine your printer's device driver information by printing a test page by performing these steps:

1. Select Start | Settings | Printers. Windows will display the Printers folders.
2. Within the Printers folder, right-click the printer you desire. Windows will display a pop-up menu.
3. Within the pop-up menu, choose Properties. Windows will display that printer's Properties dialog box.
4. Within the Properties dialog box, click the Print Test Page button.

If your printer is not working, you can use the System Information utility to determine your printer's current device driver information by performing these steps:

1. Select Start | Programs | Accessories. Windows will display the Accessories submenu.
2. Within the Accessories submenu, select System Tools | System Information. Windows will run the System Information utility.
3. Within System Information utility, expand the Component section and select Printer. The System Information utility will display version numbers and dates for the printer drivers you have installed.

Take time now to visit your printer manufacturer's Web site; see if the site offers a more recent driver, and if so, download and install the driver. In later chapters, you will examine Windows settings you can fine-tune to adjust your printer performance, as well as settings you change with respect to your PC's parallel port.

Making Sense of CD-ROM Speeds

Today, when you shop for computers, you will see CD-ROM drive speeds expressed in terms of 48X or 64X, and so on. The bigger the number that appears before the *X*, the faster the CD-ROM. To understand a CD-ROM drive's speed, you must understand that the speeds are expressed in terms of the original single-speed CD-ROM drives that could transfer data at 150 Kbps (bits per second, not bytes per second). A 2X (double speed) CD-ROM drive, therefore, transfers data at 2×150 Kbps, or 300Kbps. Likewise, a 48X drive transfers data at 48×150Kbps, or 7,200 Kbps, or about 7.2 Mbps.

CD-ROM speed is important, because multimedia data (which traditionally resides on a CD-ROM) often resides in very large files. Assume, for example, that you have a multimedia video you want to view at only 100×100 pixels (a very small image). Further assume, for simplicity, the video has been color reduced and requires only 256 colors (which we can represent using a byte). To display the video in full-motion, at 30 frames per second, the CD-ROM drive must transfer the 2.4 Mbps (which would require a 16X CD-ROM drive), as shown here:

```
Frame size = resolution × color bytes
           = 100 × 100 × 1
           = 10,000 bytes


30 frames per second requires 30 × 10,000 bytes
                = 300,000 bytes per second


Data rate in bits = 300,000 bytes/second × 8 bits/byte
                = 2,400,000 bits per second


CD-ROM Drive Speed = 2,400,000 ÷ 150,000
                = 16
```

To reduce data transmission requirements, many multimedia programs will display video at slower frame rates, such as 18 frames per second, as opposed to 30. Further, many programs can take advantage of video compression techniques to reduce each frame's size. Through this example, however, you should realize the role a fast CD-ROM drive plays in your system's multimedia capabilities. In Chapter 16, you will discover ways you can improve your CD-ROM drive's performance.

If you shop for a CD-ROM drive that can also create CDs (users refer to such drives as CDR, writeable drives, CD burners, and so on), you will normally find that the drives write data at a much slower rate than they read data. For example, it is not uncommon to find a drive that can read data at 40X, but only writes data at 16X.

USE IT   To better understand your CD-ROM drive's capabilities, you can order the CD WinBench benchmark program that measures the performance of a CD-ROM drive, the drive's control, device driver, and the system processor. To order the benchmark, visit www.etestinglabs.com/benchmarks/cdwinbench/cdwinbench.asp.

Determining Operating System Bottlenecks

When users compare operating systems, a wide range of issues can influence the system's performance, such as the amount and type of available memory, the disk drive access time, the underlying hardware (CPU type, motherboard type, bus speeds), and so on. When companies such as Microsoft release a new operating system, for which they claim improved performance, the company normally runs benchmarks against several items to analyze how the operating system manages different memory loads, program types, file types and sizes, and so on.

Throughout this book, you will examine ways you can modify operating system settings to improve your system performance. In general, these operations will focus on a specific aspect of the operating system, such as improving file system performance, reducing slow disk operations by modifying cache settings, improving TCP/IP settings for faster dial-in connections, and so on.

Often, users will upgrade to a new operating system only to find that things have appeared to slow down. That may be because the operating system's faster features are not ones you use on a regular basis. As you will recall, a performance upgrade only improves your system performance by the fraction of time you are able to use the upgrade.

USE IT To compare Windows-based systems, users often run the Winstones benchmarks. To start, the Business Winstone benchmark, which you can download from www.etestinglabs.com/benchmarks/bwinstone/bwinstone.asp, examines your system's suitability to run common business software. In addition, users often download and run the Content Creation Winstone benchmark, which measures your system's suitability to run programs such as Photoshop, Premier, Dreamweaver, and so on. You can download the Content Creation Winstone benchmark from www.etestinglabs.com/benchmarks/ccwinstone/ccwinstone.asp.

Restart Your System on a Regular Basis

For years, users have debated over when they should shut down their systems. Many companies, for example, require that users turn off their systems at the end of the day (which conserves electricity). Others will argue, that most PC failures occur when users turn their systems on and therefore, the less often users must restart their systems, the better. (Normally, however, users who experience problems when they first turn on their systems work in offices that experience high temperature differences throughout the day, so the office may be quite cold when users first turn their computers on, which causes the problem.)

Until programmers write programs that don't contain errors (bugs), I recommend that users restart their system at least once a day. When a program experiences an error (crashes), the program often fails to return resources it has allocated from Windows. If the program fails a number of times, or other programs fail, it is possible that Windows has less memory to work with, because the failed programs never gave back the memory they were using. By restarting your system, you give the original system resources back to Windows.

If your company has strict rules about leaving your computers running, make sure you take advantage of the Windows power management capabilities discussed in Chapter 3. Using the power management capabilities, you can direct Windows to place your devices in a state of hibernation when they are not in use, which will reduce their power consumption.

USE IT To monitor the resources available to Windows $9x$, you can run a special program called the Resource Meter, which, as shown in Figure 1-12, tracks various resources Windows needs to run applications. When you find that your system is slowing down, you can use to Resource Meter to determine if Windows has a sufficient number of resources. By viewing the Resource

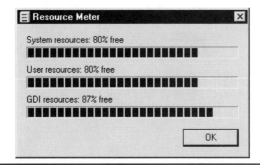

Figure 1.12   Using the Resource Meter to monitor resources available to Windows

Meter's values throughout your day, you will begin to gain an understanding of your system's normal resource use. To run the Resource Meter, perform these steps:

1. Select Start | Programs | Accessories. Windows will display the Accessories submenu.
2. Within the Accessories submenu, select System Tools | Resource Meter. Windows, in turn, will display a dialog box telling you that you can open the resource meter by clicking the Resource Meter icon that will appear on the taskbar. Select OK.
3. Click the Resource Meter icon to display the resources current available for Windows use.

Windows Runs a Myriad of Programs Behind the Scenes

Many users become frustrated by their system performance and state "I'm only running Word," or "I am only running my Web browsers." Or they may say, "I just started my system and Windows is already using a large percentage of its resources." Within the Windows environment, you need to understand that your system may be running a wide range of programs behind the scenes. You may, for example, have a virus-detection program that runs in the background that springs into action each time you open a file or receive a mail message. To determine their active programs, some users press CTRL-ALT-DEL, which displays a list of active programs, as shown in Figure 1-13.

If you are using Windows 2000, after you press CTRL-ALT-DEL, you must then select the Task Manager option. Windows, in turn, will display the Windows Task Manager dialog box, from within which you should select the Processes tab. A worthwhile exercise is to determine what each of the programs that appear in the list actually do. Later in this book, you will learn the various locations Windows starts programs from and how to disable specific programs from starting.

The application list you view by pressing CTRL-ALT-DEL tells only part of the story. Throughout this book, you will learn about key software programs you have available to help you analyze your system use. One of those programs is the System Information utility. As shown in Figure 1-14, you can use the System Information utility to view the programs that are actually running on your system, many of which you may be unaware.

Figure 1.13   Viewing programs within the task list

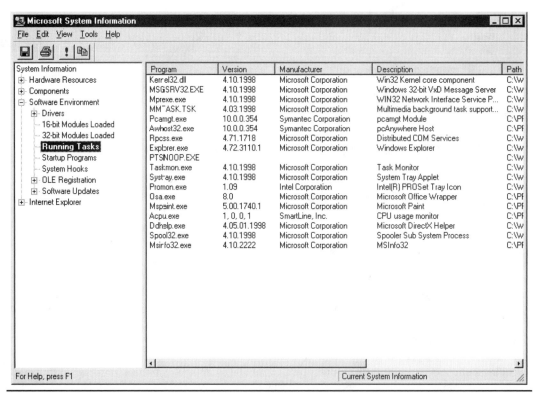

Figure 1.14   Using the System Information tool to view active programs

USE IT   If your system has the System Information tool installed, you can use it to view your system's active programs by performing these steps:

1. Select Start | Programs | Accessories. Windows will display the Accessories submenu.

2. Within the Accessories submenu, select System Tools | System Information. Windows will open the System Information window.

3. Within the System Information window, click the Running Tasks option.

If you are using Windows 2000, you can view the application list by running the System Information application from the System Tools menu by selecting the Software Environment option. The System Information application will then display a list of options from which you can select Running Tasks. In Chapter 9, you will learn how to control which programs Windows automatically runs each time your system starts.

CHAPTER 2

Touring the PC System Unit

TIPS IN THIS CHAPTER

Throughout this book's chapters, you will perform a variety of upgrades that will require you to work inside your PC system unit. In this chapter, you will open your PC chassis and identify the key components. If you are already familiar with the system unit, take time to examine the tips this chapter presents for each component. You may find one or two operations you can perform now that will either improve your system performance or simplify the operations you must perform in the future when you upgrade your system.

Taking a Closer Look at Your PC

In the past, setting up a PC for the first, or even the second time, was an adventure for most users, one that often lead to frustration. Today, most PC manufacturers simplify the PC installation process by color coding cables and ports. At the end of most new cables, you will find a colored connector or colored dot that corresponds to a matching color that appears next to the port into which you should plug the connector. Other manufacturers place small icons next to the port that contain pictures of the device you should attach to the port, as shown in Figure 2-1.

Take time now to examine your PC chassis and to note the ports that you are using and not using. For example, many systems have two serial ports, to which you can connect devices such as a mouse, joystick, or a modem. If you are not using a serial port, you may find that your CMOS setup, discussed in Chapter 7, lets you disable the port's use, which will free the port's resources, such as the interrupt request (IRQ) line, for use by other devices.

In addition to examining your PC ports, look for other items on the back of the PC. For example, as shown in Figure 2-2, many PCs have switches you can use to convert the PC's power expectations from 110V electricity, which is used in the U.S., to 220V electricity, which is used throughout Europe. Chapter 3 examines the PC's power capabilities in detail. If your system does not start, and you do not hear the fan whir after you plug in and power on your PC, the switch that selects your PC's input power type may have been switched inadvertently when the PC was moved or unpacked. Likewise, if you travel with desktop or tower PCs (which may be the case if you attend trade shows abroad), having the ability to switch between power sources in this way may eliminate your need to purchase and travel with a heavy transformer.

▶ *FACT*

Within the U.S., wall outlet current ranges between 110V and 120V. The 115V you see on the power supply in Figure 2-2 is simply an average voltage within this range. Likewise, in Europe, the current will be in the range of 220V to 240V. Again, the voltage 230V shown in Figure 2-2 is an average.

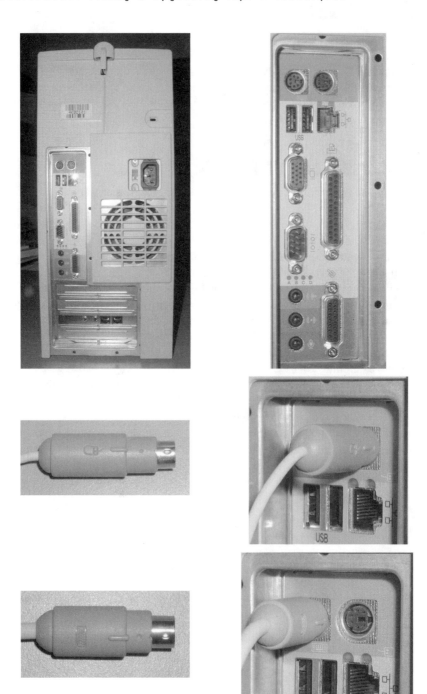

Figure 2.1   Using icons and colors to simplify port and cable connections

 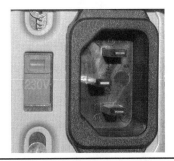

Figure 2.2   Some PCs provide a switch you can use to change their input power types from 110V to 220V.

Some Notes on Cleaning

As you examine your PC, you should take time to clean off any dust that has accumulated on the chassis or its components. The chassis fan (depending on your PC type, you may have a fan built into the power supply and a fan that vents the motherboard) tends to build up considerable dust, which may decrease the fan's effectiveness. The easiest way to clean the fan, as well as components such as your keyboard, is to use an aerosol blower, as shown in Figure 2-3. When you use the blower to blow dust off the fan, aim the blower so that it blows the dust away from, as opposed to back into, the fan. Also, do not hold the blower too close to the fan or device you are cleaning. If you hold the can too close to an object, the aerosol can's cool air can actually freeze water crystals on the object, which may damage sensitive electronic components.

As you examine your system unit, note whether you are providing your system with proper space for the fan to truly vent heat. Often, users push their PCs against a wall or their desks, which prevents the fans from venting efficiently. You might also check the top of your monitor to make sure you have not covered the monitor's vents with books, papers, or other objects.

Figure 2.3   Using canned air to clean system components

Reviewing an "Ergonomic" Setup

As you examine your PC, you should take time to evaluate the ergonomics of your workspace. To reduce wrist, neck, shoulder, and lower-back pains that accompany the long hours you spend at your PC, designers have come up with a variety of ergonomic settings you should take into consideration as you set up your PC:

- Position your monitor away from a window to reduce glare.

- Provide ample workspace lighting. Ideally, orient the lighting to reduce monitor glare and shadows.

- Provide a footrest that you can use to elevate your feet.

- Provide space on your desk where you can rest your wrist as you type. Consider a wrist pad that you place at the front of your keyboard to reduce strain.

- Provide ample desk space to hold papers and other materials such as books.

- The keyboard height from the floor should be in the range 24 to 32 inches.

- Position the monitor 24 to 30 inches from your eyes. The top of the screen should be close to the level of your nose, which causes you to look down slightly at the screen. The top of the monitor screen should tilt slightly away from you.

- Use a chair that provides lumbar and sacrum support.

Preventing Electrostatic Discharge

When you work within your PC chassis, you must take care to reduce the risk of static-electric shock to your PC's sensitive electronic devices. To damage a chip within your PC requires only 50V of electricity (sometimes less). For you to detect a shock from static electricity requires 2,000V!

At a minimum, you should always ground yourself by touching your table or another "grounded" object before you touch your PC. Ideally, you should purchase and wear an electrostatic wristband (like the one shown in Figure 2-4) while you work within the PC system unit. The wristband keeps you grounded, which, in turn, greatly reduces the possible damage to a chip from a static discharge. As you will learn in Chapter 3, a ground simply provides an alternative path that electrons (such as those caused by static) can follow, which leads them away from your sensitive electronics.

▶ *CAUTION*

Do not wear the electrostatic wristband when you work with a power supply. A power supply contains a capacitor than can hold a charge, even when the power supply is not plugged in. Should a short circuit occur, you do not want the wrist band to make you the power supply's source for a ground—such a shock would be very dangerous and possible fatal.

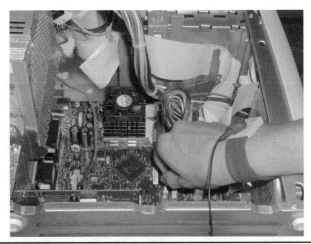

Figure 2.4   Use an electrostatic wristband to create a ground that prevents static electricity from damaging PC components.

Opening Your System Unit

Years ago, to open your system unit, you needed to unscrew several screws that held the system-unit cover in place. Today, however, most system units have one or two latches that you simply press to release the cover. Before you can open your PC, use the Start menu Shutdown option to close Windows. Then, power off your PC. Before you unplug your PC, however, examine the back of the cards that reside in the PC's expansion slots for any active lights. Although your PC's power is off, you may still see small LED lights illuminate on a network or modem card. As you will learn in Chapter 3, most power supplies provide one line that provides constant electricity to the motherboard, even after the PC is powered off. This special "constant power" line bypasses the power supply's primary transformer. In later chapters you will learn that because your PC has constant power available, you can configure your PC to "wake itself up" and power itself on at specific times or when it receives an incoming modem or network connection.

▶ *CAUTION*

Because the constant power source to the motherboard could potentially shock you, or you could inadvertently create a short circuit if you drop a tool or screw onto the motherboard, you should never work inside the system unit while the PC is plugged in.

After you unplug the PC, gently slide open the PC cover, taking care not to catch the cover on the fragile ribbon cables that reside within the PC. Regardless of your PC type, you should now see the components identified in Figure 2-5.

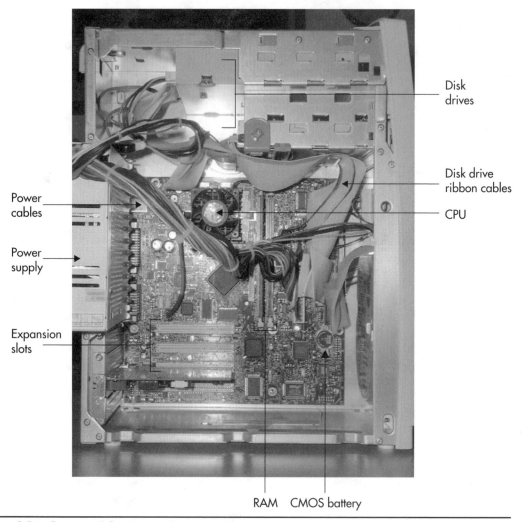

Figure 2.5 Common PC system-unit components.

Getting the Most from Your PC's Power Supply

Within your home or office, the electricity available from a wall outlet is a 110V *alternating current* (110V AC). Within the PC, the sensitive electronic devices use a low-voltage (3V, 5V, or 12V) *direct current* (DC). Alternating current is so named because it changes direction 60 times per second (in other words, it changes direction at a frequency of 60 hertz). Direct current, in contrast, flows only in one direction. The PC power supply converts the high-voltage alternating current into the low-voltage direct current. As shown in Figure 2-6, the power supply provides cables that you connect to the motherboard and disk drives within the system unit to provide their source of power.

As you will learn in Chapter 3, the power supply, depending on its type, normally provides between 300 and 800 watts of power. Depending on your system type, one or more of the power supply cables will plug into the motherboard to power the central processing unit (CPU), random access memory (RAM), and other chips, as well as the cards that reside within the expansion slots. You will connect other cables to floppy, hard disk, and CD-ROM drives. Within each set of power cables are individual cables that provide current at various voltages (normally 3V, 5V, or 12V), as well as cables that provide a ground.

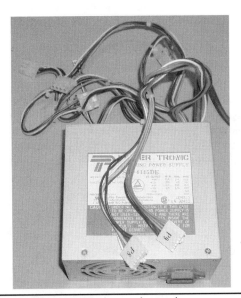

Figure 2.6 The power supply cables provide low-voltage direct current suitable for the motherboard and disk drives.

▶ *CAUTION*

Within the power supply is a device called a capacitor, the purpose of which is to hold a charge. A capacitor can hold a charge long after the power supply is unplugged. Never open a power supply. The electrical shock you may experience from a capacitor could be fatal.

USE IT   In Chapter 3, you will learn how surge suppressors protect your hardware from high-voltage electrical spikes that may travel down the power lines. Likewise, you will learn how an *uninterruptible power supply* (UPS) provides your hardware with 10 to 15 minutes (on average) of battery power should you lose wall-outlet power. If you are not currently using a *surge suppressor* (do not confuse a suppressor with a power strip into which you can plug in multiple devices, but does not provide protection from electrical spikes), you should finish reading this tip and then purchase and install either a surge suppressor or inexpensive UPS.

Because the price of an UPS has dropped considerably over the past few years (you can now purchase an UPS that is very well suited for the home or office for less than $50), you should make the addition of an UPS one of your first PC upgrades. Although an UPS won't improve your PC performance, it may protect your work in progress should you experience a loss of power. Further, most UPSs also provide surge suppression capabilities, which will eliminate your need to purchase a surge suppressor.

When you plug your devices into a surge suppressor (or an UPS that provides surge suppression), you prevent electrical spikes that are traveling down power lines from reaching your hardware. You also must protect your devices from spikes that may travel down phone lines (due to a lightning strike, for example). Most surge suppressors, as shown in Figure 2-7, provide a receptacle into which you can plug the phone cable that comes from the wall outlet. Then you plug in a second phone cable that connects to your PC modem. By running the phone cable through the suppressor in this way, you protect your PC from electrical spikes that travel down phone lines. If you are using a cable modem or other high-speed Internet connection, your Internet service provider (or an electronics store such as Radio Shack) may offer a small device into which you can plug the modem cable that provides similar spike suppression.

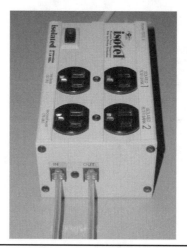

Figure 2.7   To fully protect your system from electrical spikes, you should connect your modem line to a surge suppressor

Identifying Your PC's Expansion Bus Types

In Chapter 4, you will examine in detail the motherboard expansion slots that you use to connect devices (such as a modem or video accelerator card). As you will learn in Chapter 4, when you insert a hardware card into an expansion slot, you must match the card's connector type to the bus type. Take time to note your PC's expansion slots. Most PCs have two or more bus types, as shown in Figure 2-8. The most common expansion bus slot types are 16-bit ISA slots, 32-bit EISA slots, and 64-bit PCI slots. Write down which expansion slots your system is currently using for which devices and which slots are unused. Should you need to purchase and install hardware in the future, you can refer to your notes, as opposed to having to stop and open your PC to determine which slots are available.

USE IT ▶ When you install a hardware card into an expansion slot, a myriad of conflicts may prevent the card from working properly, such as IRQ line conflicts, device-driver problems, and more. When many users encounter problems with a new card, they often fail to start their troubleshooting with the card itself. To begin, you should make sure the card is properly seated within the expansion slot. You may, as shown in Figure 2-9, have to gently rock the card back and forth slightly before the card will slide into place.

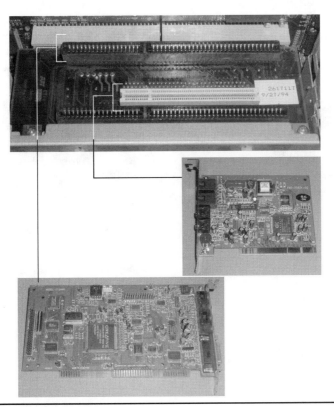

Figure 2.8   PC expansion bus types

Figure 2.9   Gently rock a card within an expansion slot to slide the card into place or to remove the card.

Before you insert a card, you should examine the card's metal connectors for fingerprints or other smudges that may interfere with the connector's ability to establish a proper electrical connection within the socket. To remove a smudge, gently rub the connector with a rubber pencil eraser and use a blower to remove any small particles of rubber that may remain, as shown in Figure 2-10.

Finally, after you properly install the card, take time to secure the small screw that holds the card in place within the expansion slot. Should you later remove the card, make sure that you replace the metal expansion slot cover (see Figure 2-11), which prevents dust from entering the chassis.

Figure 2.10   Using an eraser to clean a card's metal connectors

Securing card   Covering empty slot

Figure 2.11   Securing a card and covering an expansion-slot opening

Identifying Your System's RAM Type and Speed

As you talk with users regarding PC performance, you will normally hear that the easiest way to improve performance is to add more RAM. In Chapter 1, however, you learned ways you can determine your system's current memory use—to determine whether or not memory is a bottleneck within your system. Chapter 8 examines PC memory in detail—you will learn that before you can add more memory to your system, you must know the type of memory your system supports, as well as your current memory speed. Take time to examine your motherboard to locate your system's RAM chips, which should appear similar to those shown in Figure 2-12.

Figure 2.12   RAM chips and RAM slots on the motherboard

> ## NOTE

Memory chips and the memory expansion slots that reside on most motherboards are very fragile. As a rule, the less you touch a memory chip or memory expansion slot, the better. Repairing a broken memory expansion slot may be difficult, and, in some cases, impossible.

USE IT If your memory chips are easy to view, take time now to record any text that is written on the chips. In Chapter 8, you will learn how to decipher the text to determine the chip's storage capacity and speed.

Inventory Your System's Ports

Users connect hardware devices, such as printers, a mouse, and a monitor to various system-unit ports. Normally, most desktop or tower PCs will have the port types shown in Figure 2-13.

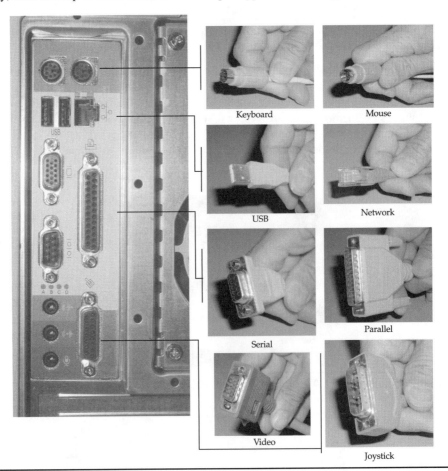

Figure 2.13 Standard PC port types

Ports and cables are categorized by gender: The term "male" describes a port or cable that has pins that plug into another connector, and "female" describes a port or cable with receptacles that receive the pins. When you shop for a cable, you must know the gender that you require. Further, user's classify ports and cables by the number of pins, such as a 9-pin or 25-pin port or cable. Figure 2-14 shows a male cable and female port.

USE IT　The "Reviewing an "Ergonomic" Setup" section earlier in this chapter examined how to set up your PC in a correct ergonomic fashion. Depending on the location of your PC, your desk size, and the number of items on your desk, you may have trouble getting your mouse, keyboard, or even your monitor at the location you desire. The cables that connect the devices to your PC simply may not be long enough to reach. In such cases, you can purchase cable extenders that may provide you with an additional six to eight feet of cable length. To use an extender, you simply plug the extension cable into the PC port and your existing device cable. Normally, you can extend a cable in this way with no adverse effects. If you extend the cable beyond one extension, you may experience power decay across the cable or potential timing programs. Normally, you can extend a printer cable 20 to 30 feet with no problems.

As you examine your system unit, pay attention to the ports you are not currently using. In Chapter 7, you will examine your PC's CMOS setup program. Many newer CMOS setup programs provide the ability to disable a port that is not in use, so you can free the port's resources (IRQs, for example) for other devices to use. Also, should you connect a device to a PC and find that the device does not work, you should check your system's CMOS settings, as described in Chapter 7, to ensure that the port is enabled for use.

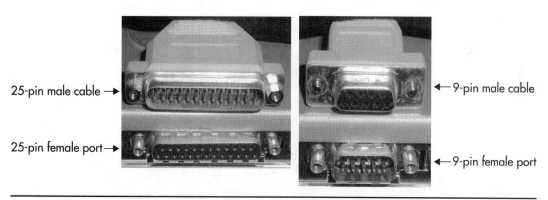

25-pin male cable →

25-pin female port →

← 9-pin male cable

← 9-pin female port

Figure 2.14　Ports and cables are described as male or female, depending on whether the port or cable plugs into another or is plugged into by another.

Locate Your Disk Drives and Note Your Disk Drive Type

In Chapter 16, you will examine disk drives in detail. You will learn how to fine-tune your disk for optimal performance, how to install additional disks, and more. For now, locate your system's floppy drives, hard drives, and CD-ROM drives. Note that each drive has a power cable that connects the drive to the power supply. Also note that each drive has a ribbon cable that connects the drive to a disk controller (the electronics that interact with the PC to control the drive). Take time to note whether your disk connects to the motherboard (which means that your drive is using a disk controller that resides on the motherboard as a chip), or whether your disk drive connects to a card that resides in an expansion slot. If your disk uses a controller that resides in an expansion slot, you may be able to disable the motherboard disk controller with the CMOS setup, as discussed in Chapter 7, to free additional system resources. Further, by disabling a disk controller that you are not using, you may shave a little time off your PC's time- consuming startup process.

USE IT   Depending on your system configuration, your hard disk may be easy to view, as it is in Figure 2-15. If your hard disk is visible, write down information that appears on the hard disk's case, which may specify the disk's type (a number, normally in the range 1 to 47), or the disk's geometry (number of cylinders, heads, and so on). Should the CMOS battery that maintains system configuration fail (as all batteries eventually will), you may need to re-enter the disk drive information within the CMOS setup program. If you take time now to record the drive information, you will not have to open your system unit to retrieve it at some point in the future.

Figure 2.15   A hard disk drive

Locate Your CPU

 Within your PC, the CPU performs the majority of the actual processing that occurs when you use your computer. Chapter 5 examines the CPU in detail and discusses steps you can take to improve your CPU's performance. If you examine your PC's motherboard, you will find that the CPU is the largest single chip. Depending on your CPU type, the CPU's shape and how you insert the CPU into the motherboard will differ. The Pentium III and IV, for example, use an edge connector (much like that of an expansion-slot card) that you insert into the motherboard. Other CPUs, in contrast, have pins that project from the bottom of the chip that you must properly align with a slot on the motherboard. Figure 2-16 illustrates the connectors for two different CPU types.

As you will learn in Chapter 5, as the CPU executes instructions, the electronic signals that pass through it can generate a significant amount of heat. To help dissipate the heat, many CPUs have an attached fan, similar to that shown in Figure 2-17.

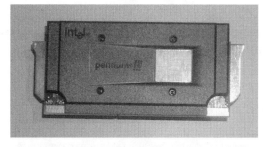

Figure 2.16   Connectors that attach the CPU to the motherboard

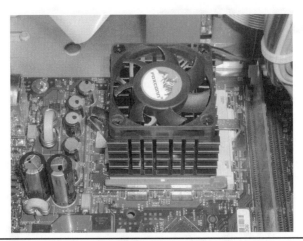

Figure 2.17   Many CPUs use a built-in fan to vent heat generated by the electronics signals that pass through the CPU.

Determine Your Sound's Card Capabilities

Today, most PCs fully support multimedia capabilities by providing a CD-ROM drive, sound card, and speakers. If you examine the expansion slots at the back of your system unit, you should find a sound card similar to that shown in Figure 2-18 that provides ports into which you can plug in speakers, a microphone, and possibly a MIDI (musical instrument digital interface) device, such as an electronic keyboard. (Because the sound card's use has become so common, many PCs provide a built-in sound card that does not consume an expansion slot.) Often, to help you to plug in the correct cables, many sound cards will label its ports with small icons that correspond to a speaker or microphone.

USE IT   When you use programs that generate music or sound, you may actually have three different ways to control the volume. First, within the Windows taskbar, you will often have a small speaker icon that you can click to display a volume control, shown in Figure 2-19.

Figure 2.18   A sound card provides ports for speakers, a microphone, and possibly a MIDI device.

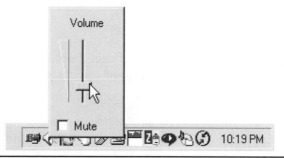

Figure 2.19   Using the taskbar volume-control slider

▶ **NOTE**

If the speaker icon does not appear on your taskbar, you can use the Control Panel's Multimedia Properties dialog box (select Start | Settings | Control Panel and then double-click the Multimedia icon) to control your volume and to place the volume-control slider's icon on the taskbar.

Second, most PC speakers provide volume control knobs you can use to adjust the volume. Third, as shown in Figure 2-20, many sound cards themselves have a volume-control knob. Unfortunately, because the sound card's volume control knob is on the back of the sound card, which is at the back of your PC (which is likely under your desk), getting to the sound card's volume control can be difficult. Because of its ease of access, most users will use the Windows volume-control slider to adjust the volume. Initially, you may want to place the volume-control slider at its middle setting and then use either the speaker's volume-control knobs or the sound card's volume control knob to fine-tune the volume for the mid-level volume. Then, in the future, you can use the Windows volume-control slider to increase or decrease the volume based on your current speaker and sound card setting.

Figure 2.20   Using a sound card volume control and speaker volume control

Fine-Tune Your Monitor Settings

Chapter 17 examines PC video processing, video-card capabilities, and monitor calibration in detail. However, as long as you are touring your PC, you should take a moment and fine-tune your monitor settings.

USE IT To start, make sure you do not have anything sitting on top of your monitor that may block the monitor's vents, which in turn, may prevent the monitor from properly dissipating the heat it generates as is displays images on the screen. Often, users will stack books, magazines, and even stuffed animals on top of the monitor, which cover the monitor vents.

As shown in Figure 2-21, most monitors have a set of controls you can use to align the monitor image (to move the image up, down, left, or right as needed). Depending on your monitor type, the controls may be readily accessible on the front of the monitor, or you may have to open a cover to reveal the controls. You can also use the controls to increase or decrease the monitor image so that the image fits properly within the screen. Finally, you can use the controls to adjust the monitor's intensity, which may make your screen easier to read.

If you are using a notebook PC, refer to your system documentation to see if your notebook provides a way for you to adjust the monitor's intensity. As you might suspect, displaying an image can consume considerable power. If you can decrease your notebook PC's monitor intensity, you may extend its battery life.

▶ *CAUTION*

Like the power supply, a monitor (and television sets, for that matter) may have a capacitor, whose purpose is to maintain a charge. Unfortunately, the capacitor may retain its charge long after you unplug the device. As a rule, never open your monitor case. The electrical shock you may receive from the monitor's electronics could be fatal.

Figure 2.21   Using monitor controls to fine-tune monitor settings

CHAPTER 3

Understanding PC Power

TIPS IN THIS CHAPTER

When you turn on your PC, quite often the first thing you will notice is the whir of the fan built into the PC's power supply. In fact, when you do not hear the fan, you have a good indication that you should check the outlets into which you plugged in your PC, and that you should check the power-cable connection between your power supply and the outlet. In general, when a PC power supply fails, it will fail completely, which makes the problem easy to identify and correct. Unfortunately, there are many times when users will experience intermittent, subtle problems they eventually trace back to the power source (not the power supply, but rather the source of power into which the user has plugged in the power supply). Such problems might include a disk write error, a memory error, or a system reboot.

This chapter first examines electricity and how it works. You will learn how the 110V alternating current (AC) arrives at your wall outlet and why it alternates. You will then learn why the PC does not use alternating current, but rather, uses a lower voltage direct current (DC), and the role the power supply plays in converting the current. This chapter's tips examine a range of power issues, including the role of surge suppressors, the troubleshooting of power problems, and the use of Energy Star devices. You will even learn ways you can use your PC's CMOS settings to automatically awaken PCs minutes before employees arrive at work.

What You Must Know About Power

PCs are electronic devices, and to run, the PC needs power. Although you plug your PC into a wall outlet, much like you would a lamp or hair dryer, internally the PC uses a much different type of power. Lamps, toasters, hair dryers, and other items use the outlet's alternating current that flows through your home or office at 110 volts (110V). The PC's sensitive electronics, in contrast, run on low voltage (less than 12 volts) of direct current.

Alternating current, as you will learn, is so named because is travels in a sine-wave-like pattern, in two directions. Direct current, in contrast, moves only in one direction. The first task of the PC's power supply is to convert the 110V alternating current into a low voltage direct current, as shown in Figure 3-1.

Gaining a Better Understanding of Current, Volts, and Watts

Most of us have likely long forgotten that the meaning of the expression "opposites attract" relates to the physical properties that cause negatively charged electrons to move toward a positive charge.

If, for example, you connect wires to a light bulb, and then to the positive and negative ends of a battery, as shown in Figure 3-2, the negative electrons (energy) will flow across the wire toward the positive charge. In the process, the electrons will provide the energy the light needs to illuminate.

The movement of energy through an object (hopefully a wire) is *current*. When you measure the amount of current that flows across a wire, you specify the amount of current in terms of Amperes, or simply *amps*.

If you examine different batteries, you will find that each battery has a voltage rating, such as 3 volts, 9 volts, and so on. In general, *voltage* represents the difference between the battery's positive and negative poles, as shown in Figure 3-3. A *battery* is really nothing more than a device that separates a negative and positive charge. When you connect a wire between the battery's poles, you provide a path across which the negatively charged electrons can flow to reach the positive charge.

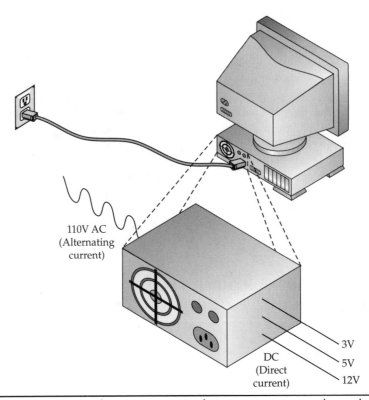

Figure 3.1 The PC's power supply converts 110V alternating current into low voltage direct current.

Voltage is a property of the battery. What happens to the voltage depends on what you attach the battery. In the previous discussion, by attaching the battery's poles to a light bulb, you enabled the flow of energy through the wire (current). The amount of current that will flow through the wire depends on the characteristics of the wire (or other material you attach to the battery, such as your tongue, if you are trying to test a 9-volt battery). All materials (because they too have electrical characteristics), will impede the current's flow. Some materials (*conductors*), such as an insulated copper wire, allow current to flow freely. Other materials (*insulators*), however, are not well suited for energy flow. We measure a material's suitability for electron flow in terms of *resistance*. The higher a material's resistance, the more the material prevents (resists) the flow of energy. Mathematically, you can view the relationship between voltage, current, and resistance as follows:

```
Voltage = Current × Resistance
```

Electricians normally use the letters *V*, *I*, and *R* to represent voltage, current, and resistance:

```
V = I × R
```

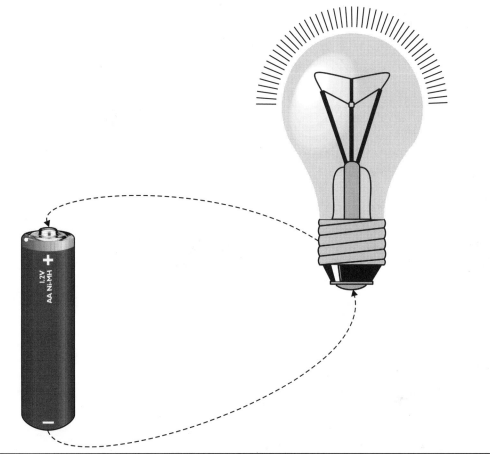

Figure 3.2 Negatively charged electrons flow to a positive charge.

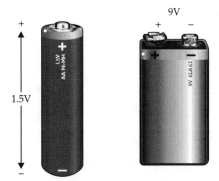

Figure 3.3 Voltage is a measure of the difference between a negative and positive energy source.

If you know a battery's voltage and a material's resistance (when you shop for wire and other materials, you can look up the object's resistance), you can determine the amount of current that will flow across the material by using the following expression:

```
Voltage
---------   =   Current
Resistance
```

Each device within a PC requires a specific current (a specific number of amps), which eventually results in the power supply having to provide a constant number of watts to power the device. Table 3-1 briefly summarizes the power of common devices.

Understanding Where Watts Come Into Play

If you shop for a PC power supply, you will find that power supplies are categorized in terms of watts, not volts or amps. Common PC power supplies provide between 200 and 600 watts. Just as we use the term current to express the measure of energy movement through an object, we use the term *watts* to express power. In general, power describes the number of volts necessary to move energy at a specific current. Mathematically, you can relate power, volts, and current as follows:

```
Power = Volts × Current
```

Here's what we have discussed so far: a device, such as a disk drive, requires a specific number of amps. Depending on the resistance of the wires that bring the current to the device, the voltage

Device	Required Watts
Hard drive	40W
CD-ROM	25W
PCI SCSI controller	60W
Sound card	10W
Network card	60W
CPU fan	2W
Floppy drive	5W
Motherboard	50W
ISA bus	12W
EISA bus	40W
VL-bus	10W
PCI bus	55W
AGP	25–110W

Table 3.1   Power Requirements for Common PC Devices

needed to force the electrons through the resistance will vary. Power is simply a measure of the energy necessary to provide a continuous source of current to a device.

▶ **NOTE**

If you are preparing for your A+ Certification, you may want to use the following modified nursery rhyme to remember the relationship between power, voltage, current, and resistance: "Twinkle twinkle, little star, voltage equals I times R. Up above the world so high, power equals V times I."

Understanding How Batteries Work

Batteries are devices that transform chemical energy into electricity. A battery consist of a positively charged section that is separated by a negatively charged section. When you place the battery within a circuit (connect wires to the battery), the electronics flow from the negative charge to positive charge. In addition to a battery's voltage, which determines the current the battery can flow through the circuit, batteries are measured by their *capacity*, which is the number of electrons the battery can produce over its lifetime.

A battery produces negatively charged electrons through a chemical reaction. Normally, on the negative side of the battery, an acid (hence the term battery acid) oxidizes lead or another element to produce a negative ion. On the positive side, the incoming charges are reduced by a second chemical reaction. Depending on the type and amount of chemical used, the batteries voltage and capacity will differ.

Understanding Alternating Current

Within the walls of your home or office, electricity travels between 110 and 120V (it's not exact). The current flows in both directions over wires following a sinusoidal wave pattern. Within the U.S., the current changes directions (and polarity from 110V to –110V) 60 times per second (60 hertz). In Europe, the current alternates at 50 hertz.

Alternating current is so named, because the electrons move back and forth on the wire, in alternating directions. When wire contains a negative charge at one end and a positive charge at the other end, the electrons in the wire will move away from the negative charge, just as they would in direct current electricity. When the current alternates (the polarity changes), the charges at the ends of the wires suddenly switch and the electrons reverse their direction. Most electric devices, such as your hair dryer or a lamp, require only that the electrons flow. The devices do not care in which direction the electrons flow. The advantage of alternating current over direct current is that alternating current voltages can be transformed into higher or lower voltages. In this way, to send electricity over long distances, such as from the power station to your home, a high voltage alternating current can be used. Then, when the power arrives at your home, a transformer can reduce the voltage to a safer level.

As you know, most power plugs within the U.S. have slots for three prongs, as shown in Figure 3-4. Within the plug, only one of the slots is "hot"—meaning, only one of the slots has alternating current present. The other thin slot connects to a neutral wire (one with no charge), and the third slot provides a safe way to discard lost electrons, called a *ground*.

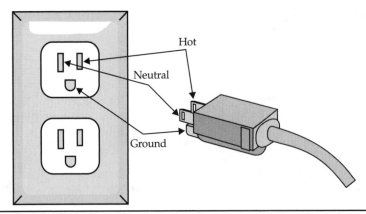

Figure 3.4 Wall outlets provide access to one hot wire, one neutral wire, and one ground wire.

As you have learned, current flows from a negative source to a positive charge. When you plug a device into a wall outlet, the alternating current will flow through the device back to the plug's neutral wire, across which the current flows back to the power company (or substation) that connects the neutral wire to a positive charge, as shown in Figure 3-5. Along the way, the current will flow through a meter that ensures that you are charged for your electrical use.

Within a plug, the ground wire exists to reduce your chance of electrical shock should electrons "leave" the hot wire (through a short circuit possibly caused by two bare wires touching that provide the electrons with a path to a different positive charge). The ground wire actually connects to the earth (hence the name ground), which provides a positive charge that attracts the electrons (hopefully away from you before you experience an electrical shock).

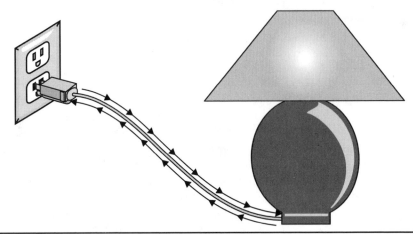

Figure 3.5 Electricity flows through a device and then back to the neutral wire, which returns the electricity a distance to a positive charge.

▶ **NOTE**

Within a wall outlet, the "hot" wire is normally black (in a PC, the black wire is normally used for ground). The wall outlet will normally use a green or bare wire for the ground and a white wire for neutral.

As you will learn next, the fundamental role of the PC's power supply is to convert alternating current to direct current that flows in one direction. In addition, the power supply "steps down" the electricity from 110V to a lower voltage better suited for the PC's sensitive electronics.

Keeping Your Home Safe

Within your house, fuses, circuit breakers, and ground-fault interrupts provide safety against things that can go wrong, such as you dog chewing on a lamp cord, which creates a short circuit, or the nail you use to hang your new family portrait piercing a power cable on the other side of the drywall, creating a short. A *short circuit* is simply a connection that allows electricity to flow across a different source. A short circuit can occur because two bare wires come in contact, or because the water on your hands creates a path from the hot wire to ground when you plug in your hair dryer.

When a power line connects directly to ground, it will send as much electricity as possible through the connection. When this electrical flow occurs, the device or the wire can become very hot, just like the elements within a toaster, and possibly burst into flames. To prevent a device or wire from heating up in this way, many devices contain a fuse that will overheat and burn out quickly, before the wire or device can become too hot. In general, a fuse contains a thin wire that simply burns up when too much current runs through it. Because you must replace fuses each time they burn out, many devices instead use circuit breakers. Rather than burning up, a circuit breaker simply *trips* a switch when the electrical overload occurs. After you identify and correct the cause of the problem, your can reset the breaker.

Also, many electrical circuits within your home (especially those near water faucets) must have a special *ground fault interrupt* (GFI) breaker that trips the circuit to reduce your risk of shock. Like a traditional breaker, when the GFI breaker trips, you can reset the breaker to restore electricity to the circuit after you correct the cause of the original problem.

The PC Power Supply's Role

Beyond the power supply, the current within the PC flows in only one direction. To convert alternating current to direct current, the PC's power supply uses a *rectifier*, which, in general, is a set of special semiconductor devices that let electricity flow in only one direction. Earlier in this chapter, you learned that a conductor is a material that readily allows current to flow. In contrast, an insulator is a material that restricts the flow of current. A *semiconductor* is a material that falls somewhere in-between a conductor and an insulator. Figure 3-6 illustrates a traditional PC power supply. On one side of the power supply, you will find a fan that pulls hot air from the supply (the process of converting currents and voltage within the power supply can generate a significant amount of heat). The power supply also has cables you use to connect to the motherboard and other devices, such as disk drives.

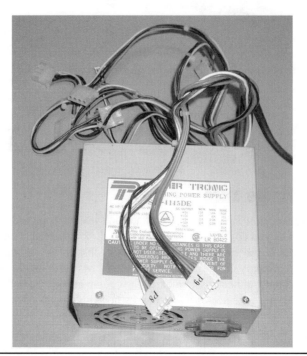

Figure 3.6 A standard PC power supply

After the power supply converts the current to direct current, the power supply distributes power (watts) to the PC components. You will recall that each component needs a specific number of amps (a specific amount of current). Watts simply expresses the amount of power necessary to deliver a continuous supply of current. Although you may hear the expression that "the power supply transforms the 110V into lower voltages (such as 3V, 5V, and 12V). The word "transforms" leads people to think of the power supply as a *transformer*, which is an electrical device that converts one alternating current voltage to another by flowing the current around an iron core to produce an alternating magnetic field. The alternating magnetic field, in turn, creates a current in a second wire that is also wrapped around the same iron core. As you will learn, the PC's power supply does not transform power, per se, but rather, power supplies use a switching technique that essentially switches incoming power off and on rapidly to reduce the incoming electricity to the voltage level it requires. As you might imagine, this rapid switching generates considerable heat, and hence the need for the power supply's internal fan.

In addition, the power supply will "condition" the power that it delivers to the PC components to ensure a higher quality, consistent current. If you are drying your hair, for example, you will not likely notice a temporary increase or decrease in the number of watts your hair dryer receives from the wall outlet. However, within the PC, the electronic components require a constant stream of power. A chip, for example, may consider a slight change in power as a directive to change its contents. Within the power supply is a *capacitor* that stores a charge to ensure that the power supply can continually supply a consistent source of power. If the power from the wall outlet decreases for an instant, the power supply uses some of the charge stored in the capacitor.

The power supply's capacitor can maintain the power it stores long after you unplug your PC. Also, the capacitor maintains enough power to kill you.

▶ *CAUTION*

Never open a power supply. The capacitor within a power supply may maintain a charge for an indefinite period of time—even if the power supply has failed or is unplugged. The energy the capacitor can discharge is sufficient to kill you.

It is important to note that you cannot buy a power supply that provides your PC with too much power. If, for example, you were to install a 200W power supply in your PC, and your PC consumes only 150W, the PC simply will not use the additional 50W. You will not consume the extra power, your electrical bill won't be more than if you had a smaller power supply, and conservationists will not picket your office. Instead, the extra watts will be available should you need them in the future if you add more hardware to your system.

Buy and Install a Surge Suppressor

On most days, current alternates up and down power lines between 110 and 120V. You plug various devices into your wall outlets and everything runs fine. If the power line suffers a slight increase or decrease for a moment, your PC's power supply will likely handle the glitch. However, if a bolt of lightning strikes the power line, the electricity on the line can jump from 110V to several hundred thousand volts!

▶ *FACT*

In 1997, lightning accounted for damage to over 101,000 laptop and desktop computers, amounting in losses over $125,000,000. (Source: Computer Security News.)

Unfortunately, your PC's power supply won't be able to smooth over such a large spike, and the electricity will likely "fry" your power supply and your PC's electronic components.

USE IT To protect your devices from such power spikes, you should install a surge suppressor. Then, you should plug each of your PC devices into the surge suppressor (including your PC, monitor, printer, scanner, and so on). Ideally, your surge suppressor will provide a plug into which you can connect your phone line and modem. That way, should the lightning hit the phone lines, it will not travel down the lines into your PC via the modem. Figure 3-7 illustrates several different surge suppressor types.

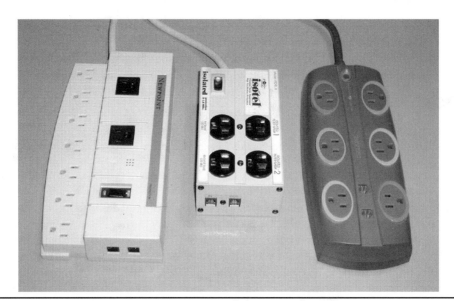

Figure 3.7   Surge suppressors come in a variety of shapes and sizes.

▶ *NOTE*

Based on historical data, lightning is four times more likely to strike a man than a woman.

Surge suppressors work by "clamping down" electrical spikes by breaking (hence the term *breaker*) the path across which the electricity can flow to your devices. Most surge suppressors contain a breaker, which you can reset following a spike by pressing a reset button on the suppressor. If you turn on your PC and nothing happens, try resetting the button on the surge suppressor. An electrical spike may have tripped the suppressor's breaker. Although a surge suppressor can protect your systems from an incoming electrical spike, a suppressor does help you should you encounter a power loss. To protect your PC from a temporary loss of power, you need an uninterruptible power supply (UPS), discussed next.

▶ *NOTE*

You should consider using surge suppressors throughout your home to protect electronic devices such as your television set, VCR, DVD player, and so on. Surge suppressors provide an inexpensive way to protect expensive electronics.

Use an Uninterruptible Power Supply (UPS) to Avoid Temporary Power Loss

An UPS provides you with the protection of a surge suppressor (an UPS will prevent electrical spikes from reaching your PC components) as well as a built-in battery backup that switches on automatically should you lose power. Normally, the battery backup will provide you with up to 15 minutes of power you can use to save your current work and shut down your applications and system normally. Like most hardware devices, the price of an UPS has dropped significantly over the past few years. In fact, today, for less than $50, you can purchase an UPS that should meet your home or office needs.

In general, you can choose from two types of UPS: an *inline* UPS and a *standby* UPS. With an inline UPS, the electricity continuously flows from the wall outlet through the UPS (and thus the battery). Should the power fail, the UPS does not need to switch power sources to get power to your PC. In contrast, in a standby UPS, electricity normally bypasses the battery (although a small amount will flow to the battery to continuously charge the battery). Should the power fail, the standby UPS will switch the PC's source to the battery. Standby UPS are normally less expensive than inline UPS. In general, the price of an UPS will differ, based on factors such as line conditioning and battery life. Figure 3-8 shows a typical PC UPS.

As you have learned, a wall outlet provides alternating current, which the PC's power supply converts to direct current. When an UPS provides power from its battery, the UPS must first convert the battery's direct current to alternating current that the PC's power supply expects. An inline UPS,

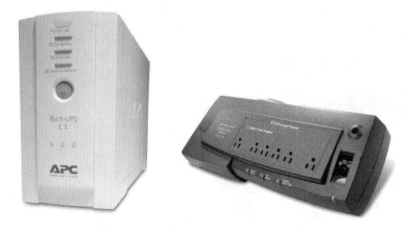

Figure 3.8   An UPS provides protection from temporary power loss.

therefore, is continuously converting the power that flows through the battery back to alternating current, whereas the standby UPS normally flows the alternating current from the wall outlet to the PC's power supply. When the standby UPS switches to battery power, it then must convert the battery's direct current to alternating current. Because the inline UPS must provide the constant conversion from direct current to alternating current, the inline UPS tends to wear out sooner than a standby UPS.

USE IT   Traditionally, because a surge suppressor costs much less than an UPS, users purchase and use a surge suppressor as opposed to an UPS. Today, however, with the price of a suitable UPS at less than $50, you should purchase and install an UPS. You do not need to plug all your devices into an UPS. Instead, you need only ensure that your PC and monitor are connected to the UPS. If you have external disk drives, you should also connect the drives to the UPS. Your goal with an UPS is to prevent lost work and data. If, for example, you do not connect your printer to the UPS, and you lose power, you can normally simply reprint your data at a later time. However, if you lose power to an external disk, you may lose data your operating system had yet to store on the disk.

You should connect the devices you do not attach to your UPS to surge suppressors to protect the devices from an electrical spike.

▶ *NOTE*

Some UPS provide a cable that connects to the PC serial port. Should a power loss occur, the UPS can notify the operating system of the power loss via the serial port connection.

Preventing Electrostatic Discharge (ESD)

If you grew up during the "shag carpet era," you have undoubtedly touched a metal door knob or possibly another person only to experience a shock from static electricity. Normally, the shocks you experience from static create about 2,000 volts. You can, however, destroy a chip or other PC component with less than 50 volts.

Some carpet types tend to create more static than others. If you begin to experience static in your office, you may want to purchase some antistatic carpet freshener that you sprinkle around your carpet on a regular basis. Further, the higher the humidity, the less likely static electricity is to occur. If you cannot move your office to Houston, you may want to monitor the humidity levels within your office and adjust your air conditioner (which removes humidity) accordingly. Some users even suggest adding plants to an office that require water and hence increase the humidity slightly.

USE IT   In Chapter 2, you learned that to reduce the risk of electrostatic discharge from damaging your PC, you should always ground yourself before you open your PC chassis. Further, when you work inside the chassis, you should wear an antistatic wristband, which keeps you grounded. Also, when you remove a card from your PC, you should store the card within an antistatic bag, as shown in Figure 3-9.

Figure 3.9   Storing a card within an antistatic bag reduces the cards risk of ESD damage.

Reducing Electromagnetic Interference

When electricity flows, it generates a magnetic field. Depending on the amount of flowing electricity, the strength of the magnetic field will differ. In the past, users went to great lengths to protect floppy disks from such electromagnetic fields. For example, the electricity that generates the "ringer" within a telephone is sufficient to create a magnetic field that can damage a floppy disk.

Within an office, electromagnetic interfaces can create electrical "noise" that is capable of causing intermittent PC, printer, or network errors. For example, if you run power cables along the ground next to data cables, it is possible that (depending on the quality of the power cables) the current flowing through the power cables can interfere with the data cables.

USE IT   If you begin to experience intermittent errors with your printer or network, make sure you are using shielded cables that reflect or possibly simply absorb the magnetic field. Also, be aware of devices within your office that are capable of producing an electromagnetic field, such as your monitor, a TV, a paper shredder, a pencil sharpener, a refrigerator, and so on. Keep these devices away from your disks and cables. Most PC chassis contain shields (as regulated by the government) that limit the amount of electromagnetic interference the system can generate.

If your office is next to power lines or a power substation, you may hear workers complain about static on their radios or TVs. Such static is caused by *radio frequency interference* (RFI), which is simply electromagnetic interference that falls within the frequency of radio waves. If your office experiences RFI on radios and TVs, make sure you use shielded data cables to connect PC devices.

Troubleshooting Power Supply Problems

Fortunately, when a power supply fails, it will normally do so in its entirety, instead of dispersing inconsistent power levels to PC components which, in turn, create intermittent errors that are very hard to troubleshoot. When a power supply fails, the fan at the back of the power supply will not spin, so you will not hear the fan's constant whir. Before you declare the power supply "dead," make sure that you check the outlet into which you have plugged the power supply to ensure it is working, that you check the reset button on a surge suppressor to ensure that the breaker has not been tripped by an electrical spike, and that you check that the UPS—to which you have hopefully attached your PC—is working.

USE IT Normally, to test the various outlets, you should employ a high-end voltage analyzer, such as a hair dryer or a lamp.

If your PC experiences intermittent errors, such a disk error or a memory error, the cause of your program may be poor power arriving to the wall outlet, which flows along to the power supply. If you are not yet using an UPS, and you suspect poor power quality, installing an inline UPS may solve your problem.

Next, you need to investigate your home or office to determine what other items may be plugged into the same circuit as your PC's wall outlet. It is possible, for example, that the office across the hall has a refrigerator whose ice-maker kicks on and briefly consumes more current than the circuit can provide, or the new high-speed espresso maker in the kitchen shares the same circuit as your PC. Is such cases, you may be able to move your PC to a new outlet, unplug your coworkers refrigerator, or ask an electrician to install a higher amp breaker on the circuit.

What to Look for When Shopping for a New Power Supply

If you must replace your power supply, keep in mind that you may not need more watts than your current power supply provides. However, like most electronic devices, power supply capabilities have increased (new power supplies simply provide more watts) as their costs have decreased.

USE IT As you shop for a power supply, in addition to identifying your power requirements, you should consider the following:

AC voltage range (VAC) specifies the range of incoming voltages that are acceptable to the power supply. Within the U.S., typical ranges include 90V to 135V. Within Europe, the ranges include 180V to 270V. In addition, you should check the power supply's frequency ranges (as you know, within the U.S., electricity alternates at 60 Hz and in Europe at 50 Hz). Most power supplies will support frequencies in the range 47 to 63 Hz.

Voltage Overload Protection specifies the amount by which the power supply's DC current can vary. The lower the value, the better. Normally variations are in the range of 120 to 150 percent.

AC to DC Efficiency measures how well (efficient) the power supply converts alternating current to direct current. During the conversion process, energy is lost. Normal conversion efficiencies range from 65 to 75 percent.

AC Voltage Hold Time specifies the amount of time the power supply will continue to produce direct current after the power supply loses power. The value may range from 2 milliseconds (low quality supply) to 20 milliseconds (a high quality supply).

Mean Time Between Failure (MTBF) estimates the life of the power supply. The MTBF value can be misleading. Often, manufacturers will test 50 to 100 power supplies. If the first power supply fails after 1,000 hours, the MTBF for 50 tested supplies would be 50,000 hours (the sum of all hours tested). No one power supply, however, actually ran for this period of time.

Replacing Your Power Supply

Relatively speaking, power supplies are one of the least expensive PC components and one of the easiest to replace. When you shop for a new power supply, keep in mind that if you don't plan on adding myriad new hardware devices to your PC, you probably do not need a much larger power supply (in terms of watts) than what you are currently using. Unlike adding a turbocharger to a car engine, adding a larger power supply won't make your PC any faster.

Further, you may want to take your existing power supply with you when you shop, so you can ensure that your new power supply will fit in your PC.

USE IT   To replace your power supply, perform these steps:

1. Unplug your system from the wall outlet. You should also unplug your monitor, which connects back to your PC by way of the video card.

2. Ground yourself before you touch the PC chassis.

3. When working with a power supply, you should *not* wear an antistatic bracelet. Should you inadvertently come in contact with the power supply's capacitor, you do not want to provide the ground source for the electrical discharge that will follow.

4. Unscrew or unfasten and remove the chassis lid. If your chassis lid uses screws to hold it in place, put the screws in a safe location, such as an envelope or plastic pill container.

5. Take note of the orientation of the power cables that connect the power supply to the motherboard, disk drives, and other devices. Then disconnect the cables.

6. Remove the screws that connect the power supply to the chassis and gently left the power supply out of the system unit. Place the screws in a safe location, such as a envelope or plastic pill container.

▶ *CAUTION*

Never open a power supply. The capacitor within a power supply may maintain a charge for an indefinite period of time—even if the power supply has failed or is unplugged. The energy the capacitor can discharge is powerful enough to kill you.

7. Place the new power supply within the system unit and replace the screws that attach the power supply to the system unit.

8. Gently plug in the cables from the power supply to the motherboard, disk drives, and other devices.

9. Replace the chassis lid carefully to ensure you do not damage any ribbon cables within the system unit. If necessary, replace the screws that hold the chassis lid in place.

10. Plug in the power supply to the wall outlet (or surge suppressor or UPS) and then turn on your PC's power.

Cleaning the Power Supply Fan

As discussed, as the power supply converts alternating current to direct current, and 110 volts to voltage more suitable for the PC's electronic devices, the power supply generates considerable heat. To help reduce the heat, the power supply has a built-in fan. Many users, in an effort to move their PC out of the way, often back the fan up to a wall, which reduces the fan's effectiveness. Ideally, the fan should have space into which it can send the hot air the power supply creates. Over time, the fan's blade will collect the majority of dust that is anywhere near your PC. When the fan blades become dusty, the fan can vent less hot hair.

USE IT   To clean the power supply fan, perform these steps:

1. Turn off your PC and unplug the power supply.

2. If you can dust the fan blades with a cloth, do so. Otherwise, you may need to may need to purchase a small air canister you can use to blow the dust off the fan. If you use a canister, try to blow the dust away from the fan, as opposed to back into it.

3. Plug your power supply back in and then power on your PC.

Using a Multimeter to Measure Amps, Volts, and Continuity

In the past, "techies" made extensive use of voltometers to measure voltage to a device. If a device did not seem to be working properly, techies (who apparently didn't own hair dryers) could use the voltmeters to troubleshoot the electrical problem. Today, voltometers have been replace by multimeters, which you can use to measure volts, amps, resistance, and continuity (which lets you determine if a connection exists between two objects—you might use continuity, for example, to determine if a wire within a cable is broken). Depending on the amount of money you spend, you can buy a high-end multimeter with a digital display for less than a $100, or a low-end analog multimeter for about $20. Figure 3-10 illustrates a multimeter device.

USE IT   Although a multimeter can provide you with a tremendous amount of information that you can use to troubleshoot power problems, misuse of the multimeter can quickly separate the trained electricians from the "electrical wannabes." If you use the multimeter incorrectly, you can shock yourself, potentially fatally. And, unfortunately, it's easy to make a simply mistake by having the multimeter on the wrong setting for the measurement you plan to take. Ideally, you should find an apprentice who will operate the multimeter as you provide expert guidance. If that is not possible, double-check your meter's systems before you take a measurement. Also, carefully read the documentation that accompanied your device.

In general, before you use a multimeter, you must first tell the device what you are measuring (voltage, current, resistance, or continuity). You must also specify if the current is alternating or direct current, as well as the input range (such as 0 to 15V within the PC or 100 to 120V from a wall outlet).

Most multimeters have two probes, one red and one black. To measure the voltage of a battery, for example, you attach red probe to the positive source and the black probe to the negative source. To measure voltage within your PC, you attach the red probe to the voltage source and black probe to the ground (within the PC, the ground is normally a black cable, so you are connecting black to black).

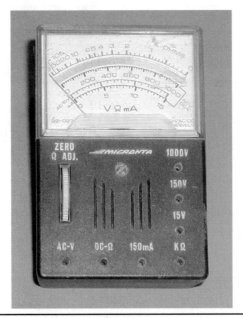

Figure 3.10   A multimeter device measures voltage, current, resistance, and continuity.

Taking a Closer Look at Power Supply Cables

If your Christmas stocking contained a multimeter, you are likely anxious to use the device to measure something. If you are using an AT power supply, you will find that power supply has two connectors, labeled P8 and P9, that connect the power supply to the motherboard.

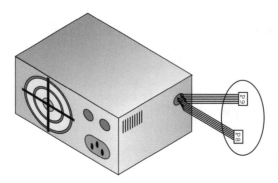

The P8 and P9 connectors each contain six leads. Table 3-2 briefly describes each lead's use.

Most motherboard power connectors contain a "power good" lead. The power supply uses this lead to notify the motherboard that it is warmed up and is providing quality power. Normally, it takes the power supply about one-tenth of one second before it can deliver stable power to the PC. The PC

Connector	Lead	Range	Color
P8	1	Power good	Orange
	2	0 or +5V	Red
	3	+12V	Yellow
	4	−12V	Blue
	5	Ground	Black
	6	Ground	Black
P9	7	Ground	Black
	8	Ground	Black
	9	−5V	White
	10	+5V	Red
	11	+5V	Red
	12	+5V	Red

Table 3.2   Summary of the Leads in the P8 and P9 Connectors on an AT Power Supply

will not begin its operations until the "power good" lead has a signal. The line will maintain a signal until the PC powers off.

If you are using an ATX power supply, you will have only one plug, that connects the power supply to the motherboard, which uses 20 leads. Table 3-3 briefly describes the ATX power leads.

Within the ATX power supply, lead 9 (the purple lead) normally remains active, providing +5V of power even when the power supply is off. Using this lead, the motherboard can provide power to devices, such as a network card, that will might awaken the PC based on an incoming connect. Lead 14, (the green lead) in contrast, lets the motherboard direct the power supply to turn itself on.

Your power supply will also have connectors that you will connect to disk drives and other devices. These devices have four leads, as described in Table 3-4.

Lead	Range	Color
1	+3.3V	Orange
2	+3.3V	Orange
3	Ground	Black
4	+5V	Red
5	Ground	Black
6	+5V	Red
7	Ground	Black
8	Power good	Gray
9	+5V	Purple
10	+12V	Yellow
11	+3.3V	Orange
12	−12V	Blue
13	Ground	Black
14	Power supply on	Green
15	Ground	Black
16	Ground	Black
17	Ground	Black
18	−5V	White
19	+5V	Red
20	+5V	Red

Table 3.3   Summary of the Leads on the ATX Power Supply Motherboard Connector

Lead	Range	Color
1	+12V	Yellow
2	Ground	Black
3	Ground	Black
4	+5V	Red

Table 3.4   Summary of Standard Power Supply Leads

▶ *NOTE*

Within a wall outlet, the black wire normally corresponds to the hot wire; within a PC, black normally corresponds to ground.

USE IT   To use your multimeter to measure voltage, first make sure you select a voltage measure on your multimeter (normally using a dial). Depending on your multimeter type, you may be able to select between a high voltage source (more than110V) and a low voltage source (less than 15V). By selecting a low voltage source for your PC components, you will get a more accurate measurement. If you select a low voltage source and then test your wall outlet, you will likely damage your multimeter. Then, connect your multimeter's red probe to the voltage source and the black probe to ground (which will also be black). If you find that your system's voltages do not match those shown here, your problem may be your power supply or your electrical outlet. You may want to move the PC to a different outlet and retest the voltages.

Splitting a Power Supply Cable

Normally a power supply provides a cable or cables you connect to the motherboard and then two or more cables you can connect to the disk drives. If you run out of power plugs within your PC, you can purchase a *power cable splitter*, which splits one plug into two.

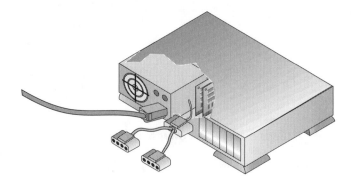

USE IT   Normally, splitting a power cable in this way does not impact the power that arrives to the device. If, however, you are concerned that splitting the cable may not provide a sufficient amount of current to each device, you might choose to connect a device that requires high amps within a device that requires low amps, or you might connect two devices that you normally do not use at the same time. In general, however, you will not experience a problem with you split a power cable and connect two devices.

Understanding Notebook Battery Power

Within a notebook computer, the battery provides the PC with a constant source of direct current. Depending on the notebook PC's components, the amount of power the PC consumes, and hence the notebook's PC's battery life, will vary. To extend your notebook's battery life, many notebook computers let you select different modes of operations. For example, you may be able to reduce your notebook's power consumption by running your notebook at a lower level of performance. Depending on your notebook type, the settings you can adjust may vary. Normally, you will access the settings from within the Control Panel Power Management icon.

USE IT   If you examine Table 3-1, you will find that different devices consume different amounts of power. To extend your notebook PC's battery life, you should minimize your use of devices such as the CD-ROM drive (or a DVD drive). Many travelers, for example, like to attach headphones to their notebook PCs and then use their CD-ROM drives to play audio CDs as they work. The CD-ROM drive, unfortunately, consumes significant power. Also, if your notebook lets you turn down your monitor's intensity, turn it down. Doing so may reduce power consumption.

▶ *NOTE*

Performing a cold boot—turning on your computer's power to start your system—consumes five times the power needed to resume from the suspend mode.

Many notebook computers let you temporarily suspend their operations (essentially letting the PC hibernate) as opposed to shutting down and later restarting Windows. If you are only going to take a few minute break (such as the time from taxi to takeoff), you should consider suspending your PC's operations as opposed to shutting down and restarting. Within the Windows Power Management Properties dialog box, you can normally direct Windows to add a Suspend option to your Start menu that you can select to place your laptop into the low power consumption suspend mode. Later, to resume operations, you simply power on your system as you normally would.

Getting the Most from Notebook PC Batteries

Notebook computers, depending on their age, use either *nickel cadmium* (NiCad), *nickel metal hydride* (NiMH), or *lithium ion* (Li-Ion) batteries. Older notebook computers used NiCad batteries, which were heavy and relatively inefficient. To improve upon NiCad batteries, NiMH batteries were introduced. In general, NiMH batteries improved upon the battery's ability to recharge. Today, most notebook computers use Li-Ion batteries, which, although they are more expensive, are much more efficient. In general, Li-Ion batteries contain internal circuitry that monitors voltage to prevent undercharging and overcharging, which may damage the battery.

For years, users have debated about "battery memory," or "memory effect," a characteristic that may limit the amount of charge a battery can store. The debate centered around when you should recharge your battery. Many users claimed that if you recharged the battery before the battery had used up its entire charge, the battery would "remember" the level at which you began to recharge it, and in the future, would not hold a charge beyond that level. Over time, a battery that once provided several hours of power may diminish to the point that it can only provide an hour or less. Fortunately, such "memory effect" impacts only NiCad and NiMH batteries. If you are using a Li-Ion battery, your battery should not suffer from being recharged before it has used its current charge. If, however, you are using a NiCad or NiMH battery, you should, in general, let the battery drain completely before you recharge it.

USE IT　In general, your batteries first few charges are the key to maximizing the charge the battery will accept. Ideally, you should let your notebook PC's battery charge completely and discharge completely three to five times before you begin using your system. To start, plug in and turn on your PC within the Control Panel, use the Power Management icon to turn off your PC's power management capabilities. Then, let the battery charge for 24 hours. Next, unplug the PC, switch on the computer and let the battery run down completely until the computer shuts down. Then, repeat this process, ideally at least three times.

Taking Advantage of Energy Star Devices

In Chapter 1, you read a little about the debate as to when users should shut down systems. To conserve energy, many companies require that their employees shut down their systems at the end of the day. Unfortunately, during the rest the day, regardless of whether the employee is using or not using his or her PC, the system is still consuming power.

Today, most PCs, monitors, and even many printers are _Energy Star_ devices, which means that the devices can hibernate (and consume less power) when they are not in use. The U.S. Government standards state that while a device is in sleep mode, the device cannot consume more than 30 watts of power.

Some devices, such as printers, will automatically hibernate when they are not in use. Later, when the user sends a file to the printer, the printer will wake up, warm up, and process the job. Depending on your printer's type, you may need to set the amount of time the printer should wait before hibernating by using the printer's menu, which appears on its front panel. For some printers, you may be able to set the value using software that accompanied your printer.

USE IT　Within the Windows environment, you can control a PC's Energy Star settings by selecting the Control Panel Power Management icon. Windows, in turn, will display the Power Management Properties dialog box shown in Figure 3-11, from which you can assign the values you

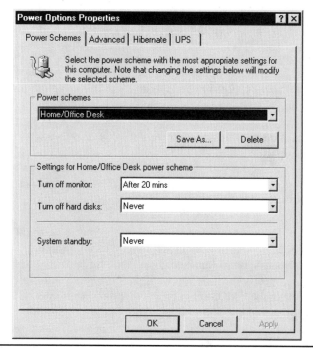

Figure 3.11   Using the Power Management Properties dialog box to control device energy use

desire. If you are using Windows 2000, Windows will display the Power Options dialog box, from which you can perform similar operations.

Using Your BIOS to Enable Power Management

In Chapter 7, you will examine the PC's CMOS settings. As you will learn, most newer PCs have a CMOS setting that lets you enable or disable the PC's power management capabilities. In general, you shouldn't disable the PC's power management. In fact, many PCs provide some cool features beyond simply using power management to direct various devices to hibernate so that they consume less power. Using power management features, for example, you can (as discussed in the next section) have your PC turn itself on at a specific time or turn itself on in response to a modem or network connection.

USE IT   To enable your PC's power management capabilities, restart your system and enter the PC's CMOS settings (as discussed in Chapter 7). Then, within the CMOS settings, locate the entry that corresponds to PC power management support and select the Enable option. Next, save your CMOS settings and exit the CMOS setup program. Your system will restart and be ready to auto start at the time you specified.

Awakening Your PC at Specific Times

In Chapter 7, you will learn about your PC's CMOS settings in detail. At that time, you will learn that many newer PCs let you automatically power on the PC without user interaction. Assume, for example, that you like to shut down your PC at the end of the day. The following morning, however, you must then patiently wait as your PC starts and loads Windows (in Chapter 9, you will examine ways to speed up your system's startup process). As an alternative, you can direct your PC to automatically start at a specific time. If you normally stroll into your office at 7:30, you can direct your PC to start at 7:00. Further, you can direct Windows to automatically launch your e-mail program so that your new e-mail messages are waiting for you. And, if you normally browse a few specific Web sites each morning before you start your day, you can direct Windows to prefetch each site's contents (Chapter 9 will show you how).

USE IT   To direct your PC to start at a specific time, restart your system and enter the PC's CMOS settings (Chapter 7 will tell you how). Within the CMOS settings, first make sure that your PCs power management support is enabled. Then, look for an "auto start" or similarly named setting. Within the setting, specify the time you want your system to automatically start. Then, save your CMOS settings and exit the CMOS setup program. Your system will restart and be ready to auto start at the time you specified.

You may be wondering how a PC can wake itself up in this way, if the power is turned off. If you examine the leads from the ATX power supply, you will find that lead 9 (the purple lead) normally maintains a constant +5V (even when the power supply is off). The lead maintains this power by bypassing the power supply's main transformer. The motherboard, in turn, can use this voltage to power a timer, a network card, or a modem (which listens for incoming connections). When, for example, the timer occurs, the motherboard can use lead 14 to direct the power supply to turn itself on.

Traveling and Your Need for Power Converters

If you travel worldwide with a notebook PC, you will need to purchase plug connectors that let you plug your PC into wall outlets that look very different than those you use within the U.S. Also, depending on your notebook type, you may also need to purchase a transformer. Unlike the U.S., which provides 110V at wall outlets, Europe provides 220V at wall outlets. If you plug your 110V device into the 220V outlet, you will likely fry your device's electronics. Figure 3-12 illustrates a collection of plug converters.

Many notebook computers, however, provide a transformer within the power supply. As such, you can (if you have the plug adapters that let you plug in your device), plug your notebook into the 220V outlet. If you examine your notebook PC's power supply, you should see a rating that states something like "Input: 110V/220V". If you are not sure whether your notebook's power supply provides a transformer, contact your manufacturer before you plug in the device, or purchase a transformer that will convert the 220V to 110V, and into which you can then plug in your device. The problem with traveling with a transformer is that they are bulky and heavy, and they generate a lot of heat.

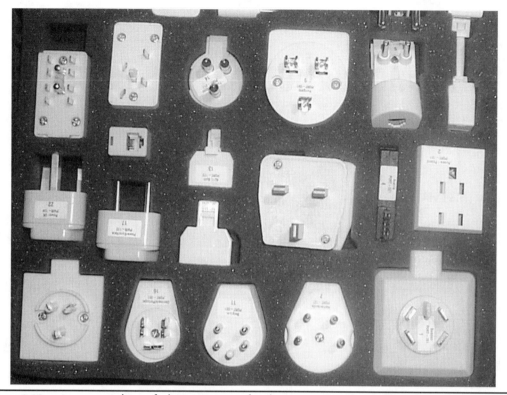

Figure 3.12   An essential set of plug converters for the international traveler

USE IT   To shop for power connectors and transformers, visit the following Web sites:

- www.radioshack.com
- www.ebags.com
- www.cdw.com

If you will be using your notebook computer to connect to the Internet while you are traveling, you will also need an adapter for your phone cable. In addition, the dial tone on European phones sounds different than the dial tone in the U.S. Some modems cannot recognize the European dial tone. You may want to check with your modem manufacturer to determine if your phone supports dial tones other than that of the U.S. In the past, I have changed my modem characteristics within Windows (using the Modem Properties dialog box within the Control Panel) so that the modem will not wait to identify the dial tone before it dials, which let me successfully place calls in Europe using my modem.

CHAPTER 4

The PC Motherboard

In Chapter 2, you opened your system unit and toured the inside of the PC chassis. Within the PC system unit, the *motherboard* houses the PC's sensitive electronic chips, such as the CPU, random access memory (RAM), and the BIOS. Further, the motherboard provides expansion slots into which users insert cards, such as modems, network interface cards, or high-speed video cards, that extend the capabilities of their PCs. Depending on your PC type, the motherboard may also house chips that provide network, video, and disk drive support.

This chapter examines the motherboard in detail. You will first examine the motherboard's key components. Then, you will examine the PC's expansion-bus types. Finally, you will learn how the PC communicates with different hardware devices and how you can resolve electronic conflicts between devices.

Touring the Motherboard

Depending on your PC type, the layout and organization of chips on your motherboard will vary. Figure 4-1, for example, shows the layout of a typical motherboard.

Regardless of the motherboard layout, the motherboard is home to such items as the CPU, RAM, the BIOS, expansion slots, as well as the buses (wires) that connect each of the electronic components. Since the release of the IBM PC in 1981, PC motherboards have experienced many evolutions, most of which have occurred as PC manufacturers have squeezed more chips closer together on the motherboard's limited real estate. Users refer to the different motherboard sizes and configurations as *form factors*. Figure 4-2, for example, illustrates the ATX form factor, which many PCs use today.

Figure 4.1   A typical PC motherboard

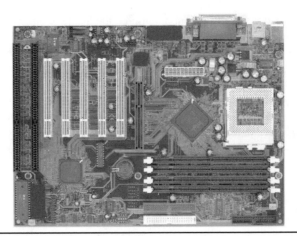

Figure 4.2 The layout of the ATX form factor

As you examine PC catalogs, books, and magazines, you will encounter the term "form factor" on a regular basis. By knowing your motherboard's form factor, a hardware technician with whom you may be talking on the phone can gain considerable insight into your motherboard's layout and circuitry. The easiest way for you to determine your PC's form factor is to refer to the technical documentation that accompanied your PC or to visit your PC manufacturer's Web site and research your PC type. Also, you can compare your motherboard size and layout to the common form factors shown in Figure 4-3.

▶ *FACT*

The processor and system bus on the original IBM PC's motherboard operated at 4.77MHz. The Pentium 4 processor supports speeds in excess of 2GHz and a system bus that operates at 400MHz.

Buses on the Motherboard Allow Chips to Communicate

The motherboard consists of a myriad of chips, connected by various buses that allow the chips to communicate. The primary motherboard bus is the *system bus*, that connects the CPU, RAM, the BIOS, and other chips within the CPU's chipset, as shown in Figure 4-4.

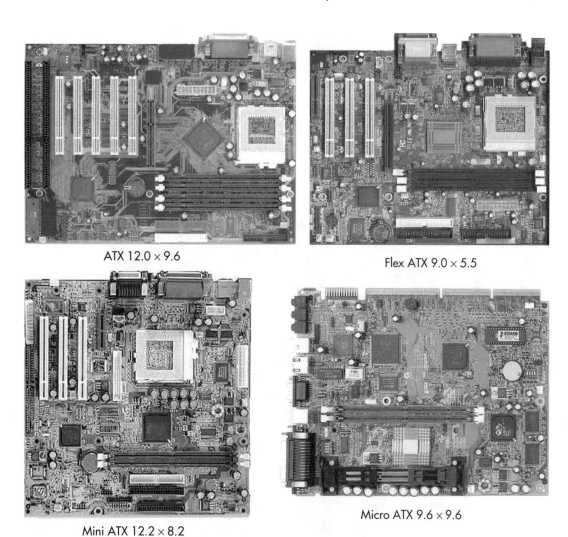

ATX 12.0 × 9.6

Flex ATX 9.0 × 5.5

Mini ATX 12.2 × 8.2

Micro ATX 9.6 × 9.6

Figure 4.3   Common PC motherboard form factors

The motherboard also houses expansion slots, into which you insert cards, such as a network interface card or modem, that "expands" your PC's capabilities, hence the "expansion slot" name. Figure 4-5 illustrates different expansion slot types on a motherboard.

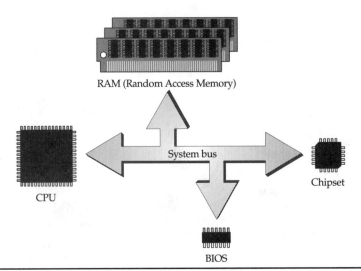

RAM (Random Access Memory)

System bus

CPU

Chipset

BIOS

Figure 4.4   The system bus connects the CPU to RAM, the BIOS, and key chips in the chipset.

Chapter 12 examines PC expansion slots and buses in detail. When you purchase a new hardware device, you must ensure that the card's connector type matches an available expansion slot on your motherboard. As you will learn in Chapter 12, since the release of the IBM PC in 1981, expansion slots (and hardware cards) have evolved to support faster speeds and transfer larger amounts of data at one time. The original IBM PC used ISA (Industry Standard Architecture) expansion slots whose

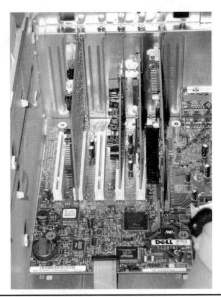

Figure 4.5   Expansion slots on the PC motherboard

bus communicated 8 bits at a time. Since that time, the ISA bus has expanded to support 16-bit data transfers at 8.33 MHz. Today, most PCs use PCI (Peripheral Component Interconnect) expansion slots that communicate 64 bits at a time (the original PCI used a 32-bit bus) at 33 MHz (although revision 2.1 of the PCI specification provides for bus speeds of 66 MHz, few PCI devices that support that speed). Further, to improve video performance, many systems have an *accelerated graphics port* (AGP) that provides a high-speed (from 66 MHz to in some cases the speed of the system bus) connection to a video card.

Different Buses on the Motherboard Operate at Different Speeds

Within the motherboard, the system bus that connects the CPU, RAM, the BIOS, and other high-speed chips in the chipset operates at the fastest speed. For years, the system bus, depending on the PC type (and CPU speed), operated at speeds from 66 MHz to 100 MHz. Today, newer Pentium 4 systems use a system bus that operates at 400 MHz. Despite its speed, the system bus remains much slower than the CPU. Chapter 5 examines ways in which hardware designers minimize the bottleneck the system bus creates within the motherboard.

As discussed, today most PCs use PCI expansion slots. The PCI bus (and the devices you insert into PCI expansion slots), typically operate at 33 MHz (although in the future the bus may operate at 66 MHz). In order to operate, a device you install within an expansion slot must be able to communicate with the CPU. To connect the slower PCI bus to the system bus, which lets the CPU and the expansion-slot devices communicate, the motherboard uses a connector that PC technicians refer to as the North Bridge, shown in Figure 4-6. (The North Bridge may also connect an AGP bus to the system bus.)

Further, to support even older ISA-based cards, which operate at 8 MHz, the motherboard connects the PCI bus to the slower ISA bus using a connector that technicians refer to as the *South Bridge*, shown in Figure 4-7.

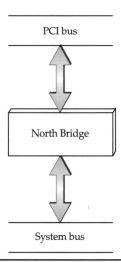

Figure 4.6   The North Bridge connects the fast system bus to the slower PCI bus.

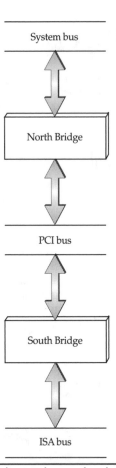

Figure 4.7   The South Bridge connects the PCI bus to the slower ISA bus.

Understanding How Devices Communicate

Within the PC, the system-unit devices communicate through the exchange of electronic signals. Each time your move your mouse, for example, the electronics within the mouse send signals to the CPU. Likewise, when your modem receives data, the modem sends signals to the CPU. Further, when your disk drive completes a disk read or write operation, the disk drive sends electronic signals to the CPU that notify the CPU of the operation's completion.

Across the motherboard, devices send the CPU signals across special wires called interrupt-request (IRQ) lines to notify the CPU that the device need's the CPU's attention. The IRQ lines are so named, because when a signal occurs on one of the lines, the CPU "interrupts" its current processing to service the device that is generating the interrupt. For example, each time you move your mouse, the mouse sends a signal that interrupts the CPU.

Each device that communicates with the CPU using interrupts has its own IRQ line, as shown in Figure 4-8.

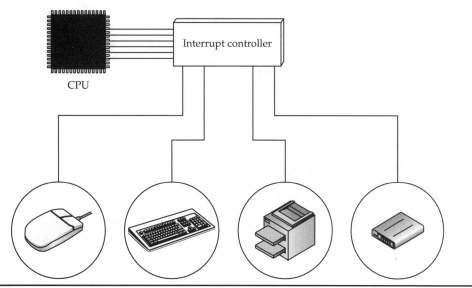

Figure 4.8   Devices that communicate with the CPU using interrupts have their own IRQ lines.

Within the PC, there are 16 IRQ lines. Table 4-1 describes the devices that traditionally use specific IRQ lines.

IRQ Line	Device
0	System timer
1	Keyboard
2	Cascaded (which provides support for interrupts 8–15)
3	COM2
4	COM1
5	LPT2
6	Floppy disk
7	LPT1
8	Real-time clock
9	Redirected as IRQ 2
10	Available
11	Available
12	Available

Table 4.1   Common Device IRQ Line Settings

IRQ Line	Device
13	Math coprocessor
14	Hard disk controller
15	Available

Table 4.1 Common Device IRQ Line Settings *(continued)*

How the CPU Responds to an Interrupt

As you have learned, a program is simply a list of instructions the CPU executes to perform a specific task. Assume, for example, that you are using a browser to surf the Web. The CPU, in turn, will spend much of its time executing the browser's instructions that download and display text and graphics. As the CPU performs such processing, your PC will respond to your mouse movements by moving the mouse pointer across your screen display. To move the mouse pointer in response to your mouse movements, the CPU responds to interrupts the mouse generates. As shown in Figure 4-9, each time you move your mouse, the electronics within the mouse will generate an interrupt, to which the CPU must respond.

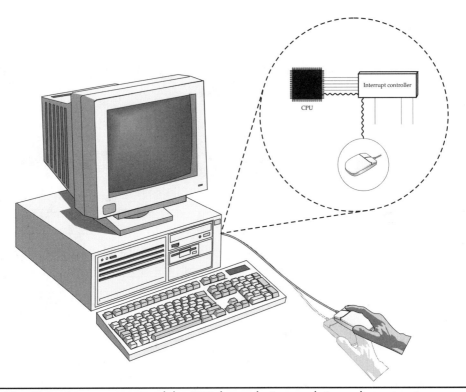

Figure 4.9 Using interrupts to signal the CPU that a device needs immediate attention

When the CPU detects an interrupt signal, the CPU stops (interrupts) its current processing to execute statements specific to the device. Users refer to the statements the CPU executes to service a device as the device's *interrupt handler*. In the case of a mouse interrupt, the CPU may execute statements that move the mouse pointer across the screen. After the CPU handles the interrupt, the CPU resumes its previous processing, which in this case, is the download and display of Web content within the browser, as shown in Figure 4-10.

If you have used Windows for any length of time, you know that sometimes when Windows performs various tasks, the mouse pointer changes into an hourglass image to inform you that the operation may take a few moments to complete. Often, when an impatient user doesn't want to wait, he or she will move the mouse back and forth in frustration. Ironically, each time the user moves the mouse, it generates an interrupt to which the CPU must respond to move the mouse pointer. The more the user moves the mouse, the more interrupts the user generates, and hence the longer the operation takes to complete.

Table 4-1 lists the devices that normally correspond to each IRQ line within the PC. However, when the CPU experiences an interrupt on line 12, the CPU does not assume the interrupt is for a mouse, nor does the CPU care which device is generating the event. Instead, the CPU maintains a table of memory addresses, whose entries correspond to each interrupt. When an interrupt occurs, the CPU starts executing the instructions (the interrupt handler) that resides at the memory address the table contains for the interrupt, as shown in Figure 4-11. The CPU does not know whether it is executing instructions for a mouse, disk drive, or modem—nor does the CPU care.

Not All Devices Use Interrupts

Not all the devices you connect to a PC require their own interrupts. As you will learn in Chapter 12, when you install a device within the PC, depending on the device type, you may connect the device to a different bus type. Remember, a bus is simply a collection of wires. The devices that you install within your PC's expansion slots will likely require their own interrupts. In contrast, devices that you connect to a universal serial bus (USB) or to a SCSI bus will use the bus to communicate with the bus

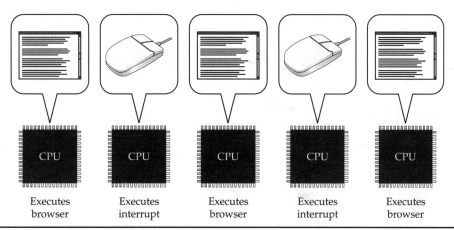

| Executes | Executes | Executes | Executes | Executes |
| browser | interrupt | browser | interrupt | browser |

Figure 4.10   Interrupts temporarily suspend the CPU's current processing while the CPU responds to a device.

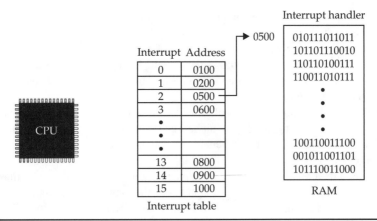

Figure 4.11 The CPU executes instructions that reside at a specific memory location when an interrupt occurs.

controller (the electronics that manage the bus), which, in turn, will use its interrupt to communicate with the CPU, as shown in Figure 4-12.

Selecting a Device's IRQ Line

Devices that communicate with the CPU using interrupts must have their own IRQ line. If two devices try to use the same IRQ line, a conflict will occur that prevents one or both of the devices from working. Users refer to such device conflicts as *IRQ conflicts*.

Depending on your device type, the steps you must perform to select the IRQ line the device will use will differ. In some cases, you will use switches, as shown in Figure 4-13, that reside on the hardware card. In other cases, you will use one or more jumpers on the card or software to specify which IRQ line the device will use.

To avoid conflicts when you install a new device, you must know how the device will communicate with the CPU. If the device connects to a USB or SCSI bus, you do not have to specify an IRQ line for the device. Likewise, as you will learn later in this chapter, if you are using a Plug-and-Play device, you may not have to specify an IRQ line. Instead, the Plug-and-Play device will communicate with other devices in the system, as well as the operating system, to determine which IRQ lines are available, and the device will then configure itself to use resources the system is not using. However, if you are installing a non-Plug-and-Play device within a motherboard expansion slot, you must determine which interrupts are currently available, and then you must configure the device to use an available IRQ line.

Determining Which Interrupts Your System is Using

For years after the PC was first released, knowing which interrupts the PC was using meant keeping track of all the devices within the PC and which interrupts you manually assigned to each device (using jumpers and switches as previously discussed). Today, you can run various software programs

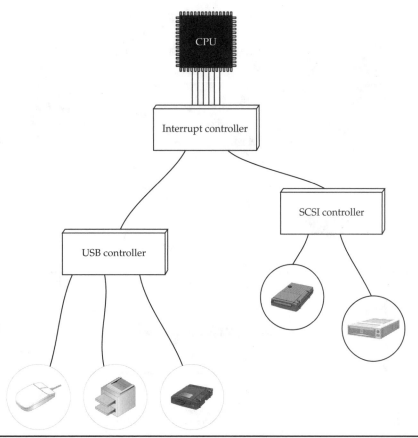

Figure 4.12   Many devices do not require their own interrupts.

to determine your system's current interrupt use, such as the System Information Utility, shown in Figure 4-14.

USE IT   To display your system's interrupt use using the System Information Utility, perform these steps:

1. Select Start | Programs | Accessories. Windows, in turn, will display the Accessories submenu.

2. Within the Accessories submenu, chose System Tools | System Information Utility. Windows will open the System Information Utility.

3. Within the System Information Utility, click the plus sign (+) that precedes the Hardware Resources option. The System Information Utility will expand its listing of hardware settings.

4. Within the System Information Utility's list of hardware settings, click the IRQ's entry.

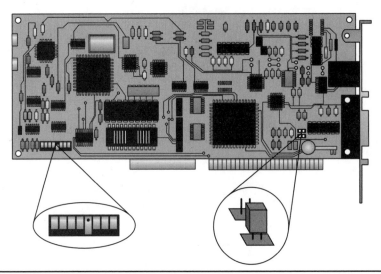

Figure 4.13 To select a device's IRQ line, you use switches, jumpers, or software.

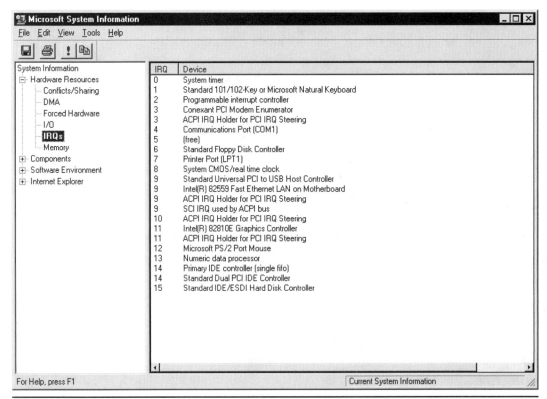

Figure 4.14 Displaying a system's interrupt use within the System Information Utility

Understanding Cascaded Interrupts

The original IBM PC, released in 1981, supported only eight interrupts. When the 80286 processor emerged a few years later, it added a second interrupt controller, which provided the PC with support for 16 interrupts. If you examine Table 4-1, you will find that IRQ 2 is *cascaded*. What that means is when the CPU receives an interrupt on line 2, the processor knows that the interrupt corresponds to an interrupt on the second controller, meaning an interrupt in the range 8–15, as shown here:

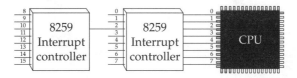

When the processor receives an interrupt on line 2, the processor examines the I/O ports 0xA0 and 0xA1 to determine which interrupt on the second interrupt controller actually occurred.

Communicating Beyond Interrupts

As you have learned, devices use interrupts to signal the CPU that the device needs the CPU to perform processing on its behalf. After an interrupt occurs, the CPU executes the corresponding interrupt handler's instructions. To perform correct processing, the interrupt handler must receive information from the device that specifies the operation the device requires the CPU to perform.

For example, when you move your mouse, the electronics within the mouse generate an interrupt on IRQ line 12. Likewise, when you click, double-click, or right-click your mouse, the electronics within mouse generate an interrupt on IRQ line 12. The interrupt handler that responds to interrupt 12 must have a way to determine which mouse operation caused the interrupt.

To communicate such information to the interrupt handler, devices use special memory locations called *input/output (I/O) ports*. These special memory locations (which reside outside of traditional RAM) are accessible by the device and the CPU, as shown in Figure 4-15.

Depending on the device type, the number of port locations the device uses to communicate with the CPU will differ. Each device that uses an interrupt to communicate with the CPU has its own unique port locations. Each port has its own unique address. The keyboard, for example, might use the following port locations:

- **0060**   Keyboard controller reset status
- **0064**   Keyboard controller command status

Just as devices must have a unique IRQ line, devices must have unique port locations. If two devices use the same port locations, errors will occur that prevent the devices from working correctly. When you install a (non-Plug-and-Play) hardware card within an expansion slot, you must ensure that the device's port settings do not conflict with an existing device. Depending on the device, the steps you must perform to set the device's port addresses will differ. Some devices will use switches, some will use jumpers, and some will let you configure the port settings by using software.

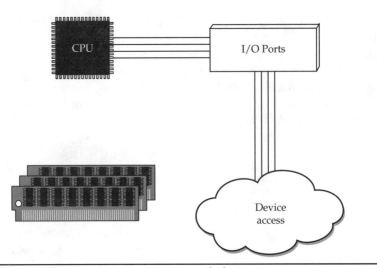

Figure 4.15   Devices use I/O ports to communicate with the CPU.

▶ *FACT*

Using PCI interrupt steering, two or more cards that reside in PCI expansion slots can share the same interrupt request line.

Determining Which Port Addresses Your System is Using

To determine which I/O ports the devices in your system are currently using, you can use the System Information Utility, shown in Figure 4-16.

 To display your system's I/O port using the System Information Utility, perform these steps:

1. Select Start | Programs | Accessories. Windows, in turn, will display the Accessories submenu.

2. Within the Accessories submenu, chose System Tools | System Information Utility. Windows will open the System Information Utility.

3. Within the System Information Utility, click the plus sign (+) that precedes the Hardware Resources option. The System Information Utility will expand its listing of hardware settings.

4. Within the System Information Utility's list of hardware settings, click the I/O entry.

Exchanging Larger Amounts of Information with a Device

If a device requires only a small amount of information, the device can communicate with interrupt handlers using I/O ports. The use of ports is ideal for a mouse, which must communicate only limited

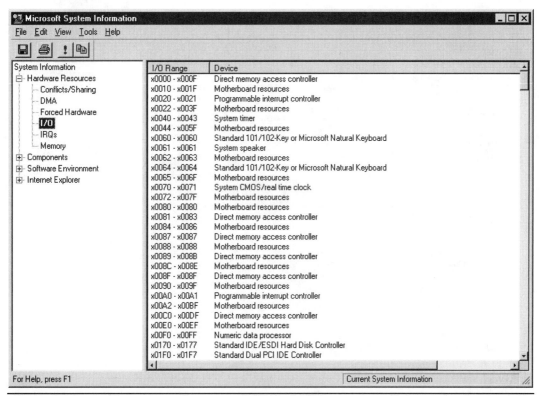

Figure 4.16   Using the System Information Utility to display a system's I/O port use

information, such as the amount the mouse has moved or that the mouse has performed a click or right-click operation (the system uses the interval of time between single-click operations to determine when a double-click operation has occurred). In contrast, devices that work with large amounts of information, such as a disk drive or CD-ROM drive, normally use standard RAM locations to hold the information the device is reading or writing. For such devices, the operating system will set a side a range of locations in RAM. Users refer to each device's starting address in memory as the device's *base address*. When you install a new device in your system, there may be times when you must specify a unique base address for a range of memory that is not currently in use by another device. To display the memory locations your system has currently set aside for various devices, you can use the System Information Utility, as shown in Figure 4-17.

USE IT   To display your system's RAM use for devices with the System Information Utility, perform these steps:

1. Select Start | Programs | Accessories. Windows, in turn, will display the Accessories submenu.

2. Within the Accessories submenu, chose System Tools | System Information Utility. Windows will open the System Information Utility.

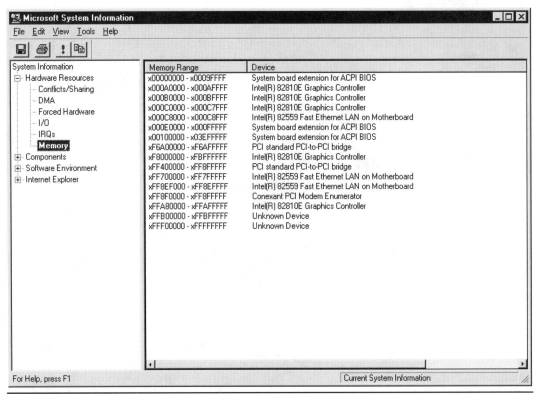

Figure 4.17   Using the System Information Utility to display memory locations reserved for specific device use

3. Within the System Information Utility, click the plus sign (+) that precedes the Hardware Resources option. The System Information Utility will expand its listing of hardware settings.

4. Within the System Information Utility's list of hardware settings, click the Memory entry.

Understanding Direct Memory Access (DMA)

As you have learned, devices use interrupts to signal the CPU that the device needs the CPU to perform processing on its behalf. Depending on the device type, the amount of processing the CPU must perform will vary. However, because the CPU has interrupted its current processing to handle the interrupt, a goal is for the CPU to complete the interrupt processing quickly, so that it can resume its previous task.

In the case of a mouse interrupt, the CPU can normally complete the interrupt processing quickly. To handle a disk read or write operation, however, the CPU might have to move a considerable amount of data between memory (RAM) and the device, which could consume considerable CPU processing time.

In Chapter 5, when you examine the CPU, you will learn how the CPU uses the system bus to communicate with RAM, the BIOS, and other chips in the CPU's chipset. Normally, the CPU controls the information that travels across the system bus. To improve CPU utilization, hardware designers developed special chips, called *DMA controllers*, whose operation the CPU can control to let the DMA chips move data between RAM and a device. By using the DMA chip to move data, the CPU alleviates itself from the task of moving each byte of data, which lets the CPU perform other tasks while the DMA chip coordinates the data movement.

For example, to read information from a disk into RAM, the CPU can configure the DMA chip by telling the chip the starting disk sector to read, the number of sectors, and the RAM location where the data should reside. The DMA controller, in turn, will perform the disk operation while the CPU performs other tasks. When the DMA controller completes the operation, the controller will use its interrupt to notify the CPU that the operation is complete. The CPU can then examine the DMA controller's ports to determine the operation's completion status.

Most newer PCs have two DMA controllers, which the systems cascade as they do interrupt controllers. Table 4-2 lists the devices that normally use specific DMA-controller lines.

To view your PC's DMA settings, you can use the System Information Utility, as shown in Figure 4-18.

USE IT To display your system's DMA settings using the System Information Utility, perform these steps:

1. Select Start | Programs | Accessories. Windows, in turn, will display the Accessories submenu.

2. Within the Accessories submenu, chose System Tools | System Information Utility. Windows will open the System Information Utility.

3. Within the System Information Utility, click the plus sign (+) that precedes the Hardware Resources option. The System Information Utility will expand its listing of hardware settings.

4. Within the System Information Utility's list of hardware settings, click the DMA entry.

DMA Line	Device
0	Available
1	Cascaded to second DMA controller
2	Floppy drive
3	Parallel port
4	Cascaded for line 1
5	Available
6	Available
7	Available

Table 4.2 Devices that Normally Use Specific DMA Controller Lines

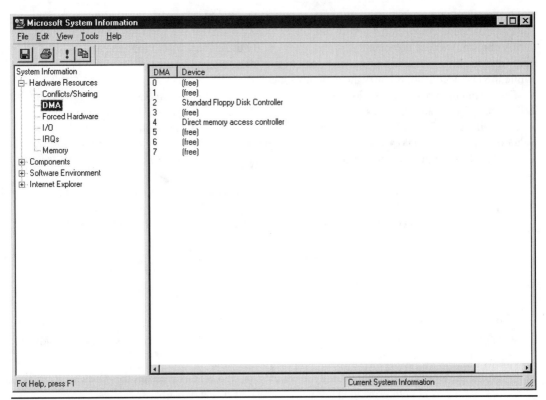

Figure 4.18   Using the System Information Utility to view DMA chip settings

Understanding Plug-and-Play Devices

As you might guess, having to assign proper values for interrupts, I/O ports, and base-memory addresses can make hardware installations quite difficult. Users refer to hardware devices that require users to manually configure such settings as *legacy devices*.

Such legacy devices might include an older internal modem, network card, multimedia sound card, and so on. Often, when users tried to install legacy devices, and the user experienced a hardware conflict, the user's only recourse was to remove and not use the new device, because troubleshooting the potential conflicts was simply beyond most user's capabilities.

USE IT   To simplify the process of installing hardware cards, device manufacturers, PC manufacturers, and operating system developers (such as Microsoft) jointly developed the Plug-and-Play specification. In general, when you install a Plug-and-Play device, the device communicates with the BIOS, other devices, and the operating system to determine which interrupts, ports, and memory locations are currently available for device use. Then the device selects from the available settings the resources its needs. Next, the device notifies the others of its resource selections.

Because Plug-and-Play devices are "self-configuring" in this way, the Plug-and-Play devices eliminate the user's need to determine available resources and the need to manually configure devices. As such, Plug-and-Play devices have made installing hardware cards much easier. Unfortunately, non-Plug-and-Play devices (legacy devices) do not participate in the communications Plug-and-Play devices use to coordinate resource use: it may possibly select resources that are actually in use by a legacy device. When such conflicts occur, one or both of the devices will not work, and you must troubleshoot the conflict.

Keep Your Motherboard Dust Free

USE IT   Over time, depending on your PC's working environment, your motherboard may accumulate dust. The primary problem dust creates within the system unit is that the dust may become a layer of insulation that traps heat within the chips. In addition, the dust can collect within unused expansion slots, which later cause the slots to fail when you install a card because the card cannot establish a proper connection. If you find that dust is accumulating within your system unit, use an aerosol blower, as shown in Figure 4-19, to blow the dust from your system.

Next, look for ways that the dust is entering your system. If you have expansion slots that are not in use, make sure that you cover the slot's opening using the metal slot cover, as shown in Figure 4-20.

Configuring Motherboard Components within the CMOS

In Chapter 7 you will learn how to use your PC's CMOS setup program to configure various settings within your PC. As you have learned, if your system has legacy devices (devices for which you must manually identify and configure interrupt, I/O port, or base memory settings), there may be times

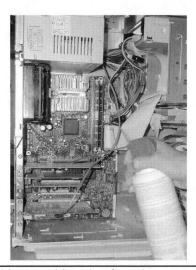

Figure 4.19   Using an aerosol blower to blow dust from the system unit

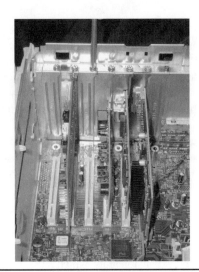

Figure 4.20 Cover unused expansion slot openings.

when one of these devices conflicts with a Plug-and-Play device that you later install in your system. As discussed, when you install a Plug-and-Play device, the device will communicate with other Plug-and-Play devices, the BIOS, and the operating system to determine which settings are currently in use. Unfortunately, legacy devices do not participate in such communication.

USE IT Depending on your PC type, your CMOS setup program may let you reserve resources that are in use by your legacy devices, as shown in Figure 4-21. Then, later, when a Plug-and-Play device queries your system regarding resources that are in use, the BIOS can ensure that a Plug-and-Play device does not try to use resources you have reserved for a legacy device.

Resolving Device Conflicts

Earlier in this chapter, you learned that when two devices try to use the same IRQ line, an IRQ conflict will occur. Likewise, if two devices use the same I/O port address or base memory address, a device conflict will occur. Normally, when such a conflict occurs, one or both of the devices will not work. Often, the Windows Device Manager will detect the conflict and will display a conflict indicator, as shown in Figure 4-22.

USE IT To use the Device Manager to check for possible conflicts, perform these steps:

1. Select Start | Settings | Control Panel. Windows, in turn, will display the Control Panel window.
2. Within the Control Panel, double-click the System icon. Windows will display the System Properties dialog box.

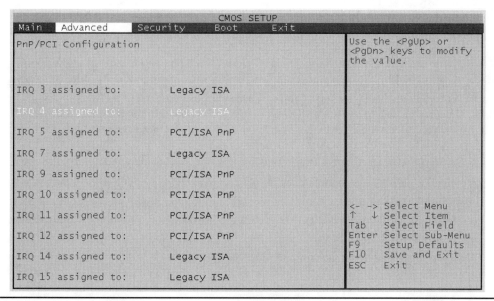

Figure 4.21 Using the CMOS setup to reserve legacy device resources

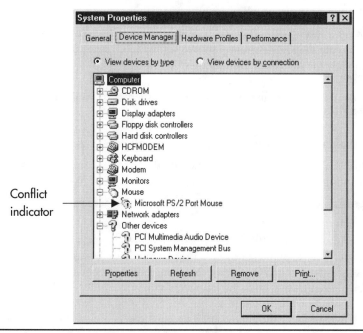

Figure 4.22 The Windows Device Manager indicates a device conflict using a yellow exclamation-mark icon.

3. Within the System Properties dialog box, click the Device Manager tab. Windows will display the Device Manager from within which you can display specifics about each of your devices, such as the device's resource use.

When such conflicts occur, you must change the resource setting for one of the two conflicting devices. Depending on the device types, you will use switches, jumpers, or software to change the settings. You may be able to use the CMOS setup to reserve resources for your legacy devices.

To display the Device Manager within Windows 2000, perform these steps:

1. Select Start | Settings | Control Panel. Windows, in turn, will display the Control Panel window.

2. Within the Control Panel, double-click the System icon. Windows will display the System Properties dialog box.

3. Within the System Properties dialog box, click the Hardware tab. Windows will display the Hardware sheet.

4. Within the Hardware sheet, click the Device Manager button.

Using the Device Manager to View or Change a Device's Resource Use

When your PC encounters a resource conflict, such as an IRQ conflict, you can use the Windows Device Manager to view your device's current resource settings. For example, Figure 4-23 uses the Device Manager to view the resources used by theCOM1 serial port.

USE IT To display device resources using the Device Manager, perform these steps:

1. Select Start | Settings | Control Panel. Windows, in turn, will display the Control Panel window.

2. Within the Control Panel, double-click your mouse on the System icon. Windows will display the System Properties dialog box.

3. Within the System Properties dialog box, click the Device Manager tab. Windows will display the Device Manager.

4. Within the Device Manager, click the device you desire, and then click the Properties button. The Device Manager will display the device's Properties dialog box. If the device is using resources, such as an interrupt or I/O address, the dialog box will contain a Resources tab. To display the device's resource use, click the Resources tab.

As you have learned, to change a device's resource settings, you may need to use jumpers or switches on the device, or you may be able to use software to configure the device. To quickly determine available resources, you can use the System Information Utility, as discussed earlier in the section "Determining Which Interrupts Your System is Using." In some cases, you can use the

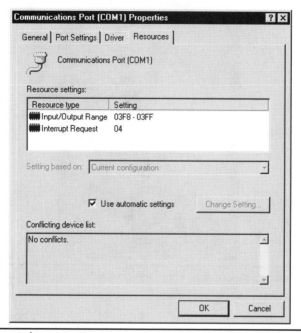

Figure 4.23   Viewing serial port resource use

Device Manager to change the device's resource settings. If a device lets you change its setting within the Device Manager, you will use the Resources dialog box similar to that shown for the COM1 serial port in Figure 4-23. To change the settings within the Resources dialog box, perform these steps:

1. Within the Resources dialog box, click the Use Automatic Settings check box to remove the checkmark.

2. Then click the Change Setting button. If the Device Manager can change the device resources, the Device Manager will display a dialog box you can use to change resource settings. Otherwise, the Device Manager will display a dialog box telling you that you cannot use it to change the device settings.

Detecting and Eliminating Heat-Related Errors

As electrical signals travel through chips and across buses on the motherboard, the signals generate heat. As briefly discussed in Chapter 3, the power supply contains a fan that carries heat from the power supply and from within the system unit. If you examine your power supply from within the system unit, you will find vents through which the fan pulls heat from inside the system unit. In addition, as shown in Figure 4-24, many systems have a second fan that may specifically vent the CPU, which is the greatest source of motherboard heat.

Figure 4.24   Many systems contain a fan within the power supply and a fan to vent the CPU.

USE IT   Unfortunately, many of the motherboard's electronic devices are quite sensitive to heat. If your PC begins to experience internal errors after you run it for a period of time (the amount of time may vary), you may have a heat problem within your system unit. When you suspect heat-related errors, open your system unit and make sure it is dust free. If necessary, use an aerosol blower to blow dust from the motherboard. Next, use the aerosol blower to clean the fans on the back of your PC. Also, make sure that you are giving your PC ample space into which it can vent the heat it generates. Many users often push their PCs against a wall or desk, which prevents the fans from venting heat effectively.

If you have overclocked your CPU or system bus to improve performance, as discussed in Chapter 5, you may need to back down your settings. You may also want to take advantage of one of the software programs Chapter 5 discusses that reduce CPU heat by halting the CPU when it is not in use.

Further, for less than $25, you can add a variety of fans to your system unit. Some such fans fit into an unused disk-drive bay, while other fans fit into and vent out of an expansion slot.

If you have a safe location where you can place your system unit, you might try running your system without a chassis cover for a few hours. If you do not experience the error when your chassis is uncovered, you can feel more confident that your problems are heat related.

▶ NOTE

To determine which chip is experiencing the error, some users will use a device such as a hair dryer to heat various chips. Exposing your chips to such heat may damage the chip. When you know you have a heat problem, the solution is to determine better ways to cool your system. Normally, the chip that will be experiencing the problem is the CPU. If you can determine the chip that is experiencing heat-related problems, you may be able to attach a "heat sink" to a chip, as discussed in Chapter 5, to better transfer heat from the chip. Before you risk your electronics with a high heat source, perform the steps this tip presents to try to reduce heat from within your system unit.

Detecting and Eliminating Power-Related Errors

If you experience intermittent errors, and you do not think that the errors are heat-related, the errors may be due to inconsistent power. As you learned in Chapter 3, the PC's sensitive electronic components must have a consistent source of correct power in order to operate correctly. Unfortunately, troubleshooting power problems can be quite challenging, particularly if the power drops occur inconsistently.

USE IT To begin, you may want to use a multimeter, as shown in Figure 4-25, to measure voltages at various sources from the power supply. Chapter 3 provides tables you can use to determine the voltages you should find at specific cable leads. In addition, you may want to download a schematic of your PC motherboard from the manufacturer's Web site that provides voltages at various motherboard locations.

If you are experiencing drops in power that occur randomly, and your power supply appears to operating correctly, you may need to install an uninterruptible power supply (UPS) that provides your PC with constant, conditioned power. If you have overclocked your CPU to improve system performance (as discussed in Chapter 5), you may need to increase the voltage to your CPU.

Pay Attention to Chip Creep

If you examine the motherboard closely, you will find that some chips are soldered to the motherboard while others reside in sockets. As a general rule, if your motherboard and system is working, do not remove chips simply as an exercise or to examine the chips. Many of the motherboard chips are very sensitive, and you can easily damage the chips from electromagnetic shock or by accidentally

Figure 4.25 Using a multimeter to measure PC voltages

dropping them. Further, many of the chips have small pins that connect the chips to the motherboard socket. As you remove and later reinsert a chip, you may break a pin or fail to get a pin back into a socket, as shown in Figure 4-26. Such pin-level problems can lead to errors that are very difficult to detect.

USE IT If you move or ship a PC, a chip on the motherboard may work itself out of the socket far enough to prevent a proper connection, as shown in Figure 4-27. Users refer to such chip movement as *chip creep*.

If your PC suddenly stops working, or if your system's power-on self-test (POST) reports a motherboard error, unplug your system, open your system unit, and gently press each motherboard chip to ensure that the chip is in place.

Disabling Motherboard Devices

Depending on your PC type, the motherboard may provide chips the PC uses for a video adapter, disk controller, a bus mouse, network interface, and so on. If you install a high-performance video adapter card or a different disk controller, you may need to disable the motherboard devices before you can use your new hardware cards. Again, depending on your motherboard type, you may disable the motherboard device using a jumper, or you may be able to use the CMOS setup program (discussed in Chapter 7) to disable the motherboard device.

USE IT Further, the motherboard may provide chips that drive a serial port or parallel port. If you are not using these devices, you can disable them and use their resources (the IRQ line, I/O address, and so on) for other devices. To determine whether your CMOS setup program lets you enable and disable devices, restart your system and enter the CMOS setup, as discussed in Chapter 7. Within your CMOS program, look for an entry, such as that shown in Figure 4-28, which you can use to disable the device. After you use the CMOS setup program to enable or disable a device, save your changes and exit the program. Your system will restart with your changes in effect.

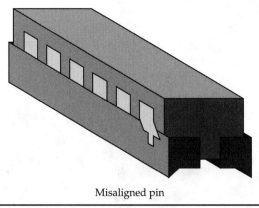

Misaligned pin

Figure 4.26 Failure to correctly place a pin within a socket

Figure 4.27 Chip creep may prevent a proper electrical connection.

Using Sandra to Display Motherboard Specifics

USE IT Throughout this book, several tips will take advantage of the SiSoftware Sandra (**S**ystem **AN**alyser, **D**iagnostic and **R**eporting **A**ssistant) program, which you can use to provide low-level device information and to run various benchmarks. Using Sandra, you can display specifics

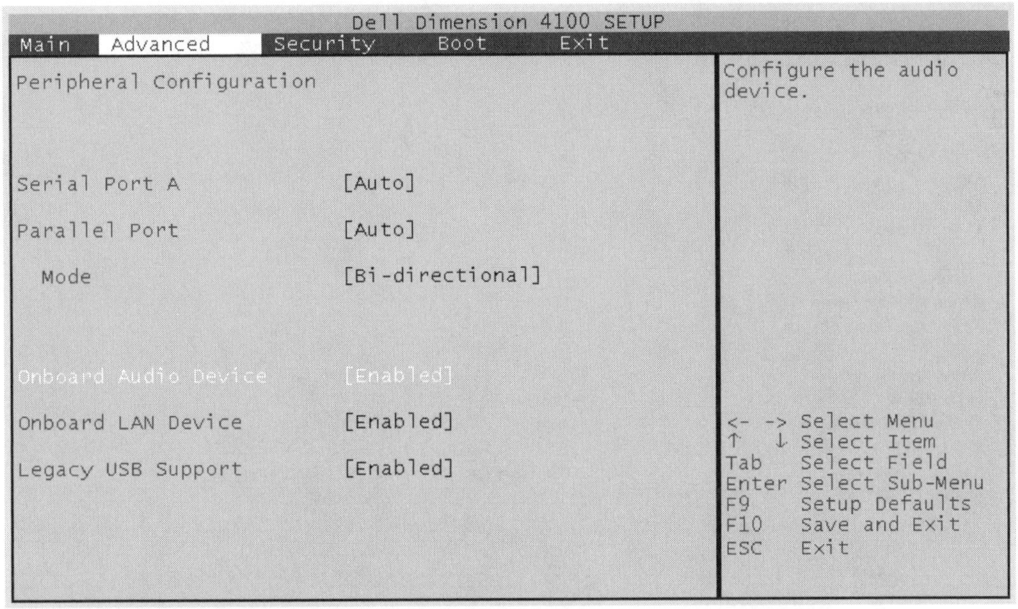

```
                        Dell Dimension 4100 SETUP
  Main    Advanced      Security    Boot      Exit
  Peripheral Configuration                            Configure the audio
                                                      device.


  Serial Port A            [Auto]

  Parallel Port            [Auto]

   Mode                    [Bi-directional]



  Onboard Audio Device     [Enabled]

  Onboard LAN Device       [Enabled]                  <- -> Select Menu
                                                      ↑   ↓ Select Item
  Legacy USB Support       [Enabled]                  Tab   Select Field
                                                      Enter Select Sub-Menu
                                                      F9    Setup Defaults
                                                      F10   Save and Exit
                                                      ESC   Exit
```

Figure 4.28 Using the CMOS setup program to enable or disable motherboard devices.

about your motherboard, such as manufacturer, serial number, chipset, RAM, and more, as shown in Figure 4-29.

To download the Sandra program, visit the SiSoftware Web site at www.sisoftware.demon.co.uk.

Viewing Shared Interrupt Settings

If you examine IRQ assignments within System Information Utility, as shown in Figure 4-30, you may find that several devices share the same interrupt, which seems to be a direct violation of this chapter's discussion that each device must have a unique interrupt.

As it turns out, interrupt sharing is fairly common among PCI-based devices. When two or more devices share the same interrupt, the PC will essentially chain each device's interrupt handling code together, giving the first handler a chance to respond to the interrupt, followed by the second, and so on. The interrupt handler (the instructions the PC executes when the interrupt occurs) may interrogate various port values to determine if its device is the one generating the interrupt. The operating system will continue to run one interrupt handler after another until one of the chained handlers responds to the interrupt.

Even if your device supports shared interrupts, you should try to assign your device an unused interrupt to reduce complexity and to improve system performance. Because the process of identifying which device generated the interrupt takes time, chained interrupts reduce your system performance.

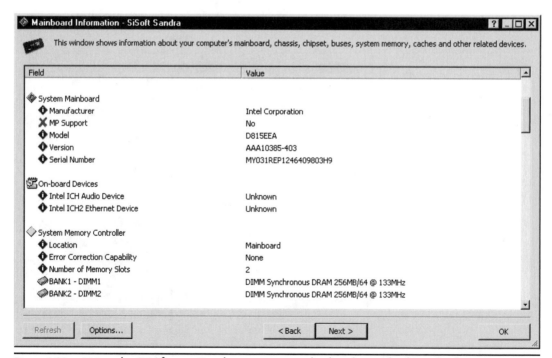

Figure 4.29　Using the SiSoftware Sandra program to display the motherboard information

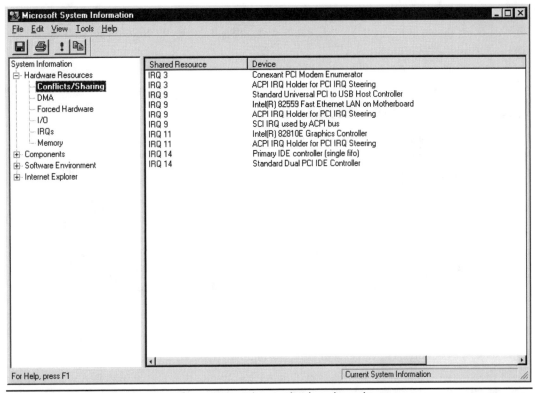

Figure 4.30   Using the System Information Utility to display shared interrupts

Understanding Chipsets

The CPU is the largest single chip on the motherboard. Throughout this book, as well as in articles you read in magazines and on the Web, you will encounter the term "chipset." In general the *chipset* is a collection of chips (normally five or less chips) that implements the key motherboard operations. The chipset essentially performs the same operations that required over 100 separate components on the original IBM PC. In general, the chipset is responsible for managing the flow of communication between the CPU, RAM, the BIOS, and other key motherboard components.

Most chipsets, as you might guess, are developed at Intel. Each chipset has a unique name, such as Intel i820 chipset. Because chipsets evolve over time, the capabilities each chipset supports may differ. For example, newer chipsets provide support for the accelerated graphics port (AGP), the universal serial bus (USB), power management operations such as ACPI (discussed in Chapter 3), as well as different RAM types. Normally, to upgrade your chipset, you upgrade your motherboard. Chapter 5 discusses steps you must perform to upgrade your processor. Before you install a new processor, you must ensure that the new processor is compatible with your existing chipset.

USE IT To view your system's current chipset, you can use the SiSoftware Sandra program, as shown in Figure 4-31. You can download Sandra from the SiSoftware Web site at www.sisoftware.demon.co.uk.

Replacing the Motherboard

If your system fails to start, or if your system's power-on self-test reports a motherboard error, you may need to replace your motherboard. For most users, the thought of replacing the motherboard may conjure up a wide range of fears. Actually, however, removing one motherboard and inserting another is actually not that difficult.

USE IT To replace your motherboard, perform these steps:

1. Power off and then unplug your system unit.

2. Remove each of the expansion-slot cards your system contains and (ideally) place the cards into an antistatic bag.

3. Open your system unit. As you examine your current motherboard, write notes that describe the connectors that attach to your motherboard and their orientation. (Often, the motherboard sockets label pin 1. The cables will normally highlight pin 1 by changing its cable's color.)

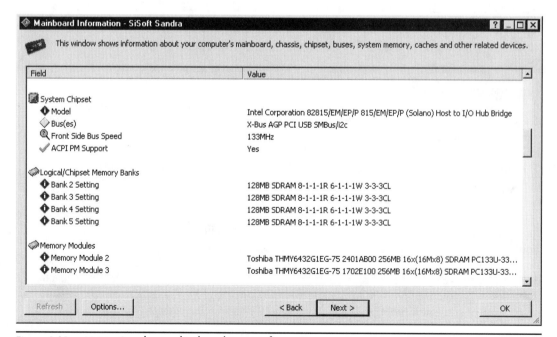

Figure 4.31   Using Sandra to display chipset information

4. Gently remove each of the wire connectors that attach to the motherboard.

5. Normally, the motherboard is attached to the chassis with several screws or clips. Remove the screws or gently move the motherboard over the clips that hold the motherboard in place. Again, ideally place the motherboard within an antistatic bag.

6. Insert and secure the new motherboard.

7. If you are replacing only your motherboard and not your CPU as well, gently remove the CPU from your old motherboard and insert the CPU onto the new one.

8. Reattach the cables you removed from the previous motherboard to the new motherboard.

9. Replace the expansion-slot cards you previously removed from your system.

10. Replace your system unit cover, plug in your system, and restart your PC.

If your system fails to start, the problem may be related to jumper or switch values that are different on the new motherboard. Closely compare each motherboard's jumper or switch settings.

CHAPTER 5

Getting the Most from Your Central Processing Unit (CPU)

TIPS IN THIS CHAPTER

Within the PC, the CPU is the workhorse that performs the majority of the processing. When you run a program, for example, the CPU executes the instructions the program contains. The faster a PC's CPU, the faster the computer. Today, most users refer to the CPU as a "Pentium processor." Although the Pentium, a CPU made by Intel, is widely used, other CPU types exist (such as those made by Advanced Micro Devices). In addition, the Macintosh CPU is a Motorola processor that is very different from the Pentium.

This chapter examines the CPU in detail. You will learn how the CPU works and the difference between CPU types, such as the Pentium, Pentium II, Pentium III, and Pentium IV. You will learn how to monitor your CPU's performance and ways you may be able to improve it. In addition, this chapter explains the CPU's built-in cache (users refer to the CPU caches as L1 and L2 caches), and how you may improve your system's performance by "overclocking" your system bus and the CPU.

Understanding the CPU's Role

A computer program is a list of instructions the computer performs to accomplish a specific task. A program may be quite simple, perhaps displaying only a message such as "Hello, World!" on your screen, or the program may be complex, such as a word processor or Web browser. In any case, a program is nothing more than a list of instructions that the CPU executes. As shown in Figure 5-1, the CPU is a chip that resides on the motherboard.

Figure 5.1 The CPU is normally the largest single chip on the motherboard.

Each CPU has a specific set of instructions that the CPU understands, called the *CPU's instruction set*. The instruction set for the Intel Pentium, for example, is much different from the instruction set for the Mac's Motorola processor, which is why you cannot run a program written for a Intel-based PC on a Mac, and vice-versa.

Depending on the complexity of the instruction set, computer engineers categorize CPUs as either a RISC- or CISC-based processor. RISC is an acronym for *reduced instruction set computer*. In general, a RISC-based processor may provide simple instructions such as load, store, add, compare, and so on. The concept behind a RISC-based processor is to design the processor so that it can execute the simple instructions very fast (every instruction within an RISC-based processor, for example, should execute within one clock tick). Because the RISC-based instructions are simple, it may require the processor several instructions to perform an operation.

In contrast, CISC stands for *complex instruction set computer*. A CISC-based PC may have several powerful instructions that can perform, in one step, the same operations that would require a RISC-based processor many instructions to perform. Depending on the complexity of the instruction, the instruction may require more than one clock tick to complete its processing. However, because the complex instructions reduce the number of operations the processor must perform, the CISC-based processor is normally very fast.

From a processor-design perspective (which is important to engineers at companies like Intel), a RISC-based processor is easier to design and implement. However, a CISC-based processor, as discussed, provides more processing power per instruction. The question, therefore, becomes, which processor type is better? The answer depends. For some benchmark programs, a RISC-based processor may outperform a CISC-based processor. Likewise, for multimedia-based game programs that perform complex video operations and graphics processing, the CISC-based processor will normally perform better. Although many marketing pieces categorize the Intel Pentium as a CISC-based processor, the Pentium is probably more accurately described as a hybrid that falls between a RISC- and CISC-based architecture.

Understanding the Programming Process

A program is simply a list of instructions that the CPU executes to accomplish a specific task. Internally, computers operate based on the presence or absence of electronic signals. You can think of the CPU as consisting of billions of small electronic switches that are either *on* (have a signal present) or are *off* (no signal).

The first computer programmers created programs using switches that resided on the outside of large mainframe computers. To add the numbers 2 and 5, for example, the programmers would set the switches that selected the add operation and then use different switches to enter the data values 2 and 5. After the computer completed its calculation, the computer would display its results by illuminating lights that appeared next to the switches.

The switches on the mainframe computer could be either on or off—which meant they could be in only one of two possible states. The programmers recognized that they could represent these two states by using the values 1 (signal on) or 0 (signal off). The computer designers next built computers that the programmers could program without having to use the switches. Instead, the programmers could use paper tape or punch cards to enter the instructions and data the CPU was to process. The programmers entered the data and instructions using long sequences of ones and zeros (binary data). To add the numbers 2 + 5, for example, the programmer might enter the string of zeros 11000101110000101111, which corresponded to the following:

- **1100 0101**   Load the value 5
- **1100 0010**   Load the value 2
- **1111**   Add the values

As you might imagine, using the ones and zeros to specify program instructions was an error-prone process. Further, locating the cause of the errors was a very tedious and time-consuming task. To reduce the number of errors that working with a sequence of ones and zeros created, programmers started using the hexadecimal (base 16 number system) to represent the sequences of ones and zeros. As shown in Table 5-1, the hexadecimal numbering system uses the values 0–9 and the letters A–F to represent the values 0 to 15 (16 different numbers—hence, the name "base 16" numbering system).

Decimal Value	Binary	Hexadecimal
0	0000	0
1	0001	1
2	0010	2
3	0011	3
4	0100	4
5	0101	5
6	0110	6
7	0111	7
8	1000	8
9	1001	9
10	1010	A
11	1011	B
12	1100	C
13	1101	D
14	1110	E
15	1111	F

Table 5.1   The Hexadecimal (Base 16) Number System

Using the hexadecimal numbering system, for example, the previous program might use the following symbols:

- **C5**   Load the value 5
- **C2**   Load the value 2
- **F**   Add the values

As you might guess, it was easier for a programmer to detect an error in hexadecimal than in binary. Using the previous example, it would be easier for a program to note the use of D5 (as opposed to C5) than the use of 11010101 (as opposed to 11000101). Although the hexadecimal numbering system was an improvement over binary, writing and debugging long programs using hexadecimal values was still quite challenging. As a solution, programmers started using mnemonics, such as ADD, SUBT, and LOAD to write program. Using such mnemonics, the previous program might become

- **LOAD**   2
- **LOAD**   5
- **ADD**

As you can see, the mnemonics made the program much easier for the programmers to read. However, keep in mind that the computer understands only ones and zeros, and that it does not understand mnemonics such as ADD and LOAD. After the programmers would write their programs using the mnemonics (which the programmers referred to as *assembly language*), the programmers would run a special program called an *assembler* that, as shown in Figure 5-2, would convert the mnemonics into the ones and zeros the computer understands.

Today, programmers use high-level programming languages such as Visual Basic or C++ to create programs. To write a program, the programmer uses the programming language to specify the program statements (the program's instructions). The programmer places the statements within a text file the programmers refer to as the program's *source file*. Then, as shown in Figure 5-3, the programmer uses a special program called the *compiler* that converts the program statements into the ones and

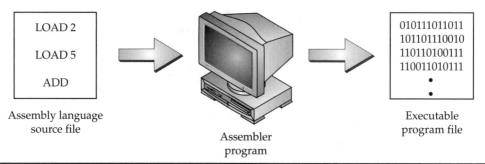

| LOAD 2 |
| LOAD 5 |
| ADD |

Assembly language source file

Assembler program

010111011011
101101110010
110110100111
110011010111

Executable program file

Figure 5.2   Using an assembler to convert assembly-language code into binary ones and zeros

zeros the CPU understands. The compiler stores the ones and zeros in an executable file that, within the Windows environment, has the .exe file extension. Each programming language, such as C or Visual Basic, has its own compiler, which is specific to that language. The following program, written in C, displays the result of the addition of 2 and 5:

```
void main(void)
{
  int result;

  result = 2 + 5;

  printf("The sum of the numbers is %d", result);
}
```

When the compiler creates an executable program, the compiler targets a specific family of processors. This means that the compiler creates an executable program file whose ones and zeros correspond to a specific processor's instruction set, such as the Intel Pentium running within the Windows environment.

Look for the Ones and Zeros within the CPU's Transistors

As you have learned, the PC operates internally based on the presence or absence of electronic signals. As you will learn in Chapter 13, the PC holds the electronic signals within billions of small electronic switches, called transistors. Each transistor within the PC serves a specific purpose. In general, the more powerful a PC's CPU, the greater number of transistors the processor contains. Table 5-2 lists the number of transistors that reside in the various PC CPUs that have evolved over the years.

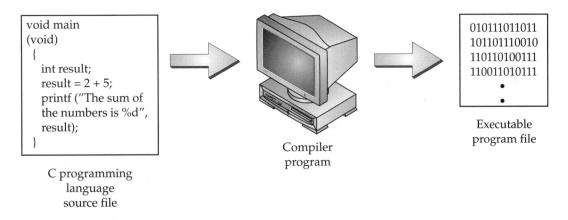

Figure 5.3   Converting programming language statements into the ones and zeros the CPU understands

CPU	Number of Transistors
8088	29,000
80286	134,000
80386	275,000
80486	1,200,000
Pentium I	3,100,000–3,300,000
Pentium I MMX	4,500,000
Pentium II	7,500,000
Pentium III	28,000,000
Pentium IV	42,000,000

Table 5.2   The Number of Transistors in Various Intel CPUs

The System Bus Lets the CPU Communicate with RAM and the BIOS

Within the PC, the electronic signals that let one device communicate with another travel down groups of wires collectively known as *buses*. One bus, for example, lets the CPU interact with cards that reside within the PC's expansion slots. Another bus may let the PC interact directly with the video card. As shown in Figure 5-4, the primary motherboard bus—known as the *system bus*—connects the CPU to the other members of the chipset, such as the BIOS.

▶ *NOTE*

Many books and articles refer to the system bus as the front side bus, or FSB.

To coordinate the exchange of signals across its wires, the system bus operates at a fixed frequency, meaning that the CPU, for example, may place data on the bus that it wants to store in RAM. The data (the electronic signals) reside on the bus wires for a specific period of time—in this case, long enough for the memory controller to receive and place the data into RAM. Then, depending on the operation the CPU is performing next, the contents of the system bus will change.

Years ago, when the IBM PC was first released, the system bus ran at 8 MHz. As processor speeds increased, so too did the speed of the system bus. For many years, the system bus operated, depending on the PC, at a speed in the range 66 MHz to 100 MHz. A PC with a system bus speed of 66 MHz, for example, placed signals onto the bus over 66 million times per second.

As you have learned, the CPU can operate at speeds of several gigahertz. Each time the CPU's clock ticks, the CPU performs an instruction. Unfortunately, if the CPU instruction requires a memory operation, the CPU must stop and wait for the data to travel across the system bus—which

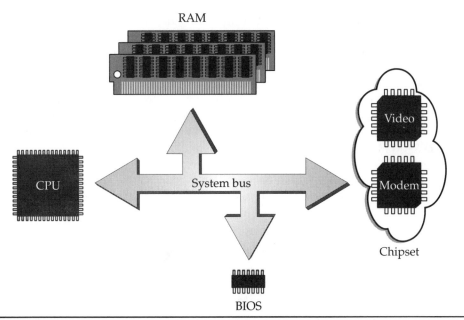

Figure 5.4   The CPU communicates with RAM and the BIOS via the system bus.

significantly decreased the PC's performance. The fast CPU was forced to sit and wait on the slow system bus. The system bus, as you might have guessed, is a considerable bottleneck within the PC. By now, you may be wondering why the system bus speed is not the same as the CPU speed.

Several factors prevent the system bus from running at the same speed at the CPU. First, the CPU is able to operate at gigahertz speeds because the electronic signals it uses internally have to travel only very minute distances, which means that the signals must reside only on the CPU's internal buses an instant in time. Because the signals traveling from the CPU to RAM, for example, have to travel a much greater distance, the signal must spend more time on the bus.

Second, the system bus must operate at a slower speed than the CPU because other members of the chipset, such as RAM, simply can't keep up with the CPU—the chip's technology is simply slower.

Level 1 and Level 2 Cache Reduce the System Bottleneck

As it executes instructions, the CPU stores its temporary results in storage locations called *registers*. Because the registers reside within the CPU itself, the CPU can access the register's contents very quickly.

Unfortunately, as the CPU executes a program, most instructions and data reside in RAM. In the best case, to retrieve an instruction from RAM, the CPU must come to a screeching halt and wait for two slow system bus operations to complete (the first operation requests the instruction from RAM and the second returns the instruction from RAM to the CPU).

To reduce the number of slow operations the PC must perform, the engineers who design CPUs placed an expensive RAM (relative to the price of traditional RAM) and high speed (again relative to traditional RAM) within the CPU itself. Users refer to the CPU's onboard RAM as the *CPU cache*.

In general, the CPU cache reduces slow system bus operations as follows. Normally, when a program runs, the CPU will execute many program instructions sequentially, one instruction followed by the next, followed by the next. Before the CPU can execute an instruction, the CPU must load the instruction from RAM. Prior to the onboard CPU cache, the CPU would retrieve one instruction at a time—a slow process. By taking advantage of the cache, the CPU can preload many program instructions at a time from RAM into the cache.

Then, when the CPU needs its next instruction, it can retrieve the instruction from the fast onboard cache, which eliminates the slow system bus operation, as shown in Figure 5-5.

When the CPU later needs an instruction that is not in the cache, it retrieves the instruction from RAM, but at the same time, it preloads more instructions.

▶ *FACT*

Programs spend 80 percent of their processing with 20 percent of a program's code. Programmers refer this phenomenon as the 80/20 rule.

Over the years, by monitoring program execution, programmers have learned that programs (on average) spend 80 percent of processing time within only 20 percent of the program instructions (the programs do not execute the instructions, or do not frequently repeat the instructions in the remaining 80 percent of the code).

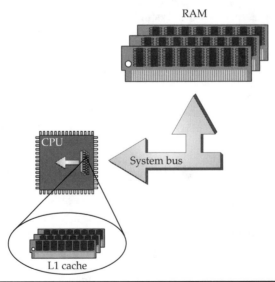

Figure 5.5 The CPU cache reduces slow system-bus operations.

If you think about how you use most of your programs, you will better understand why this is the case. Consider, for example, your word-processing program. Normally when you use your word processor, you simply type. Before you print your document, you may spell check and then save the document to disk. To perform these operations you use less than 20 percent of the word processor's capabilities. You do not, for example, normally manipulate margins, use a wide range of fonts, create tables, insert graphics, change text colors, and so on. Instead, you simply type, print, and save documents.

To further improve the effectiveness of the CPU cache, most systems provide an instruction cache and a data cache. Further, as shown in Figure 5-6, many systems provide a second-level cache, (which users refer to as the *L2 cache*). This second-level cache typically resides outside of the processor, and uses memory that is faster and more expensive than traditional RAM, but normally not as expensive as the L1-cache memory. Normally, the L2 cache is at least twice the size of the L1 cache.

Say you have a large 1MB program and that your CPU has a 256KB cache. In most cases, because you will normally make extensive use of only 20 percent of your program, the program will fit nicely into the cache memory.

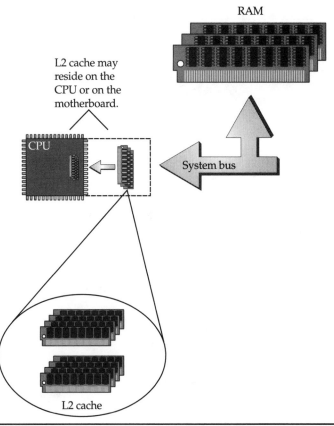

Figure 5.6   Using a second-level cache to further improve performance

▶ *FACT*

Many books and articles refer to the bus that connects the processor to the L2 cache as the "back side bus."

Taking a Closer Look at a System Bus

In general, a bus is simply a set of wires, across which devices communicate by exchanging signals. As shown in Figure 5-7, the system bus consists of a data bus, address bus, and a control bus.

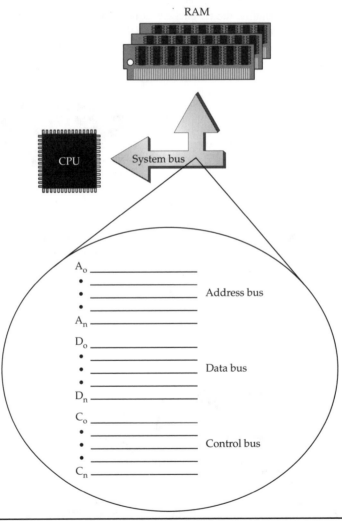

Figure 5.7 A system bus consists of separate buses for data, addresses, and control signals.

Depending on your PC type, the number of wires in each bus will differ. For example, the original IBM PC, for example, used an 8-bit data bus and a 16-bit address bus. Today, in contrast, the Pentium 4 processor uses a 64-bit data bus and a 64-bit address bus.

The data bus contains the data values (and instructions) the CPU is storing or retrieving from RAM. The address bus contains the memory location (the memory address) to which the CPU is placing data (or an instruction) or the address from which the CPU is retrieving data (or an instruction). The control bus specifies the operation the CPU is performing across the bus, such as a memory-read or memory-write operation. The larger the data bus, the more information the bus can transfer within one bus cycle. The larger the address bus, the more RAM the PC can use. The control bus wires contain signals that tell the other devices the current bus operation. For example, when the CPU retrieves data from memory, the control bus contains signals that correspond to a memory-read operation. Likewise, when the CPU stores data in memory, the control bus contains signals that correspond to a memory-write operation.

▶ *FACT*

The Pentium 4 system bus operates at 400 MHz.

Tracking the PC's CPU Evolution

As discussed, the original IBM PC used a 4.33 MHz CPU with an 8-bit data bus and a 20-bit address bus (which could address 1MB of RAM). Today, newer Pentium IV processors support speeds of several gigahertz and use 64-bit data and address buses. Table 5-3 briefly describes the stages in the evolution of the PC's CPU.

CPU	Data Bus (in Bits)	Address Bus (in Bits)
8088	8	20
8086	16	20
80286	16	24
80386SX	16	24
80386DX	32	32
80486	32	32
Pentium	64	32
Pentium II	64	36
Pentium III	64	36
Pentium IV	64	64

Table 5.3   Stages in the Evolution of the PC's CPU

CPUs Use Pipelining to Increase Performance

As you have learned, the CPU normally executes one instruction per clock cycle. A 2 GHz processor, for example, can execute over 2 billion instructions per second. To further increase performance, CPUs take advantage of a technique called *pipelining*, which lets the CPU process several instructions at the same time, using an assembly-line fashion, during each clock tick. To perform pipelining, the CPU must be capable of performing multiple operations at the same time. To better understand how pipelining can improve performance, consider the following simple program:

```
A = B + C

D = E + F

G = H + I
```

To begin, the CPU will execute the statement A = B + C. To perform this simple addition, the CPU must perform the following instructions:

- Load the value of B
- Load the value of C
- Add the values
- Store the results in A

To execute the entire program, the CPU performs the following instructions:

- Load the value of B
- Load the value of C
- Add the values
- Store the results in A
- Load the value of E
- Load the value of F
- Add the values
- Store the results in D
- Load the value of H
- Load the value of I
- Add the values
- Store the result in G

Pipelining improves performance by taking advantage of the fact that when the CPU is performing the addition operation, A + B, for example, the CPU can also retrieve the value for C. Assuming a simple pipeline that lets the CPU perform an operation and transfer data across the system bus (provided the bus is not in use because of instruction), the previous program can overlap two instructions as shown here:

- Load the value of B
- Load the value of C
- Add the values; Load the value of E
- Store the results in A
- Load the value of F
- Add the values; Load the value of H
- Store the results in D
- Load the value of I
- Add the values
- Store the result in G

Behind the scenes, the steps the CPU must perform to implement and coordinate pipelining can be quite complex. However, the performance payoff that pipelining provides is very significant.

As you read about a CPU's pipelining capabilities, you may encounter the term *branch prediction*. To perform their processing, programs must often make decisions. For example, if one value is larger than another, the program may perform one specific set of instructions. If the first value is instead smaller than another, the program may perform a different set of instructions. The following C programming statements illustrate how a program can use an if-else statement to perform specific processing based on a condition. In this case, the program code retrieves the temperature within a nuclear reactor. If the temperature is greater than 200 degrees, the reactor is experiencing a meltdown, and the program initiates a reactor shutdown. If the temperature is not greater than 200 degrees, the program displays a status message telling the plant operators that all is well:

```
Temperature = GetCoreReactorTemperature();

if (Temperature > 200)
  BeginEmergencyNuclearReactorShutdownProcedures();
else
  DisplayConsolesMessage("The reactor is A-OK");
```

As you have learned, to take advantage of pipeline operations, the CPU tries to execute specific instructions in advance. When a program uses an if-else statement, similar to that just shown, the CPU often tries to determine (takes an educated guess) as to which condition is likely to execute. In other words, the CPU tries to predict which branch of the if-else statement the program will execute so that the CPU can pipeline the corresponding statements. If the CPU guesses correctly, it can use the statements it has in the pipeline. If the CPU guesses wrong, it discards the statements in the pipeline. This "guessing process" illustrates the concept of *branch prediction*.

Understanding Single Instruction Multiple Data (SIMD) Operations

As you read about processor capabilities, an acronym you encounter is SIMD, which stands for *single instruction multiple data*. Many high-end programs, such as multimedia or game applications, often require that the CPU perform the same instruction over and over on a wide range of data. For example, within a multimedia application, for example, the CPU may copy data from RAM that represents a video image (the data may reside in several hundred thousand memory locations) to the video card. Years ago, to move the data, the CPU would have to loop through memory locations one at a time. Today, however, the CPU may have an instruction (the "single instruction," or SI, in SIMD) that lets it move all the video data (the "multiple data," or MD, in SIMD) in one step. By consolidating several hundred thousand instructions into one instruction, the CPU improves your system performance. The Pentium IV processor provides over 100 SIMD instructions.

Improving CPU performance is a cumulative process. The designer's goal is to improve performance using a cache, to gain further performance improvements using pipelining, and to gain yet more performance using SIMD instructions.

Using Multiple Processors to Increase Performance

As you know, operating systems such as Windows and Linux let you run multiple programs at the same time. Actually, the operating system simply creates the illusion that the PC is running two more programs at once. Within the PC, the CPU is only capable of running one program's instructions at any one time.

For years, computer engineers and programmers have wrestled with the question that if the user is running multiple programs at the same time, wouldn't it make sense to build multiple processors into the PC? In general, the answer is "yes"—having multiple processors would improve performance. However, keep in mind that most users can rarely sustain 20 percent utilization of their CPU's processing power. The CPU is rarely a system bottleneck.

A multiprocessor system is one that contains two or more processors. Today, most computer magazines advertise high-performance servers that support two or more processors. Typically, such servers are well suited for database, network, or Web operations. Because of their complex electronics (both processors, for example, must electronically coordinate bus, memory, and device use), multiprocessor systems are expensive. Further, not all operating systems support multiprocessors.

With the price of PCs becoming readily affordable, you should weigh the benefits of buying two PCs, as opposed to a single multiprocessor-based system. By having the two PCs, you can share the workload. Further, should one PC fail, you do not have a single point of failure as you would with a single-processor system.

Understanding the Role of the Math Coprocessor

Computers, as you know, are very well suited for performing complex arithmetic operations. That said, complex floating-point math operations are much more time consuming for the PC to perform than standard LOAD and MOVE instructions. For years after the IBM PC was first released, users would purchase and install on their motherboards a special chip called the *math coprocessor*. The CPU would perform the standard operations and the math coprocessor, in turn, would perform the complex arithmetic operations. The 80386 (or simply, the 386), for example, had a math coprocessor named the 80387 (or 387). Today, the math coprocessor is built into the CPU itself. In fact, some of the processor's floating-point instructions are the most complex in the CPU's instruction set.

Understanding Hyperthreading

As you have learned, using pipelining, the CPU performs multiple operations within one clock cycle. To squeeze even more performance from the CPU, engineers and software developers have developed a technique called *hyperthreading*. Programmers often refer to the sequence of instructions the CPU executes as a thread. Many programs today are written to let two or more threads exist at one time. Within a word processor, for example, one thread of execution might print your document in the background, while a second thread performs a spell checking operation.

The basis for hyperthreading is that during a clock cycle, the CPU often does not require the entire cycle to perform its operation. In such cases, the CPU should be able to quickly switch to another thread of execution and process its instructions during the available time. Using hyperthreading, the engineers at Intel have benchmarked 30 percent performance improvements.

Unfortunately, before the CPU can take advantage of hyperthreading, programmers must rewrite applications to support multiple threads and the operating system itself must support hyperthreading. In the future, however, hyperthreading may play an important role in driving greater system performance.

▶ Revisiting CPU Processor Utilization

In Chapter 1, you learned how to determine your PC's processor's utilization by using the Windows 2000 Task Manager or the Active CPU shareware program. If you have not yet run these programs to determine your system's CPU use, do so, as shown in Figure 5-8.

Later, in the tips "If You Are Going to Overclock, Start with Your System Bus" and "CPU Overclocking Using a System Bus Multiplier," you will learn how to improve your system performance by overclocking your CPU and system bus. Assume, for example, that by overclocking your system, you can improve performance by 15 percent. If, however, your PC uses the CPU only 20 percent of the time on average, the performance increase you can expect from overclocking your system is 20 percent of the 15 percent, or simply 3 percent. This means that you may not want to invest the time and effort for such a small increase in performance.

USE IT   If you are using Windows 2000, you can use the Windows Task Manager Processes sheet to determine how much processor time each active application has consumed since the application began, as shown in Figure 5-9. When the CPU is not running another program within Windows 2000, the CPU runs a special idle (or do nothing) application. Normally, within the list the Task Manager displays, the idle application has consumed the most CPU time.

Figure 5.8   Monitoring a system's CPU use

To view CPU use with the Windows 2000 Task Manager, perform these steps:

1. Press CTRL-ALT-DEL. Windows 2000 will display the Windows Security dialog box.
2. Within the Windows Security dialog box, click the Task Manager button. Windows will display the Task Manager dialog box.
3. Within the Task Manager dialog box, click the Processes button. Windows 2000 will display the Processes sheet, as shown in Figure 5-9.

▶ **NOTE**

In the "Using Software to Cool the CPU" tip later in this chapter, you will learn how to download the Amn Refrigerator program to reduce the amount of heat an overclocked CPU generates. The program also lets you view the current CPU use.

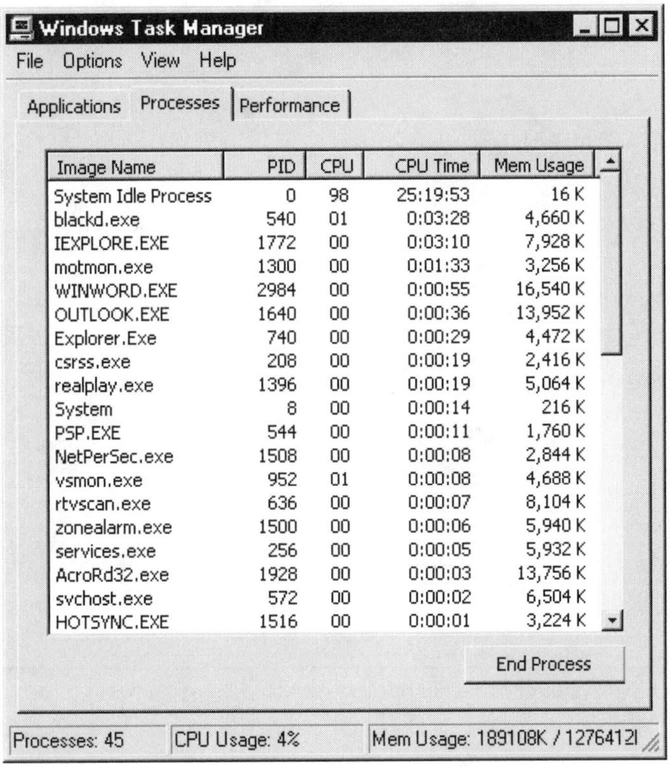
Windows Task Manager
File Options View Help
Applications Processes Performance
Image Name PID CPU CPU Time Mem Usage
System Idle Process 0 98 25:19:53 16 K
blackd.exe 540 01 0:03:28 4,660 K
IEXPLORE.EXE 1772 00 0:03:10 7,928 K
motmon.exe 1300 00 0:01:33 3,256 K
WINWORD.EXE 2984 00 0:00:55 16,540 K
OUTLOOK.EXE 1640 00 0:00:36 13,952 K
Explorer.Exe 740 00 0:00:29 4,472 K
csrss.exe 208 00 0:00:19 2,416 K
realplay.exe 1396 00 0:00:19 5,064 K
System 8 00 0:00:14 216 K
PSP.EXE 544 00 0:00:11 1,760 K
NetPerSec.exe 1508 00 0:00:08 2,844 K
vsmon.exe 952 01 0:00:08 4,688 K
rtvscan.exe 636 00 0:00:07 8,104 K
zonealarm.exe 1500 00 0:00:06 5,940 K
services.exe 256 00 0:00:05 5,932 K
AcroRd32.exe 1928 00 0:00:03 13,756 K
svchost.exe 572 00 0:00:02 6,504 K
HOTSYNC.EXE 1516 00 0:00:01 3,224 K
End Process
Processes: 45
CPU Usage: 4%
Mem Usage: 189108K / 1276412I

Figure 5.9 Using the Task Manager to display each application's CPU use

Determining Your System's CPU Type

USE IT Before you can "tweak" your system's CPU performance, you should know specifics about your CPU type. Within Windows, you can view general information about the CPU using the System Properties dialog box, shown in Figure 5-10.

In Chapter 7, you will examine your PC's CMOS setup program in greater detail. Often, the CMOS setup program will display specifics about the current processor, such as its type and speed. Also, in Chapter 1 you learned now to use the Ziff Davis WinBench benchmark programs. Within the WinBench program, you can select the Windows menu System Info option to display the CPU type, speed, and the amount of system cache, as shown in Figure 5-11.

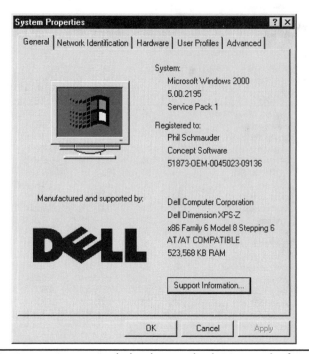

Figure 5.10   Using the System Properties dialog box to display general information about your CPU type

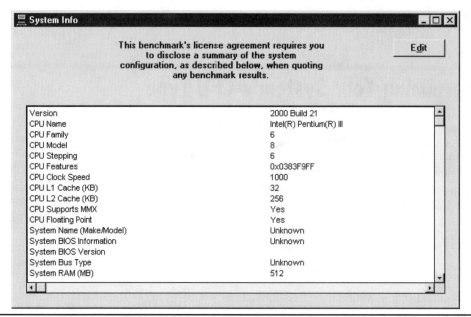

Figure 5.11   Using the WinBench benchmark program to display CPU specifics

Determining Your System Bus Speed

As you learned in this chapter, the CPU uses the system bus to communicate with the other chips within its chipset (such as RAM and the BIOS). Because the system bus operates at a slower speed than the CPU, the system bus will always be a bottleneck. Later in this chapter's tips, you will learn that your system may let you improve its performance by increasing (overclocking) the system bus. Before you begin, you may want to know the speed at which your system bus is operating.

USE IT Depending on your CMOS setup program, you may be able to view your PC's current system bus speed within the setup, which, if you can, means you can later use the CMOS setup program to increase your system bus speed.

Also, if your have the technical documentation for your motherboard (which you can likely download from your PC manufacturer's Web site), you should be able to locate jumpers on the motherboard that control the system bus speed. By examining the current jumper positions, you can determine the current bus speed.

Finally, as shown in Figure 5-12, you can use the SiSoftware Sandra (System ANalyser, Diagnostic and Reporting Assistant) program to display your current system bus speed.

To down use the Sandra program, visit the SiSoftware Web site at www.sisoftware.demon.co.uk.

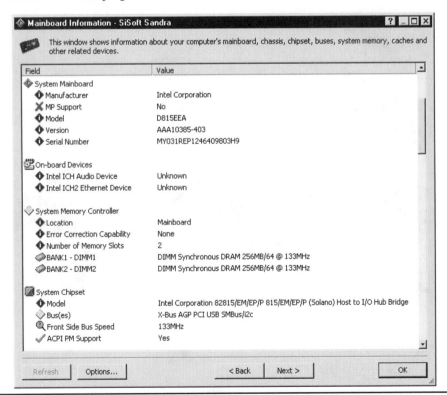

Figure 5.12   Using the SiSoftware Sandra program to display the system bus speed

Enable Your Processor's Onboard Cache

Today, to reduce the number of slow system bus operations the CPU must perform, most CPUs provide one or more built-in caches. Most CPUs have two layers of cache memory, which users refer to as L1 and L2. Periodically, a PC will encounter a power-on self-test error or other related problem that may cause the PC to disable the processor cache—which, in turn, significantly downgrades the system performance.

USE IT   To enable the processor cache (or to simply verify that the cache is enabled), you can use your CMOS setup program. Chapter 7 discusses CMOS operations in detail. Normally, as shown in Figure 5-12, the CMOS setup program will contain options you can select to enable or disable the L1 and L2 cache. Make sure you enable both. Then exit the CMOS program after saving your changes. Your system will restart with processor cache enabled.

Replacing Your Existing CPU with a Faster CPU

USE IT   Depending on your existing CPU type and chipset, you may, as shown in Figure 5-13, be able to upgrade your existing CPU simply by removing your current CPU and plugging in a newer, faster CPU that fits into your CPU's slot.

The CPU is a chip that resides within a slot on the motherboard. Depending on your CPU, chipset, and motherboard type, the CPU's slot type will differ. Figure 5-14 illustrates common CPU slot types that have evolved over the years.

As you have learned, the CPU communicates with RAM, the BIOS, and the chipset by using the system bus. Depending on the processors type (and age), the number of wires in the system bus will

Figure 5.13   Upgrading a CPU with a faster slot-compatible CPU

vary. The socket into which you insert the CPU connects the chip to the system bus, a power source, and so on. As you might guess, therefore, a newer CPU that uses a larger database or address bus needs more pin-connectors than an older CPU. Thus, many CPUs will not be slot-compatible, which means that the newer CPU won't fit into your existing CPU slot. Also, some newer Pentium processors use an edge connector, shown in Figure 5-15, as opposed to slot-based pins.

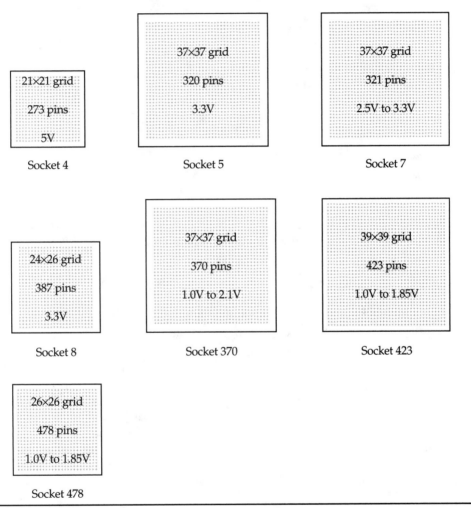

Figure 5.14 Common CPU slot types

Figure 5.15 Newer Pentium processors use edge connectors.

Under the right conditions, upgrading a CPU by installing a newer, faster CPU within the socket may make sense. First, the upgrade process is easy: you simply take one chip out and put another in its place. Second, the newer chip may come with its own built-in fan and heat sink, so you do not have to worry about excess heat the faster chip may generate. Third, the processor will likely come with more L1 and L2 cache memory, which may likely have a larger performance impact than the processor's faster clock speed.

The problem (or shortcoming) of upgrading only the CPU is that the new CPU may introduce yet a larger disparity between the CPU clock speed, the system bus, and possibly other chips in the chipset. Unfortunately, the only way you can resolve that issue is to upgrade your motherboard.

Because of its reliance on its fast chipset, users cannot, for example, upgrade a Pentium III processor to a very high-performance Pentium IV processor (the two processors simply are not pin-compatible).

Some third-party hardware manufacturers offer cards you can plug into an expansion slot, or in some cases, plug into the CPU slot that provides you with a way to use a newer CPU in a system that does not provide pin-level compatibility. In general, although these cards may let you use a faster CPU, the cards introduce their own overhead (which will consume some of the performance gain), and you will still have an imbalance between the CPU speed, bus speed, and chipset. With the cost of motherboards becoming more affordable, a better alternative is to upgrade your motherboard.

Overclocking May Destroy Your Processor

Within the CPU is a built-in clock that controls when the CPU executes instructions. Likewise, the system bus uses a clock to coordinate the exchange of data between the CPU, RAM, the BIOS, and other chips within the chipset. Normally the system bus runs at a much slower speed than the CPU.

To ensure compatibility and increase chip longevity, the CPU and system bus do not operate at their full potential. Instead, PC manufacturers may back off a CPU that is capable of running at 500 MHz, for example, to 400MHz when they install the CPU within a PC. Likewise, the PC manufacturer may back off a system bus that is capable of running at 85 MHz to 66 MHz. By backing off speeds in this way, the PC manufacturers increase compatibility (among chips in the chipset), increase reliability, and reduce heat (which the electronic signals within the bus and CPU generate). What this means is that your expensive, state-of-the-art PC that you just unboxed and set up is not running as fast as it can.

To improve system performance many (very technically astute) users will increase either their CPU clock speed, bus speed, or both. Users refer to the process of speeding up their system in this way as *overclocking.*

USE IT By overclocking the CPU or system bus, you can gain a significant performance gain at little cost (you may, for example, need to add another fan to your system unit to help eliminate excess heat). That said, overclocking can be a challenging process, and it is not a task for the "faint of heart" or the "faint of wallet." By overclocking your system, you may overheat and destroy your CPU or your motherboard, in which case you will get the opportunity to improve your system performance by replacing it.

▶ *CAUTION*

Unless you have considerable technical knowledge, or you can afford to discard a PC you destroy, do not overclock your system.

▶ *NOTE*

Many users successfully overclock their systems to drive maximum performance. Many other users destroy their systems in the process. If you have a system that you are not using and you do not need in the future, that system should be the first one you try to overclock.

Before and After You Overclock, Run Benchmarks

USE IT If you plan to overclock your system bus or CPU, you should first run an extensive set of benchmarks. Then save the benchmark results so that you can use them to determine the improvement overclocking adds to your system performance.

If you can successfully start Windows after you overclock your system, you should immediately run benchmarks—not just to determine the performance improvement overclocking has introduced, but to put your system through extensive testing. Often, overclocking a system will cause the system bus or CPU to generate more heat, which may eventually lead to intermittent errors after the system has been running for a period of time. One of the best ways to determine if heat is going to be a problem in your system is to "put your system through the wringer," so to speak, but letting it run benchmarks for several hours. If your system executes several hours of benchmarks successfully, you will likely not encounter heat-related errors in the future.

If You Are Going to Overclock, Start with Your System Bus

The CPU uses the system bus to access RAM, the BIOS, and other chips within the chipset. Because the system bus operates at speeds much slower than that of the CPU, the system bus creates a significant bottleneck within your system.

If you decide to overclock your system, start with the system bus first. Do not try to overclock the system bus and the CPU at the same time—should your system fail, you would then need to determine whether the system bus or the CPU was at fault. Instead, start with the system bus.

Earlier in this chapter, you learned how to monitor your system's CPU use. Most users utilize only a small portion of their CPU's processing power. Many PC benchmarks have shown that if you must choose between overclocking your system bus or your CPU (in cases where the system does not run if you try to overclock both), you will get better performance by choosing to overclock the system bus.

USE IT In Chapter 7, you will examine your PC's CMOS in detail. Many CMOS programs let you increase or decrease the system bus speed. If your CMOS program lets you increase the system bus speed, increase the speed one step at a time. After you change the bus speed, restart your system and then run several benchmark programs to verify that your system is working correctly. Then, repeat the process with yet a faster system bus speed.

If your system's CMOS setup program does not let you change the system bus speed, you will have to use motherboard jumpers to increase the speed. Within your PC's technical documentation (which you can likely download from your PC manufacturer's Web site), you will find jumper settings you can use to change your system bus speeds.

When you change your system bus speed, do so one step at a time. This means that if your system bus is currently running at 66 MHz, and your bus supports 75 MHz, 85 MHz, and 100 MHz, first select the 75 MHz bus speed and then restart your system. After you are satisfied that your system is running correctly, you can try yet a faster bus speed.

Troubleshooting a System Bus Overclocking Error

USE IT If your system fails to start after you overclock your system bus, the problem may be due to an incompatibility between the system bus speed and the CPU speed. In the "CPU Overclocking Using a System Bus Multiplier" section later in this chapter, you will learn how to change your CPU's clock speed. When you increase your system bus speed, you may need to decrease your CPU speed before the two will work in unison. Many PCs set the CPU clock to a multiple of the system bus speed. Common multiples include 2, 2.5, 3, 3.5, and so on. If your system fails after you overclock the system bus, you may simply need to reduce the CPU clock multiplier.

You may be questioning why, if the goal is faster performance, you would want to decrease your CPU clock speed. Many benchmarks have shown that having a faster system bus and a slightly slower CPU often drives better total system performance than having a slower system bus and a fast CPU.

The only way you will know which setting gives your system the best performance is to try the setting and then run the benchmarks discussed in Chapter 1.

If you find that after overclocking your system bus, your PC runs fine for a while and then begins to experience intermittent errors, the problem is probably due to excess heat in your system unit, which is generated by the signals traveling across the bus at the faster speeds. In such cases, you may need to install another fan to better dissipate the heat from within your system unit. If you can place your PC in a safe location, you might try running the PC for a few hours without the system unit cover (which will let the hot air exit the chassis) to see if the same errors occur.

Venting Your System Unit Better to Remove Excess Heat

If you talk to the "overclocking experts," they will tell you that increasing (or decreasing) the temperature within the system unit by only a few degrees can have a substantial influence on the life of the motherboard's sensitive electronic components (which includes the CPU). Many users can probably reduce the heat within their system units today, simply by moving their PCs a little farther away from the walls or their desks so that the PC's existing fans can better vent heat from the system.

Excess heat is the biggest threat to your system when you overclock the CPU or system bus. Should you begin to experience errors after your system has been running for some time, the errors are probably heat-related.

 USE IT   To reduce heat within your system unit, you should install an additional fan. If you shop on the Web, you will find a wide range of fans available for under $25. One type of fan will slide into one of your PC's unused drive bays. A second fan type will slide into one of your PC's expansion slots, venting heat out the back of the slot. To power the fans, you simply connect the fan to one of the power supply cables.

CPU Overclocking Using a System Bus Multiplier

USE IT   Depending on your system type, the steps you must perform to overclock your CPU will differ. Often, you will select the CPU speed that you desire as a multiple of the system bus speed (common multipliers include 2, 2.5, 3, 3.5, and so on). As is the case for overclocking your system bus, many PCs will let you overclock your CPU by using the CMOS setup program or by changing jumpers that appear on the motherboard (which will be specific to your system type).

If you have not yet tried overclocking your system bus, do so before you try overclocking your CPU. In some cases, you may not successfully overclock your system bus and your CPU. Often, users will get better system performance by increasing the system bus speed.

Depending on your CPU, motherboard, and chipset, the exact steps you must perform to successfully overclock your system will differ. Fortunately, someone else has very likely already tried to overclock a system similar to yours and has quite likely recorded the correct steps you must perform on a Web site, such as that shown in Figure 5-16. Before you set out with your Web-based instructions in hand, take a few moments to examine the Web site's quality and technical content. Remember, overclocking your system can destroy your CPU or motherboard. If you find the instructions suspect, continue your search.

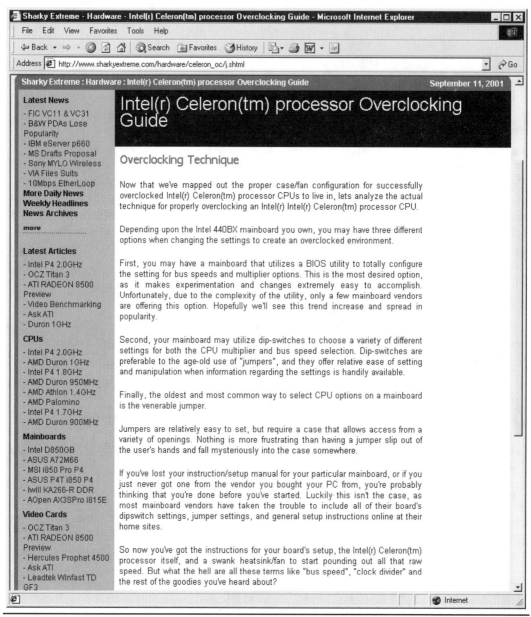

Figure 5.16　You may find step-by-step instructions for overclocking your PC on the Web.

Further, several sites on the Web offer databases that provide optimal CPU and system bus settings for a wide range of CPUs and chipsets. One of the most complete databases is at www.sysopt.com/ocdatabase.html, shown in Figure 5-17. Using the information the performance database, you may better target the clock speeds for your system.

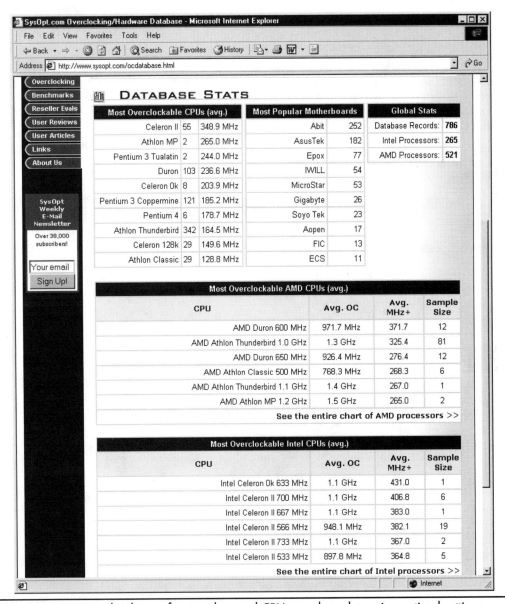

Figure 5.17   Using a database of system bus and CPU speeds to determine optimal settings

Troubleshooting a CPU Overclocking Problem

Troubleshooting a CPU overclocking error is quite similar to troubleshooting an error that occurs as a result of overclocking your system bus. Normally, should your system start, run for a period of time, and then fail, the problem is heat-related.

USE IT To reduce heat within the CPU, users will sometimes attach a fan to the CPU, similar to that shown in Figure 5-18.

Depending on your CPU type, the size and shape of the fan you attach to your CPU will differ. A good source for CPU fan information on the Web is at www.cpucooling-overclocking.com/products.htm. Again, depending on the fan's type, the connector you will use to power the fan may differ. Many fans will use a TX3 connector, whereas others will connect to a standard connector from the power supply.

Figure 5.18   Using a fan to vent heat from the CPU

Using Software to Cool the CPU

Sometimes, depending on their CPU type, users run special programs that halt the CPU during idle times, which in turn reduces the amount of heat the CPU generates. Across the Web, you can find several programs that perform such operations, such as the Amn Refrigerator shown in Figure 5-19.

USE IT   Heat is the most likely cause of failure for a CPU overclock operation. If you overclock your CPU and begin to experience intermittent errors, you likely have a heat problem. Before you turn to other sources, such as a CPU fan or heat sink, you may want to try using software to cool your CPU. In such cases, visit the Amn Software Web site at www.amn.ru and download the Amn Refrigerator freeware program that halts your CPU when it is not in use to reduce the heat the CPU produces.

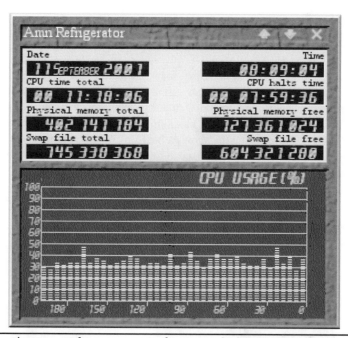

Figure 5.19   Using the Amn Refrigerator to "software cool" the CPU

If Heat Is Not the Problem, Increase the Voltage

USE IT   If, after overclocking your CPU, you begin to experience intermittent errors that do not seem heat-related, the problem may be that your CPU requires more voltage to run at the faster clock speed. If you are lucky, you may find an article on the Web specific to your CPU, motherboard, and chipset that discusses the steps you must perform to increase the CPU's base power. Further, if you are very lucky, the article will not use the terms "soldering iron" and "resistor." Many motherboards provide jumpers you can use to increase the CPU's base power.

When you increase the voltage to the CPU, you will also increase the heat within the chip (more voltage and faster signals generate more heat). If you create too much heat, you will destroy the CPU. As a rule, you should not increase the CPU voltage more than 20 percent. Further, as you increase the voltage through the CPU, you may need to install a fan—as discussed in the "Venting Your System Unit Better to Remove Excess Heat" section—that helps vent heat away from the CPU.

Using Heat Sinks

USE IT   To reduce heat within the system unit, many users add additional system unit fans. Further, to better cool the CPU, many users will attach fans directly to the CPU itself. Sometimes, a fan alone is not sufficient to cool a chip. In such cases, you may need to add a *heat sink* to the chip. In general, a heat sink is a piece of metal that you glue (using a special heat sink glue) or connect to a chip. Figure 5-20, for example, shows a heat sink on a Pentium processor. The metal conducts heat away from the chip, which the fan can more easily dissipate. Most electronics stores sell heat sinks and the adhesive you will need to attach the sink to the chip.

Figure 5.20   A heat sink conducts heat away from the chip.

Using a Heat Sensor

USE IT   As you have learned, excess heat within your system can damage your PC's sensitive electronic components. To reduce the risk of damage from heat, you may want to install a small heat sensor within your system unit. When the temperature within the system unit reaches a specific level, the heat sensor will sound an audible alarm. When the alarm occurs, you can shut down and power off your system. Then you may need to add another fan within the system unit or disable overclocking until you can provide an adequate heat sink.

CHAPTER 6

Upgrading the PC BIOS

TIPS IN THIS CHAPTER

I n Chapter 5, you learned that within your PC, the CPU is the workhorse that executes the instructions within each program you run. Without the CPU, the PC could not perform meaningful work. In this chapter, you will examine the Basic Input Output System (BIOS), which users pronounce as "bye-ose." The BIOS plays several key supporting roles within the PC's operations. To begin, each time your system starts, the first instructions the CPU executes reside within the BIOS. These BIOS-based instructions initiate and control the PC's power-on self-test (POST).

Second, the BIOS provides the CMOS setup program you will use in Chapter 7 to configure key system settings (such as your disk-drive type, amount of RAM, processor-cache control, and power-management options). Finally, the BIOS, true to its name, provides a set of "basic" input and output services (programming instructions) that the operating system (such as Windows) can build upon to interact with devices such as the keyboard, mouse, disk drives, video, and printer, as well as a wide range of Plug and Play devices.

Most users will never have to upgrade their system BIOS. However, depending on new hardware cards you install or operations you perform (such as CPU overclocking, as discussed in Chapter 5), you may need to update your PC BIOS. This chapter examines the steps you must perform to upgrade your BIOS, which as you will learn, has become much easier over the past few years.

The BIOS Resides on the Motherboard

The BIOS contains the instructions the PC executes when you first power on your system, as well as instructions that programs (such as the operating system) can use to interact with various devices. These instructions reside within one or more chips, which sit on the motherboard. In older PCs, the BIOS consisted of two chips, which users referred to as the *odd* and *even* BIOS chips. Today, most systems have a single flash-based BIOS chip, similar to that shown in Figure 6-1, that users can upgrade simply by running a software program.

Assume, for example, that hardware manufacturers create a high-speed wireless network device that connects to a parallel port. Unfortunately, because the device is new, most BIOS chips within existing PCs will not support the device. However, because the flash BIOS is software upgradeable, users who want to take advantage of the device may be able to download a BIOS upgrade from their PC manufacturer's Web site, which they can run to install support for the new device.

▶ *NOTE*

To improve performance, most operating systems no longer use BIOS-based code; instead, they provide their own code to implement tasks the BIOS previously performed.

Reviewing the Three-Key BIOS Components

As discussed, and as shown in Figure 6-2, the BIOS provides three key roles within the PC. First, the BIOS oversees the PC startup process and runs the PC's POST. Second, the BIOS provides the CMOS setup program and houses key system settings within the CMOS memory. Finally, the BIOS

Figure 6.1   Most PCs today use a flash BIOS that is software upgradeable.

provides instructions that programs can use to interact with a wide range of hardware devices, including support for Plug and Play hardware. In fact, the operating system builds its support for most hardware devices on top of the BIOS input/output routines.

Newer Operating Systems Make Less Use of the BIOS

As you have learned, conceptually, the operating system sits on top of the BIOS. In the past, operating systems such as MS-DOS made extensive use of the BIOS to perform input and output operations. Today, however, newer operating systems such as Windows 2000 may not use the BIOS at all after your system completes its POST and starts the operating system's boot process.

To perform the operations that BIOS once performed, such as video and disk operations, operating systems simply provide their own program instructions. As a result, many operations that users used to perform to improve BIOS performance, such as shadowing the BIOS by directing the PC to use a

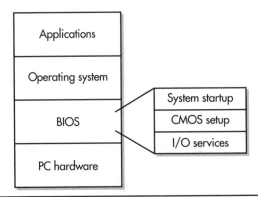

Figure 6.2   The PC BIOS plays three key roles: startup, setup, and device I/O.

RAM-based copy of the BIOS (as opposed to accessing the BIOS from the slower ROM chip), no longer provide users with a performance improvement. In fact, by leaving such operations enabled (in Chapter 7 you will learn how to enable and disable such operations using the CMOS setup program), users may consume system resources, RAM specifically, to hold a copy of the BIOS that the system never uses. Today, the BIOS exists to start the PC's boot process, to provide the user with a way to access CMOS settings, to assist in the PC's power-management capabilities, and to provide operating system support for Plug and Play devices.

On the Web, in books, and in magazines, you may encounter many ways to tweak your BIOS for optimal performance. Unfortunately, many of the techniques, which *did* improve performance a few years ago, no longer apply, either due to newer operating systems or hardware upgrades.

Understanding the Power-On Self-Test (POST)

As you have learned, when you turn on your PC, the BIOS initiates the PC's POST. Depending on the BIOS type, the tests and the order in which the BIOS performs them may vary. Table 6-1 briefly describes common tests the POST performs. To determine the specific tests your BIOS performs, visit your BIOS manufacturer's Web site. Within this chapter's tips, you will learn how to troubleshoot the startup process by tracking a test code value the post places at I/O port 80H as it begins a test. By examining the status value, you can determine which tests your PC successfully passes and which test is causing the error.

Test	Purpose
CPU test	Sets and examines various CPU status flags using specific operations. In some cases, it runs a test program built into the CPU itself.
CMOS battery	Verifies that the CMOS battery is providing power capable of maintaining the CMOS settings.
CMOS checksum	Calculates a checksum value for CMOS settings and compares the value with the result stored in the CMOS checksum. If the checksums are not equal, a setting error has occurred.
Memory test	Examines the PC's memory to ensure that it can be written and read correctly.
Video ROM test	Performs a series of video operations to ensure that the video card and its video memory are working correctly.
Keyboard test	Interacts with keyboard controller (that resides within the keyboard) to ensure that the keyboard is working and is accessible.
Port detection and initialization	Verifies that the serial and parallel ports are accessible and initializes the ports to their default settings.

Table 6.1   Sample Tests Performed During the System's POST

Test	Purpose
Disk controller test	Interacts with the floppy and hard disk controllers to ensure that the disks are accessible.
BIOS checksum	Calculates a checksum for the BIOS itself and compares the value to the checksum the BIOS maintains. If the two values are not equal, the BIOS chip has likely failed.

Table 6.1   Sample Tests Performed During the System's POST (*continued*)

Understanding the BIOS Services

In general, the BIOS is a set of instructions that reside at specific locations within a chip. To access the BIOS instructions, the programs either branch to a specific memory address, or programs generate a specific interrupt (Chapter 4 discusses interrupts in detail), which results in the PC branching to the instruction's specific memory address. To give you an overview of the BIOS operations, Table 6-2 briefly summarizes the BIOS services, which the operating system or other programs can use to perform specific tasks.

Interrupt Number (in Hexadecimal)	Service
00H	Divide-by-zero error handler
01H	Single step (debugging)
02H	Nonmaskable interrupt
03H	Breakpoint
04H	Arithmetic overflow handler
05H	Print screen contents
06H	Invalid operation code (OP code) handler
07H	Coprocessor not available
08H	System timer services
09H	Keyboard device services
0AH	Cascaded interrupt controller
0BH	Serial port services (COM2)
0CH	Serial port services (COM1)
0DH	Parallel port services (LPT2)
0EH	Floppy disk services
0FH	Parallel port services (LPT1)

Table 6.2   A Summary of the BIOS Services

Interrupt Number (in Hexadecimal)	Service
10H	Video services
11H	Get equipment list service
12H	Get conventional memory service
13H	Hard disk services
14H	Serial communication services
15H	System services
16H	Keyboard services
17H	Parallel printer services
18H	Load ROM BASIC service
19H	Load DOS service
1AH	Timer services
1BH	CTRL-BREAK service
1CH	User timer service
1DH	Video control parameters
1EH	Floppy disk parameters
1FH	Video graphics service
40H	Floppy disk (revector) service
41H	Hard disk (drive C) parameters
42H	EGA video driver
43H	Video graphics characters
44H	Novell Netware services
46H	Hard disk (drive D) parameters
4AH	User alarm
67H	EMS services
70H	Real-time clock
71H	Redirect interrupt cascade
75H	Math coprocessor exception
76H	Hard disk support
77H	Suspend request

Table 6.2 A Summary of the BIOS Services *(continued)*

The Evolution of BIOS Chips

Originally, the PC BIOS consisted of two chips, an odd BIOS chip and an even BIOS chip. To upgrade the BIOS, the user had to replace both chips. These two BIOS chips were actual integrated circuits. The instructions the BIOS performed where essentially hardwired into the chips. Over time, these two chips where replaced by an EPROM (erasable programmable read-only memory) chip. An EPROM chip is programmable (and hence, you can change its contents), but to reprogram the chip, you must have a *prom burner* that sends an ultraviolet light through an opening in the chip. To upgrade their BIOS, users normally still had to replace the BIOS chip. The advantage of the EPROM chip was that the chip was easier for manufacturers to update.

Today, most PCs contain a flash BIOS chip, which users can update by simply running a program. The flash BIOS provides a very easy way for users to upgrade their system BIOS.

Determining Your BIOS Type

With the motherboards and chips becoming smaller and smaller, determining which chip is actually the BIOS can be a difficult process. If you are using a newer PC, your system likely contains a flash BIOS. However, as previously shown in Figure 6-1, a flash BIOS looks very much like any other chip. An EPROM BIOS, in contrast, contains a small window on the top of the chip through which chip manufacturers (and technicians who own a prom burner) can reprogram the chip.

In some cases, the chip may simply have the name of the BIOS manufacturer, such as AMI, Award, Intel, or Phoenix. After you locate the BIOS, write down the information printed on top of the chip. You can use this information later when you search the manufacturer's Web site to determine if an upgrade is available.

If you cannot readily identify the BIOS chip, you should turn to your PC manufacturer's Web site. You may be able to find a motherboard schematic you can use to determine the BIOS chip's location, or you may find a part number for the BIOS (which will normally appear in small numbers on the chip itself) that you can then use to search your motherboard for the chip.

Using Your System to Display BIOS Information

Normally, each time your system starts, it will briefly display your BIOS information on the screen. In addition, if you enter the CMOS setup program, as discussed in Chapter 7, you can display specifics about your BIOS, as shown in Figure 6-3.

Within Windows, you can also determine information about your BIOS, such as your BIOS date, version, and manufacturer. To display the BIOS information, perform these steps:

1. Select Start | Run. Windows will display the Run dialog box.

2. Within the Run dialog box, type **REGEDIT** and press ENTER. Windows will run the Registry Editor.

3. Within the Registry Editor, select Edit | Find. The Registry Editor will display the Find dialog box.

4. Within the Find dialog box, type **BIOS** and press ENTER. The Registry Editor, in turn, will begin searching its entries for the string "BIOS". Depending on your Registry's entries, you may need to press the F3 (find next) key several times before the Registry Editor displays your BIOS date and version information, as shown here.

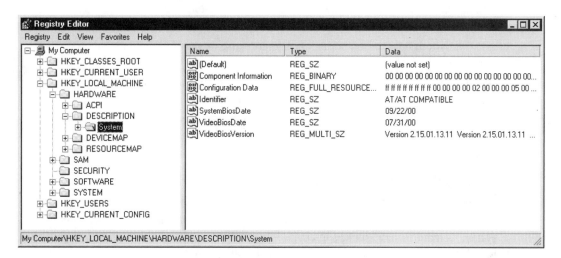

Figure 6.3   Using the CMOS setup program to display BIOS information

In addition to using the Registry Editor, you can use the System Information utility to display BIOS information by performing these steps:

1. Select Start | Programs | Accessories. Windows will display the Accessories submenu.

2. Within the Accessories submenu, select System Tools | System Information. Windows will run the Microsoft System Information utility.

3. Within the System Information utility, click your mouse on the plus sign (+) that precedes Components. The System Information utility will expand its list of components.

4. Within the system component list, click your mouse on the System entry. The System Information utility will display its list of system components.

5. Within the System Component list, click on the Advanced radio button and then scroll through the list to locate the motherboard BIOS entry.

Understanding the Plug and Play BIOS

Over the past few years, hardware upgrades have become much easier for users to perform due to Plug and Play support. In general, a Plug and Play hardware card identifies itself to the system and tells the system its requirements, such as interrupt-request (IRQ) settings. The operating system, in turn, will tell examine the PC's available resources and then assign resources as necessary to the Plug and Play card. In the past, users had to track their system's IRQ use and then manually configure new cards by using jumpers and switches.

To perform Plug and Play operations, a PC must have a Plug and Play BIOS chip and must be running an operating system, such as Windows, that supports Plug and Play. In general, any PC BIOS chip manufactured in the last five years should provide Plug and Play support.

During the system startup process, the Plug and Play BIOS resolves hardware resource conflicts so that the operating system can successfully run. In addition to having the ability to interact with Plug and Play–based devices, the Plug and Play BIOS also provides support for legacy (non–Plug and Play hardware) devices. In Chapter 7, you will learn that most newer CMOS setup programs let you reserve hardware resources such as IRQ and memory addresses for legacy cards. The CMOS stores this information within a CMOS memory location that users refer to as the Extended System Configuration Data (ESCD).

When to Upgrade Your BIOS

As you have learned, to upgrade a flash BIOS, you simply download a program that you run to perform the upgrade. Because of the simplicity of the upgrading the BIOS, many users wonder why they simply just shouldn't upgrade their BIOS each time a new version is available. In general, the answer falls back to the old adage "if it's not broken, don't fix it."

If your system is working, you should think twice about upgrading your BIOS. Although the new BIOS may provide new capabilities, the new BIOS may introduce an error that prevents your PC or a specific device from working. So, unless you have a specific objective in mind, you may put off upgrading your BIOS. Should you upgrade your BIOS only to find that your system no longer works, turn to the "Recovering from an Errant BIOS Upgrade" tip later in this chapter.

Learning More About Your BIOS

Earlier in this chapter, you learned how to determine specifics about your BIOS, such as its version number, date, and manufacturer. With this information in hand, you can turn to the Web to determine more information about your BIOS, such as whether an upgrade is available, as well as the upgrade's purpose. Further, if you are using a flash BIOS, you can likely download the upgrade program. To help you get started, Table 6-3 lists the Web sites for several BIOS manufacturers. In addition, you should visit your PC manufacturer's Web site and search for BIOS upgrade information. You may find, for example, that an upgrade to your BIOS exists. However, when you visit your PC manufacturer, you may learn that the BIOS upgrade is not compatible with your PC motherboard.

USE IT   Perhaps the easiest way to locate information on your BIOS is to use a search engine, such as Yahoo or Google. Simply type in your BIOS specifics, such as 82802AB. As shown in Figure 6-4, the search engine will likely locate your BIOS manufacturer's site, as well as sites that may provide you with additional insight to your BIOS.

BIOS Manufacturer	Web Site
Abit	www.abit-usa.com/
Acer	www.acer.com/
ALI (Acer Laboratories)	www.acerlabs.com/
American Megatrends	www.megatrends.com
AMI	www.megatrends.com
Amptron	www.amptron.com/html/bios.html
ASUS	www.asus.com.tw/Products/motherboard/bios.html
Award	www.award.com/
Biostar	www.biostar-usa.com/Bios/bios_index_page.htm
Dell	www.dell.com
Compaq Computer	www.compaq.com
Gateway	www.gateway.com/
Intel	www.intel.com/
Micron	www.micron.com/
Mylex	www.mylex.com/products/flashbios/index.html
Phoenix	www.phoenix.com/
Tekram Technologies	www.tekram.com/
Toshiba	www.csd.toshiba.com/tais/csd/support/products/bios/
Tyan	www.tyan.com/support/html/bios_support.html

Table 6.3   Key BIOS Sites on the Web

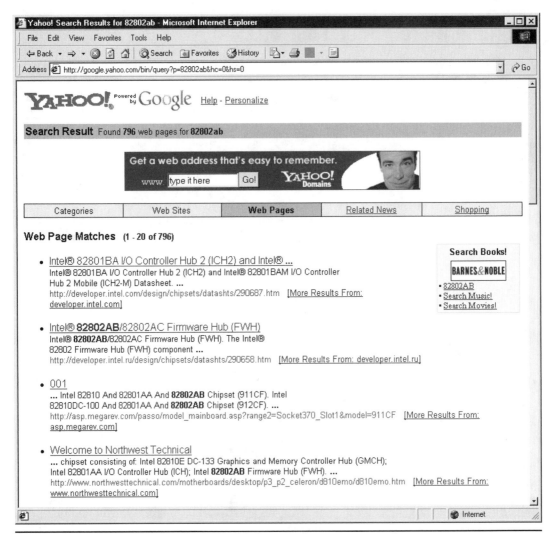

Figure 6.4 Using a search engine to quickly locate information regarding your BIOS

Determining Your Motherboard and Chipset Information

Before you download an upgrade for your BIOS, you may need to know specifics about your motherboard and your chipset, so you can ensure that the upgrade is compatible with your system. Chapter 4 examined the motherboard and chipsets in detail.

In the past, you could examine the motherboard itself to find a description that you could use to identify the motherboard type. Today, with real estate on the motherboard harder to come by, there is less descriptive information regarding the motherboard or its chips. In the past, for example, you could readily find chips that were labeled "BIOS." Today, finding specific chips on the motherboard is much more difficult. To determine your PC's motherboard type, your motherboard, you should first visit your PC manufacturer's Web site, where you can normally find a wide range of information, from chipsets to schematics.

Depending on your BIOS type, the BIOS identifier string (which the BIOS may display as your system starts, or which you may be able to view from within the CMOS setup program) may contain information you can use to track down your motherboard. For example, within the AWARD BIOS identification string, characters 6 and 7 correspond to the motherboard manufacturer. Likewise, within the AMI BIOS, the third set of numbers within the serial number provide motherboard information. Across the Web, one of the most useful sites for tracking down motherboard information from the BIOS is at www.computercraft.com/docs/mbid.html. In addition, if you have a device's identification number, you may be able to learn more about the device, such as its manufacturer by entering the number into the equipment search engine at the Federal Communications Commission's Web site at www.fcc.gov/oet/fccid/.

To determine your PC's chipset, you again likely must turn to your PC manufacturer's Web site. Your CPU and your BIOS are the two largest and most significant chips within the chipset. By knowing your CPU and BIOS information (type, version number, and so on), you can normally locate the corresponding chipset ID at your manufacturer's Web site. If you install a BIOS upgrade that is not specific to your chipset, the upgrade will likely fail, and your system may not run.

Upgrading a Flash BIOS

As you have learned, to upgrade a Flash BIOS, you simply must run a BIOS-upgrade program that corresponds to your motherboard and chipset. The upgrade program, in turn, will "reprogram" your BIOS.

 As discussed, you can normally find a BIOS-upgrade program at your PC manufacturer's Web. If, for some reason, you cannot get an upgrade from your PC manufacturer, you should then look to your BIOS chip manufacturer's site. The advantage of getting the BIOS-upgrade program from your PC manufacturer is that the program is likely to be correct for your system's motherboard and chipset. Before you upgrade your flash BIOS, be doubly sure that your BIOS upgrade program is compatible with your motherboard and chipset. If the program is not compatible with your system, you may leave your system in an unbootable state.

Download the BIOS upgrade program and place it on a bootable floppy disk. To simplify your recovery process should the BIOS upgrade fail, you should also download a copy of the program file that corresponds to your current BIOS and place it on the bootable floppy disk as well. Each BIOS version will reside in a file whose name corresponds in some way to the version number. You can place both files, therefore, onto the same floppy disk.

Next, restart your system, booting from the floppy. When the operating system displays its command-line prompt, type in the program's filename to run the upgrade program. After the upgrade completes, remove the floppy disk and restart your system.

Recovering from an Errant BIOS Upgrade

To recover from an errant upgrade to your flash BIOS, you must run a program that installs your previous BIOS. Normally, you can find a program that corresponds to your previous BIOS on your PC manufacturer's Web site. Before you upgrade your flash BIOS, you should download a copy of the program that you can use to reinstall your current BIOS.

USE IT If you cannot find a program at your PC manufacturer's Web site that you can use to restore your BIOS, visit the Micro Firmware Web site at www.firmware.com/support/recovery. The Site maintains a list of BIOS recovery programs for a wide range of BIOS chips. Next, from a PC you can use to access the Web, download the BIOS recovery program file and place it onto a bootable floppy disk. Next, restart your system from the floppy disk. After your system starts, run the BIOS recovery program.

Improving Performance by Shadowing the BIOS

Compared to the fast speeds of the PC's RAM, a read-only memory (ROM) chip is quite slow. As you will learn in Chapter 8, typical access speeds for RAM chips is 50 to 70 nanoseconds (ns), whereas the access time for a ROM chip is normally twice as slow, in the 120 to 200 nanosecond range.

To improve system performance, many older CMOS setup programs let users *shadow* the BIOS by copying the BIOS instructions and data values from the slower ROM chip into the faster RAM. As shown in Figure 6-5, when the PC later needed to use BIOS instructions or data, the PC would access the data from the faster RAM locations, which improved performance significantly.

Prior to Windows 95, operating systems such as MS-DOS, and even Windows 3.1, made extensive use of the BIOS. Today, most newer operating systems do not use the BIOS instructions. Instead, the operating systems provide their own instructions to perform the capabilities the BIOS provides. By implementing the BIOS features using software (which is easier to upgrade), the operating system can provide greater flexibility with respect to interacting with devices. Today, the only time the BIOS instructions may execute is when the system starts. After the PC loads the operating system, the operating system may not use the BIOS at all. Because newer operating systems make little use of the BIOS, most newer CMOS programs have removed the user's ability to shadow the BIOS.

USE IT If you are using a newer operating system, and you have set your CMOS settings to shadow the BIOS, you may simply be consuming RAM resources to shadow the BIOS that your PC is never uses. To disable BIOS shadowing, restart your system and enter the CMOS setup program as discussed in Chapter 7. Next, look for entries that correspond to shadowing the BIOS. Before you disable the entries, press SHIFT-PRINT SCRN to print the setting's current values. Then

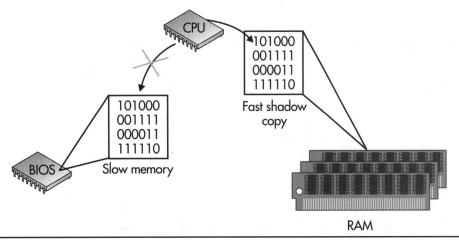

Figure 6.5 Using a shadowed copy of the BIOS that resides in the PC's RAM

disable the shadowing, save your changes, and exit the CMOS. Your system will restart without copying the BIOS to RAM, which will give your system a little more physical memory that it can use to hold other programs.

Configuring the Video ROM

If you examine the list of BIOS services, you will find that the PC BIOS provides routines that programs can use to perform video-screen output. These routines, which programmers refer to as the *BIOS video services*, provide functions that programs can use to display characters at specific screen locations, to set the video mode (for the display of text or graphics, for example), to set the screen resolution and color support, to draw colored pixels at specific locations, and so on. Like the BIOS setup program and other BIOS routines, the BIOS video services are simply instructions that reside within the BIOS chip.

As video cards evolved, most video-card manufacturers provided their own set of instructions, which were specific to their video cards. The manufacturers placed their card-specific instructions on a ROM chip that resided on the video card itself. Users and programmers began to refer to the chip whose instructions defined the PC's video capabilities as the *video ROM*. Depending on a PC's hardware configuration, the video ROM might be the original BIOS instructions, or it might be the instructions that reside on the video card.

USE IT   Chapter 17 examines the PC's video processing in detail. Depending on your PC's BIOS and the video card you may have installed, there may be times when you must manually disable your PC's built-in video ROM before your PC will recognize the new video card. To disable the PC's video ROM, enter the CMOS setup program, as discussed in the Chapter 7, and look for a Video ROM setting. Using the setup program, disable the PC's ROM BIOS, which the setup program may refer to as the primary video.

As you learned in the previous tip, in the past, users improved their system performance by shadowing the ROM BIOS by directing the PC to use a copy of the BIOS instructions that the PC had placed within its faster RAM. Because the BIOS video instructions resided in a ROM chip, many setup programs provided users with the ability to shadow the video ROM as well. Today, most newer operating systems make little use of the BIOS. Instead, the operating systems provide their own instructions that implement the BIOS services. In a similar way, most operating systems rely on the video card's device driver (software that interacts with the card) to implement video operations. When your system starts, the operating system will load the device driver into your PC's fast RAM. Most users, therefore, will not improve performance by shadowing the video ROM. In fact, shadowing the video ROM may simply consume your PC's RAM unnecessarily.

Using the BIOS Power Management Capabilities

In Chapter 3, you examined power, the PC's power supply, and the PC's power-management capabilities in detail. As you learned, most new PCs provide a wide range of power-management capabilities. The base (foundation) of a PC's power management begins with the BIOS. When PC's first began to provide power management, BIOS manufacturers provided a set of BIOS-based instructions users referred to as the PC Advanced Power Management (APM) capabilities. In general, the APM defines a hardware-independent interface the operating system could use to reduce power consumption and increase battery life. The primary shortcoming of the APM services was that because much of the capabilities resided within the BIOS, the operating system could not fully leverage its knowledge of the user's current level of activity.

Today, operating systems, such as Windows, have built upon the BIOS capabilities, to provide support for the Advanced Configuration and Power Interface (ACPI) specification, which is an open industry specification that provides the operating system with a standardized access to the PC's power management capabilities. In general, the ACPI specification defines a set of routines (some the operating system implements and some which are built into the BIOS, such as APM support) that programs can use to interact with the PC's power-management capabilities.

USE IT   Support for power management has become a key BIOS service. As you will learn in Chapter 7, most CMOS setup programs provide you with access to a range of power-management settings. Using the power-management settings, for example, you can direct your PC to hibernate when it is not in use, which in turn, causes the PC to consume less power. You can also use the power-management settings to automatically turn your PC on at a specific times or to turn itself on when it receives an incoming modem or network connection. In general, you should also enable your PC's power-management capabilities. To enable your PC's settings within the CMOS, restart your system and enter the CMOS setup program as discussed in Chapter 7. Many CMOS setup programs will have a screen (which you can view by selecting a power setup or power management option) whose entries relate specifically to the PC's power-management capabilities. After you configure the settings you need, save your settings and exit the CMOS setup program.

Understanding BIOS Beep Codes

As the BIOS performs the PC's POST, there may be times when the BIOS encounters an error so severe that the BIOS simply cannot continue processing. In some cases, the BIOS may display an error message that describes the error. At other times, the BIOS will sound a series of beeps that correspond to the error. Users refer to these beeps as the BIOS *beep codes*. Each BIOS has its own set of codes, the meaning of which are specific to the BIOS. Often, the BIOS may generate short and long beeps as well, much like Morse code. Table 6-4 lists sample beep codes for various BIOS chips.

 Most users, unfortunately, do not have a "secret decoder ring" they can use to decode their BIOS beep codes. In fact, many users do not know the BIOS beep codes exist, until one day when they turn on their system only to encounter a cryptic series of beeps and a blank screen.

Take time now to visit your BIOS chip manufacturer's Web site and download or print your BIOS beep codes. Often, you can find your beep codes on the Web simply by entering your BIOS chip type followed by the key words "beep codes," in a search engine, such as the AMI BIOS beep codes shown in Figure 6-6.

Using a POST Board to View Post Codes

To help PC technicians troubleshoot system startup problems, the BIOS will place a code within a specific location (I/O port 80H) that corresponds to the current step within the POST. By monitoring the values, the technician can determine which tests the PC successfully completed as well as the test the PC failed to complete (which will be the last value in the port location). Depending on the BIOS chip, the meaning of the status code value may differ.

BIOS	Beep Code	Meaning
AMI	1 long	POST successfully passed
AMI	5 short	CPU has failed
AMI	1 long, 3 short	Memory chip failed
Award	1 long, 2 short	Video adapter error
Award	1 long, 3 short	Video adapter memory error
Phoenix	Beep, pause, beep, pause, 2 beeps	CPU has failed
Phoenix	Beep, pause, beep, pause, 3 beeps	CMOS read/write error
Phoenix	Beep, pause, beep, pause, 4 beeps	BIOS checksum error

Table 6.4   A Sampling of BIOS Beep Codes

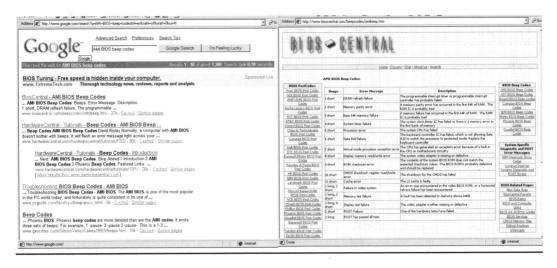

Figure 6.6   Searching the Web for BIOS beep codes

To view the status value, technicians install a *POST analyzer* card into the PC. Normally, the card will contain a small LED display that shows the current test number or a series of lights the technician can translate into a status number.

USE IT   If you troubleshoot a failed PC on a regular basis, a POST analyzer card may save you considerable time and experimentation. Depending on the card's capabilities, the card's price will vary. Some cards, for example, provide extensive diagnostics you can run to better troubleshoot the error. Further, some cards let you monitor IRQ and DMA activity to troubleshoot hardware conflicts. For information on POST analyzer cards, visit the following Web sites:

- **PC Engines**   www.pcengines.com/test.htm
- **TriniTech**   www.pcdiagnostics.net/omni.htm
- **Micro 2000**   www.micro2000.com/postprobe/index.htm
- **pcwiz**   www.pcdiag.com/index.htm

To use a POST-analyzer card, you must know your BIOS chip's status values. Normally, your BIOS manufacturer's Web site will contain a page of status values specific to your BIOS that you can download or print.

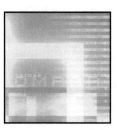

CHAPTER 7

Getting the Most from Your CMOS Settings

When you turn on your PC, the system begins the startup process by running instructions that are built into the BIOS (Basic Input Output System). These instructions direct the PC to run diagnostics against key system components. After the PC performs and successfully passes its power-on self-test (which users simply refer to as the POST), the PC reads into RAM information from the hard disk (or a floppy disk) called the operating system's boot record, which contains instructions the PC then performs to load the rest of the operating system from disk into RAM.

Before the PC can perform the POST, and before the PC can read the boot record from a disk, the PC must know some specific configuration information about the PC and its devices, such as the number and type of disk drives, which disk the PC should boot the operating system from, and so on. The PC stores configuration information within a special battery-powered memory, which users refer to as the CMOS. This chapter examines the PC's CMOS memory in detail. You will learn how and when you may need to change CMOS settings, you will examine CMOS settings that may improve your system performance, and you will learn how to change your CMOS battery should it fail.

Years ago, the CMOS contained only information about the system date and time, the floppy disk type, the disk type, and so on. Today, in contrast, there are CMOS settings that influence your PC's power management capabilities, entries that provide Plug and Play support, and a few entries you may use to improve your system performance—either by changing clock or bus speeds or by changing the CPU's cache use.

▶ FACT

CMOS memory, (complimentary metal oxide semiconductor memory) is unique in that it requires minimal power (3V to 5V) to retain its contents, which the PC provides using a small battery.

Accessing Your PC's CMOS Settings

Within your PC, the CMOS settings reside in a special battery-powered memory, that lets the PC "remember" the settings after you power off your system. When you purchase a PC, the manufacturer will preconfigure your CMOS settings as part of the manufacturer's "burn in" process. As you will learn throughout this book, or as you install new hardware, sometimes you must update the CMOS settings. Further, should the battery that powers the CMOS memory fail, you must manually reenter each of the CMOS settings.

Depending on your PC, how you will access your CMOS settings may differ. Normally, you must restart your system (or turn your system on). As your system is performing the POST (before it starts to load Windows), you must press a specific key. In some cases, your system may display a helpful message, such as this:

```
Press F2 to enter Setup
```

If your system does not display such a message, and you no longer have your system documentation that explained which key you should press, you may need to experiment by restarting your system a few times and pressing one of the following commonly used keys:

- F2
- DELETE
- ESC
- CTRL-ALT-ESC
- CTRL-ESC

▶ **NOTE**

If you are using an older system (such as a 286 or 386), the CMOS settings program is not built into your system. Instead, you must boot the settings programs from a floppy disk. If you do not have a setup program on a floppy disk, you may be able to use a different PC (assuming that your PC won't start) to surf the Web, where you may find several programs that provide access to CMOS settings.

Depending on your system, the appearance and functionality of your CMOS program may differ. Figure 7-1 illustrates a traditional CMOS setup program.

▶ **CAUTION**

Never make changes to settings within the CMOS that you do not thoroughly understand. Should you assign an errant value to a CMOS setting, you may prevent your system from working.

Normally, within the CMOS settings program, you will use your keyboard arrow keys to highlight a specific menu or entry. Then, you will press either the SPACEBAR or ENTER to select the item. Next, depending your program, you will use the arrow keys, the SPACEBAR, TAB, or ENTER to cycle through values you can assign to the entry. After you change the settings you need, you will normally select a menu option that lets you save your changes and exit. Should you decide that you want to discard your changes, you can normally select a menu option that lets you exit the setup program without saving your changes. After you exit the setup program, your system will restart to put your settings into effect.

▶ **NOTE**

Should you make an errant entry within the CMOS setup program that prevents your system from running, restart your system and again enter the setup program. Within the setup program, look for a menu option that will restore the system's default settings. After you restore the default settings, your

```
                      Dell Dimension 4100 SETUP
   Main   Advanced    Security      Boot      Exit
  BIOS version           A05                          Enabling this option
                                                      enables the processor
                                                      serial number feature.
  Processor Type         Intel(R) Pentium(R)III       Disabling this option
  Processor Speed        1 GHz                         disables the
  System Bus Frequency   133 MHz                      processor serial
                                                      number feature.
  Cache RAM              256 KB
  Service Tag            ABC1234

  Total Memory           512 MB
  Memory Bank 0          256 MB (PC133)
  Memory Bank 1          256 MB (PC133)
                                                      <- -> Select Menu
                                                      ↑  ↓  Select Item
  Processor Serial Number [Disabled]                  Tab   Select Field
                                                      Enter Select Sub-Menu
  System Time            [18:52:16]                   F9    Setup Defaults
  System Date            [Sun 08/19/2001]             F10   Save and Exit
                                                      ESC   Exit
```

Figure 7.1   Using a setup program to change CMOS settings

system should again run with the same capabilities it had when it left the manufacturer. If you have changed hard drives since you purchased the system, you may need to change the hard drive's information within the setup program before your system will use the device

You Can't Do Everything You Once Could Do Within the CMOS

Over the past few years, CMOS setup programs have changed. In the past, many, CMOS setup programs provided users with access to settings that users could tweak to improve system performance. For example, compared to the speed of RAM, the BIOS read-only memory was quite slow. Rather than suffer a decrease in performance each time the PC had to access BIOS settings or run BIOS code, users would use a technique called *BIOS shadowing*, which would make a copy of the BIOS contents in RAM. Then, whenever the PC needed to perform a BIOS operation, the PC would access the RAM-based version, which improved performance. Today, however, many CMOS setup programs no longer let you select options that shadow RAM. In a similar way, users often used the CMOS settings to tweak items such as memory wait states (Chapter 8 discusses wait states in detail) to squeeze out higher system performance. Again, few CMOS setup programs today provide access to wait state settings.

As a result, users looking to CMOS for ways of improving system performance no longer have many CMOS items with which they can experiment. PC manufacturers probably decided to remove some of these capabilities after having to help so many users restore settings they had tweaked during such experiments. In addition, with newer technologies, some of the timing issues that existed in the past are gone. As a result, the CMOS no longer must address them. If your CMOS setup program still provides access to these settings, you may want to turn to the chapters that address the corresponding topic, such as Chapter 8 (memory wait states) and Chapter 6 (BIOS).

Understanding the CMOS Memory Layout

The CMOS settings contain a range of values your PC uses during the startup process. Although newer PC may provide support for additional (or different) values, most CMOS settings contain the values listed in Table 7-1.

Size	Description
1 byte	Real-time clock current seconds
1 byte	Real-time clock alarm seconds
1 byte	Real-time clock current minutes
1 byte	Real-time clock alarm minutes
1 byte	Real-time clock current hours
1 byte	Real-time clock alarm hours
1 byte	Real-time clock day of week
1 byte	Real-time clock current day
1 byte	Real-time clock current month
1 byte	Real-time clock current year
4 bytes	Status registers
1 byte	Diagnostic status
1 byte	CMOS shutdown status
1 byte	Floppy drive types
1 byte	System configuration settings
1 byte	Disk 1 type
1 byte	Keyboard typematic settings
1 byte	Installed equipment flags
1 byte	Base memory amount low order byte
1 byte	Base memory amount high order byte
1 byte	Extended memory amount low order byte
1 byte	Extended memory amount high order byte
1 byte	Hard disk 0 extended information
1 byte	Hard disk 1 extended information
1 byte	User-defined drive C cylinders low order byte
1 byte	User-defined drive C cylinders high order byte

Table 7.1   The Contents of the Traditional CMOS Settings

Size	Description
1 byte	User-defined drive C number of heads
1 byte	User-defined drive C Write precompensation low order byte
1 byte	User-defined drive C Write precompensation high order byte
1 byte	User-defined drive C Control byte
1 byte	User-defined drive C Landing zone low order byte
1 byte	User-defined drive C Landing zone high order byte
1 byte	User-defined drive C Sectors per cylinder
1 byte	User-defined drive D cylinders low order byte
1 byte	User-defined drive D cylinders high order byte
1 byte	User-defined drive D number of heads
1 byte	User-defined drive D Write precompensation low order byte
1 byte	User-defined drive D Write precompensation high order byte
1 byte	User-defined drive D Control byte
1 byte	User-defined drive D Landing zone low order byte
1 byte	User-defined drive D Landing zone high order byte
1 byte	User-defined drive D Sectors per cylinder
1 byte	System operation flags
1 byte	Checksum low order byte
1 byte	Checksum high order byte
1 byte	Actual extended memory low order byte
1 byte	Actual extended memory high order byte
1 byte	Century date in binary coded decimal
1 byte	Power-on self-test information
2 byte2	BIOS and Shadow flags
1 byte	Chipset information
1 byte	Password seed information
6 bytes	Encrypted password
1 byte	Extended CMOS checksum high order byte
1 byte	Extended CMOS checksum low order byte
1 byte	Model number
6 bytes	Serial number

Table 7.1 The Contents of the Traditional CMOS Settings *(continued)*

Size	Description
1 byte	CRC
1 byte	Century byte
1 byte	Date alarm
2 bytes	Control registers
2 bytes	Reserved
2 bytes	Real-time clock address
1 byte	Extended RAM address low order byte
1 byte	Extended RAM address high order byte
12 bytes	Reserved

Table 7.1 The Contents of the Traditional CMOS Settings *(continued)*

Understanding CMOS Memory

CMOS is an acronym for *complimentary metal oxide semiconductor*. The term CMOS describes a type of chip. CMOS memory is unique in that it requires minimal power to retain its contents. In fact, within your PC, the CMOS is powered by a small 3V battery (although some systems may use a 5V battery), as shown in Figure 7-2.

Like all batteries, the CMOS battery will eventually run out of power and will fail. When the CMOS battery fails, you must replace the battery. Unlike traditional RAM, which requires constant power, the CMOS memory may retain its contents for a period of time after the battery fails—which means that if your timing was perfect and you detect the battery failure as it occurs, you could, in theory, remove the failed battery and insert a new one without losing the CMOS contents. Unfortunately, most users do not know their CMOS battery has failed until they turn on their system and receive a message such as:

```
Invalid CMOS settings - run Setup
```

Figure 7.2 The CMOS is powered by a small 3V battery.

Replacing the CMOS Battery

Replacing the CMOS battery is actually quite simple. The challenge comes, when you must restore the CMOS settings that were lost when the battery failed. To restore the battery itself, perform these steps:

1. Turn off your computer and unplug your system from the wall outlet.
2. Ground yourself before you touch the PC chassis.
3. If you have an antistatic bracelet, you should wear it while you replace the battery.
4. Unscrew or unfasten and remove the chassis lid. If your chassis lid uses screws to hold it in place, put the screws in a safe location, such as an envelope or plastic pill container.
5. Within the motherboard, you should find either a small nickel sized battery or a small battery pack, shown in Figure 7-2. Replace the battery with a new battery.
6. Carefully replace the chassis lid to ensure that you do not damage any ribbon cables within the system unit. If necessary, replace the screws that hold the chassis lid in place.

Plug in the power supply to the wall outlet (or surge suppressor or UPS) and then turn on your PC's power. As your system starts, press the system-specific key that directs your center to run the CMOS setup program. You must now restore your CMOS settings. Normally, the CMOS setup program will have a menu option that lets you restore the default settings. If the system still knows its defaults, many are likely to be settings you will want. Select the default settings. If you have previously recorded the values of your CMOS settings, restore the settings now. Otherwise, you may have to experiment for a while, trying new settings and restarting your system until you get the correct settings restored.

Understanding the Extended System Configuration Data (ESCD) Settings

Many of the CMOS settings have existed since the days of the IBM PC AT, in the early 1980s. Over the years, new technologies such as Plug and Play have placed new demands on the PC's startup process. Today, the PC must identify myriad devices when it starts, avoid conflicts between the devices, and provide the operating system with information it can use to access the devices.

Just as it was convenient for the PC to place general information within the CMOS memory, it is also convenient to record information about specific hardware within an extended CMOS memory area that users refer to as the Extended System Configuration Data (or ESCD) settings. In general, the ESCD settings provide a link between the PC's BIOS and the operating system. When you install a new device, such as a Plug and Play card, Windows will store information about the card within the ESCD memory region. To avoid device conflicts, Windows also stores information about legacy (non–Plug and Play devices) within the ESCD settings.

By placing information about devices within the ESCD settings, the PC does not have to query each device during the startup process, which would be a very time-consuming process. Depending on your CMOS setup program, you may or may not have access to the ESCD settings.

Back Up Your CMOS Settings

You should never change a CMOS setting without first writing down the setting's original value. Should the change cause your system to fail, you can restore the original setting by restarting your system and running the CMOS settings program.

USE IT   Further, you should take time now to print a copy of each of your CMOS setting values. To print the CMOS settings, simply display each page within the CMOS setup program and then press SHIFT-PRINT SCRN. Your PCs BIOS, in turn, will print the current screen contents. After you print each page of CMOS settings, place your printouts in a safe location.

▶ *NOTE*

When you perform a SHIFT-PRINT SCRN operation, your printer will not automatically eject a page each time you perform the operation. Instead, you must manually take your printer offline, press the form feed (or page eject) button, and then place your printer back online.

On the Web, you may encounter several programs that will copy your current CMOS settings to a floppy disk. Should you later need to restore the CMOS settings (perhaps your CMOS battery failed), you can use the program to restore the settings from the floppy disk, which saves you the time of manually restoring your settings from your printouts. Make sure, however, that the program you are downloading to save your CMOS entries is compatible with your BIOS. The exact information that BIOS stores in a CMOS setting may differ from that of another BIOS—which means you could potentially restore incorrect values to your CMOS settings. Although it may take a little longer, you are probably safer to print copies of your CMOS settings, restore default settings, and then make changes to settings from your printouts that differ from the defaults.

▶ *FACT*

Many CMOS setup programs provide a menu option you can select to restore the system's default settings. Should your CMOS battery fail, you can restore many settings to their correct values by restoring the default values.

Password-Protecting a User's System

If you work in an office where users log into their systems, such as an office that uses Windows 2000 or Windows NT workstations, the user must specify a username and password before he or she can access the system. However, should a user create a bootable floppy disk (or series of disks depending on the operating system), the user may be able to start another user's PC using the floppy disks and then later access files that reside on the user's hard disk.

Many CMOS setup programs let you assign a password that the user must enter before he or she can access the PC in any way. Before a user could boot the system using floppy disks, for example, the user would have to know the CMOS-based password. By assigning passwords to systems in this way, you create yet one more layer of security within your system.

USE IT If you are a system administer within an office, you may want to assign each user a CMOS-based password, which you record and store in a secure location. Then, as discussed in the next section, you should assign a different password to each system's CMOS, that the users do not know, which prevents them from changing CMOS settings that include their passwords.

Preventing Users from Changing CMOS Settings

As you have learned, by assigning an errant value to a CMOS setting, a user may render his or her system unusable. Most businesses, therefore, probably do not want their users to have the ability to access the CMOS settings. In addition to assigning a password a user must enter before he or she can access a system, the CMOS also lets you specify a different password someone (hopefully the system administrator) must enter before he or she can access the CMOS settings.

USE IT By password-protecting the CMOS settings, you prevent users from being able to assign an errant value to a system setting. Further, you prevent a disgruntled employee, for example, from assigning a password to the system that locks you out (at least temporarily, as discussed in the next section). Within an office, you should use the CMOS setup program to password-protect the CMOS.

▶ *NOTE*

Some CMOS setup programs provide a field that you can use to temporarily disable the system and CMOS password protection. For example, if you're troubleshooting a system, and you must continually restart the system and access the CMOS settings, continually having to enter the passwords could become quite time consuming. By temporarily disabling the password protection, you may save time. To disable the password protection, you must have password access to the CMOS settings.

Recovering from a Forgotten CMOS Password

If you assign CMOS-based passwords to a PC, and you later forget the password, or worse yet, if someone else locks you out of your own PC by assigning a password you do not know, do not panic.

  First, many systems have a jumper on the motherboard whose setting you can change to clear the CMOS password. If you have your system documentation, it may specify the jumper location. Also, some motherboards will label the jumper with something like "Password." Further, if you can gain access to another PC, you may be able to find out information for the CMOS password jumper location through your PC manufacturer's Web site.

If you cannot use a jumper to clear the password, many systems have a jumper you can use to clear the contents of the entire CMOS (the contents of which you hopefully previously recorded). Again, your system documentation should identify the jumper's location on the motherboard.

Finally, if you cannot clear the CMOS settings by using a jumper, you can clear it by removing the CMOS battery. To start, unplug your system, ground yourself, and then remove the chassis lid. Next, locate the CMOS battery on the motherboard and remove it. As briefly discussed, the CMOS memory may hold its charge for an indefinite period of time after you remove the battery. Some technicians will speed up the rate at which the battery drains by creating a short circuit within the battery. Given that after you get the battery drained, you are going to have to reenter the CMOS contents manually, you may want to call it a day.

After the CMOS contents clear, place the CMOS battery back into place, close your system unit, plug in your PC, and then power it on. Then, within your CMOS settings programs, you may first want to look for a menu option that lets you restore the system defaults. After you restore the defaults, you should have fewer entries you have to manually update.

▶ *NOTE*

If given ample time, someone who is trying to break into your password-protected system can drain the CMOS battery in this way and then later restart your system to gain access to your file. Before the user can drain the CMOS battery, he or she must gain access to it within the system chassis. Some newer CMOS settings let you enable an intrusion detection setting that notifies you when the system unit has been opened. Depending on your system type, the notification you receive may vary.

Changing Your PC's Boot Device Sequence

Normally, when you power on your PC, your system will first try to boot from a floppy disk in drive A. If the floppy drive contains a disk, but the disk is not a bootable disk, your system will display an error message similar to the following:

```
Non-System disk or disk error
Replace and strike any key when ready
```

If the floppy drive is empty, the system will then normally try to load the operating system from the hard drive.

USE IT   By changing your system's boot device order, so that your system boots from the hard drive first, you may prevent a floppy disk left in drive A from preventing your system from starting. In addition, because your system does not have to check drive A, you may speed up your system startup process.

Sometimes, Windows will crash due to a virus or corrupt file, and your system will no longer be able to start. In such cases, your only recourse may be to start the system with a CD-ROM disk that came from your manufacturer, which restores Windows from scratch. Unfortunately, during this process, you will lose all the information you have previously stored on your system. (Hence the importance of maintaining backups). To boot from the CD-ROM, you must change your CMOS settings so that your system first tries to boot from the CD-ROM drive. Then, simply insert the manufacturer's CD-ROM in the drive and restart your system. Remember, when you reinstall Windows in this way, you will destroy all the information previously stored on your hard disk.

Controlling Your PC's Power Management Settings

In Chapter 2, you examined PC power in detail. At that time, you learned how to use your PC's advanced power management capabilities to direct your various system devices to hibernate when the devices are not in use. When the devices hibernate, they consume less power. Many CMOS setup programs let you turn the PC's power management capabilities on or off. You should always enable your PCs power management capabilities.

In addition, the CMOS setup program may let you specify the duration values for various settings, such as the length of inactivity the PC will wait until it spins down a hard disk in order to conserve power. You may also be able to specify how you want a PC that has lost power to behave when power is restored. For example, you may want the PC to remain off, you may want the PC to restart, or you may want the PC to resume its previous state, meaning if it was on when the power died, restart. And if it was off, stay off.

USE IT Further, some CMOS programs let you specify a time at which you want the PC to automatically start. Assume, for example, you work in an office where all employees power off their systems at night before they leave. Then, the following morning, each employee starts his or her system and patiently waits for the systems to start. Using the PC's CMOS-based auto-start capability, you can direct the PCs to automatically start each morning, say at 7:50, so when the employee enters the office at 8:00, his or her PC is ready for action.

In addition, some CMOS programs lets you direct the PC to auto-start when the PC receives a remote connection, such as a dial-in connection from a modem or a network connection. Again, given the company scenario, you could create a simple program that contacts each user's computer at the specific time you want the computer to wake up and start.

Speeding Up Your System's Startup Process

Earlier in this chapter, you learned that by changing your PC's sequence of boot devices, you may be able to eliminate the PC's need to examine the floppy drive each time it starts, which in turn, speeds up the startup process. In addition, some CMOS setup programs provide a "fast boot" option you can select, which directs the PC not to perform specific (less critical) tests during the POST. By directing the PC to skip the tests, the PC will complete the POST faster, which lets your system start sooner.

In my opinion, if the hardware engineers who designed the tests felt that the tests were important enough to leave in the POST, I would prefer that my PC ran them to make sure everything is working correctly, especially considering that the tests will likely consume less time than it will take me to delete my first Spam message of the day.

USE IT That said, however, using the fast boot option is one way you can speed up your system's startup process. (In Chapter 9, you will examine other ways you may further speed up the process.) If you enable fast boot operations, and you don't later encounter intermittent errors, great. Should you encounter strange errors in the future, you can always enable the tests and see if the POST identifies a cause.

▶ *NOTE*

In addition to letting you skip memory tests by selecting a fast boot option, many CMOS setup programs let you enable a memory "click" that directs the BIOS to sound an audible click as it tests your PC's memory: "click, click, click, click, click, ..." Normally, every office has at least one employee for whom this annoying audible click is well-suited.

Setting Your System's Real-Time Clock

Within the PC is a real-time clock that the PC uses to determine the current time and date. When Windows, for example, displays the current time in the lower-right corner of the screen, Windows calculates the time by using the real-time clock. By maintaining the real-time clock within the CMOS settings, the battery that powers the CMOS can run the clock, which in turn, maintains the current date and time.

Years ago, the only way to set the PCs real-time clock was to use the CMOS setup program or to write a program that interacted with the BIOS. The MS-DOS DATE and TIME commands originally did not change the real-time clock. As a result, the real-time clock remains as a CMOS entry today.

 Using a CMOS setup program, you can update your system's date and time, which, in turn, will update the real-time clock. However, you can also now update the real-time clock simply by using Windows.

Floppy Drive Settings Your Operating System Will Likely Ignore

Most CMOS setup programs have one or more settings you can use to configure, disable, or possibly even write-protect a floppy drive. For example, assume that you work with sensitive information (perhaps you are system administrator at the CIA), and there are times when you want to ensure that employees cannot copy information onto a floppy disk. Rather than removing all the floppy drives from their systems, you may be able to use a CMOS setting to write-protect the floppy drives. In this way, users will not be able to use the drive to store information on a disk. Unfortunately, most operating systems will ignore the CMOS read-only setting. You may find a version of Linux that will support the read-only drive.

Annoyed by the fact that his or her floppy disk is now a read-only device, a disgruntled employee could use the read-only disk to read a virus into his or her PC, which they then release across your network. Again, rather than removing the floppy drives, you may be able to use the CMOS settings to disable the drives completely. Unfortunately, Windows and other operating systems have an uncanny ability to locate disk drives, even when you try to hide them.

USE IT   The most common use of the CMOS floppy disk drive settings is simply to identify a
new disk to the system and to specify the drive's type, such as a 1.44MB drive. Normally,
however, even if you do not specify your floppy disk type within the CMOS, Windows will locate,
and determine the drive's correct settings.

Enabling Your System's Use of the Processor Cache

In Chapter 5, you examined your PC's CPU operations in detail. At that time, you learned that to
improve performance, many CPUs have a small amount of high-speed memory built into the CPU
chip that serves as a cache between the CPU and traditional RAM. Most CPUs employ two levels of
cache, named L1 and L2. Depending on the CPU, L1 may reside on the CPU and L2 may not, or both
may reside on the CPU.

When programs execute, the CPU must retrieve the program instructions and data from RAM. As
the information moves from RAM to the CPU, the information passes through the caches, as shown
in Figure 7-3.

Should the CPU need a specific instruction a second time or need to access specific data a second
time, the CPU can retrieve the data from the fast cache, as opposed to retrieving the information again
from the slower RAM.

USE IT   If your CPU has cache memory (L1 or L2 cache), make sure that you use the CMOS
settings to enable the cache memory use. Normally, the cache will always be enabled.
Depending on the operating systems you have used in the past on your system, however, an operating
system may have disabled the cache use due to a system conflict. Also, some PCs might disable the
cache should the PC's POST encounter a memory error.

▶ NOTE

*Some CMOS setup programs let you specify the speed at which the processor will read from the
cache. Normally, you express these speeds in terms of clock cycles. The fewer clock cycles, the faster
the read. Chapter 5 examines CPU operations in detail, which gives you a better understanding of
how the CPU communicates with the cache. Normally, the CMOS settings for cache timing, if you can
access the settings, are set to ensure compatibility. However, depending on your CPU type, memory
type, and bus speeds, you may be able to reduce the settings and improve your system performance.
Make sure, however, before you change the settings that you record the original values.*

Controlling Bus Speeds

As you learned in Chapter 5, the CPU communicates with RAM and other devices by exchanging
signals over high-speed connections called buses. For compatibility reasons, PC manufacturers often run
CPU and buses at slower speeds than the maximum speed the CPU or bus may support. In Chapter 5,
you learned that by overclocking your system, you can often improve your system's performance for
little cost. Depending on your system type, you may need to use motherboard jumpers to change the
bus speeds. Some CMOS setup programs, however, provide access to the bus speeds.

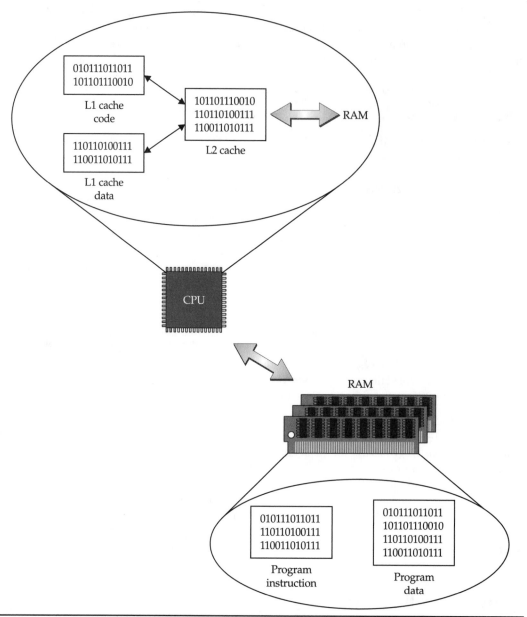

Figure 7.3 Using CPU caches to store information

USE IT   As discussed in Chapter 5, if you want to overclock your system, you should step up the bus speed one speed at a time, and then test your system to determine if it can run at the slightly faster speed. If your system runs successfully, you can then bump up the speed to the next level and repeat your testing. However, before you change your bus speeds, make sure you write down the original settings that work.

Specifying a Hard Disk's Geometry

In Chapter 16, you will learn about hard disks in detail. To store information, disks first divide the storage platter into concentric circles that users refer to as *tracks* or *cylinders* (in the case of multiple storage platters). Then, the disk further divides each track or cylinder into fixed-size storage locations called *sectors*. Depending on the disk's type and size, the number of tracks (cylinders) and sectors will differ. Users refer to the disk's structure as the disk's *geometry*. In Chapter 16, you will learn that users include other attributes within the term "disk geometry".

USE IT   Before the PC BIOS (and later the operating system) can access a hard disk, the BIOS must know the disk's geometry. If you install or replace a hard disk, you must use the CMOS setup program to specify the new disk's geometry. To simplify the process, the CMOS setup knows about a wide range of disk types, each of which uses a unique geometry. For example, a type 1 disk contains a 10MB drive with 306 cylinders, 17 sectors per cylinder, and 4 read/write heads. Often, if you examine the outer casing of a hard disk, you will find that the casing contains a type number. Within the CMOS setup program, you can normally simply specify the type number, as opposed to having to enter the disk's individual settings. If you are not sure about your disk's type, check the disk manufacturer's Web site. Normally, within the site's technical information, you can look up your disk type number. If, for some reason, your CMOS settings do not recognize your disk type number, you will need to specify your disk's individual settings by hand. Again, you can likely find the setting values you need on the disk manufacturer's Web site.

▶ *NOTE*

Most newer CMOS setup programs have an AUTO setting you can select for the disk type that lets the BIOS determine the disk's geometry. Normally, you can use the AUTO setting to successfully configure your hard drive. If, for some reason, however, the AUTO entry does not work, you will need to determine your drive's type or specify the individual settings.

Selecting a Disk Drive Controller

As you will learn in Chapter 16, a disk drive communicates with the PC BIOS via special electronics called a *disk controller*. In the early days of PCs, the disk controller resided on a card that you inserted within a PC expansion slot. Today, many motherboards will provide a built-in controller, and many disks have their own controller logic built in. In fact the letters "IDE" in the term "IDE disk" stand for integrated drive electronics—a fancy term for disk controller.

USE IT If you install a new (possibly faster) disk controller, you can use the CMOS settings to disable the motherboard's controller, or at least indicate to the controller that it has no drives attached. The new disk controller will contain BIOS information the system will need to communicate with the disk. In most cases, you will set the motherboard's disk controller to auto, which directs the controller to determine if it has any devices attached, and if so, to support them.

Enabling Parallel Port Features

In Chapter 18, you will learn that although just about every PC has a parallel port, not all parallel ports are created equal. A parallel port, for example, may only output data, or the port may support bidirectional communication, which lets the printer send data back through the port (perhaps, for example, to notify the operating system that the printer needs paper). Further, a parallel port can be an EPP (enhanced parallel port) or ECP (extended capabilities port). By using these port types, you may increase your printer performance by as much as a factor of 10.

As you will learn in Chapter 18, ECP and EPP are bidirectional ports that significantly improve data transmission rates. ECPs are common for high-speed printer use. In fact, an ECP may use direct memory access (DMA) to speed communication. EPPs often connect other peripheral devices, such as scanners.

USE IT To use an ECP or EPP, you must have the following:

- Your parallel port must be ECP or EPP.
- You must have a device (such as a printer) that supports an ECP or EPP connection.
- You must have an IEEE 1284–compliant cable.
- You must have ECP or EPP device drivers for your operating system.

If you meet these four criteria, within the CMOS settings, you can enable parallel port attributes.

Enabling and Disabling DAC Snooping

If you are using an older ISA-based video card, or a third-party video capture card, you may have newer PCI-based cards that must snoop at the video card's digital-to-analog converter (DAC) to determine your system's capabilities. In general, when a device snoops, it examines the current VGA palette to determine the colors the system can use. Normally, you will not need to enable DAC snooping on your system. However, if you add a video card and your system displays incorrect colors, blank windows, and other video errors, you should use the CMOS settings to enable DAC snooping to see if the error goes away.

Keeping the Data-Entry Folks in Finance and Accounting Happy

USE IT OK, I will agree that compared having your PC autostart at a specific time, controlling the initial state of the keyboard's NUM LOCK key is not that exciting. However, because most CMOS setup programs let you enable or disable the Num Lock state, a chapter on CMOS settings probably ought to at least mention it. When you enable the Num Lock state, the numeric keys at the right end of the keyboard will function as number keys. When you disable the Num Lock settings, the keys move the cursor, functioning instead as arrow keys.

Assume, for example, that you want to stay on the good side of the folks in Finance who oversee your MIS budget, and you further want to impress the folks with your knowledge of the PC's inner workings. To do so, you might volunteer to "fix" their PCs so that they always start with Num Lock enabled, so they are ready for their high-speed data entry operations. To enable or disable Num Lock's initial state, you can assign the CMOS setting you desire.

Controlling On-Board Devices

Many motherboards come with built-in support for a range of devices, such as video cards, disk controllers, mice, and so on. If you do not use the motherboard-based devices, you may need to disable the devices to avoid potential conflicts or to free up resources (such as IRQs) for use by other devices. Within most CMOS setup programs, you can enable, disable, and configure such motherboard-based devices.

USE IT If you install new hardware and your system does not recognize the card, examine your CMOS settings to determine if the device conflicts with a device for which the motherboard already provides support. If you cannot disable the motherboard device through the CMOS, there is likely a jumper on the motherboard itself, which you can use to disable the device.

Managing PCI Devices and Reserving Interrupt Requests (IRQs)

Today, most PCs support a Plug and Play BIOS, which lets Windows recognize new devices as you install or later remove the device. In the past, when users installed new hardware cards, the users had to ensure that the new device did not conflict with an existing card. Normally, the user had to manually set IRQ settings and possibly the device's address ports. Plug and Play devices, in contrast, identify themselves to the system when you install them and query the system to determine which resources (such as IRQs) are available. When a Plug and Play device makes such a request, the other Plug and Play devices can respond, or Windows can respond on their behalf.

The problem, however, is that older devices, such as PCI-based cards, do not participate in the Plug and Play discussion. As a result, although the Plug and Play devices report that IRQ 3, for example, is available, a PCI card may be using the device.

To avoid such conflicts, most CMOS setup programs let you specify resources that PCI cards in your system are using, and they let you reserve various system resources, such as specific IRQs. The systems store this information within the ESCD, which is available to Windows for use in supporting Plug and Play devices.

USE IT If you experience conflicts between a Plug and Play card and a PCI-based device, try using the CMOS settings to reserve resources in order to resolve the conflict.

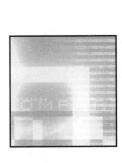

CHAPTER 8

Random Access Memory (RAM)

TIPS IN THIS CHAPTER

efore the PC's CPU can execute a program, the program's instructions and data must reside within the PC's RAM. This chapter examines how RAM stores information, why the contents of RAM are volatile (meaning why the contents of RAM are lost when you power off your PC), how various types of RAM differ, ways you can determine if RAM is a bottleneck within your system, and more.

On the Web, in books, and in magazines, you may encounter a broad range of recommendations for the amount of RAM your PC needs. Many articles will state that a user should have a minimum of 64MB to 128MB to perform traditional PC operations, that programmers should have 256MB to 512MB as they develop applications, and that servers should have 512MB to several GB of RAM. In reality, the amount of memory a user, programmer, and server requires depends on the applications each runs, the system's use or traffic in the case of a server, and, most importantly whether the system is currently running short on RAM. Only by monitoring your system under normal conditions can you determine the amount of RAM your system needs.

Understanding Storage Layers

Within the PC, disks provide long-term storage that lets you save information from one PC session to the next, or for long periods of time ranging from months to years. Disks store information by magnetizing data to the surface of the disk. Because the disk stores information magnetically (as opposed to electronically), the disk is a *nonvolatile* storage device, meaning that the disk does not require constant power in order to maintain the information it contains. PC memory (RAM), in contrast, is volatile, which means that the memory loses its contents when power is lost.

Users often categorize storage technologies in terms of speed, cost, and storage capacity. Because disk drives are mechanical devices, the drives are much slower than the PC's electronic memory. Figure 8-1 illustrates the common levels of storage devices within the PC, from the fastest (registers within the CPU) to the slowest (mechanical disk drives). To maximize performance, the PC makes use of each of its various storage levels.

▶ **NOTE**

As the speed of a storage technology within the PC increases (say moving from disk drives to RAM, or RAM to cache memory, or cache memory to a CPU-based register), so too does the cost per byte of storage.

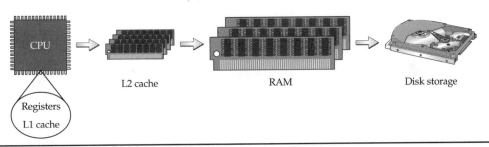

Figure 8.1   Storage technologies within the PC

Understanding the Data Flow from RAM to the CPU

When the CPU requests a data or an instruction, the CPU first examines the contents of its L1 onboard cache. If the CPU does not find the item within the L1 cache, the CPU then looks within the L2 cache, which is normally external to the CPU (depending on the processor type). If the L2 cache does not contain the item, the CPU must then request the item from memory RAM by sending the item's memory address across the system bus to a memory controller chip. The memory controller, in turn, uses the item's address to locate the corresponding data or instruction. After the memory controller retrieves the item, it sends the item back across the system bus to the CPU.

At each step from the CPU's data request until the data arrives back at the CPU, time is consumed. To improve system performance, newer memory technologies search for ways to reduce memory-access time delays.

Understanding How the PC Organizes RAM

RAM stores the program instructions the CPU executes, as well as the program data. As you learned in Chapter 5, programs consist of ones and zeros that correspond to the specific instructions the CPU executes. RAM, therefore, is organized to store ones and zeros. In general, you should picture RAM as consisting of many rows of storage locations. Programmers often think of RAM as grouping bits into a "word" that matches the size of the CPU's data bus. CPUs that use a 32-bit data bus would use a 32-bit word and CPUs that use a 64-bit data bus would use a 64-bit word. Behind the scenes, however, programs can (and often do) access individual address bytes within RAM. As shown in Figure 8-2, you can think of each byte location in RAM as having its own unique address. To retrieve information from a specific storage location or to store information into memory, the CPU must specify the location's memory address.

In Chapter 12, you will examine the PC's buses that transfer information from one chip on the motherboard to another. As you will learn, the system bus, which connects RAM and the CPU, provides wires across which data is sent as well as wires across which the memory address the CPU is wanting to read or write is sent. The number of bits in the address bus specifies the amount of memory the PC can address. For example, a system with a 32-bit address bus can address up to 2^{32}, or 4GB, of address. Likewise, a system with a 64-bit address can address up to 2^{64}, or 18,446,744,073,709,551,616, memory locations.

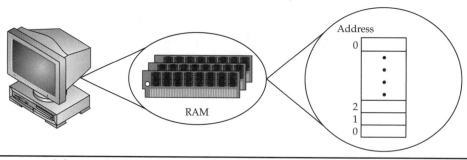

Figure 8.2   Each byte within RAM has a unique address.

▶ *FACT*

The Pentium IV processor contains 42,000,000 transistors. A 256MB DRAM chip uses over 268,435,456 transistors.

Understanding Dynamic Random Access Memory (DRAM)

Because of their speed, storage density, and low costs, most PCs make extensive use of dynamic random access memory (DRAM) chips. To store one bit of information, a DRAM chip uses a transistor and a capacitor. The capacitor stores the bit's current value. The problem with using a capacitor to store data is that the capacitor can sustain its charge for only a finite period of time, and then its must be refreshed. To refresh the capacitor's value, the memory controller reads the capacitor value, which means drains the capacitor's contents. The memory controller must then restore the value back into the capacitor. Normally, the memory controller must refresh its bit's contents at 66 MHz.

Further, when the CPU requests the contents of memory stored in RAM, the memory controller must drain the capacitor's current contents to determine the data the capacitor is storing. If the capacitor contained a 1, the memory controller must then refresh the capacitor's contents. Because the capacitor loses its contents when the memory controller reads the capacitor's value, users refer to the process as a *destructive read*.

Because the memory controller must continually refresh the DRAM chips, the chips are slower than other memory technologies. However, because the DRAM chips require only a capacitor and a transistor to store one bit of information, the chips are very high density—which means they can store large amounts of data.

Understanding Static Random Access Memory (SRAM)

Because of their high density and low costs, most PCs make extensive use of DRAM chips to implement the PC's main memory. As you have learned, however, to improve performance, PCs make extensive use of a high-speed (and more expensive) cache memory. Normally, cache memory uses the static random access memory (SRAM) technology.

Unlike DRAM chips within which the capacitor requires constant refreshing to maintain its contents, a SRAM chip does not require refreshing. Further, the memory controller can read the SRAM chips contents without performing a destructive-read operation. As a result, SRAM chips support access times of 10 nanoseconds or less.

Although the SRAM chip eliminates the capacitor and hence the need for the memory controller to constantly refresh the chip's contents, the SRAM chip requires several transistors (as many as five or six) to store a single bit of information. Because each chip requires a larger number of capacitors, the SRAM chips can store less data than a comparably sized DRAM chip. Because of its high speed, lower storage capacity, and higher price, the SRAM chip is better suited for use as cache memory than standard RAM.

Understanding RAM Packaging

As discussed in Chapter 4, RAM resides on the motherboard in one or more memory slots, as shown in Figure 8-3. Depending on the motherboard's design, the number of memory slots and the type of chip (size and speed) the slots support will differ.

In general, a RAM chip consists of multiple memory chips. RAM chips are categorized as SIMM or DIMM chips, based on the chip's electronics. SIMM is an acronym for single inline memory module. A SIMM is essentially a small circuit board that contains memory chips and a connector that you plug into a SIMM socket on the motherboard. DIMM is an acronym for dual inline memory module. A DIMM chip looks very much like a SIMM. The difference between the two is that the DIMM's electrical contacts that plug into the DIMM socket are electronically independent, whereas the SIMM chip ties together the leads on each side of the chip. Figure 8-4 illustrates a SIMM chip.

Depending on the type of memory chip the SIMM or DIMM contains, the amount of data the chip can store will differ. For example, older SIMMs held 256KB by using eight smaller 32KB chips. SIMM and DIMM chip storage capacities and speeds have evolved over time. Originally, SIMM chips used 30-pin connectors. Today, most SIMMs use 72-pin connectors, and most DIMMs use 168-pin connectors. The 72-pin SIMM can transfer 32 bits of a data at one time, whereas the 168-pin DIMM can transfer 64 bits of data at one time. When you upgrade your system's RAM, you must know whether your system supports SIMM or DIMM chips. Table 8-2 briefly describes the pinouts on a standard 72-bit SIMM (with parity).

Figure 8.3   RAM chips reside in memory slots on the motherboard.

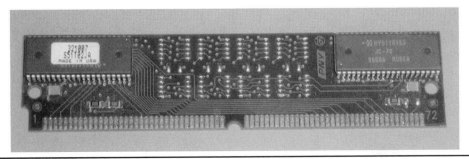

Figure 8.4   A SIMM chip contains a socket connector and memory chips.

Pin	Purpose	Pin	Purpose
1	Ground	37	Parity bits 8–15
2	Data bit 0	38	Parity bits 24–31
3	Data bit 16	39	Ground
4	Data bit 1	40	Column address strobe 0
5	Data bit 17	41	Column address strobe 2
6	Data bit 2	42	Column address strobe 3
7	Data bit 18	43	Column address strobe 1
8	Data bit 3	44	Row address strobe 0
9	Data bit 19	45	Row address strobe 1
10	+5V	46	Not connected
11	Not connected	47	Write enable
12	Address bit 0	48	Not connected
13	Address bit 1	49	Data bit 8
14	Address bit 2	50	Data bit 24
15	Address bit 3	51	Data bit 9
16	Address bit 4	52	Data bit 25
17	Address bit 5	53	Data bit 10
18	Address bit 6	54	Data bit 26
19	Address bit 10	55	Data bit 11
20	Data bit 4	56	Data bit 27
21	Data bit 20	57	Data bit 12

Table 8.1   Pinouts from a Standard 72-Pin SIMM

Pin	Purpose	Pin	Purpose
22	Data bit 5	58	Data bit 28
23	Data bit 21	59	+5V
24	Data bit 6	60	Data bit 29
25	Data bit 22	61	Data bit 13
26	Data bit 7	62	Data bit 30
27	Data bit 23	63	Data bit 14
28	Address bit 7	64	Data bit 31
29	Address bit 11	65	Data bit 15
30	+5V	66	Not connected
31	Address bit 8	67	Presence detect 1
32	Address bit 9	68	Presence detect 2
33	Row address strobe 3	69	Presence detect 3
34	Row address strobe 4	70	Presence detect 4
35	Parity bits 16–23	71	Not connected
36	Parity bits 0–7	72	Ground

Table 8.1 Pinouts from a Standard 72-Pin SIMM *(continued)*

The row access strobe "latches" the row address and initiates each memory cycle. It is required at the beginning of every operation. The column access strobe latches the column address and initiates a memory read or write operation. The PC uses the presence-detect bits to determine the speed and capacity of the chip that resides in the memory socket. The Joint Electronics Devices Engineering Council (JEDEC) at www.jedec.org defines a specification that relates the presence-detect bits to a specific memory type.

Understanding Memory Banks

You install memory chips into slots on the motherboard that users sometimes refer to as memory banks. More specifically, a bank corresponds to a group of sockets that provides enough data bits to match the number of data bits in the system bus. For example, assume that the system bus (and CPU) are 64-bit. If you are using 32-bit memory chips, you would need to group two chips in order to provide the 64 bits the bus requires.

When you install memory, you must normally fill a bank. In the previous example of a 64-bit bus, you could not add one memory chip that provides only 32-bits of data. Instead, you would need to install two chips.

Depending on your PC manufacturer (more specifically the motherboard manufacturer), you may have other requirements you must satisfy when you install memory chips. Often, the motherboard will require that that the chips you place into the bank be the same size, meaning, you cannot place a 32MB chip in the first slot and a 128MB chip in the second. Also, a motherboard may require that the chips you place in a bank are the same speed.

Often, you can place different size chips in different banks, meaning, you may be able to place two 32MB chips in the first two slots (to fill one bank) and then place two 16MB chips in the next two slots. Before you purchase memory, refer to your system's technical documentation to determine restrictions your motherboard may place on the memory banks.

Making Sense of Chip Speeds

Random access memory is so named because the CPU can access any location in RAM, at random, in the same amount of time. In contrast, the amount of time it takes a disk drive to access a disk section will vary based how far the disk drive must move its read/write head to locate the sector's track and the amount of time the drive must wait for the sector to spin past the read/write head.

Users refer to the amount of time a memory chip needs to return a value as the chip's *access time*. Different chip technologies support different access times. Common DRAM chip access times, for example, are in the range 60 ns to 70 ns. Likewise, faster SRAM chips have access times of 10 ns or less. Over the past 10 years, several different memory technologies have emerged. In general, each technologies goal was simply to reduce memory-access times. Table 8-1 briefly summarizes several of the memory technologies this chapter presents.

Technology	Time Frame	Access Time
Fast Page Mode (FPM)	1987	50 ns
Extended Data Out (EDO)	1995	50 ns
Synchronous Dynamic RAM (SDRAM)	1997	66 MHz (PC66 SDRAM)
SDRAM	1998	100 MHz (PC100 SDRAM)
RAMBUS Dynamic RAM (RDRAM)	1999	800 MHz (16-bit)
SDRAM	1999	133 MHz (PC133 SRAM)
Double Data Rate Synchronous Dynamic RAM (DDR SDRAM)	2000	266 MHz

Table 8.2 PC Memory Technologies

Understanding CPU Wait States

Within the PC, the CPU operates at a clock speed that is much faster than the system bus and must faster than RAM. Assume, for example, you are using a CPU that is running at 100 MHz. The CPU's cycle time, in turn, becomes 1 ns. In contrast, most DRAM chips operate at 60 ns. When the CPU needs data or an instruction that resides in RAM, the CPU must essentially "do nothing" while it waits for the data or instruction. Given the 1 GHz CPU and 60 DRAM chips, the CPU would need to wait for at least 6 CPU cycles. Users refer to the CPU's unused cycles as *wait states*. When the CPU is experiencing wait states, the CPU does no meaningful work.

Fortunately, because the CPU often finds data and instructions within its cache memory, the CPU can reduce its number of wait states significantly, which, in turn, greatly improves the system performance. Normally, the system's cache memory consists of SRAM chips, whose access time is 10 ns. Given a 100 MHz processor and a SRAM operating at 10 ns, the CPU would not have to wait on the memory to retrieve data that resides in the cache.

Understanding Memory Technologies

Although programmers and users often view memory as a long column of individually addressable byte locations, memory chips actually organize data within rows that consist of columns. The number of rows and columns depends on the chip's packaging. One row within a chip, for example, has millions of columns of bit-storage locations. To locate a byte location within a memory chip, the memory controller (the chip that oversees memory read and write operations) must first determine the row that contains the data. After that, the controller must determine the column location within the row where the data begins.

Assume, for example, that a DRAM memory chip has a 60-nanosecond access time. Part of the chip's access time corresponds to the row lookup operation (possibly as much as 15 ns). Next, part of the access time corresponds to the column lookup (say another 15 ns). The remainder of the access time corresponds to the process or reading or writing the memory contents.

As programs execute, the programs tend to execute instructions and access data that reside in close proximity to one another—a characteristic that programmers refer to as *locality of reference*. Often, a program may spend 80 percent of its processing time within 20 percent of its code and data. To take advantage of a program's locality of reference, newer memory technologies typically try to improve performance by reducing the access time for subsequent memory references, meaning that the first memory reference may require the program to look up row and column information. Subsequent memory references, however, can use the previous row information to reduce the chip's access time. As you examine various memory technologies, you may run into numeric ratings for the technology, such as 5-3-3-3. The numbers tell you the number of memory cycle types the first memory access requires, and the remaining numbers tell you the cycle times for subsequent memory-access operations. Given the rating 5-3-3-3, the first memory access requires five cycle times and subsequent accesses require three.

Understanding Memory Interleaving

Much the time consumed during a memory reference is due to the processing the memory controller must perform to locate a value within the memory chip. To start, the controller must determine the value's row and then determine the value's column. Memory interleaving is an older technique that systems use to improve memory performance by placing a value's bytes into different memory banks. As the first bank's memory controller is looking up the row and column location for the first byte, the second byte's memory controller can perform the same processing, which makes the bytes available at the same time.

Understanding Fast Page Mode (FPM) Memory

Fast page mode memory (which emerged in the late 1980s) improved system performance by reducing the memory access times by letting the memory chip "remember" the row location of the previous memory operation. For example, if the first memory reference requires 60 ns, and 15 ns correspond to the row-lookup operation, subsequent memory references for locations in close proximity to the previous reference (that use the same row) would require only 45 ns.

Fast page mode memory divides memory into fixed-sized pages, which, depending on the implementation, may range from 512 bytes to as much as 4KB. Each page uses the same row location within the memory chip. By tracking page references, the memory chip can reduce the access time for subsequent memory references.

Understanding Extended Data Out (EDO) Memory

Around the 1995 timeframe, Pentium processors switched from the fast page mode–memory technology to extended data out (EDO) memory. Like fast page mode–chips, the EDO chips improved performance by reducing access time of subsequent memory references. EDO RAM reduced the cycle time by eliminating the column setup time by performing subsequent column lookup operations while the memory chip is outputting data for the previous request.

Understanding Synchronous Dynamic Random Access Memory (SDRAM)

As memory chips continued to improve their speeds, performance was still restricted because the chips operated at speeds different from the system bus. By the late 1990s, synchronous dynamic random access memory (SDRAM) chips improved system performance by synching memory chip operations with the system bus. Because SDRAM chips synchronize with the system bus, you will normally find their speeds specified in megahertz. To determine the cycle time of an SDRAM chip, simply divide 1 by the corresponding speed. For example, an SDRAM chip running at 100 MHz has an access time of 10 ns. To further drive memory speeds, in support of 200 MHz system buses, memory manufacturers have released double data rate SDRAM chips (DDR SDRAM) and enhanced SDRAM (ESDRAM). The double data rate RAM improves performance by transferring data twice during a clock cycle. Likewise, the ESDRAM improves performance using its own built-in cache.

Understanding RAMBUS Memory

In 1999, Rambus memory came on the scene, improving system performance by using a high-speed special bus to transfer the data between RAM and the CPU. The special RAM bus transfers 16 bits of data at speeds of 800 MHz. The Rambus technology uses a special memory chip called a RIMM (Rambus inline memory module). The RIMM chip requires a unique 168-pin RIMM slot. A unique aspect of the RIMM bus is that each RIMM slot must either contain a RIMM chip or a special continuity module that completes the bus.

Understanding Video RAM

Chapter 17 examines PC video operations in detail. At that time, you will find that most video cards provide memory to store the current video image. To improve video performance, many video cards use a special dual mode chip that supports simultaneous read and write operations. Using a dual-mode memory chip, the video controller can update the video memory's contents, while the cards digital-to-analog converter reads the memory contents in order to send the image to the monitor for display.

Understanding Parity and Error Correcting Codes

As discussed, the PC stores information as bits. Although such errors are rare, there are times when a value the memory controller is to store in memory encounters an error during the write process that causes an errant assignment to bit value (a one value, for example, is stored as a zero). To help the memory controller identify such errors, some memory chips employ a special parity bit.

Using the parity bit, the memory controller will either make the total number of bits whose value is 1 in byte an even number or an odd number. For example, given the data bits 00000111, there are three bits in the group that are one, meaning an odd number of bits. If the memory chip uses *odd parity*, the parity bit would be 0, so that when you count the number of bits set to 1, the total will remain odd. In contrast, if the memory controller uses even parity, the parity bit would be set to 1, so when you add up the number of data bits that are set to 1 (three), and you add the parity bit you would get an even value (four). The following table illustrates the parity bit value to maintain an odd parity:

Data Bits	Parity Setting	Total Bits	Result
00000000	1	1	Odd
00000001	0	1	Odd
00000011	1	3	Odd
01010101	1	5	Odd

The problem with using a parity bit is that parity lets only the memory controller recognize a single-bit error. For example, assume that the memory chip uses odd parity. Next, assume that the memory controller is to store the value 00001100 and that parity value 1. Unfortunately, during the memory-write operation, an error occurs that causes the memory chip to store the bit values 11000000 and the parity bit 1. In this case, because the number of bits set to one is still an odd value (three), the memory controller is not aware that an error occurred. Because parity can detect only a one-bit error, many memory chips simply do not use a parity bit. In fact, because memory-write errors are rare, some CMOS Setup programs let you disable the use of parity within RAM. When you shop for memory, you must know whether your system requires memory chips that support parity operations. A memory chip that supports parity must provide storage for a parity bit for each byte of data. A SIMM chip that supports 256KB and parity, for example, will provide eight 256KB chips to store 8 bits and a ninth 256KB chip to store the corresponding parity bits. Because chips that support parity are more expensive and because many systems do not use the parity support, you will normally purchase chips that do not provide parity support or that provide high-end error detection and correction technologies.

Because parity checking can detect only single-bit errors, some memory chips employ error-correcting codes (ECC) that cannot only detect a multibit error within a byte, the technology can correct the error. The electronics that implement error-correcting codes adds significant overhead and costs to the memory chip. Normally, only servers that perform a critical role will merit the expense of memory chips that support error-correcting codes. When you shop for memory chips, you will normally find chips labeled as ECC chips or non-ECC chips. The non-ECC chips will be significantly less expensive.

Understanding Windows Virtual Memory

Chapter 10 examines operating system issues in detail. At that time, you will learn that Windows uses a technique called virtual-memory management to give each program the illusion that it has its own 4GB address space (meaning that the program has up to 4GB of RAM it can use to hold instructions and data). To implement the large virtual memory, Windows combines space on RAM with space on the hard disk to store each program's instructions and data. When the PC's RAM becomes full, Windows moves some of the contents from RAM to a special file on disk called the page file, in order to make room for programs to store information in RAM. Later, if a program needs to access instructions or data Windows has swapped to disk, Windows will move other data or instructions from RAM into the page file and swap the previous contents back into RAM. By moving data between RAM and the hard disk in this way, Windows gives its program the illusion that it has an unlimited amount of RAM. Further, because each program references its own virtual address space, one Windows program cannot overwrite another program's memory contents. Windows keeps each program's memory contents distinct. Chapter 10 examines Windows virtual memory in detail.

Making Sense of Memory Types

Using virtual memory, Windows gives each program the illusion that the program has an essentially limitless amount of available memory. However, unlimited memory was not always the case. Only a few years ago, programs running within the MS-DOS environment had to work around much more restricted memory use. Within the MS-DOS environment, programs used the following memory technologies:

- Conventional memory
- Expanded memory
- Extended memory

- High memory
- Upper memory

Today, most Windows users no longer run MS-DOS–based programs and, in general, can ignore the MS-DOS memory types. However, depending how you have upgraded your operating systems over the years, your system may still be providing support for these memory types, and as a result, consuming resources its does not use. Because users may encounter discussions of the MS-DOS memory types in other books and magazines, the sections that follow briefly describe the various memory-management techniques MS-DOS provided users to expand the user's capabilities. Then, within the Tips section you will learn how to fine-tune Windows to better meet your true needs.

Understanding MS-DOS Conventional Memory

As you have learned, the number of bits in the memory-address space define the amount of memory the operating system can reference. The MS-DOS environment used a 20-bit address, which let MS-DOS and the programs users ran within MS-DOS use 2^{20} memory locations, or 1MB of memory. Within the MS-DOS environment, the first 640KB of memory was called the PC's conventional memory. Most MS-DOS-based programs, as well as MS-DOS itself, ran within this conventional-memory space.

As shown in Figure 8-5, the PC used the 384KB of memory that sits above the conventional memory area for video memory, device drivers, and the ROM-BIOS.

Because most MS-DOS–based programs were relatively simplistic, most normally fit within the boundaries of the conventional memory. However, as the complexity of the data programs needed to manipulate increased, so too did the program's memory requirements.

Using Expanded Memory to Provide Older MS-DOS–Based Programs with More Memory for Data

As discussed, within the MS-DOS environment, programs were restricted to the PC's 640KB of conventional memory. As programs became more complex, and the amount of data the programs required increased (such as larger spreadsheets or larger databases), programs quickly outgrew the available 640KB. To provide more memory to hold data, Lotus, Intel, and Microsoft designed a memory-management technique that tricked the PC into thinking it had available memory beyond the 640KB conventional memory called the *expanded memory specification* (also known as *EMS* or *LIM-EMS* for Lotus, Intel, and Microsoft EMS).

Lotus, Intel, and Microsoft actually designed EMS for the original IBM PC, which used the 8088 processor. Using a special EMS-memory card and EMS device-driver software, programs divided their data into 64KB sections, storing all the data within the EMS memory. Next, the software would allocate a 64KB memory region within conventional memory that it would use to hold pieces of data. When the program needed to access specific data, the EMS software would move the data from the EMS memory card into the 64KB region (within conventional memory) the PC could access. By swapping memory between conventional and EMS memory in this way, a program could access large amounts of data, such as a several megabyte spreadsheet. Unfortunately, the swapping of data between expanded and conventional memory was quite time consuming, which decreased the system's performance. Eventually, therefore, expanded memory was replaced by extended memory.

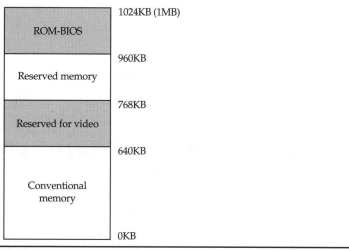

Figure 8.5   Within the MS-DOS environment, conventional memory is the PC's first 640KB of RAM.

Using Extended Memory to Provide MS-DOS–Based Programs with More Memory for Data

As just discussed, expanded memory lets programs running within the original IBM PC access data beyond 640KB. However, because of the swapping it performed (to move data between conventional and expanded memory), expanded memory was slow. Fortunately, with the advent of the 80286-based PC-AT came a new memory-management technique called *extended memory*. The extended memory specification (also known as XMS) defines PC memory that resides above 1MB, as shown in Figure 8-6. Unlike expanded memory, which required data swapping between conventional and expanded

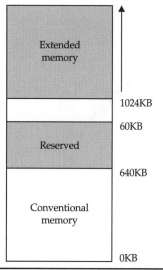

Figure 8.6   Extended memory lets program access data beyond 1MB.

memory, extended memory let programs directly access the memory beyond 1MB, which greatly improved system performance.

> ## NOTE
>
> *Within the MS-DOS operating system, programs could store only data within expanded or extended memory. All program instructions had to reside within the 640KB conventional-memory space.*

Using Upper-Memory Area and High-Memory Area to Provide MS-DOS—Based Programs with More Memory

As discussed, within the MS-DOS environment, the 384KB above the 640KB conventional area memory (which users sometimes referred to *upper-memory area*) was reserved for device drivers and video memory. Often, much of this memory area was unused. Beginning with MS-DOS version 5, users could install a device driver that let them later install memory-resident programs and device drivers into the upper-memory area. Also, MS-DOS let programs load device drivers into the high memory, which was the first 64KB above 1MB, as shown in Figure 8-7.

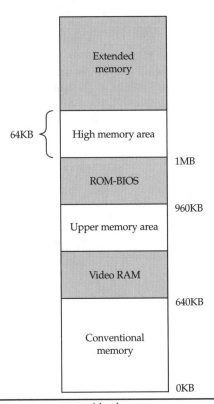

Figure 8.7   Using the upper-memory area and high-memory area to store device drivers and memory-resident programs

Monitoring Your System's Memory Use

Ask most Windows-based users the best way to improve system performance and you will likely hear the response "add more RAM." Before the CPU can execute a program, including Windows, the program must reside within RAM. Within the Windows environment, many programs run in background, behind the scenes, to perform key support operations. For example, the print spooler is a background process that oversees your printer operations. Likewise, before Windows can interact with various hardware devices, the corresponding device-driver software must reside in memory. Windows itself, therefore, can consume a considerable amount of memory. If you normally have several other programs active at the same time (such as your browser, e-mail, word processor, virus detection software, and more), you can quickly consume your PC's available RAM.

However, unless your system is actually running very low on physical memory, you will not improve your system performance by adding more RAM. To monitor your system's memory use within Windows, you can use several different programs. For example, Figure 8-8 illustrates your system's available resources within the System Information utility. The available resources the System Information utility displays relates primarily to available memory.

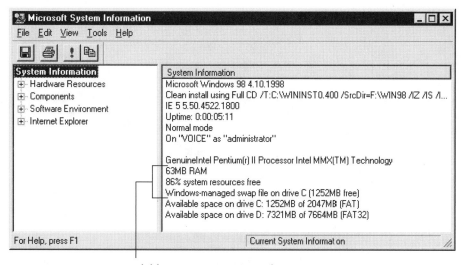

Available resources correspond
to available memory.

Figure 8.8   Displaying available resources within the System Information utility

USE IT   To view your system's available resources within the System Information utility, perform these steps:

1. Select Start | Programs Accessories. Windows will display the Accessories submenu.
2. Within the Accessories submenu, select System Tools | System Information. Windows will display the System Information utility, whose main screen displays available resources.

As you work, however, you may find that using the Windows Resource Monitor lets you easily track your system's available resources. When your system becomes low on resources, you may want to end one or more applications or possibly restart your system. Figure 8-9 illustrates the Windows Resource Meter.

Using the Windows Resource meter is a convenient way to monitor your system resources because normally, as you use your system, the Resource Meter will display a small taskbar icon you can view to monitor your available resources as you perform other operations.

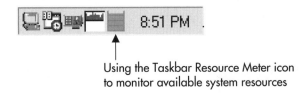

Using the Taskbar Resource Meter icon
to monitor available system resources

To run the Windows Resource Meter, perform these steps:

1. Select Start | Programs | Accessories. Windows will display the Accessories submenu.
2. Within the Accessories submenu, select System Tools | Resource Meter. Windows will display the Resource Meter icon within the taskbar.
3. To display the Resource Meter window, click the Resource Meter taskbar icon.

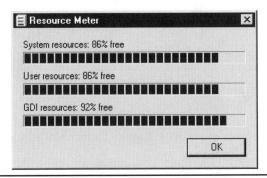

Figure 8.9   Using the Windows Resource Meter to monitor available system resources

The best way to fully understand your system's memory use is to use the System Monitor. Using the System Monitor, you can view your system's unused physical memory (which is your best indicator as to whether adding more memory will improve your system performance). Figure 8-10 illustrates the System Monitor.

To use the Windows System Monitor to observe memory operations, perform these steps:

1. Select Start | Programs | Accessories. Windows will display the Accessories submenu.

2. Within the Accessories submenu, select System Tools | System Monitor. Windows will display the System Monitor window.

3. Within the System Monitor, select Edit | Add Item. The System Monitor will display the Add Item dialog box.

4. Within the Add Item dialog box, select the Memory Manager entry. The System Monitor will display a list of items you can monitor.

5. Within the item list, select the Unused Physical Memory entry (you may also choose other items you want to monitor) and then click OK.

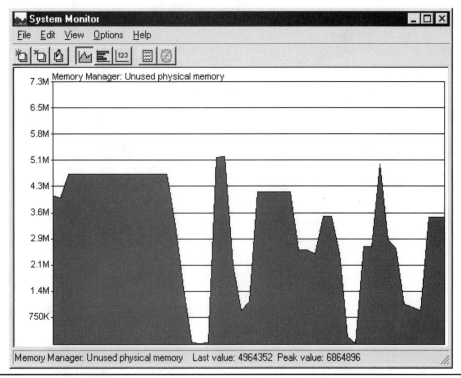

Figure 8.10   Using the System Monitor to observe unused physical memory

To monitor memory operations within Windows 2000, perform these steps:

1. Select Start | Settings | Control Panel. Windows will open the Control Panel window.
2. Within the Control Panel, double-click the Administrative Tools icon. Windows will display the Administrative Tools window.
3. Within the Administrative Tools window, double-click Performance. Windows will display the Performance Monitor.
4. Within the Performance Monitor, click the Add button (+). The Performance Monitor will display the Add Counters dialog box.
5. Within the Add Counters dialog box, use the Performance Object pull-down menu and select Memory. The Performance Monitor will display a list of counters you can monitor.
6. Within the counter list, select the counters you want to display and then click Add. The Performance Monitor will display your memory settings, as shown in Figure 8-11.

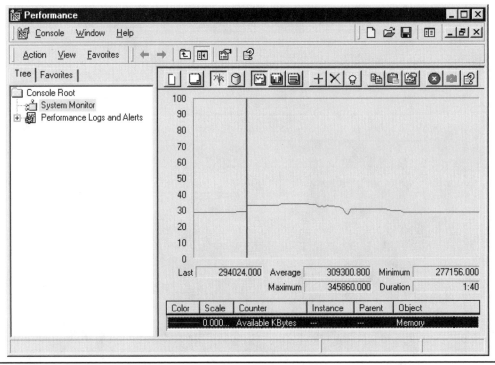

Figure 8.11   Monitoring memory settings within Windows 2000

Running Memory Benchmarks

USE IT   In Chapter 1, you learned that to monitor your system's performance and to identify potential bottlenecks, you should run benchmarks. On the Web, you may find several different memory benchmarks, such as MemTach (shown in Figure 8-12), which you can download from www.cpureview.com. Using the MemTach benchmark, you can gain insight into your system's memory bandwidth capabilities. You can compare your system's results to others, and you can submit your results for inclusion in the Web site's database.

MemTach v0.89 *ALPHA* - FREE benchmarking utility by http://www.CPUReview.com

File   Tests   Help

Test System	Value		Test Name	Min MB/sec	Avg MB/sec	Max MB/sec
Processor Brand	x86 Family 6 Model 8 Stepping 6		memset	230.4	232.6	234.0
Processor MHz			memcpy	156.5	160.0	163.3
Processor FSB			Fill - double	215.1	226.2	231.8
Motherboard Brand			Fill - int	220.8	226.5	230.2
Motherboard Model			Fill - short	227.9	230.6	232.8
Chipset Type			Fill - char	224.3	227.5	228.9
Chipset FSB			Sum - double	816.5	846.1	872.0
Memory Brand			Sum - int	524.3	528.9	533.5
Memory Type			Sum - short	259.4	262.0	264.1
Memory chip markings			Sum - char	215.1	221.8	227.6
BIOS memory settings			PSum - double	764.2	794.0	832.0
Operating System			PSum - int	468.3	478.2	485.2
Version			PSum - short	362.7	382.0	390.4
Service Pack			PSum - char	336.2	338.7	342.6
Your Name			ASum - double	924.1	935.4	945.1
Email Address			ASum - int	285.3	386.5	440.4
Web Address			ASum - short	168.5	209.3	261.3
Comments			ASum - char	211.0	223.4	229.4

Benchmark took a total of 55.83 seconds to run

	APSum - double	802.5	816.4	822.5

Choose Your Browser
(◉) Netscape   (○) Internet Explorer

	APSum - int	462.8	477.3	490.5
	APSum - short	364.7	376.9	392.1

Advanced Options
☑ Prefetch   ☐ Analyze   ☐ Longer Test (4x)

	APSum - char	332.9	336.5	342.0
	Random - int	391.0	398.6	409.2

[Start Tests]   [View Other Results]   [Submit Your Results]

Analyze 1			

[Help!]   [Visit the official MemTach page at CPUReview]

Analyze 2			

Figure 8.12   Using the MemTach benchmark to analyze your system's memory bandwidth

Displaying Windows Memory Information Using Sandra

Throughout this book, several tips have taken advantage of the SiSoftware Sandra (**S**ystem **AN**alyser, **D**iagnostic, and **R**eporting **A**ssistant) program, which you can use to provide low-level device information and to run various benchmarks. Using Sandra, you can display specifics about your system's memory use, as shown in Figure 8-13.

USE IT   To download the Sandra program, visit the SiSoftware Web site at www.sisoftware .demon.co.uk. After you install and run the Sandra software, double-click the Windows Memory Information icon to display information about Windows memory use. The Sandra software also provides a memory benchmark you can run by double-clicking on the Memory Benchmark icon.

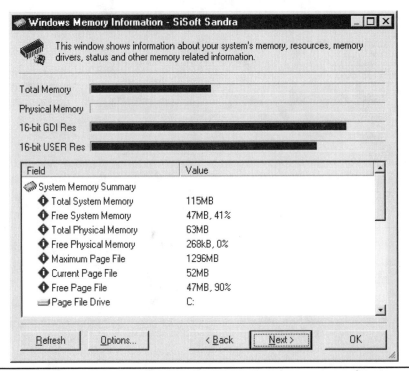

Figure 8.13   Using the SiSoftware Sandra program to display the memory information

Preparing to Upgrade Your Memory

After you make the determination that adding more memory will improve your system performance, you need to do some homework before you set out to buy your new RAM. To start, you need to examine your PC's technical documentation to determine the memory types, speeds, and sizes your system supports. Some PCs, will use SIMMs, some DIMMs, and some will use Rambus-based RIMMs. Next, you must determine your system's bank requirements, so you can purchase the correct number of memory chips. Normally, you can determine your system's memory requirements at your PC manufacturer's Web site. In fact, many manufacturers provide Web pages to help you configure your memory upgrade.

After you know your system's requirements, you must know the specifics for the memory you are currently using. Often, your system's CMOS Setup program, discussed in Chapter 6, will display information about the chips that make up each bank, as shown in Figure 8-14.

USE IT   Within the motherboard, you insert memory chips within a memory slot. Before you purchase memory chips, examine the sockets (or your PC's technical documentation) to determine if the sockets use tin or gold connectors. Then, purchase memory that matches the connector type. Many users have reported compatibility errors when they try to use a memory chip that uses tin-plated connectors in a socket that uses gold-plated connectors.

```
                        Dell Dimension 4100 SETUP
  Main    Advanced    Security    Boot       Exit
  BIOS Version              A05              Enabling this option
                                            enables the processor
                                            serial number feature.
  Processor Type      Intel(R) Pentium(R)III Disabling this option
  Processor Speed           1 GHz           disables the
  System Bus Frequency      133 MHz         processor serial
                                            number feature.
  Cache RAM                 256 KB
  Service Tag               ABC1234

  Total Memory              512 MB
  Memory Bank 0       256 MB (PC133)
  Memory Bank 1       256 MB (PC133)
                                            <- -> Select Menu
                                            ↑   ↓  Select Item
  Processor Serial Number  [Disabled]       Tab    Select Field
                                            Enter  Select Sub-Menu
                                            F9     Setup Defaults
  System Time         [18:52:16]            F10    Save and Exit
  System Date         [Sun 08/19/2001]      ESC    Exit
```

Figure 8.14   Viewing memory bank information within the CMOS Setup program

Finally, before you handle and install a memory chip, you should purchase and use a grounded wristband, as discussed in Chapter 2, which reduces the chance of electrostatic discharge damaging a sensitive memory chip.

Upgrading Your System Memory

USE IT Regardless of whether you are installing the SIMM, DIMM, or RIMM chip, the steps you will perform to install the memory are quite similar:

1. Shut down, power off, and unplug your system.

2. Gently remove your chassis cover.

3. Before you touch any of your PC's electronic components, make sure you ground yourself by first touching your desk or an object other than your PC. Ideally, wear a grounded wristband as you perform your memory installation.

4. If you are replacing or moving any memory chips, gently remove the chip(s) from its memory slot. To remove a chip, you must gently push back the edge connectors that hold the chip in place.

5. Gently insert your new memory chip into the memory slot. If you are inserting a SIMM chip, you may need to slightly angle the chip in order to slide the chip into place, as shown in the following illustration. Note that the edge connectors hold the SIMM chip in place are very sensitive. If you break a connector, you may not be able to use the memory slot (and possibly slots beyond that slot).

6. If you are inserting a DIMM or RIMM chip, make sure you close the edge connectors that hold the chip in place, shown as follows. Also, if you are installing a RIMM check, make sure that you place a continuity RIMM in each unused slot.

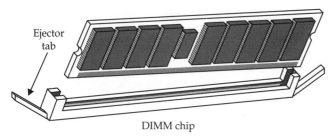

Ejector tab

DIMM chip

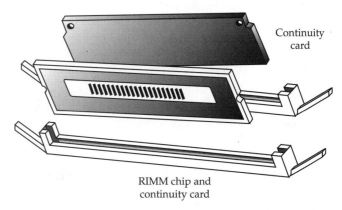

Continuity card

RIMM chip and continuity card

7. Gently replace your system's chassis cover.

8. Plug in and power on your system. As your system starts, the power-on self-test should display a count of your system's memory, which includes your newly added memory.

Troubleshooting a Memory Installation

USE IT Normally, after you install more RAM, your system should immediately start and Windows should put its new resources to use. However, if your system fails to start, perform the following troubleshooting techniques:

• If your system fails to start, power off and unplug your system. Within your system unit, make sure that each chip is seated securely within its socket. Again, take care to prevent damage to the connectors that hold the pins in place. Replace your chassis cover and try restarting your system.

• If your system fails to restart, verify again that your chips are compatible with your motherboard. If, for example, you are using 16MB EDO 72-pin SIMM chips, verify that your system does not require 16MB FPM 72-pin SIMM chips instead.

- If your memory chips are compatible, compare the chips you have placed in each bank with the motherboard's bank requirements. If for example, you are using 32-bit memory chips, and your system uses a 64-bit bus, you must install an even number of chips to properly fill each bank.

- If your system still will not start, and you are installing several chips, try installing the minimum number of chips you can in order to fill one bank. Then try starting your system. Also, one or more of your new memory chips may possibly be damaged.

- A bad connection may be causing a chip to malfunction. Gently remove and examine each chip's connectors. A smudge from a fingerprint may prevent a connector from properly functioning. If a connector is dirty, gently rub the connector with a pencil eraser. Then use an aerosol blower to blow off any eraser remnants that remain. Next, use the aerosol blower to blow out the memory slot as well.

- If your system starts, but the power-on self-test fails, take time to examine the corresponding error message. In some cases, the error message may inform you of a defective chip. Also, your problem may be a BIOS incompatibility. You may need to restore your system to its original memory configuration so that you can determine if a BIOS upgrade is available from your manufacturer's Web site, as discussed in Chapter 7.

- Normally, your system will automatically detect and use the new memory. Some systems, however, will require that you update your CMOS settings, as discussed in Chapter 6, to specify the amount of memory each memory bank contains.

Eliminating Expanded and Extended Memory Use Within Windows

Within the MS-DOS environment, programs used expanded and extended memory to increase the amount of memory programs could use to store data. MS-DOS also used the upper-memory area and high-memory area, but to do so, MS-DOS had to install an extended-memory device driver. If you run MS-DOS–based programs within the Windows environment, your programs can use expanded and extended memory. Because Windows uses virtual memory, Windows-based programs will not use expanded or extended memory. If you do not run MS-DOS–based programs from within Windows, or the programs you run do not require expanded or extended memory, you may be able to free up system resources by directing your system not to install the MS-DOS expanded memory and extended memory device drivers.

Each time Windows starts, Windows examines the contents of the config.sys file, which resides in root directory of your boot drive. Within the config.sys file, you specify MS-DOS–based device drivers that Windows uses when you open an MS-DOS window or run an MS-DOS–based program.

USE IT To view your system's MS-DOS memory use, perform these steps:

1. Select Start | Run. Windows will display the Run dialog box.

2. Within the Run dialog box, type **command** and press ENTER. Windows will open an MS-DOS window.

3. Within the MS-DOS window, type **mem**, which will yield the following results:

```
C:\WINDOWS> mem   <Enter>

Memory Type         Total        Used         Free
----------------    --------    --------     --------
Conventional          636K         44K          592K
Upper                   0K          0K            0K
Reserved                0K          0K            0K
Extended (XMS)      65,468K           ?      392,012K
----------------    --------    --------     --------
Total memory        66,104K           ?      392,604K

Total under 1 MB      636K         44K          592K

Largest executable program size        592K (606,624 bytes)
Largest free upper memory block          0K       (0 bytes)
MS-DOS is resident in the high memory area.
```

If your system is using extended or expanded memory, Windows will display the corresponding amounts within the MEM command's output.

To prevent Windows from loading either the expanded-memory or extended-memory device drivers in the future, perform these steps:

1. Select Start | Run. Windows will display the Run dialog box.

2. Within the Run dialog box, type **notepad \config.sys** and press ENTER. Windows will open Notepad, displaying the contents of the config.sys file, as shown next.

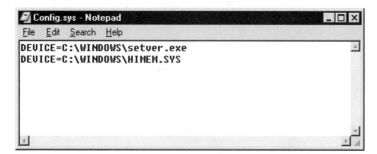

3. Within the config.sys file, look for a DEVICE= entry that loads the emm386.sys (or emm386.exe that corresponds to the expanded memory device driver) or the himem.sys (extended memory device driver). If you find such entries, type the letters **REM** at the start of the entry, which will direct Windows to ignore the entries the next time it starts:

```
REM DEVICE=C:\WINDOWS\HIMEM.SYS
```

The next time you restart your system, Windows will not load the device drivers.

Controlling the Amount of Physical RAM Windows Uses

USE IT Each time your system starts, the BIOS performs its power-on self-test. Normally, during the self-test, the BIOS will examine your PC's memory to make sure it is in working order. Should the BIOS encounter a memory error, it will normally display an error message on your screen and will stop the startup process. Normally, when such errors occur, you should simply power your system off and back on to repeat the power-on self-test. If the error persists, and you need to access your system, you may be able successfully start your system by using the CMOS Setup program discussed in Chapter 6 to disable RAM testing during the power-on self-test. Then, after your system starts, you may be able to restrict Windows from using the damaged memory region by reducing the amount of physical memory Windows will use by performing these steps:

1. Select Start | Programs | Accessories. Windows will display the Accessories submenu.

2. Within the Accessories submenu, select System Tools | System Information. Windows will run the System Information utility.

3. Within the System Information utility, select Tools | System Configuration Utility. Windows will run the System Configuration utility.

4. Within the System Configuration utility, click Advanced. The System Configuration utility will display the Advanced Troubleshooting Settings dialog box, as shown here.

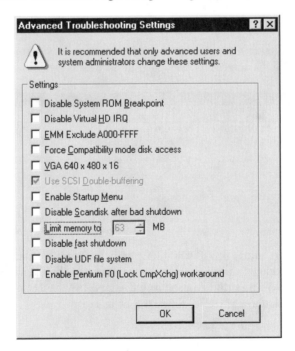

5. Within the Advanced Troubleshooting Settings dialog box, click the Limit Memory To checkbox, placing a checkmark in the box. Then specify the amount (in megabytes) of physical memory want Windows to use.

6. Click OK and then restart your system to put your change into effect.

Later, after you replace the errant memory chip, remember to use the System Configuration utility to remove your memory restriction. One way to better understand how RAM impacts your system performance is to reduce the amount of physical memory Windows can use and then to run a variety of programs. As you run the programs, you can use the System Monitor to view the amount of paging Windows must perform to move data and instructions between disk and memory. Often, programmers have high-end PCs with large amounts of RAM. To test a program's performance, the programmer may want to reduce the amount of physical memory Windows has to work with to better learn how the program will run in a user environment.

CHAPTER 9

Speeding Up and Troubleshooting System Startup

If computers can land a man on the moon, oversee trades on the stock exchange, and coordinate traffic patterns to ensure safe air travel, why then, does a Windows-based system so long to start? If a gigahertz processor can execute over one billion instructions per second, what possibly can a system be doing during its seemingly endless startup process?

This chapter examines the PC's startup process in detail. To start, you will examine the role the BIOS plays within the startup process. Next, you will learn how an operating system loads itself into RAM from a bootable system disk. Finally, you will learn which programs your system may automatically run each time your system starts, and ways you may disable the programs in the future. Within the tips this chapter presents, you will find ways you may be able to shave time off your system's startup process.

Years ago, users could configure lots of settings to "tweak" various system settings to improve the speed at which their system started. Today, however, many of those settings are no longer available. In some cases, PC manufacturers have removed the user's ability to access the settings for compatibility reasons. In most cases, the operating system has eliminated the setting's need or purpose. However, just as the operating system has eliminated some settings, it has also introduced others. In this chapter, you will use the new capabilities to streamline or troubleshoot the system startup process.

Stage One: The BIOS and the Power-On Self-Test (POST)

To perform useful work, computers (specifically the CPU) execute program instructions that direct it to perform a specific task. A program is nothing more than a list of instructions the CPU executes. When you first power on your PC, no programs are currently running. So, the PC directs the CPU to start running instructions that are built into the BIOS. Chapter 6 discussed the PC BIOS in detail.

During the startup process, the BIOS instructions initiate the PC's POST, which directs the PC to examine its key components, such as RAM, to make sure everything is in working order. If the POST encounters a problem, your PC may display an error message that you can use to start your troubleshooting process, or your PC may simply sound one of the cryptic beep codes described in Chapter 6.

If the self-test is successful, the BIOS then examines your system's CMOS settings to determine from which disk it should start (boot) the operating system. After the BIOS identifies the "boot" disk, the BIOS will read the disk's first sector into RAM. Users refer to the disk's first sector as the "boot record" or "boot sector." A disk's book record contains information about the disk, as well as a set of instructions the CPU can execute to load the operating system from disk. Figure 9-1 illustrates a simple floppy disk boot record.

Address	Field
00H	JMP instruction
03H	OEM name
0BH	Bytes per sector
0DH	Sectors per cluster
0EH	Number of reserved sectors
10H	Number of file allocation tables
11H	Number of root directory entries
13H	Total disk sectors
15H	Media descriptor
16H	Sectors per file allocation table
18H	Sectors per track
1AH	Number of heads
1CH	Number of hidden sectors
20H	Huge sector count
24H	Drive number
25H	Reserved
26H	Extended boot record signature
27H	Volume serial number
28H	Volume label
36H	File system type
3EH	DOS loader

Figure 9.1   The boot record contains information about the disk and instructions the PC uses to load the operating system.

Stage Two: Loading the Boot Record into RAM

As you know, before the CPU can execute a program, the program's instructions must reside within the PC's RAM. The operating system is no exception. Before the operating system can run, it must reside in RAM. After the BIOS completes the POST and locates the boot record on disk, the system loads the boot record in to RAM, as shown in Figure 9-2. The boot record contains instructions the CPU executes to load the remainder of the operating system from disk into RAM.

The previous discussion about the boot record actually simplified the process by omitting a few hard disk–related issues. If you are booting your system from a floppy disk, the BIOS can simply read the floppy's boot record into RAM. However, if you are booting from a hard disk, which may contain multiple partitions, the BIOS must first determine which partition it should boot.

To determine the bootable partition, the BIOS reads the hard disk's *master boot record*. Just as the floppy disk's boot record contains information about the floppy disk, such as the disk's sector size, the master boot record contains information about each hard disk partition, such as the partition's starting cylinder number. The master boot record also specifies which partition is the boot partition. After the BIOS knows which partition to boot, the BIOS reads that partition's boot record into RAM.

Normally, if the floppy disk or hard disk partition is bootable, that is, the disk contains the files the operating system needs in order to start, the BIOS will hand off the startup process over to the instructions that reside within the boot record. If the disk is not bootable, however, your system will display a message similar to the following, and the startup process will stop:

```
Non-System disk or disk error
Replace and strike any key when ready
```

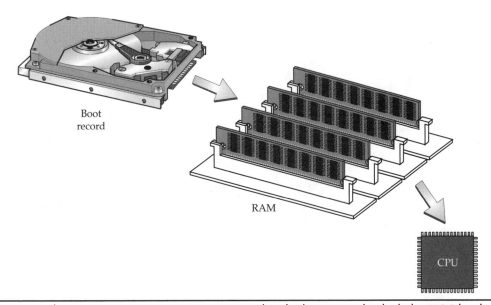

Boot record

RAM

CPU

Figure 9.2   The CPU executes instructions contained in the boot record, which the BIOS loads into RAM.

As an aside, the BIOS does not display the nonsystem disk message. Instead, the program that resides within the boot record displays the message. When you format a disk for use, you can make the disk bootable by directing the format process to copy the files to the disk that the operating system needs to boot. If you do not create a bootable disk, the format process will place the instructions in the disk's boot record that displays the nonsystem disk message should a user try to boot the disk.

Stage Three: The Operating System Loads Itself into RAM

Depending on the operating system you are running, the files the system loads during stage 3 of the startup process will differ. However, regardless of the operating system, the process is the same: the operating system must load into RAM the files it needs to start. The more complex the operating system, the larger the size or number of files the operating system will need, and hence, the longer the startup process will require.

For those of you who used computers before they had mice, you will likely recall how fast MS-DOS loaded itself into memory and displayed its system prompt telling you it was ready for work. Table 9-1 briefly describes the files the MS-DOS operating system loaded from disk into RAM during the system startup process.

In a similar way, Table 9-2 describes the files Windows 95 and 98 load during the startup process.

▶ **NOTE**

If you are using Windows 2000, turn to your documentation and take time to review the Boot.ini file. Within the Boot.ini file, you can place entries that configure operating system settings and which control the boot process.

File	Purpose
Io.sys	Builds upon the BIOS input and output routines
Msdos.sys	Contains the MS-DOS system services that perform file operations, date and time manipulation, and more
Command.com	Contains the MS-DOS command-line processor
Config.sys	Contains single-line entries the user can use to customize various system settings and install device drivers
Autoexec.bat	Contains one or more commands (programs) the operating system will automatically run each time the system starts

Table 9.1   Files Loaded by MS-DOS During the System Startup Process

File	Purpose
Io.sys	Contains a real-mode operating system that loads the device drivers and other files Windows will eventually need to operate.
Msdos.sys	A text file that contains single-line entries that control the Windows startup process.
Logo.sys	Windows displays its logo on your screen.
Dblspace.bin	If your system is using drive compression, the Dblspace.bin driver is loaded, which lets Windows read the disk.
System.dat, user.dat	Windows examines the Registry contents.
Config.sys	Windows loads any real-mode device drivers it needs that are listed in the config.sys file.
Autoexec.bat	Windows loads any specified terminate-and-stay-resident programs (TSRs).
Win.com	Windows is run.
Device driver files	Windows loads its virtual device driver files.
Network support	Windows performs necessary network operations.
Startup folder	Windows launches programs that reside in the Startup folder.

Table 9.2   Files Loaded by Windows 9x During the System Startup Process

Stage Four: The Operating System Runs a Slew a Programs

If the operating system loaded only files listed in the preceding tables, most users would likely tolerate the amount of time the startup process consumed. Unfortunately, before you can begin working, the operating system runs several other programs—some of which you may know about—some of which you may need—and some of which will simply waste your time and consume system resources.

To better understand the number of programs your system may start, use either the System Information utility—or if you are using Windows 2000, you can use the Task Manager—to view active tasks, as discussed in the sections that follow.

Within the Windows environment, to determine which programs are running, users typically examine the taskbar, which normally appears at the bottom of their screens. As shown in Figure 9-3, the taskbar contains icons for active programs on which users can click to switch quickly between programs.

Figure 9.3   Using the taskbar, users can switch between active programs.

Normally, the taskbar contains icons only for programs the user has run by selecting the application from a Start menu option or by double-clicking on an application icon. The taskbar may also show icons for programs Windows has started automatically for the user via the Start menu Startup folder (which contains entries for programs that the user wants Windows to launch automatically each time the system starts). The taskbar does not, however, contain an icon for every program your system is running.

USE IT To view more programs that are running within Windows 9*x*, press CTRL-ALT-DELETE. Windows, in turn, will display the Close Program dialog box that you can use to end a program that is *hung* (not responding), as shown in Figure 9-4.

Normally, users will use the Close Program dialog box to end a program that is not responding. However, within the dialog box, you can view the names of programs beyond those with icons that appear on your taskbar, that are currently running within with your system. Most users are surprised to see the list of programs they may not have known were running. Later, in this chapter's tips, you will learn how to identify each program's purpose.

▶ *NOTE*

When a program stops responding to user input, and you cannot end the program by clicking on the program's close button or by using the program's File menu to exit the program, you can normally end the program by using the Close Program dialog box. To display the Close Program dialog box, press the CTRL-ALT-DELETE keyboard combination. Then, within the dialog box, click the program you want to end and click the End Task button. In some cases, Windows may immediately end the application. In other cases, you may need to repeat these steps two or three times before Windows successfully ends the application. You should only use the Close Program dialog box to end applications you cannot close using normal Windows-based operations. If you close an application for which you have unsaved work in progress, you will likely lose your work.

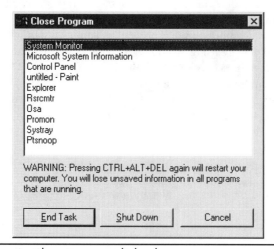

Figure 9.4 The Windows 9*x* Close Program dialog box.

Using the System Information Utility to Display Running Programs

As you just learned, while using the Close Program dialog box, you can display the names of programs that are running on your system of which you may not have been aware. However, the Close Program dialog box still does not show you all the programs that are currently running. To display all the active programs in your system, you must use the System Information utility, which, as shown in Figure 9-5, will display a long list of programs.

 USE IT   To display running programs within your system using the System Information utility, perform these steps:

1. Select Start | Programs | Accessories. Windows will display the Accessories submenu.

2. Within the Accessories submenu, select System Tools | System Information. Windows, in turn, will open the Microsoft System Information utility.

3. Within the Microsoft System Information utility, click the plus sign (+) that appears in front of the Software Environment entry. The System Information utility will expand its list of software options.

4. Within the list of software options, click the Running Tasks entry. The System Information utility will display a list of the programs currently running on your system, similar to that previously shown in Figure 9-5.

Depending on your system configuration and the applications you are currently running, the number of programs that appear within the active tasks list can be very long. Take time now to examine the description the System Information utility will display for each program. You may be surprised by the programs Windows must run behind the scenes to support programs such as your dial-up modem connection or your network connection.

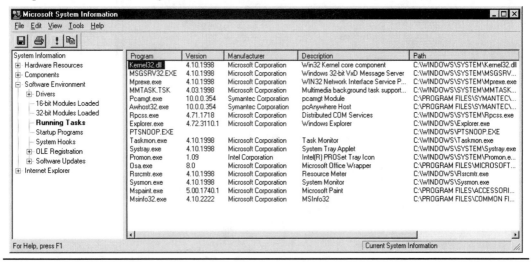

Figure 9.5   Using the System Information utility to display programs that are running within your system

If you consider Windows normally takes a second or two to launch a program, you will soon realize the amount of overhead running the programs listed in the active task list can place on your system startup process (however, as you will learn later in this chapter, not all of these programs launch when your system starts). Within this chapter's tips, you will learn how to control which applications Windows automatically starts.

Displaying Running Programs within Windows 2000

If you are using Windows 2000, you can use the System Information utility as just discussed to view information on running tasks. In addition, you can use the Windows Task Manager dialog box Processes sheet to display information about your system's running programs, as shown in Figure 9-6. Within the Processes sheet, you can view not only which programs are running, but the amount of memory each program consumes, as well as the amount of CPU time the program has used since it was active.

Image Name	PID	CPU	CPU Time	Mem Usage
System Idle Process	0	96	3:28:33	16 K
System	8	00	0:00:53	212 K
smss.exe	132	00	0:00:01	348 K
csrss.exe	160	00	0:00:13	1,916 K
winlogon.exe	180	00	0:00:08	472 K
services.exe	208	00	0:00:05	4,956 K
lsass.exe	220	00	0:00:01	1,052 K
explorer.exe	276	01	0:00:34	2,580 K
svchost.exe	380	00	0:00:00	3,176 K
PSP.EXE	404	00	0:00:39	2,020 K
SPOOLSV.EXE	416	00	0:00:00	2,808 K
blackd.exe	464	00	0:00:16	3,240 K
defwatch.exe	476	00	0:00:00	988 K
svchost.exe	492	00	0:00:04	6,888 K
rtvscan.exe	520	01	0:01:44	7,820 K
vptray.exe	544	00	0:00:00	2,904 K
SynTPLpr.exe	576	00	0:00:00	1,096 K
regsvc.exe	636	00	0:00:00	756 K
mstask.exe	656	00	0:00:00	2,912 K
MSGSYS.EXE	668	00	0:00:05	2,740 K
winmgmt.exe	676	00	0:00:31	1,228 K
SynTPEnh.exe	1140	00	0:00:00	2,108 K
point32.exe	1168	00	0:00:00	1,584 K
blackice.exe	1224	00	0:00:01	3,156 K
bkclient.exe	1256	00	0:00:01	7,164 K
Sprint PCS Dial	1264	00	0:00:02	2,400 K
NetPerSec.exe	1288	00	0:00:00	2,832 K
taskmgr.exe	1416	02	0:00:01	2,384 K
WINWORD.EXE	1452	00	0:00:52	13,580 K

Processes: 29   CPU Usage: 5%   Mem Usage: 104112K / 310740K

Figure 9.6   Viewing active programs within Windows 2000 using the Task Manager dialog box Processes sheet

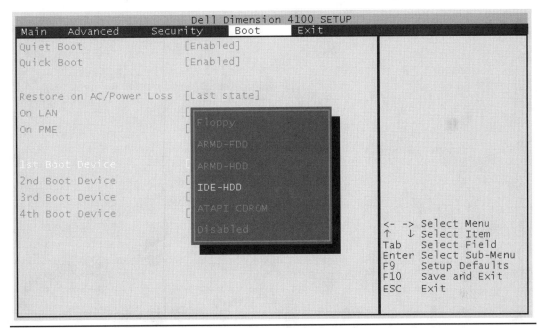

Figure 9.7   Using a CMOS setup program to change the boot device sequence

Should you ever encounter a hard-disk error that prevents your system from starting, you can again use the CMOS setup program to change the boot disk sequence, this time putting your floppy disk first in the boot device order. Then, you can boot your system from a floppy disk in drive A. Also, there may be times when you must rebuild Windows using the CD-ROM that you received from your computer manufacturer. In such cases, you will likely need to boot your system from the CD. Using the CMOS setup program's boot device sequence, you can place the CD-ROM drive first in the list, which will direct your system to boot from the CD.

Using the CMOS Fast Boot Option

As discussed earlier in this chapter, each time your system starts, the BIOS initiates the PC's POST. Depending on your system type, the CMOS setup program may provide an option you can choose to disable part of the self-test, which, in turn, speeds up your system's startup. Chapter 6 examines various components of the POST. Normally, when you use the CMOS setup program to select a "fast boot" option, the POST will not test all of your PC's RAM, which, depending on the amount of RAM your system contains, may shave noticeable time off of the startup process.

USE IT   To direct your PC to perform a fast boot operation, restart your system and enter the CMOS setup program. Within the setup program, look for and enable fast boot option, as shown in Figure 9-8.

```
                    Dell Dimension 4100 SETUP
  Main    Advanced    Security    Boot     Exit
  Quiet Boot              [Enabled]              Allows BIOS to skip
  Quick Boot              [Enabled]              certain tests while
                                                 booting. This will
                                                 decrease the time
  Restore on AC/Power Loss [Last state]          needed to boot the
  On LAN                  [Power On]             system.
  On PME                  [Stay Off]

  1st Boot Device         [ATAPI-CDROM]
  2nd Boot Device         [ARMD-FDD]
  3rd Boot Device         [IDE-HDD]
  4th Boot Device         [Disabled]
                                                 <- -> Select Menu
                                                 ↑  ↓  Select Item
                                                 Tab   Select Field
                                                 Enter Select Sub-Menu
                                                 F9    Setup Defaults
                                                 F10   Save and Exit
                                                 ESC   Exit
```

Figure 9.8   Using the CMOS setup program to enable a fast boot operation

Many users will argue that disabling part of the POST is a risky process, and that they would prefer that the system checks out as "ready for use," before they start their work. If you enable the fast boot option and later begin to experience intermittent errors, you should disable the option and let your system perform its complete self-test.

Also, many CMOS setup programs provide users with the ability to enable and disable an audible tone (a click) that the POST generates as it examines your system's memory. Although most users will disable the click because they find it annoying, you should disable the click because it removes yet one more operation the PC must perform during the startup process.

▶ **NOTE**

Many CMOS programs also let you enable the display of boot-time diagnostics. If you are experiencing problems within your system startup, you may want to use your CMOS setup to display the results of the diagnostics the BIOS runs as your system starts.

Using the System Information Utility to Determine Which Applications Windows Automatically Starts

Using the Windows System Information utility, you can display a list of the programs that are running within your system. Many of the programs the System Information utility displays are programs that

Windows automatically starts each time your system boots. To determine which programs it should start automatically, Windows examines three sources: the Startup folder, entries within INI files (initialization files that carry over from older versions of Windows), and entries within the Windows Registry. Using the System Information utility, you can display information that tells from where Windows is receiving the directive to automatically start various programs.

 To use the System Information utility to display information about the programs Windows automatically starts each time it boots, perform these steps:

1. Select Start | Programs | Accessories. Windows will display the Accessories submenu.

2. Within the Accessories submenu, select System Tools | System Information. Windows, in turn, will open the Microsoft System Information utility.

3. Within the Microsoft System Information utility, click the plus sign (+) that appears in front of the Software Environment entry. The System Information utility will expand its list of software options.

4. Within the list of software options, click the Startup Programs entry. The System Information utility will display a list of the programs Windows automatically runs each time your system starts, as shown here.

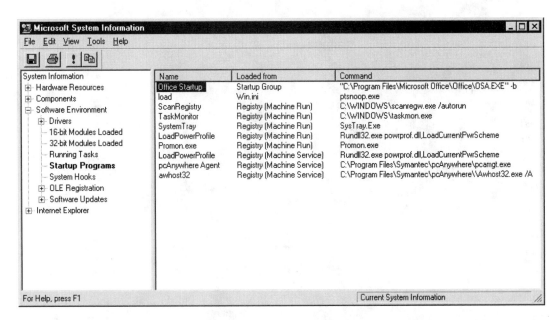

Within the System Information utility, the Loaded from column tells you where Windows is getting the directive to load the program. In the next tip, you will learn how to remove the entry that directs Windows to automatically run the program.

Remove Programs You Don't Regularly Use from the Start Menu Startup Folder

Each time Windows starts, Windows automatically runs a range of programs, some of which you will know about and some which run behind the scenes—which you may or may not want running.

To let you specify programs you want Windows to automatically start each time it runs, Windows provides a special Startup folder (which appears within the Start menu Programs option). Each time your system starts, Windows will automatically run programs that you place within the Startup folder. You might, for example, use the Startup folder to automatically start your e-mail program or your word processing program. To view the contents of your Startup folder (and hence the programs Windows thinks you want to automatically start each time it boots), select Start | Programs | Startup. Windows, in turn, will display the Startup folder's contents, as shown in Figure 9-9.

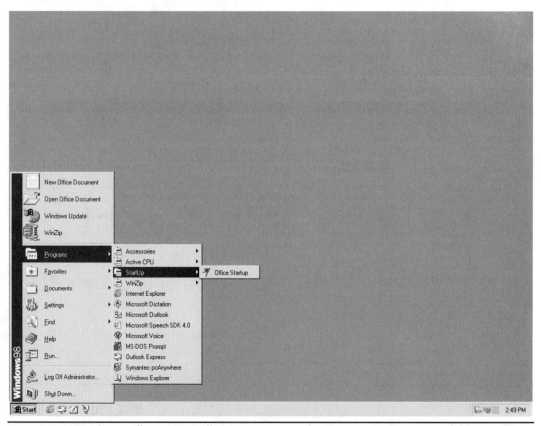

Figure 9.9   Windows will automatically start programs that appear in the Startup folder each time your system starts.

USE IT To add a program to the Startup folder, perform these steps:

1. Select Start | Settings | Taskbar & Start menu. Windows will display the Taskbar Properties dialog box.

2. Within the Taskbar Properties dialog box, select the Start Menu Programs tab. Windows will display the Start Menu Programs sheet, as shown here.

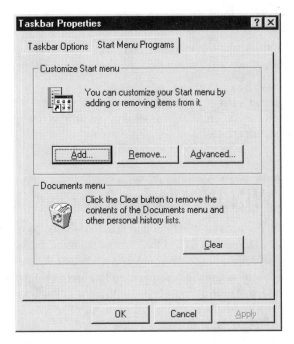

3. Within the Start Menu Programs sheet, click Add. Windows, in turn, will display the Create Shortcut dialog box.

4. Within the Create Shortcut dialog box, click Browse. Windows will display the Browse dialog box.

5. Within the Browse dialog box, traverse the folders on your disk to locate the executable program file for the application you want Windows to automatically run each time it starts. Double-click the program file. Windows will return you to the Create Shortcut dialog box.

6. Within the Create Shortcut dialog box, click Next. Windows will display the Select Program Folder dialog box.

7. Within the Select Program Folder dialog box, click the Startup folder and then click Next. Windows will display the Select a Title for the Program dialog box.

8. Within the Select a Title for the Program dialog box, type the title that you want to appear on the Start menu and then click Finish. Windows will add your program to the Startup folder.

To remove a program from the Startup folder, perform these steps:

1. Select Start | Settings | Taskbar & Start menu. Windows will display the Taskbar Properties dialog box.

2. Within the Taskbar Properties dialog box, select the Start Menu Programs tab. Windows, in turn, will display the Start Menu Programs sheet, previously shown in Figure 9-11.

3. Within the Start Menu Programs sheet, click Remove. Windows, in turn, will display the Remove Shortcuts/Folders dialog box.

4. Within the Remove Shortcuts/Folders dialog box, click the plus sign (+) that precedes the Startup folder. Windows will expand the folder's contents, listing the programs the folder contains.

5. Within the Startup folder's list of programs, click the program you want to remove and then click Remove. Windows will remove the program from the Startup folder. When you are done removing programs, click Close.

Examining the WIN.INI File for Run= and Load= Entries

Prior to Windows 95, users customized Windows and Windows-based programs using files with the .INI extension, such as WIN.INI and SYSTEM.INI. Within these INI files (INI is an abbreviation for *initialization*), users would place single-line entries that directed Windows to perform specific operations. To direct Window to automatically run programs, users would place run= and load= entries within the WIN.INI file. The difference between the run= and load= entries is that the run= entry directs Windows to run the program within an open window, whereas the load= entry directs Windows to run the program minimized as an icon. To provide compatibility for early Windows versions, Windows today still searches the WIN.INI file for load= and run= entries. As such, Windows may still run programs that were used under Windows 3.1, for example, that you no longer need, simply because the WIN.INI file contains a load= or run= entry.

USE IT Take time now to examine your system's WIN.INI file for load= and run= entries, and if you find one or more, decide if you still want Windows to run the corresponding program. If not, delete the corresponding entry within the file. To quickly examine the WIN.INI file's content, perform these steps:

1. Select Start | Run. Windows, in turn, will display the Run dialog box.

2. Within the Run dialog box, type **SYSEDIT** and press ENTER. Windows, in turn, will run the System Configuration Editor program, which as shown in Figure 9-12, loads several files for your review.

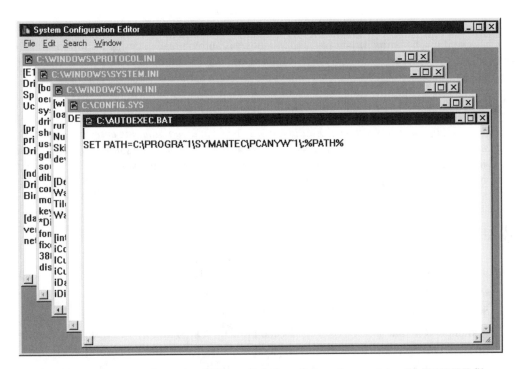

3. Within the System Configuration Editor, click the window that contains the WIN.INI file. Then, scroll through the file's contents for a `load=` or `run=` entry. If you encounter an entry, try to determine the corresponding program's purpose.

4. If you decide you do not need the program, place a semicolon in front of the entry. The WIN.INI uses the semicolon to indicate the start of a *comment*. By placing the semicolon at the start of the line, you essentially "comment out" the entry, which directs Windows to ignore it. Should you later find that the program performed an operation you require, simply edit the file once again and remove the semicolon.

5. After you make and save your changes to the WIN.INI file, select File | Exit to close the System Configuration Editor.

6. If you make any changes to the to WIN.INI file, you must restart your system for the changes to take effect.

Examining the Registry for Entries that Launch Programs

Each time your system starts, Windows automatically runs a range of programs. Windows determines which programs it should automatically run by examining the Startup folder and the WIN.INI file (for `run=` and `load=` entries), and via entries that reside within the Windows Registry. As you have learned, using the System Information utility, you can determine which source Windows is using to launch a specific application. If you find that Windows is automatically starting an application you do not need because of an entry in the System Registry, you can use the Registry Editor to remove the entry, and thus, prevent Windows from running the program each time your system starts.

▶ *CAUTION*

Before you change or delete a Registry setting, make sure you understand the entry's purpose. To start and later to operate, Windows relies upon the Registry to provide key settings. If you errantly delete the wrong setting, you may prevent Windows from running. Should you experience a Registry error, turn to the Chapter 10 tips that discuss restoring a Registry backup.

USE IT To locate and remove an entry from the Registry that is launching a program, perform these steps:

1. Within the System Information utility, note the application's complete program name, such as WinMenu.exe or Supercache.exe.

2. Select Start | Run. Windows, in turn, will display the Run dialog box.

3. Within the Run dialog box, type **regedit** and press ENTER. Windows will open the Registry Editor.

4. Within the Registry Editor, select Edit | Find. The Registry Editor will display the Find dialog box.

5. Within the Find dialog box, type the program's filename and press ENTER. The Registry will search for the entries that contain the filename.

6. When the Registry locates the entry, make sure that the entry resides in a folder named Run, as shown in Figure 9-10. Then, select Edit | Delete to remove the entry from the Registry. Select File | Exit to close the Registry Editor.

Using the System Configuration Utility to Control Applications that Windows Automatically Starts

In the preceding tips, you learned how to use the Startup folder, the WIN.INI file, and the Registry to control which programs Windows automatically starts each time your system boots. You can also quickly and easily enable or disable a program's automatic execution by using the Windows System Configuration Utility. As shown in Figure 9-11, the System Configuration Utility provides a Startup sheet that you can use to direct Windows to run or not run specific programs each time Windows starts.

USE IT To use the System Configuration Utility to disable a program's automatic execution by Windows at startup, simply click the check box that precedes the program name, to remove the check mark. Before you disable a program's execution, however, you should understand the program's purpose.

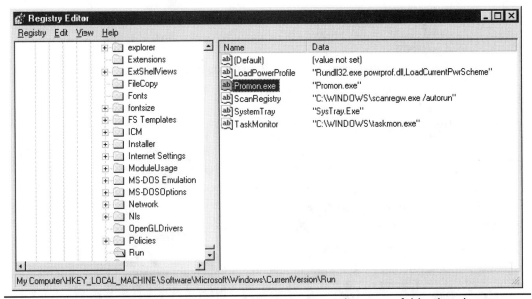

Figure 9.10   Using the Windows Registry to locate an entry within a Run folder that directs Windows to automatically run a program each time the system starts

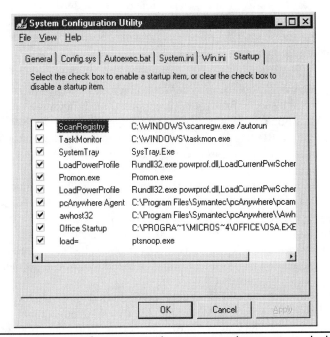

Figure 9.11   Using the System Configuration Utility's Startup sheet to control which applications Windows automatically starts

You can run the System Configuration Utility in one of two ways. First, you can run the program simply typing the program's name within the Run dialog box, by performing these steps:

1. Select Start | Run. Windows will display the Run dialog box.

2. Within the Run dialog box, type **msconfig** and press ENTER.

You can also start the System Configuration Utility from within the System Information utility, by performing these steps:

1. Select Start | Programs | Accessories. Windows will display the Accessories submenu.

2. Within the Accessories submenu, select System Tools | System Information. Windows, in turn, will open the Microsoft System Information utility.

3. Within the Microsoft System Information utility, select Tools | System Configuration Utility.

Examining the Windows 9x Startup Log File Bootlog.txt

Each time your system starts, Windows loads a set of operating system programs into RAM. Next, Windows begins to load device drivers (the software that lets the operating system interact with a device, such as a keyboard, mouse, or disk). Depending on the hardware devices connected to your PC, Windows may load device drivers that are unique to your system, such as the device driver for a scanner, TV video card, and so on. Unfortunately, there may be times when a device driver causes the Windows startup process to fail.

USE IT To help you troubleshoot your system startup process, Windows 9x logs the names of the device drivers it successfully (or unsuccessfully) loads during the startup process to a root directory file named Bootlog.txt. Even if your system started successfully, you should take time to examine the contents of the Bootlog.txt file, shown in Figure 9-12 within the Windows WordPad accessory. As you can see, the file contains one or two line entries that tell you whether or not Windows successfully loaded specific device drivers.

If you examine the contents of the Bootlog.txt file, you will find that each time your system starts, Windows loads the files listed in the Fonts folder, so that the fonts are ready for use. In the next tip, you will learn how to improve Windows performance by reducing the number of fonts Windows must load each time it starts. Within Windows 2000, you can enable boot logging from the Windows 2000 Advanced Options menu, which you can access by pressing the F8 key during the startup process. Windows 2000, in turn, will log the startup information to the file Ntbtlog.txt that resides within the %windir% directory, which is typically C:\WINNT.

If your system fails to start, you may need to boot Windows within Safe Mode, as discussed in this chapter's "Booting Your System in Safe Mode" tip. After your system is running, you can perform the following steps to view the contents of the Bootlog.txt file. Within the Bootload.txt file, you may be able to determine that a device driver is causing your system to hang. Using the Control Panel

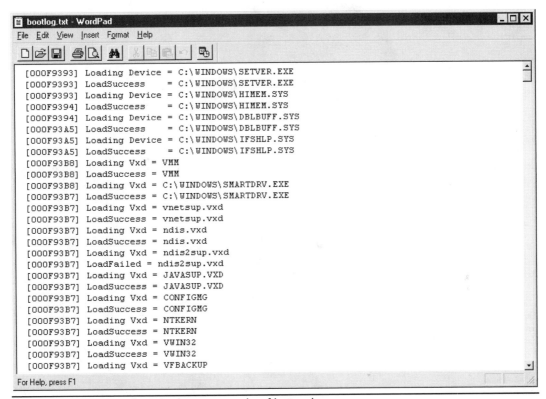

Figure 9.12 Viewing the Windows startup log file Bootlog.txt

Device Manager, you can remove the device from the Windows configuration, in which case, Windows will not try to load the device driver the next time it starts. Chapter 4 discusses the Windows Device Manager. To view the Windows startup log, perform these steps:

1. Select Start | Run. Windows will display the Run dialog box.

2. Within the Run dialog box, type **Wordpad \Bootlog.txt** and press ENTER. Windows, in turn, will start the Wordpad editor, loading the root directory Bootlog.txt file for your review.

Remove Unnecessary Fonts

Each time your system starts, Windows loads the fonts specified within the Windows Font folder. Depending on the number of fonts your Font folder contains, you may be adding significant overhead to the Windows startup process for fonts you do not use.

USE IT To view the fonts your system currently supports, perform these steps:

1. Select Start | Settings | Control Panel. Windows will open the Control Panel window.

2. Within the Control Panel, double-click the Font icon. Windows will display the contents of the Fonts window, as shown in Figure 9-13.

If you are like most users, your system has many fonts that you will likely never use. Rather than delete the fonts that you don't think you will use, simply move the fonts to a different folder. Should you ever need the fonts in the future, you can move them back into the Fonts folder. In the meantime, the fonts will simply consume disk space.

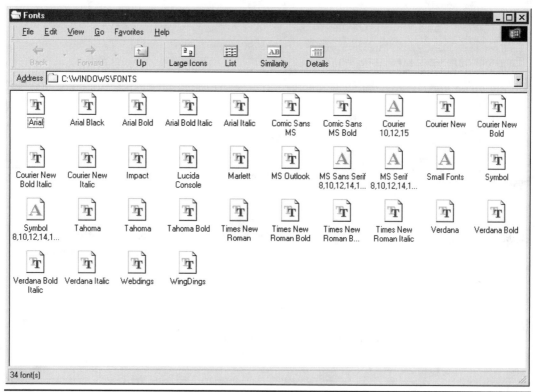

Figure 9.13 Displaying system fonts within the Fonts window

Booting Your System in Safe Mode

If Windows fails to start, you may be able to start Windows in Safe Mode, which directs Windows to load a "scaled down" version of the operating system that you can then use to troubleshoot your system. When you start Windows in Safe Mode, Windows will disable network operations, will not process the System Registry (and hence will not respond to the Registry's entries that direct it to run specific programs), and Windows will not load a range of device drivers. Within Safe Mode, Windows does not provide all the functionality you would have within a normal system. However, Safe Mode operations do let you run programs, edit system configuration files, and perform other operations that may help you to detect and correct the problem that is keeping your system from starting.

USE IT To start Windows in Safe Mode, power on your PC. As the BIOS is performing your system's POST, press the F8 function key. Windows, in turn, will display the following menu:

```
Microsoft Windows 98 Startup Menu
============================
    1. Normal
    2. Logged (BOOTLOG.TXT)
    3. Safe mode
    4. Step-by-Step confirmation
    5. Command prompt only
    6. Safe mode command prompt
```

Within the Startup menu, select option 3 to boot Windows in Safe Mode. After you complete your troubleshooting options, select Start | Shutdown and restart your system. If your troubleshooting was successful, Windows should boot for normal operations. If the error persists, reboot your system in Safe Mode and continue your troubleshooting. You might, for example, view the root directory file Bootlog.txt to determine if a device driver is preventing your system from starting.

To access Safe Mode within Windows 2000, you again press F8 during the startup process. Windows 2000, in turn, will display the Windows 2000 Advanced Options menu, from which you can select Safe Mode operations.

Controlling How Windows Will Start Next

In the preceding section, you learned that when Windows will not successfully start, you may be able to boot Windows in Safe Mode, by pressing F8 as your system is starting. In addition, by using the System Configuration Utility, you can specify—before you shut down (or restart) Windows—how you want the system to start (Normal mode; Diagnostic mode, which lets you interactively select the device drivers you desire; or using a selective startup that lets you control the files the startup will use, such as Config.sys and Autoexec.bat). As shown in Figure 9-14, the System Configuration Utility's General tab provides options you can use to control the startup process.

USE IT As before, to run the System Configuration Utility, perform use either of the following techniques:

1. Select Start | Run. Windows will display the Run dialog box.
2. Within the Run dialog box, type **msconfig** and press ENTER.

You can also start the System Configuration Utility from within the System Information utility by performing these steps:

1. Select Start | Programs | Accessories. Windows will display the Accessories submenu.
2. Within the Accessories submenu, select System Tools | System Information. Windows, in turn, will open the Microsoft System Information utility.
3. Within the Microsoft System Information utility, select Tools | System Configuration Utility.

To use the System Configuration Utility to control how Windows will start next, click the radio button that corresponds to the type of startup you want Windows to perform next. If you choose a selective startup operation, click the check boxes that correspond to the options you want to enable or disable. To enable an option, place a check mark within the check box. To disable an option, remove the check mark.

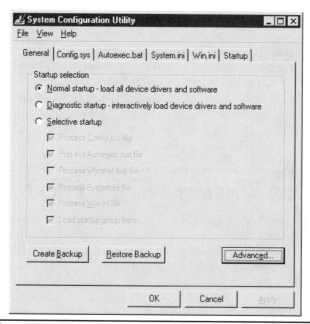

Figure 9.14 Using the System Configuration Utility to control how Windows will start the next time you reboot

Controlling Advanced Windows Startup Options

As you have learned, the Windows System Configuration Utility provides you with numerous capabilities you can use to control your system's startup processing. If you are troubleshooting a startup problem, you may want to take advantage of the System Configuration Utility to control specific startup operations. As shown in Figure 9-15, the System Configuration Utility's Advanced Troubleshooting Settings dialog box lets you enable or disable a wide range of startup operations.

 USE IT To use the System Configuration Utility to control specific startup options, perform these steps:

1. Start the System Configuration Utility as discussed in the preceding tip.

2. Within the System Configuration Utility, click Advanced. The System Configuration Utility, in turn, will display the Advanced Troubleshooting Settings dialog box.

3. Within the Advanced Troubleshooting Settings dialog box, click the check box you desire, adding or removing a check mark to enable or disable the option's processing.

4. After you have selected the options you desire, click OK.

To help you better understand the startup processing you can use the System Configuration Utility to perform, Table 9-4 briefly discusses each option's purpose.

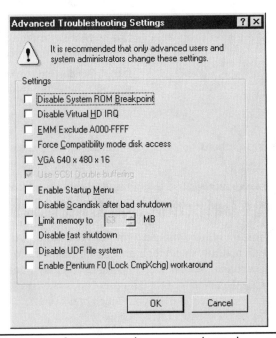

Figure 9.15   Using the System Configuration Utility to control Windows startup processing

Option	Purpose
Disable System ROM Breakpoint	Specifies that Windows should not use ROM addresses in the range 0 through 1MB for breakpoint.
Disable Virtual HD IRQ	Specifies that Windows should let the ROM BIOS handle interrupts from the hard disk controller.
EMM Exclude A000-FFFF	Prevents Windows from using the upper-memory area.
Force Compatibility mode disk access	Directs Windows to perform real-mode disk operations.
VGA 640 × 480 × 16	Forces Windows to use the standard VGA driver.
Use SCSI Double-buffering	Directs Windows to perform double-buffer operations for SCSI-based devices.
Enable Startup Menu	Directs Windows to automatically display its startup menu when the system boots.
Disable Scandisk after bad shutdown	Normally, if Windows does not shut down successfully, Windows will automatically run the Scandisk utility. This check box directs Windows not to run Scandisk in such cases.
Limit memory to…MB	Specifies the maximum amount of physical memory Windows will use.
Disable fast shutdown	Directs Windows to perform a slower shutdown operation that notifies each device driver the system is shutting down.
Disable UDF file system	Directs Windows not to use the Universal Disk Format file system supported by newer DVDs.
Enable Pentium FO (Lock CmpXchg) workaround	Directs Windows to provide a software patch that protects Pentium processors from an instruction sequence that may interfere with the processor's normal execution.

Table 9.4 Windows Startup Options You Can Control Using the System Configuration Utility

Reschedule Virus Detection and Other System Utilities

To increase the likelihood that most users will perform virus checking on their system, many virus-detection programs automatically begin their processing each time Windows starts. Although performing virus checks on a regular basis is very important, you may want to reschedule virus operations in order to decrease the amount of time it takes your system to start. You might, for example, schedule a virus check to occur during your lunch break or after you have left for the day.

Most virus-detection programs provide the ability to examine your incoming e-mail for viruses (if your software does not, you should upgrade your virus-detection program). If you reschedule when your virus-detection software runs, make sure you do not inadvertently disable the software's e-mail detection, which you will want active at all times.

Within many offices, system administrators use system startup as a time to run programs such as ScanDisk, which examines your disk and the operating system's file system for errors, or the Disk Defragmenter program, which improves your system's disk performance by correcting fragmented files. Again, although these are key utilities you should run on a regular basis, there are times other than your system's startup that you may find more convenient for running the programs.

USE IT　To help you schedule when you want your system to perform key operations, Windows provides a special program you can use to schedule when Windows automatically runs specific tasks, such as a disk defragmentation operation. To use the Windows Scheduled Task facility, perform these steps:

1. Select Start | Programs | Accessories. Windows will display the Accessories submenu.

2. Within the Accessories submenu, select System Tools | Scheduled Tasks. Windows will display the Scheduled Tasks window, as shown here.

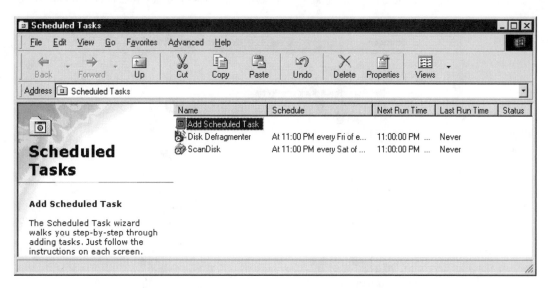

3. Click the Add Scheduled Task icon. Windows, in turn, will launch the Scheduled Task Wizard—special software that will walk you through the process of scheduling when you want a program to run.

To remove a program from the schedule, click the program's entry within the Scheduled Task window and click the Delete icon.

Examine Your Network Settings

If your system is part of a local area network, Windows must perform additional processing each time your system starts to establish a range of network settings and to determine available resources. If you later remove your system from the network, you should disable your system's network settings (you may have a notebook PC that you attach to a network when you are in the office) to eliminate Windows need to perform the startup network processing.

 USE IT To view your current network settings, perform these steps:

1. Select Start | Settings | Control Panel. Windows will open the Control Panel window.

2. Within the Control Panel, double-click the Network icon. Windows will display the Network dialog box, as shown in Figure 9-16.

Chapter 15 examines network operations in detail. At that time, you will learn which network settings your system may need to support your dial-up network connections. Within the Network Properties dialog box, remove the network settings your system does not need for dial-up connections. You may, for example, want to take advantage of Windows hardware profiles, discussed in the next tip.

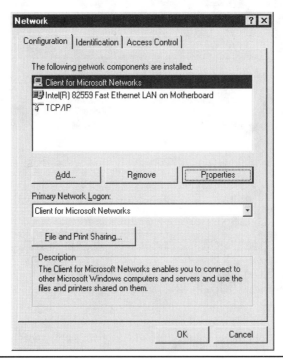

Figure 9.16 Using the Network dialog box to view network settings

You can also increase the speed of your startup by directing Windows to not to connect to network drives until you use them, by performing these steps:

1. Within the Network dialog box, select the Client for Microsoft Networks option and then click Properties. Windows, in turn, will display the Client for Microsoft Networks Properties dialog box.

2. Within the Client for Microsoft Networks Properties dialog box, click the Network Logon Options field Quick Logon button and then click OK.

When you direct Windows not to reestablish connections to network drives until you use them, your system will start faster; however, you may have to wait longer when you first connect to a remote drive.

Take Advantage of Windows Hardware Profiles

Today, many users have notebook PCs that they plug into docking stations at their offices, which, in turn, gives them instant access to larger keyboards, mice, and monitors, and possibly to network connections. To make it easier for users to maneuver between the hardware that is available when their PC is docked versus when it is undocked, Windows lets users define hardware profiles.

While using the System Properties Hardware Profiles sheet, shown in Figure 9-17, a user can create, in this case, a profile named Docked and one named Undocked. Within each profile, the user can then specify the available hardware. Later, each time the system starts, it will display a menu asking the user to select the corresponding profile. Depending on the profile the user selects, Windows will load software support for the different hardware devices.

 To speed up your startup operations, you may want to define your own hardware profiles. You might, for example, create one profile that you name Fast Boot and one that you name Full Boot. Within the Fast Boot profile, you can specify only that hardware that you use on a regular basis. You might, for example, not specify remote printers, for example. By reducing the number of hardware devices in the profile, you reduce the number of device drivers Windows must load, which in turn, speeds up the startup process.

Using the CMOS Auto-Start Setting

Today, most newer PCs have a built-in auto-start capability that most users fail to exploit. Using your PC's CMOS setup program, discussed in Chapter 7, you may find an auto-start option that lets you specify a time when you want your PC to automatically turn itself on. If, for example, you normally get to your office at 8:00, you can direct your PC to turn itself on at 7:50. Then, by the time you walk into the office, your system has completed its startup process and is ready for use.

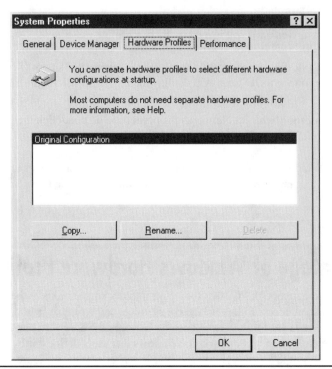

Figure 9.17   The System Properties Hardware Profiles sheet

USE IT   You may be wondering how the PC can turn itself on, when the system is powered off. As it turns out, most newer power supplies provide one power source that provides constant power, even when the power supply itself is turned off. This power source plugs into the motherboard. Although your PC is powered off, the BIOS continues to monitor the system clock. When the clock's time corresponds to the auto-start time, the BIOS will send a single back to the power supply that directs it to power the PC on.

To auto-start your PC at a specific time, restart your system and enter the CMOS setup program, as discussed in Chapter 7. Within the CMOS setup, look for an entry that corresponds to auto-start, as shown in Figure 9-18. Within the entry, specify the time you want the BIOS to automatically turn on your system. Then save your changes and exit the setup program.

```
                                         SETUP
  Main    Advanced        Security     Boot       Exit
  Quiet Boot                   [Enabled]                    Allows you to set the
  Quick Boot                   [Enabled]                    time and days of the
                                                            week to turn on the
  Restore on AC/Power Loss     [Last state]                 computer system
  On LAN                       [Power On]                   automatically. You
  On PME                       [Stay Off]                   can set Auto Power On
  Auto Power On                [Disabled]                   to turn on the system
                                                            either every day or
                                                            every Monday through
                                                            Friday
  1st Boot Device              [ATAPI-CDROM]
  2nd Boot Device              [ARMD-FDD]
  3rd Boot Device              [IDE-HDD]
  4th Boot Device              [Disabled]                   <- ->  Select Menu
                                                            ↑  ↓   Select Item
                                                            Tab    Select Field
                                                            Enter  Select Sub-Menu
                                                            F9     Setup Defaults
                                                            F10    Save and Exit
                                                            ESC    Exit
```

Figure 9.18   Using the CMOS setup program to enable the PC's auto-start capabilities

Create a Bootable Floppy System Disk

To boot an operating system, either from floppy disk or from a hard disk, the disk must be a system disk containing the files that the operating system needs in order to load itself into RAM. To boot your system from floppy disk, you must format the disk as a bootable disk. To ensure that you can access your system should a hard-error occur that prevents your system from booting from the hard disk, you should create a bootable floppy disk that you keep in a safe location.

USE IT   Windows makes it quite easy to create a bootable floppy disk. After you create the floppy disk, place it in a safe location (perhaps in the same location where you placed the printouts of your CMOS settings that you created earlier). To create a bootable floppy disk, which is also referred to as an *emergency boot disk*, perform these steps:

1. Select Start | Settings | Control Panel. Windows, in turn, will open the Control Panel window.

2. Within the Control Panel, double-click the Add/Remove Programs icon. Windows will display the Add/Remove Programs Properties dialog box.

3. Within the Add/Remove Programs Properties dialog box, select the Startup Disk tab. Windows will display the Startup Disk sheet, shown here.

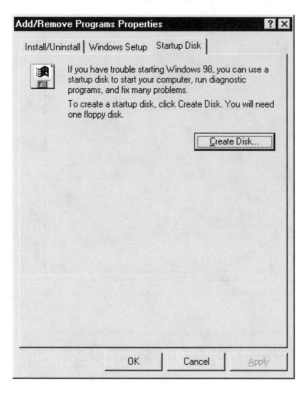

4. Insert an unused floppy disk into your disk drive, then click Create Disk. Windows will format the disk and copy over the files that it needs to start. To create the bootable floppy disk, Windows may prompt you to insert your original Windows CD so that Windows can copy files directly from the CD to the floppy.

5. Label the disk as "Windows Boot Disk" and place the disk in a safe location.

Using a Notebook Computer's Standby Option

If you travel with a notebook PC, you could spend considerable time starting and later shutting down the PC. For example, when your airplane is getting ready to taxi, you must shut down your system. Then, a few minutes later, after the plane has reached a safe altitude, you must sit through your PC's long startup process. Likewise, if you use your PC to present information to clients, a client might become annoyed if he or she has to wait for your PC to start or to later shut down.

Fortunately, most notebook PCs support a standby mode, which essentially freezes the notebook's current operations. (If you have programs open, the programs remain open when you suspend operations—however, I do recommend that you save your work before you suspend your system.) If you suspend your notebook PC, the next time you turn on your notebook's power, your system will resume right where you left off. You will not have to wait for your system to restart, nor will you have to reload programs.

The notebook's standby operations provide an ideal way to quickly stop and later resume your PC operations. Keep in mind, however, that to maintain its current state while it is standing by, the notebook PC must consume power. (However, because the PC is not performing work or accessing disk drives or other devices that consume power, the notebook PC's power consumption during the suspend process is minimal.)

USE IT   Normally a notebook PC's Shut Down menu will contain a Standby option. To place your notebook into standby mode, perform these steps:

1. Select Start | Shutdown. Windows will display the Shut Down Windows dialog box.

2. Within the Shut Down Windows dialog box, click Stand by and then click OK.

If your Shut Down Windows dialog box does not have a Standby option, and your computer supports standby operations, perform these steps:

1. Select Start | Settings | Control Panel. Windows will display the Control Panel Window.

2. Within the Control Panel, double-click Power Management. Windows, in turn, will display the Power Management Properties dialog box.

3. Within the Power Management Properties dialog box, select the Advanced tab. Windows will display the Advanced sheet.

4. Within the Advanced sheet, you should find a check box that lets you enable the display of a Standby option on the Shut Down menu.

Determining How Long Your System Has Been Running

In previous chapters, you have learned that as a general rule, you should restart your system at least once a day. As you run programs throughout the day, errors in different programs (errors that may or may not cause the program to fail) may use Windows resources (such as memory) that the program does not return to Windows when the program ends. The only way to recover the resources is to restart your system. Using the System Information utility, you can determine how long your system has been running (and hence how long it has been since your last reboot). The same screen that shows the system uptime also shows the amount of resources currently available to Windows, as shown in Figure 9-19.

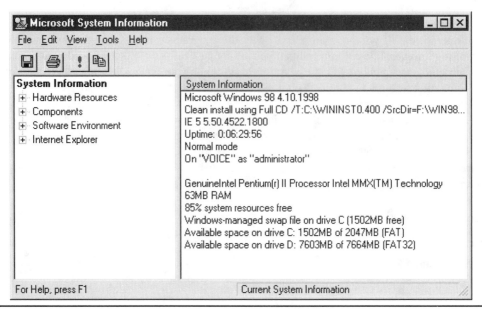

Figure 9.19   Using the System Information utility to determine your system's uptime and available
Windows resources

USE IT   To display your system's current uptime using the System Information utility, perform
these steps:

1. Select Start | Programs | Accessories. Windows will display the Accessories submenu.

2. Within the Accessories submenu, select System Tools | System Information. Windows, in
   turn, will open the Microsoft System Information utility. As shown in Figure 9-19, the System
   Information utility's opening screen contains the system uptime and percentage of available
   resources.

Using the Windows Fast Shutdown Option

If you must restart your system, the speed at which Windows shuts down can be as important to you
as the speed at which Windows restarts. To improve the speed at which it shuts down, Windows, by
default, performs a fast shutdown operation. During the fast shutdown, Windows does not assign
values to its installed device drivers to notify the drivers of the shutdown (in other words, Windows
does not "uninitialize" the drivers). In most cases, Windows will shut down successfully using the
fast shutdown. However, there may be times when, based on the device drivers you are using, the
Windows shutdown process may hang and fail to complete. In such cases, you may want to disable
fast shutdown operations.

USE IT   To disable Windows fast shutdown operations, perform the following steps:

1. Start the Windows System Configuration Utility, as previously discussed in the "Using the System Configuration Utility to Control Applications that Windows Automatically Starts" tip.

2. Within the System Configuration Utility, click Advanced. The System Configuration utility, in turn, will display the Advanced Troubleshooting Settings dialog box.

3. Within the Advanced Troubleshooting Settings dialog box, click the Disable fast shutdown check box, placing a check mark within the box. Then click OK to put your change into effect.

If your system does not have the System Configuration Utility installed, you can disable fast shutdown operations by using Windows Registry by performing these steps:

1. Select Start | Run. Windows, in turn, will display the Run dialog box.

2. Within the Run dialog box, type **regedit** and press ENTER. Windows will open the Registry Editor.

3. Within the Registry Editor, select Edit | Find. The Registry Editor will display the Find dialog box.

4. Within the Find dialog box, type **Fastreboot** and press ENTER. The Registry will search for the FastReboot entry.

5. When the Registry locates the entry, shown in Figure 9-20, select Edit | Modify and then assign the entry the value 0 to disable fast shutdown operations, or assign the value 1 to enable fast shutdown.

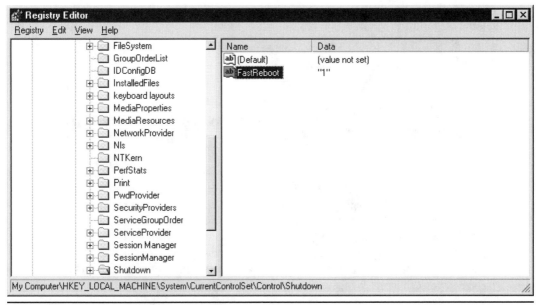

Figure 9.20   Using the Windows Registry to enable or disable fast shutdown operations

Launching Your Favorite Web Sites to Eliminate Your Download Delay

USE IT   By using the Windows Startup folder, you can direct Windows to automatically run specific programs each time your system starts. You may, for example, want Windows to automatically run your e-mail program each time it boots, so that your e-mail is waiting for you when you get to the office. Further, many users have Web sites they like to view at the start of each day, such as the New York Times, Business Week, or even Ebay. Using the Startup folder, you can direct Windows to launch a browser window for each site you desire, so that the site's content is waiting for you, completely downloaded when you get to your office. To direct Windows to automatically download a specific Web page each time it starts, perform these steps:

1. Select Start | Settings | Taskbar & Start menu. Windows will display the Taskbar Properties dialog box.

2. Within the Taskbar Properties dialog box, select the Start Menu Programs tab. Windows will display the Start Menu Programs sheet.

3. Within the Start Menu Programs sheet, click Add. Windows will display the Create Shortcut dialog box.

4. Within the Create Shortcut dialog box, type the address of the Web site you desire, such as www.BusinessWeek.com, and click Next. Windows will display a list of folders within which you can place the shortcut.

5. Within the folder list, click the Startup folder and then click Next. Windows will display the Select Title for the Program dialog box.

6. Within the Select Title for the Program dialog box, type in a meaningful site name, such as Business Week, and then click Finish. Click OK to close the Taskbar Properties dialog box.

Skipping Device Drivers During the System Startup Process

USE IT   As you have learned, when Windows starts, the Windows logs the boot operations to the root directory file Bootlog.txt. If you examine the log file and determine that Windows is encountering an error when it tries to load a specific device driver, you may be able to direct Windows to skip the driver using the Automatic Skip Driver agent, shown in Figure 9-21.

When the Windows startup process determines that Windows encountered a problem with a driver, Windows will add the driver to the list that appears within the Automatic Skip Driver agent. Using the agent, you can direct Windows to skip the driver the next time it starts. If you can only

Figure 9.21   Using the Automatic Skip Driver agent to direct Windows not to load a problem driver

start your system in Safe Mode, you may want to use the Automatic Skip Driver agent to direct Windows to ignore one or more drivers. To run the agent, perform these steps:

1. Select Start | Programs | Accessories. Windows will display the Accessories submenu.

2. Within the Accessories submenu, select System Tools | System Information. Windows, in turn, will open the Microsoft System Information utility.

3. Within the Microsoft System Information utility, select Tools | Automatic Skip Driver Agent.

4. Within the Automatic Skip Driver Agent, click your mouse on the check box that corresponds to each driver you want Windows to skip, placing a check mark within the box. Then click your mouse on the OK button to close the dialog box.

CHAPTER 10

Operating-System Performance

TIPS IN THIS CHAPTER

hroughout this book, you will examine ways to improve the performance of your PC's hardware devices. To maximize your system's performance, you must also examine your operating system, which sits between your hardware and the programs you run. Depending on which version of Windows you are running, the steps you can take to "tweak" your operating system's performance will differ. This chapter examines several specific operations—available under most versions of Windows—you can perform to improve your system performance.

Understanding the Operating System's Role

When programmers wrote the first programs for computers over 50 years ago, they had to include instructions within their code that loaded the program into RAM, accepted input from various switches, and displayed output by illuminating various lights (the combination of which represented the program's result). Each time a programmer created a new program, the programmer had to include these statements within his or her code.

Eventually, the programmers created a special "monitor" program they could use to load new programs into RAM and with which programs could interact to perform input and output operations. Because this monitor program was always in RAM, it eliminated the programmer's need to build such processing into every program. Over the years, this special monitor program evolved into the operating systems that we use today.

Operating systems exist to make it easy for you to run programs and store and retrieve information. Further, as shown in Figure 10-1, the operating system provides programs with access to hardware devices, such as the keyboard, mouse, video, disk drives, modems, and more. Operating systems interact with devices by using special software programs called *device drivers*. For many devices, such as the keyboard, the operating system provides its own "generic" device driver. For other devices, the operating system uses device driver software you install after you add a new device to your PC.

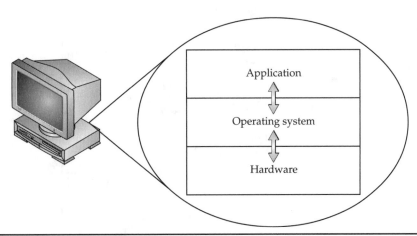

Figure 10.1   Operating systems provide your applications with an interface to your hardware.

When to Upgrade Your Operating System

As is the case with many key software programs, such as e-mail applications, word processors, and Web browsers, software developers constantly work on enhancements and fixes to operating system code. Depending on the extent of the code changes, the developers may release a patch (normally to fix a specific error, such as a security bug), or the developers may release a new version of the software. Again, depending on the extent of the changes, the developers will categorize the new version as a major or minor version release.

For years, users could easily track operating system versions by examining the operating system's major and minor version numbers. In the case of MS-DOS version 3.2 "3" is the major version number and "2" is the minor. For a minor operating system release, MS-DOS version 3.2 became 3.3. Likewise, for a major version upgrade, MS-DOS version 3.3 become version 4.0. With operating systems such as Windows 95, 98, 2000, and XP, Microsoft still uses release numbers. Unfortunately, most users are unaware of the release numbers.

 To display your system's operating system release number, perform these steps:

1. Select Start | Settings | Control Panel. Windows will open the Control Panel.
2. Within the Control Panel, double-click the System icon. Windows will display the System Properties dialog box, which displays the Windows release number, as shown in Figure 10-2.

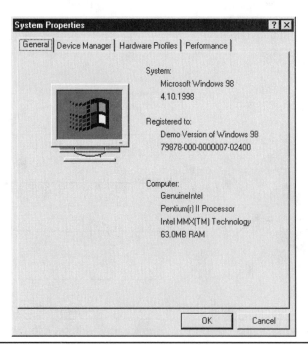

Figure 10.2   Displaying the Windows release number within the System Properties dialog box

Users frequently debate over when is the best time to upgrade to a new operating system. Many users, in pursuit of the fastest possible performance or the greatest hardware support, frequently visit the Microsoft Web site, as discussed later in this chapter, to download and install each patch Microsoft provides for Windows and Windows-based programs. Most users, however, approach operating system upgrades from the "if it is not broken, don't fix it" point of view—meaning that if their systems essentially work and meet their performance needs, they are not going to download and install patches or perform upgrades that may introduce compatibility errors on their systems.

Normally, when Microsoft releases a major-version release of an operating system, the "early adopters" are users who feel comfortable troubleshooting potential conflicts that may arise. Novice users may avoid problems users experience with an initial software release by waiting a few months (or more) for Microsoft to release the first minor version release.

Why You Should Upgrade the Operating System

The operating system is involved in just about every operation you perform with your PC. When you run a program, the operating system loads the program file from disk into memory so that the CPU can execute the program instructions. When you create, open, or save a file, the operating system manages the file's contents on disk. When you browse the Web, the operating system provides your browser with access to the TCP/IP protocol that programs use to exchange messages across the network, and the operating system oversees (through device drivers) the actual exchange of data the modem or network card performs. Further, the operating system provides software that implements the graphical user interface that programs use to manage the display of information within windows and dialog boxes.

Operating system developers (the programmers who write the operating system's program code—who may number in the thousands for Windows-based operating systems) are always looking for ways they can fine-tune operations the operating system performs to eliminate bottlenecks and to maximize performance. Normally, when the developers release an upgrade to the operating system, they include the patches they previously released to fix errors, code to improve the performance of key operating system components, and code to provide new security enhancements.

Unfortunately, as operating systems become more powerful and complex, the operating system itself requires more system resources—in particular, RAM. The Windows XP operating system, for example, requires a minimum of 64MB of RAM, and for reasonable performance, you should have 128MB. For one user, upgrading a system to support a new operating system may not be an expensive proposition. However, for a small company that may have a few hundred employees, upgrading the PC resources can require a significant investment.

Looking for Operating System Bottlenecks

As you can imagine, the operating system is a large, complex program. Programmers estimate that the Windows 2000 operating system contains 30 to 40 million lines of code! Within those millions of program statements are many locations that will emerge as system bottlenecks after users put the operating system to work. Eventually, the developers will release patches and future version updates to improve performance.

The ideal way to approach improving your operating system performance is to start with the 80/20 rule—focus your efforts on the 20 percent of the operating system code where you spend 80 percent of your time. For example, if you spent considerable time surfing the Web, you should strive to maximize your system's network performance. In contrast, if you seldom print large documents, you don't want to spend time trying to fine-tune your system's printer and spooler operations.

Normally, you should focus your efforts on maximizing the operating system's performance with respect to memory management, program execution, video processing, file operations, and network operations.

Understanding Virtual Memory

As you have learned, before the CPU can run a program, the program's instructions and data must reside within the PC's RAM. Within RAM, each storage location has a unique address. When the CPU needs to place data into or retrieve data from RAM, the CPU specifies the corresponding memory address.

When the IBM PC was first released in 1981, the MS-DOS operating system let users run only one program at a time. When a program referenced a memory location, the program used the actual address (sometimes called the *real address*) of the memory location. If the program contained an error (a bug), it was possible that the program could overwrite itself in memory, or worse yet, the program could overwrite the MS-DOS operating system. In such cases, the user would have to restart his or her system to reload MS-DOS into memory.

The Windows operating system, in contrast to MS-DOS, lets you run multiple programs at the same time. When you run two or more programs simultaneously, each program must reside within RAM before the CPU can execute the program. Managing multiple programs in memory introduces several issues the operating system must resolve. First, depending on the programs a user runs, the programs may consume much or all of the available RAM. Second, if a program contains an error, the programs should not have the ability to overwrite the other programs in memory. Third, if a program requires large amounts of data, the program should still run on a PC that has a minimal amount of RAM.

To address these memory issues, operating systems employ *virtual-memory management*. In general, virtual memory combines RAM and space on the disk drive to provide programs (including the operating system itself) with the illusion that the system has more memory than what is physically present within the PC. Within Windows 98, for example, which is a 32-bit operating system, each program has the illusion that it has 4GB (2^{32} bytes) of memory available for use. In other words, even if your PC has only 64MB of RAM, Windows virtual memory gives the program the illusion that it has 4GB, as shown in Figure 10-3.

Further, if you are running multiple programs, Windows virtual memory gives each program the illusion that it has its own 4GB memory region. As it turns out, programs actually get only 2GB of memory they can call their own. Windows places instructions in the top 2GB of memory that programs share, such as operating-system code, as shown in Figure 10-4. Because the shared memory contains code (which programs cannot change), sharing the operating system in this way is quite efficient because Windows must maintain only one copy of the operating system in RAM.

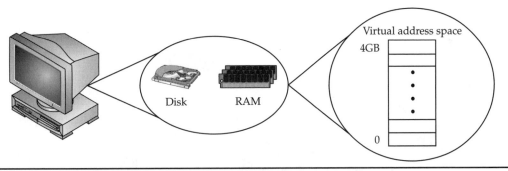

Figure 10.3   Within Windows, each program receives up to 4GB of virtual memory.

Understanding Paging

Virtual memory is so named because unlike physical memory that actually exists within your PC (that you can physically touch), virtual memory does not physically exist. Rather, virtual memory is an illusion. To create the illusion of unlimited memory (or at least of 4GB of memory), Windows combines physical RAM with space on your disk space called the *page file*. Next, as shown in Figure 10-5, Windows divides your applications into smaller pieces (typically 512 bytes) called *pages*. As an application executes, the entire application does not have to physically reside in RAM. Instead, Windows loads the pages that correspond to the program instructions the CPU is currently executing, as well as the pages that contain the data the program instructions are currently using. As the program executes, Windows will load pages into RAM as necessary.

When the CPU executes a program, the CPU refers to the program's virtual-memory address. Behind the scenes, the Windows virtual-memory management software maps the virtual addresses to the corresponding physical addresses in RAM. When the CPU tries to access a virtual-memory address

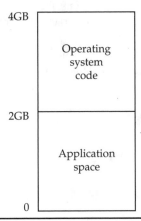

Figure 10.4   Windows applications share 2GB of memory that normally contains operating-system code.

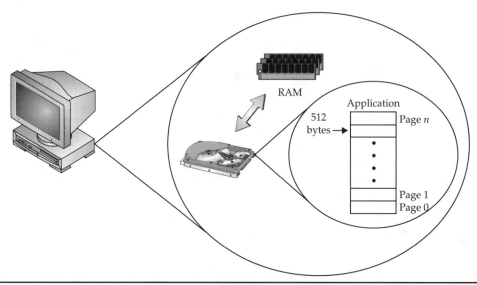

Figure 10.5   Windows divides a program and its data into fixed-sized pages it can move into and out of RAM on an as-needed basis.

that maps to instructions or data that do not currently reside in RAM, a *page fault* occurs, which directs Windows to load the corresponding page from disk into RAM.

Depending on the amount of RAM your system contains, there may be times when a program consumes all available RAM. In such cases, the Windows virtual-memory management software will move pages from RAM into the page file that resides on your hard disk, in order to make room in RAM for the new pages. Should the CPU later need a page that has been moved from RAM into the page file, the Windows virtual-memory management software will move other programs from RAM to the page file to free up locations into which the program can load new pages, as shown in Figure 10-6.

When you use Windows to run multiple programs, the process becomes slightly more complex in that Windows virtual-management software must track each application's pages (those that reside in RAM and those that reside in the page file).

By moving pages between RAM and the page file in this way, the Windows virtual-memory-management software gives each program the illusion of having 4GB of RAM.

▶ *FACT*

Windows XP 64-bit edition provides applications with a 13TB (terabyte) virtual address with 2^{64} storage locations!

Virtual Memory Protects One Application from Another

When multiple programs reside in RAM, one program (either intentionally or accidentally) should not be able to access another program's memory locations. Windows achieves such protection

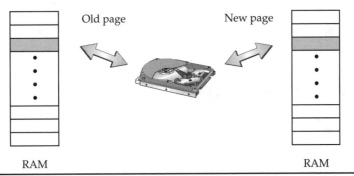

Figure 10.6   To free up physical RAM, Windows moves pages from memory to disk.

through the use of virtual-memory management. As you have learned, within Windows, each program uses a unique virtual-memory address space. Programs do not refer to physical locations within RAM. Because a program cannot access memory locations beyond its virtual-address space, one program cannot access the memory of another application.

Understanding Protected Mode

The original IBM PC—in fact, all models of the PC that used the MS-DOS operating system—did not use virtual memory. Instead, the PCs ran in "real mode," which meant the memory addresses programs used, corresponded to the real (or physical) addresses in RAM. In contrast, when programs use virtual memory, the operating system and the PC's underlying hardware map the program's virtual addresses to real addresses.

Within real mode, any program could access any memory address. As such, an errant (or malicious) program could overwrite its own program statements in memory, as well as those used by the MS-DOS operating system. In contrast, when the PC operates in protected mode, programs can access only their own virtual address space, which prevents one program from overwriting another. MS-DOS is a real-mode operating system. Windows 95 and later typically perform all their operations in protected mode.

Understanding File Systems

Operating systems exist to help you run programs and store and later retrieve information using files on disk. Within the operating system, users refer to the software that manages file operations as the *file system*. In general, the file system keeps track of the folders (directories) you create and the file and subfolders each folder contains. Further, the file system tracks the specific locations on disk where each of your files reside.

Each time you create, open, save, rename, or delete a file, you use the operating system's file system. Different operating systems use different file systems, each of which offers various capabilities. Common file systems include the NTFS (NT file system), FAT16, and FAT32, as well as the CDFS (used for CD-ROM) and UDF (used for DVDs).

In some cases, your operating system will let you choose between different file systems. The file system you select may directly impact your system performance. Chapter 16 examines Windows file systems in detail.

Understanding Network Operations

To support network operations, most operating systems provide built-in support for the TCP/IP network (the network that drives the Internet and World Wide Web). In addition, Microsoft operating systems normally also provide support for the Microsoft Networks interface. Chapter 16 examines network operations in detail.

Understanding Device Drivers

The operating system provides programs with the ability to use your PCs various hardware devices. Within the operating system, users refer to the software that interacts with hardware devices as *device drivers*. As shown in Figure 10-7, the operating system has a device driver specific to each hardware device.

Some device drivers are built into the operating system itself, such as drivers for disk controllers, buses such as the PCI bus, and so on. For other devices, such as a video card, you must install the device driver that accompanies the device.

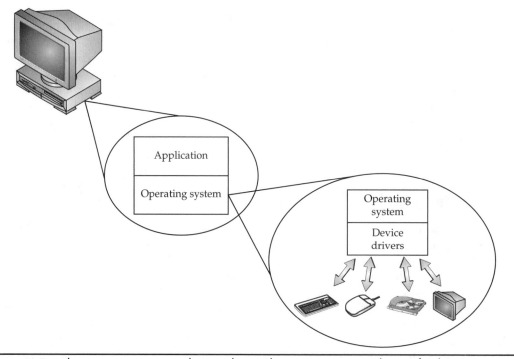

Figure 10.7 The operating system relies on device drivers to interact with specific devices.

In Chapter 4, you learned that devices communicate with the CPU by generating an interrupt. Each time an interrupt occurs, the CPU executes the corresponding *interrupt handler*—the instructions that direct the CPU to perform device-specific operations in response to the interrupt. Normally, the instructions the CPU executes for the interrupt are part of the device driver, as shown in Figure 10-8.

Because Windows must use the device driver every time you use a device, it is important that the device driver's code execute quickly. In this chapter's tips, you will learn how to update your device drivers to the most recent version. Normally, in addition to providing new functionality, a new version of a device driver will also offer better performance.

Understanding the Windows Registry

Prior to Windows 95, Windows stored its initialization information (configuration settings) in a series of files with the .ini extension, such as system.ini, win.ini, and so on. The .ini file extension indicated to users that the file contained initialization settings. Within the INI files, Windows would store settings that directed it to run specific programs each time your system started, settings that corresponded to your screen resolution and color choices, settings for device drivers, and more. Often, third-party programs would also place their configuration settings within the INI files. The INI files were text files that users could edit using a text editor, such as the Windows Notepad. Each time Windows started (and each time an application started), it would examine the file's contents and configure itself accordingly.

Windows 95 replaced the INI files with a database known as the Registry. Windows, as well as applications, use the Registry to store a wide range of settings. Each time Windows starts (and when applications start), it uses the Registry entries to configure itself.

Using RegEdit, the Registry Editor

To fine-tune operating-system and application settings, there may be times when you must edit a Registry entry's value.

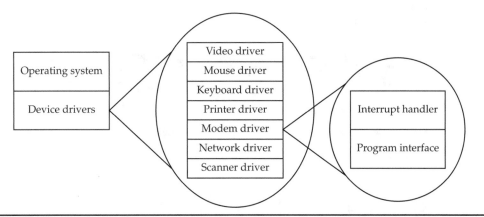

Figure 10.8   The device driver contains the code that executes to handle a device interrupt.

▶ **CAUTION**

The Windows Registry contains many key settings that Windows uses to configure itself each time your system starts. If you make an errant change within the Registry or delete a needed entry, you may prevent your system from starting. Never make a change to a Registry entry that you do not fully understand. Also, do not make changes to your Registry's contents without first backing up the Registry, as discussed in the tip "Checking the Registry's Contents."

In the sections that follow, you will use the Registry Editor to view several different settings. To start the Registry Editor, perform these steps:

1. Select Start | Run. Windows will display the Run dialog box.

2. Within the Run dialog box, type **regedit** and press ENTER. Windows will open the Registry Editor, as shown in Figure 10-9.

The Registry Organizes Data Using a Treelike Structure

The Windows Registry normally stores thousands of entries. To better organize those entries, the Registry groups related settings into a treelike structure, much like you would use folders and subfolders to organize the files you store on disk. Table 10-1 briefly describes the primary Registry branches. By knowing each branch's purpose, you can often restrict your Registry search operations to a specific branch, which will significantly reduce your search time.

Within the Registry Editor, you view entries by expanding and then traversing the tree branches. To expand a branch, click the plus sign (+) that precedes the branch entry. Figure 10-10, for example, illustrates branches within the HKEY_LOCAL_MACHINE branch.

Searching for and Modifying a Registry Entry

Normally, when you must change a Registry setting, the document you are reading will tell you the name of the specific entry. To locate the entry within the Registry, you can use the Registry Editor's Find dialog box, shown in Figure 10-11.

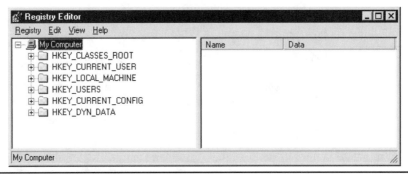

Figure 10.9   The Registry Editor

Registry Branch	Purpose
HKEY_CLASSES_ROOT	Contains entries that associate file types (extensions) with a specific application.
HKEY_CURRENT_USER	Windows lets multiple users configure various Windows settings. The HKEY_CURRENT_USER branch contains the settings that correspond to the current user (based on the user's login name and password).
HKEY_LOCAL_MACHINE	Stores settings about the system's hardware and software.
HKEY_USERS	Stores information about each user that logs into the system.
HKEY_CURRENT_CONFIG	Stores settings for the current hardware profile.
HKEY_DYN_DATA	To improve performance, Windows stores a copy of the Registry entries in RAM. The HKEY_DYN_DATA key corresponds to the current RAM settings.

Table 10.1   The Purpose of Key Branches in the Windows Registry

As discussed, the Registry stores many Windows configuration settings. For example, the Registry stores the current keyboard delay and repeat rate settings within the HKEY_CURRENT_USER branch. If you use the Find dialog box to search for the KeyboardDelay setting, the Registry Editor will display the setting's current value, as shown in Figure 10-12.

Never change an entry's value within the Registry Editor without first writing down the entry's original value, in case you must restore the value at a later time. Then, to change a value, click the setting and then choose Edit | Modify. The Registry Editor, in turn, will display a dialog box into which you can type the value you desire.

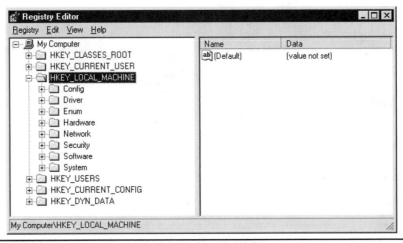

Figure 10.10   Expanding branches within the Registry Editor

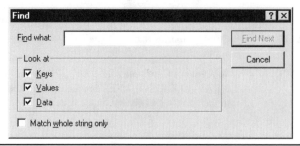

Figure 10.11   Using the Find dialog box to locate a Registry entry

Viewing Your System's Device Drivers

To support various old and new devices, Windows uses a wide range of device drivers. Some drivers are 32-bit, some are 16-bit, and some exist to provide support for MS-DOS applications. In some cases, your system may be loading device drivers you do not need—which consumes resources unnecessarily. Using the System Information utility, you can view the your system's kernel-mode, user-mode, and MS-DOS device driver, as shown in Figure 10-13.

USE IT   To view device-driver types within the System Information utility, perform these steps:

1. Select Start | Programs | Accessories. Windows will display the Accessories submenu.
2. Within the Accessories submenu, select System Tools | System Information. Windows will open the System Information utility.

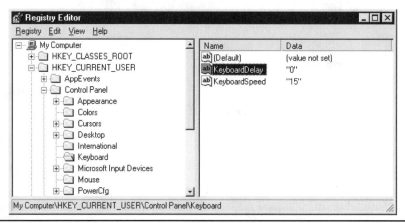

Figure 10.12   Locating an entry within the Windows Registry

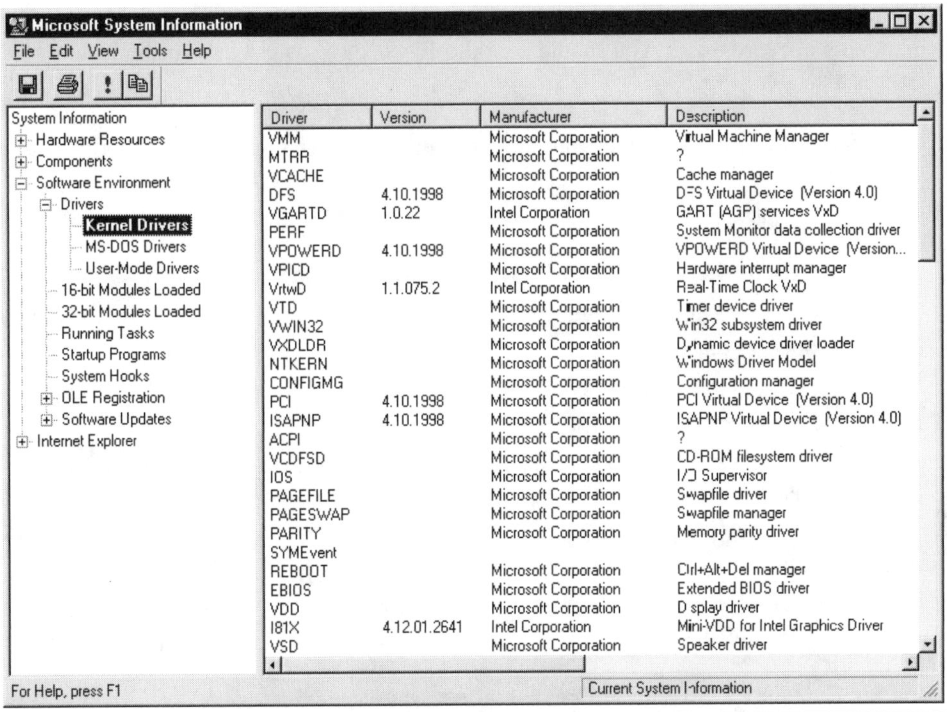

Figure 10.13   Using the System Information utility to view device driver types

3. Within the System Information utility, click the plus sign (+) that precedes the Software Environment entry. Next, click the plus sign that precedes the Drivers entry. The System Information utility will expand the Drivers list to let you view kernel mode, user mode, and MS-DOS–based drivers.

▶ **NOTE**

In Chapter 9, you learned that to decrease your system startup time—to free system resources (primarily RAM) for use by other applications—you should remove device drivers your system is not using.

Viewing Device Driver Specifics

To interact with a device, Windows makes extensive use of the corresponding device driver. In general, if your system is working, you can normally ignore the version number of most of the device drivers your system is using. In fact, if your system is working, there may be times when installing a newer version of a device driver may introduce problems. However, for the devices your system uses most of often (the 20 percent of device drivers your system uses 80 percent of the time), such as a video, modem, or network card driver, you should periodically check to determine whether a new version of a driver is available.

USE IT Normally, you can search your hardware manufacturer's Web site to determine whether a new driver is available. To determine the device driver you are currently using, perform these steps:

1. Select Start | Settings | Control Panel. Windows will open the Control Panel window.

2. Within the Control Panel window, double-click the System icon. Windows will open the System Properties dialog box.

3. Within the System Properties dialog box, click the Device Manager tab. Windows will display the Device Manager sheet.

4. Within the Device Manager sheet, click the plus sign (+) that precedes the device type you desire. The Device Manager will expand the list to show the specific drivers.

5. Click the device entry you desire and then click Properties. The Device Manager will display the device's Properties dialog box. Within the dialog box, click the Drivers tab. The Device Manager will display the Drivers sheet that shows the current device-driver version number, as shown in Figure 10-14.

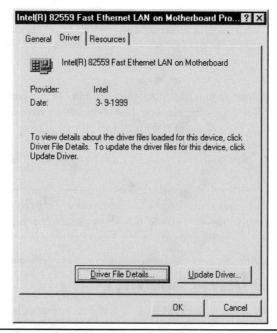

Figure 10.14   Viewing a device driver's version information

You can also use the System Information utility to display device driver information and device resource use, as shown in Figure 10-15. To view device driver information using the System Information utility, perform these steps:

1. Select Start | Programs | Accessories. Windows will display the Accessories submenu.

2. Within the Accessories submenu, select System Tools | System Information. Windows will open the System Information utility.

3. Within the System Information utility, click the plus sign (+) that precedes the Components entry. Windows will display a list of your system's components.

4. Within the component list, click the device you desire. Then click the Advanced Information radio button. The System Information utility will display the specifics about the device's drivers and resource settings, as shown in Figure 10-15.

Upgrading a Device Driver

Each time Windows interacts with a device, Windows must use the device's device-driver software. Periodically, hardware manufacturers (and in some cases Microsoft) will make new drivers available

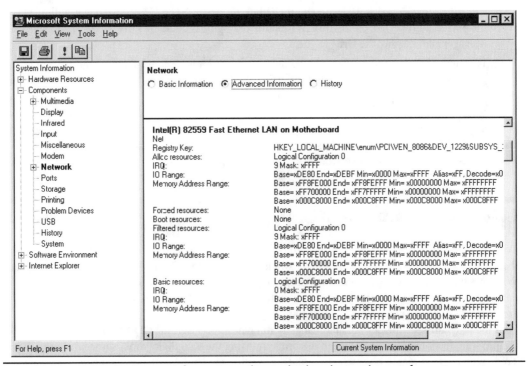

Figure 10.15   Using the System Information utility to display device-driver information

for a device. Normally, the device-driver upgrade may fix bugs, provide additional functionality, and often, improve performance. Because the speed at which a device driver performs its processing can have a significant impact on your system performance, programmers spend considerable time trying to make device drivers execute faster.

That said, any time you install software on your system, you run a risk of introducing an incompatibility problem that prevents your system from working correctly. Therefore, with respect to device drivers, you may not install every device-driver upgrade that becomes available. Instead, you focus your upgrades on the drivers your system uses most often.

USE IT Windows makes it very easy for you to learn if a device driver upgrade is available and then to install the driver, by performing these steps:

1. Select Start | Settings | Control Panel. Windows will open the Control Panel window.

2. Within the Control Panel window, double-click the System icon. Windows will open the System Properties dialog box.

3. Within the System Properties dialog box, click the Device Manager tab. Windows will display the Device Manager sheet.

4. Within the Device Manager sheet, click the plus sign (+) that precedes the device type you desire. The Device Manager will expand the list to show the specific device drivers.

5. Click the device entry you desire and then click Properties. The Device Manager will display the device's Properties dialog box. Within the dialog box, click the Drivers tab. The Device Manager will display the Drivers sheet.

6. Within the Drivers sheet, click the Update Driver button. Windows will start the Update Device Driver Wizard that will walk you through the upgrade processing. On the wizard's third screen, you can select the location where you want the wizard to look for a new driver. Make sure you select Microsoft Windows Update. The wizard, in turn, will search the Microsoft Web site for a driver update. If the Wizard locates a new driver, it will give you a chance to download and install the driver. If your driver is current, the Wizard will display a box telling you that you are using the most recent version.

Installing and Removing Programs Correctly

To install most Windows-based programs, users normally run a special installation (or *setup*) program that resides within the file setup.exe. Often, when you insert the CD-ROM that contains the program, Windows will automatically run the setup program. In such cases, the CD-ROM contains a special file named autorun.inf that Windows examines when you insert the CD-ROM. Within the autorun.inf file are instructions Windows follows to automatically run the setup.

If the program's setup does not automatically run when you insert the CD-ROM, or if you download the program from the Net, you can run the program using the Run dialog box, shown in Figure 10-16. To display the Run dialog box, select Start | Run. Within the Run dialog box, you can click Browse to

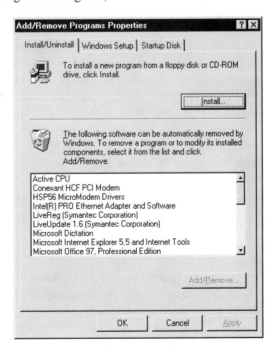

Figure 10.16   Using the Run dialog box to launch a program.

search your disk for the program file you want to run, or if you know the program's location, you can simply type in the corresponding path and press ENTER.

USE IT   The Windows Control Panel also provides a way for you to install and remove programs, which you should use whenever possible. By using the Control Panel's Add/Remove Programs icon to install an application, you ensure Windows will track (log) information it needs to later successfully remove the application should the installation fail or you no longer need the program. To install a program from the Control Panel, perform these steps:

1. Select Start | Settings | Control Panel. Windows will open the Control Panel.

2. Within the Control Panel, double-click the Add/Remove Programs icon. Windows will display the Add/Remove Programs dialog box, as shown here.

3. Click Install. Windows, in turn, will launch a wizard that walks you through the installation process.

To remove (uninstall) a program you no longer need, perform steps 1 and 2 to display the Add/Remove Programs dialog box. Within the Add/Remove Programs dialog box list of removable programs, click the entry that corresponds to the program you want to remove. Next, click Add/Remove. Windows will display a dialog box asking you to confirm that you want to remove the program from your disk. Click Yes.

Validating Your System Files

The Windows operating system consists of a variety of programs and support files, such as dynamic-link library (DLL) files. A DLL file contains program code (it is a library of routines programs can use) that performs a specific task. Windows might use one DLL to handle printer operations, another for modem operations, and so on. By placing the code within a DLL file, programs can share code. In other words, when a program must print a document, the program relies on code that resides within the DLL to handle the printing. By using the DLL-based code, each program does not have to include its own code to perform the tasks, which makes the programs easier to write and smaller. If you are like most users, your system may actually have thousands of DLL files.

If your system hangs, shuts down due to a power loss, or experiences a disk error (or possibly a virus), one or more Windows system files may become damaged (corrupted). In some cases, the file error may prevent Windows from starting. At other times, the corrupted file may cause intermittent errors that are hard to troubleshoot.

USE IT   To help you identify possibly corrupt system files, the System Information utility provides a File Checker that examines the Windows system files. If the File Checker encounters an incorrect file, it will display a dialog box describing the corrupted file. Within the dialog box, you can direct the File Checker to reinstall the corrupt file from your original Windows CD-ROM. To use the System File checker to examine your system files, perform these steps:

1. Select Start | Programs | Accessories. Windows will display the Accessories submenu.

2. Within the Accessories submenu, select System Tools | System Information. Windows will run the System Information utility.

3. Within the System Information utility, select Tools | System File Checker. Windows will run the System File Checker, as shown in Figure 10-17.

▶ NOTE

The System File Checker lets you customize the processing it performs, letting you add or exclude specific directories. To configure the System File Checker settings, click the Settings button that appears on the program's opening dialog box.

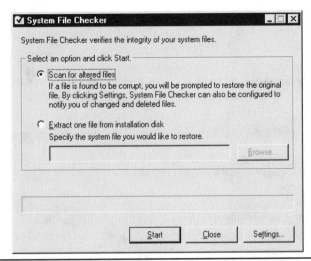

Figure 10.17   Using the System File Checker to validate key system files

Checking the Registry's Contents

As you have learned, Windows uses the Registry to store key system configuration information and program settings. Each time your system starts, Windows reads the Registry file and uses its contents to configure various operating system settings. If Windows does not encounter any Registry errors during the startup process, Windows will make a backup copy of the Registry's contents. That way, should you make an errant change to the Registry or should the Registry file become corrupt, you can restore the backup.

USE IT   To help you verify that your Registry is in order, the System Information utility provides the Registry Checker application, which can validate the Registry's contents. Further, if you have not yet backed up the Registry's contents today (which likely means you have not restarted your system today), the Registry Checker will let you do so. To run the Registry Checker, perform these steps:

1. Select Start | Programs | Accessories. Windows will display the Accessories submenu.
2. Within the Accessories submenu, select System Tools | System Information. Windows will run the System Information utility.
3. Within the System Information utility, select Tools | Registry Checker.

Taking a Closer Look at the Registry Entries

USE IT   One of the best ways to understand how Windows uses the Registry is to look at the Registry's various entries. One way to view the entry values is simply to click through the entries within the Registry Editor. A better way, however, is to direct the Registry to print a copy of its current settings. Within the Registry Editor, you can print the entire Registry contents, or you can print entries for a specific branch, by performing these steps:

1. If the Registry Editor is not currently running, select Start | Run. Windows will display the Run dialog box. Within the Run dialog box, type **regedit** and press ENTER. Windows will open the Registry Editor.

2. Within the Registry Editor, select Registry | Print. The Registry Editor will display the Print dialog box.

3. Within the Print dialog box, click All to print the entire Registry or click Selected Branch to print the current branch. Then click OK.

In addition to printing the Registry entries, you may want to export the Registry settings to a text file whose contents you can later view or search using a text editor or word processor. To export the Registry entries, perform these steps:

1. Within the Registry Editor, select Registry | Export Registry File. The Registry Editor will display the Export Registry File dialog box.

2. Within the Registry Export File dialog box, select the folder within which you want to place the file and then type the filename you desire. Then click OK.

Restoring a Registry Backup

Windows stores the Registry using several hidden files that reside in the Windows folder. The two primary files are system.dat and user.dat. The system.dat file contains key hardware and software settings. The user.dat file contains settings specific to a user. (The system will have a user.dat file for each user who can log into the system.)

USE IT   Each time Windows successfully starts, it makes a backup copy of the Registry's current contents, which it stores compressed in a CAB file in the Windows\Sysbckup folder. By default, Windows will keep five backup copies of the Registry. Should Windows encounter a Registry error, Windows will automatically fall back to a previous version. Sometimes, however, you may realize that you have made and saved an errant change to the Registry. In such a case, you can restore a previous backup of the Registry yourself by performing these steps:

1. Close your current applications.

2. Select Start | Shutdown. Windows will display the Shut Down Windows dialog box.

3. Within the Shut Down Windows dialog box, select the Restart In MS-DOS Mode option and click OK. Windows will restart your system in MS-DOS mode displaying the MS-DOS prompt.

4. At the system prompt, type **scanreg /restore** and press ENTER. Windows will restore your Registry to its previous backup.

▶ *NOTE*

Windows uses a special INI file named scanreg.ini that you can use to specify the number of backup copies of the Registry Windows maintains. To edit the file's contents, you can use a text editor such as the Windows Notepad.

Checking Your System's INI Files

Prior to Windows 95, Windows (and many Windows-based applications) stored configuration information within several key INI files. To maintain compatibility, Windows still examines the system.ini and win.ini files each time it starts. Depending on the settings the files contain, your system may be loading device drivers or applications that run behind the scenes that you no longer need. To maximize your system's performance (and security), you should take time to examine the system.ini and win.ini files closely. If you encounter an entry you do not think that you need, do not delete the entry, but rather, place a semicolon at the start of the entry that tells Windows to ignore the entry. In this way, if you later learn that you need the entry, you simply must remove the semicolon to restore the entry's use.

The easiest way to view the key INI file contents is to run the System Editor program, which, as shown in Figure 10-18, displays several windows, each of which contains an INI file or related system configuration file.

USE IT To run the System Editor, perform these steps:

1. Select Start | Run. Windows will display the Run dialog box.
2. Within the Run dialog box, type **sysedit** and press ENTER.

If you change a file's contents within the System Editor, you must choose File | Save to save your changes.

Avoiding System File Conflicts

When you install a new operating system, your system may contain versions of files that are more recent than those the operating system is to install. Normally, to avoid conflicts, the operating system will move your existing file into a folder and install its older version (which will work when the installation completes). The operating system installation normally moves the conflicting files into the folder Windows\vcm. Using the Version Conflict Manager, you can display a list of files the operating system has moved that shows the file's version, as well as the version your system is currently using, as shown in Figure 10-19.

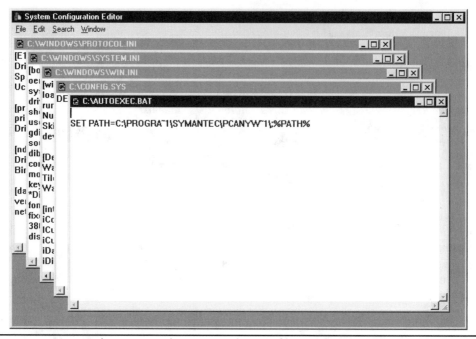

Figure 10.18 Running the System Editor to view key INI files

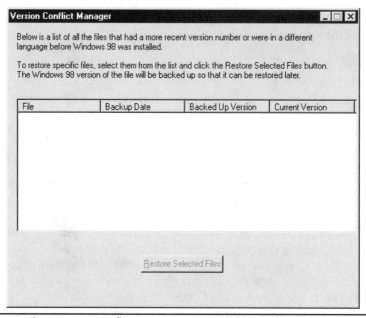

Figure 10.19 Using the Version Conflict Manager to track file conflicts

If your system is working, you may simply want to continue using the older version. However, you may want to spend some time researching each file's use and then testing key files by first saving a copy of the current (older) file and then moving the newer file from the Windows/vcm folder into the Windows/System folder (or the folder containing the conflicting file). If your system restarts and runs properly, you may later (after you have thoroughly tested your system) want to move the older file to floppy disk for safekeeping and then remove the file from your hard disk.

USE IT To run the Version Conflict Manager, perform these steps:

1. Select Start | Programs | Accessories. Windows will display the Accessories submenu.
2. Within the Accessories submenu, select System Tools | System Information. Windows will start the System Information utility.
3. Within the System Information utility, select Tools | Version Conflict Manager.

Monitoring Kernel Mode Operations

Within the operating system is key collection of software capabilities around which the rest of the operating system is developed, which programmers refer to as the *kernel*. Within the kernel, the operating system performs such key operations as virtual-memory management, process and thread management, and file-system support, as well as interfacing to device drivers. Every time a program interacts with a device, code within the kernel executes. When you switch from one program to another, or when a background process runs, code within the kernel executes. When you save a file on disk, code within the kernel executes. To maximize system performance, the kernel code must execute quickly. Within the Windows environment, all programs, including Windows itself, shares the same kernel code.

Using the Windows System Monitor, you can monitor various kernel-mode operations, as shown in Figure 10-20.

USE IT To monitor kernel-mode operations within the System Monitor, perform these steps:

1. Select Start | Programs | Accessories. Windows will display the Accessories submenu.
2. Within the Accessories submenu, select System Tools | System Monitor. Windows will open the System Monitor window.
3. Within the System Monitor, select Edit | Add Item. The System Monitor will display the Add Item dialog box.
4. Within the Add Item dialog box Category list, click the Kernel entry. The System Monitor will display the list of kernel-mode operations you can monitor in the Item list.
5. Within the Item list, click the item you want to monitor and click OK.

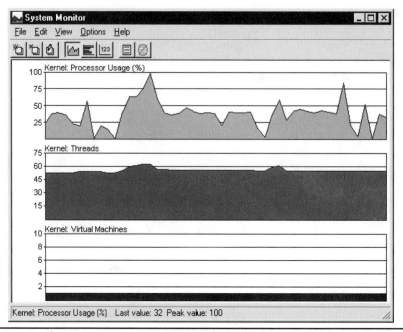

Figure 10.20 Using the System Monitor to monitor kernel-mode operations

If you find that your system is spending considerable time in kernel mode, you need to dig a little deeper to determine why. For example, if your system is short on memory, Windows must perform more page faults to programs in and out of memory—which will lead to more kernel-mode operations for disk operations and memory management. By monitoring the number of kernel-mode threads that are running, you may find that you are simply overtasking your program, possibly by running more applications than your system's resources can support. Increased kernel mode operations are normally an indicator that the operating system is juggling a wide range of operations.

The 80386 processor introduced a capability called the *virtual machine*, which let an operating system create a session, such as an MS-DOS window, that created the illusion that the session had its own 1MB environment—complete with its own copy of operating system, video RAM, and so on. Each time you open an MS-DOS window, Windows creates a virtual machine. By placing each MS-DOS session within its own virtual machine, one MS-DOS session cannot lock up the system. Using the System Monitor, you can track the number of virtual machines your system is using. Normally, your system has one virtual machine, which corresponds to Windows. Each time you open or close an MS-DOS window, the system will increment or decrement its virtual machine count.

Monitoring Your System's Virtual Memory Use

Windows uses a virtual-memory management system that gives users the illusion that they have an essentially unlimited amount of memory. To implement virtual memory, Windows divides programs (the instructions and data it loads into memory) into fixed-sized pages. As the CPU executes the program, Windows loads the corresponding pages into memory. When the CPU tries to execute an instruction (or access a data value) whose page is not in memory, the system generates a page fault that directs Windows to load the page from disk into RAM.

Unfortunately, to load the page into RAM, Windows must first perform a slow disk-read operation. In some cases, before Windows can move the page into RAM, Windows must swap other pages out of RAM to disk to make room for the new page (which means Windows must also perform a slow disk-write operation to store the page it is removing within the page file). The more page faults Windows must perform, the slower the system performance. By monitoring your system's page-fault statistics, you can determine whether your system may need more RAM. By increasing the amount of RAM available for Windows to place program instructions and data, you reduce the amount of swapping Windows must perform, which reduces slow disk operations. Figure 10-21 shows the System Monitor tracking the memory-management settings.

USE IT   To monitor your system's page faults, perform these steps:

1. Select Start | Programs | Accessories. Windows will display the Accessories submenu.

2. Within the Accessories submenu, select System Tools | System Monitor. Windows will display the System Monitor.

3. Within the System Monitor, select Edit | Add Item. The System Monitor will display the Add Item dialog box.

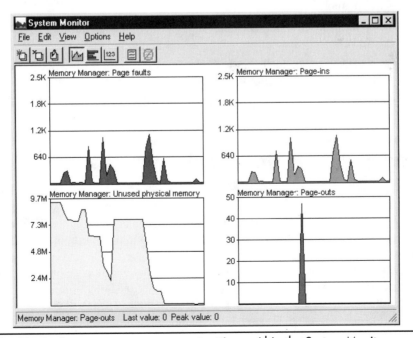

Figure 10.21   Monitoring memory-management settings within the System Monitor

4. Within the Add Item dialog box Category list, click the Memory Manager entry. The System Monitor will display the list of memory-management operations you can monitor in the Item list.

5. Within the Item the list, click the item you want to monitor and click OK.

As you examine the various statistics, you should be more concerned with the number of page outs than page ins. Before the CPU can execute a program, the program's instructions and data must reside in RAM. Therefore, you are always going to have page faults to load any program you run (page ins). When Windows cannot load a page without first moving one or more pages temporarily to disk, a page out occurs. If you are experiencing a large number of page outs, you need more RAM. You can also determine whether adding RAM will improve performance by monitoring the amount of unused physical RAM.

Some key programs (often operating system code) will *lock* their pages into memory to prevent Windows from paging them to disk. Programs should only lock memory for very critical code that executes on a frequent basis. If you find that a specific program is locking a large number of pages, that program may have an adverse performance impact on other programs you run.

To monitor your system's virtual memory use under Windows 2000, perform these steps:

1. Select Start | Settings | Control Panel. Windows will open the Control Panel window.

2. Within the Control Panel, double-click the Administrative Tools icon. Windows will display the Administrative Tools window.

3. Within the Administrative Tools window, double-click Performance. Windows will display the Performance Monitor.

4. Within the Performance Monitor, click the Add button (+). The Performance Monitor will display the Add Counters dialog box.

5. Within the Add Counters dialog box, use the Performance Object pull-down menu to select Memory. The Performance Monitor will display a list of counters you can monitor.

6. Within the counter list, select the counters you want to display and then click Add.

Fine-Tuning Virtual Memory Operations

Most users should normally let Windows manage the system's virtual memory settings. However, if you are running low on disk space, or if you want to move your swap file to a faster disk, you may want to override Windows virtual-memory settings. For example, by default, Windows places its swap file on the boot disk. Depending on your hardware configuration, the boot disk may not be your fastest disk.

If your system performs a large number of page-out (memory to disk page fault) operations, you can improve your system performance by moving your swap file to a faster disk. If Windows performs a large number of page-in (disk to memory page fault) operations (which will occur when Windows must load a program into memory for execution), as opposed to page out operations, you probably will not improve your system performance by moving the swap file. Each time you run a program, Windows must load the program file from disk into memory. The page faults that occur when Windows is loading a program do not use the swap file. To monitor page out faults, use the Windows System Monitor as discussed in the tip "Monitoring Your System's Virtual Memory Use."

USE IT   To move the swap file to a different disk, perform these steps:

1. Select Start | Settings | Control Panel. Windows will open the Control Panel window.

2. Within the Control Panel, double-click the System icon. Windows will open the System Properties dialog box.

3. Within the System Properties dialog box, click the Performance tab. Windows will display the Performance sheet.

4. Within the Performance sheet, click Virtual Memory. Windows will display the Virtual Memory dialog box, as shown here.

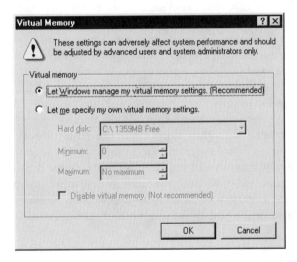

5. Within the Virtual Memory dialog box, click the Let Me Specify My Own Virtual Memory Settings button. Then, use the Hard Disk pull-down list to select your system's fastest drive. Click OK. You then must restart your system to put your change into effect.

To fine-tune the virtual memory settings within Windows 2000, perform these steps:

1. Select Start | Settings | Control Panel. Windows will display the Control Panel window.

2. Within the Control Panel, double-click the System icon. Windows will open the System Properties dialog box.

3. Within the System Properties dialog box, click the Advanced tab. Windows will display the Advanced sheet.

4. Within the Advanced sheet, click Performance Options. Windows will display the Performance Options dialog box.

5. Within the Performance Options dialog box, click Change. Windows will display the Virtual Memory dialog box.

6. Within the Virtual Memory dialog box, select the drive upon which you want the paging file to reside and then select the initial and maximum sizes for the file.

7. Click OK to close each dialog box and to apply your changes.

Changing Thread Priorities in Windows 2000

A program consists of a series of instructions the CPU executes to perform a specific task. Programmers often refer to the program instructions the CPU executes as a *thread of execution*. Although it is normally not readily apparent to the user, many Windows applications make use of several threads of execution, which, much like programs in a multitasking operating system, appear to run at the same time. For example, when you print a document within your word processor, the word processor may create a thread of execution that runs to oversee your printing, while a second thread runs that continues to let you edit your document. Likewise, within a browser, one thread of execution might manage the display of text or graphics on your screen, while one or more threads download files from a remote server.

When a programmer creates a multithreaded application, the programmer can assign different priorities to threads, which causes the higher-priority thread to execute more often than a lower-priority thread. Normally, programmers should assign only the "normal" priority to applications (and the threads the applications create), which causes each application to get the same amount of processor time. However, a programmer may sometimes assign a higher priority to an application to improve the application's performance. Unfortunately, although the application executes faster, the system performance may decrease because the application's higher priority threads are getting the majority of the processor time.

USE IT   If you are using Windows 2000, you can view the number of threads an application is running along with the application's base priority within the Task Manager dialog box Processes sheet, as shown in Figure 10-22.

To view an application's thread count and base priority using the Task Manager, perform these steps:

1. Right-click within an empty area on the taskbar. Windows will display a pop-up menu.

2. Within the pop-up menu, select Taskbar. Windows will display the Task Manager. Within the Task Manager, click the Processes tab. Windows will display the Processes sheet within which you can display the thread count and base priority information. (If the Base Priority and Thread Count columns do not appear within the Processes sheet, select View | Select Columns to display the Select Columns dialog box. Within the Select Columns dialog box, select Base Priority and Thread Count.)

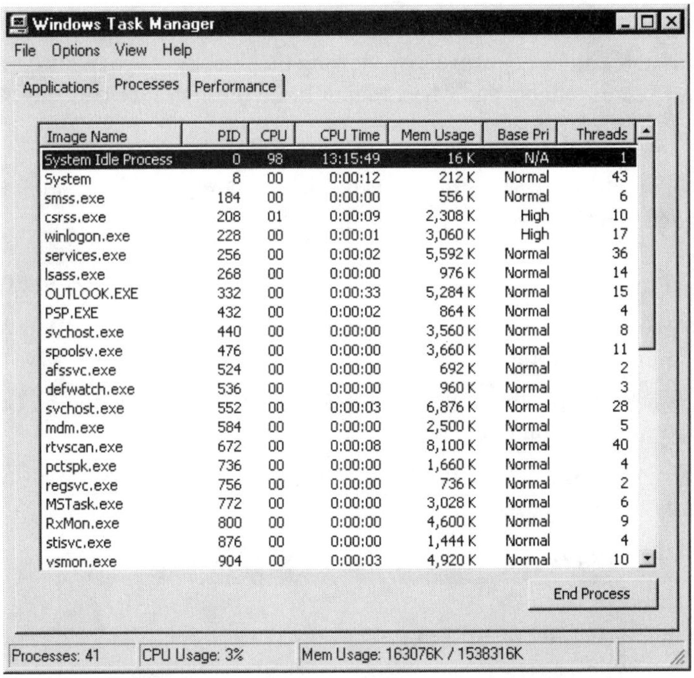

Image Name	PID	CPU	CPU Time	Mem Usage	Base Pri	Threads
System Idle Process	0	98	13:15:49	16 K	N/A	1
System	8	00	0:00:12	212 K	Normal	43
smss.exe	184	00	0:00:00	556 K	Normal	6
csrss.exe	208	01	0:00:09	2,308 K	High	10
winlogon.exe	228	00	0:00:01	3,060 K	High	17
services.exe	256	00	0:00:02	5,592 K	Normal	36
lsass.exe	268	00	0:00:00	976 K	Normal	14
OUTLOOK.EXE	332	00	0:00:33	5,284 K	Normal	15
PSP.EXE	432	00	0:00:02	864 K	Normal	4
svchost.exe	440	00	0:00:00	3,560 K	Normal	8
spoolsv.exe	476	00	0:00:00	3,660 K	Normal	11
afssvc.exe	524	00	0:00:00	692 K	Normal	2
defwatch.exe	536	00	0:00:00	960 K	Normal	3
svchost.exe	552	00	0:00:03	6,876 K	Normal	28
mdm.exe	584	00	0:00:00	2,500 K	Normal	5
rtvscan.exe	672	00	0:00:08	8,100 K	Normal	40
pctspk.exe	736	00	0:00:00	1,660 K	Normal	4
regsvc.exe	756	00	0:00:00	736 K	Normal	2
MSTask.exe	772	00	0:00:00	3,028 K	Normal	6
RxMon.exe	800	00	0:00:00	4,600 K	Normal	9
stisvc.exe	876	00	0:00:00	1,444 K	Normal	4
vsmon.exe	904	00	0:00:03	4,920 K	Normal	10

Figure 10.22 Viewing an application's thread count and base priority

In addition, within the Task Manager's Processes sheet you can change an application's base priority by right-clicking the application and then choosing Set Priority from the pop-up menu Windows displays. Next, Windows will display a second menu of priorities you can select.

Taking a Closer Look at the Windows 98 Log Files

Within an office environment, you may sometimes want to know (perhaps for troubleshooting reasons, or perhaps to monitor an employee's performance) what applications a user is running. Often, system administrators will first look at the user's Document menu to determine the files the user has recently opened. However, under Windows 98, you can take advantage of application log files to better understand what programs users are running.

In Chapter 16 you will use the disk defragmentation program to defragment the files that reside on your disk. To improve your system performance, the disk defragmentation program tries to move files that you run on a frequent basis to more optimal locations on the disk. To help the disk defragmentation program know which programs you run, Windows 98 logs information about each program (and the program support files, such as DLL files) you use within a log file that resides in the Windows/applog folder. The files in the applog folder have the extension .lg*x* where *x* corresponds to the disk drive where the application resides. For example, applications that reside on drive C will have the extension .lgc.

The applog folder is a hidden folder, which means it normally does not appear within directory listings or within the Windows Explorer. However, by viewing the directory's contents, you can learn exactly which applications a user is running and when. Figure 10-23 illustrates the contents of a log file within the Windows Notepad accessory.

USE IT   By creating the log files, Windows adds overhead to every application you run. To disable the log-file creation, perform these steps:

1. Select Start | Programs | Accessories. Windows will display the Accessories submenu.

2. Within the Accessories submenu, select System Tools | System Information. Windows will run the System Information utility.

3. Within the System Information utility, select Tools | System Configuration Utility. Windows will run the System Configuration utility.

4. Within the System Configuration utility, click the Startup tab. The System Configuration utility will display the Startup sheet, as shown here.

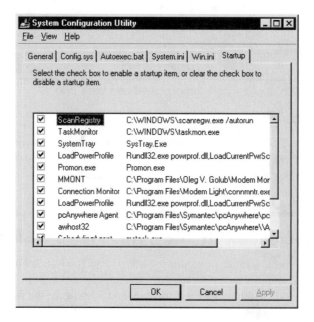

5. Within the Startup sheet, click the TaskMonitor check box, removing the check mark from the box and then click OK. Windows will display a dialog box asking you if you want to restart your system. Because you have removed the TaskMonitor task from the startup programs, Windows will not run the application the next time your system starts.

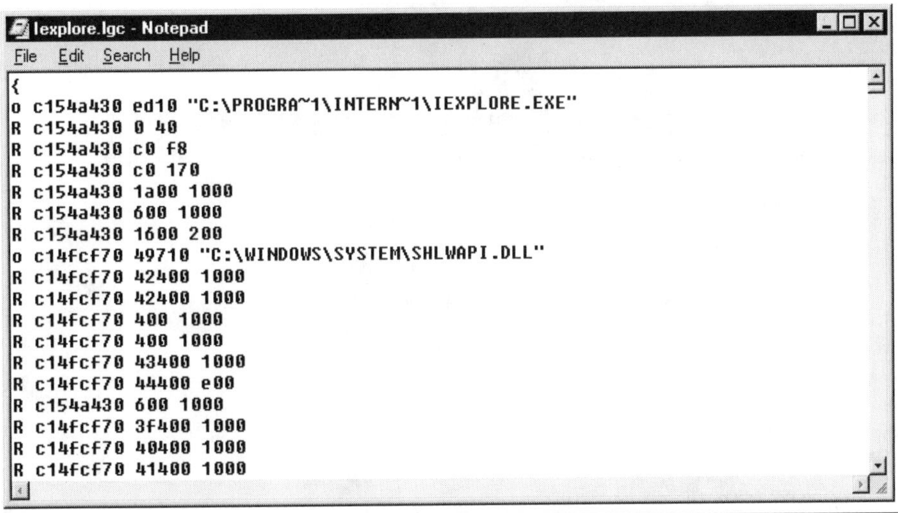

```
Iexplore.lgc - Notepad
File   Edit   Search   Help

{
o c154a430 ed10 "C:\PROGRA~1\INTERN~1\IEXPLORE.EXE"
R c154a430 0 40
R c154a430 c0 f8
R c154a430 c0 170
R c154a430 1a00 1000
R c154a430 600 1000
R c154a430 1600 200
o c14fcf70 49710 "C:\WINDOWS\SYSTEM\SHLWAPI.DLL"
R c14fcf70 42400 1000
R c14fcf70 42400 1000
R c14fcf70 400 1000
R c14fcf70 400 1000
R c14fcf70 43400 1000
R c14fcf70 44400 e00
R c154a430 600 1000
R c14fcf70 3f400 1000
R c14fcf70 40400 1000
R c14fcf70 41400 1000
```

Figure 10.23   Viewing an application log file within the Windows Notepad

CHAPTER 11

Understanding Cables and Ports

TIPS IN THIS CHAPTER

s you work with a PC, you will connect numerous cables to ports in order to attach different devices to your system. Normally, to get things up and running, you simply must match the correct cable and port. However, if you experience errors, or if you want to optimize performance, you will need a basic understanding of cables, ports, and techniques you can use to troubleshoot each. This chapter examines cables, ports, and connectors in detail.

You may be asking yourself "how much could there be to understand about cables?" The best way to respond to such as question is to visit Belkin on the Web at www.Belkin.com. You will find that the company sells hundreds of different types of cables for PCs. By the time you finish this chapter, you will be able to explain the differences between cable categories (such as the common "CAT 5" cable), the cabling issues you must address if you want to implement a gigabit Ethernet, the differences between a standard parallel port and one that supports ECP or EPP capabilities, how to troubleshoot cables, and how 10Base-T Ethernet differs from 10Base-F Ethernet, as well as others.

Cables: Sometimes You Get What You Pay For

If you have ever shopped for a parallel printer or an extension cable for your mouse or keyboard, you may have found a considerable pricing disparity among cable manufacturers. You may, for example, find inexpensive "unshielded" cables that cost less than $10, while the shielded counterparts cost twice the price.

As you will learn in this chapter, shielded cables generate less electromagnetic interference (EMI; electrical noise that interferes with the signals that travel across the cable's wires) and are much less likely to experience interference from outside sources that may generate EMI. Further, a shielded cable, due to its higher cost, may have slightly higher quality connectors, which may better withstand the cable's everyday use.

Is the shielded cable worth the additional cost? It's hard to say. In most cases, an inexpensive unshielded printer cable that you set away from other cables and devices, and, which you rarely move, will long outlive your printer and PC. However, cable problems, such as a broken pin or wire within the cable, can be very difficult and frustrating to troubleshoot.

When you shop for a cable for a single PC, paying a few dollars more for one or two cables may not require a substantial investment on your part. However, when you must cable an office building in preparation for a computer network, the cost of the cable can become very significant. In fact, some analysts estimate that the cost of cable alone makes up 10 percent (or more) of the cost a network installation. As you will learn in this chapter, having the wrong cable can cause you to experience a tremendous decrease in your network performance.

Cables, Heat, and Others Choosing Your Cable Type for You

Cables exist for one purpose, to transmit electronic signals from one device to another. As you learned in Chapter 3, as an electronic signal travels across a wire, the signal generates heat (resistance within the wire essentially creates friction as the signal passes through the wire, which results in heat). Depending on the signal's strength, the resistance of the cable, and the material that insulates the cable, it is possible for a cable to get so hot that the cable will melt or catch fire.

Because of the risk of fire, you simply cannot just use any cable you want to connect PCs within an office network. For example, to run cable in the space above a drop-down ceiling (the space where air ducts reside), the cable must be certified as a *plenum* cable. Likewise, to run a cable between floors, the cable must meet different fire-resistant characteristics. As it turns out, government agencies specify the types of cables you can run within the walls, ceilings, and even under the carpet within an office. Depending on the size and layout of the office you must cable, the restrictions on the cables you must consider will differ.

Revisiting Voltage, Current, and Resistance

As you learned in Chapter 3, the voltage (v) across a wire is the product of current (i) times the cable's resistance (r):

```
v = i × r
```

You measure voltage in volts, current in Amperes (amps), and resistance in ohms.

As you examine cables (or advertisements for cables), you will find that most cables are copper and that users often classify cables by their resistance and the cable's diameter (or more specifically, the cable's gauge). Within the United States, the American Wire Gauge (AWG) describes cable diameters. As shown in Table 11-1, as the AWG value becomes larger, the cable's diameter actually becomes smaller.

AWG	Diameter	AWG	Diameter
10	2.6mm	26	0.404mm
11	2.3mm	27	0.361mm
12	2.05mm	28	0.32mm
13	1.83mm	29	0.287mm
14	1.63mm	30	0.254mm
15	1.45mm	31	0.226mm
16	1.29mm	32	0.203mm
17	1.15mm	33	0.18mm
18	1.02mm	34	0.16mm
19	0.912mm	35	0.142mm
20	0.813mm	36	0.127mm
21	0.724mm	37	0.114mm

Table 11.1   Common Cable Diameters and their AWG Descriptions

AWG	Diameter	AWG	Diameter
22	0.643mm	38	0.102mm
23	0.574mm	39	0.089mm
24	0.511mm	40	0.079mm
25	0.455mm	41	0.069mm

Table 11.1   Common Cable Diameters and their AWG Descriptions *(continued)*

Determining a Cable's Pin One

As you work with different cables, sometimes a cable's connector does not number the connectors (most connectors will specify pin 1 so you can correctly align the cable). If you are connecting a ribbon cable, the cable manufacturer will normally either make pin 1's jacket dark or will place some type of marking on the wire's jacket that distinguishes it from the others. By knowing pin 1, you can align the cable correctly.

Just How Fast Do Signals Travel Across a Cable?

Within a fiber-optic cable, signals travel at the speed of light, which is about 300 million meters per second. How fast is that? If a fiber-optic cable reached to the moon (238,857 miles), a signal could travel to the moon and back in less than three seconds.

Copper wire cables have a characteristic called the Nominal Velocity of Propagation (NVP) that users express in terms of the speed of light. A copper wire with an NVP value of 50, for example, travels at 50 percent of the speed of light. Likewise, signals on a cable with an NVP of 67 percent would travel at 201 million meters per second. As users discuss signals, they will periodically use the term "propagation delay," which corresponds to the length of time a signal travels from its start to its finish.

Within a computer (or network), signals are sent down cables at specific frequencies. A category 5 (CAT 5) cable, for example, supports frequencies of 100 MHz (meaning the signal changes over 100 million times per second).

Understanding Twisted-Pair

Many common PC cables consist of one or more "pairs" of cables. Depending on the cable's type, the number of pairs within the cable will differ. For example, the popular category 5 cable contains four pairs of cables. Within a cable, the related pairs can be twisted or "untwisted," as shown in Figure 11-1.

Within a twisted-pair cable, the related cable pairs twist around one another. The higher a cable's quality, the greater the number of twists the cable contains. Normally, the cables will twist between 2 and 20 times per foot, depending on the cable's type. By twisting the cable pairs around one another, engineers have found that they can reduce the impact of electromagnetic interference (EMI) that occurs at high signal speeds.

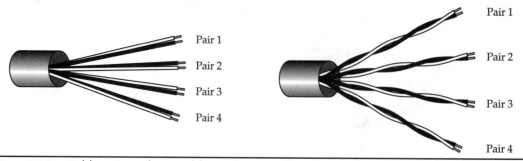

Figure 11.1   Cable pairs within a cable can be twisted or untwisted.

Shielded Versus Unshielded Twisted-pair

As signal speeds increase, so too does the possibility of EMI. To reduce EMI problems, shielded twisted-pair cables place a shielded "jacket" around the cable pairs (not individual pairs) as shown in Figure 11-2. As you might guess, shielded twisted-pair cables are more expensive than unshielded cables. However, at higher data rates, shielded cables normally perform much better than their unshielded counterparts.

Understanding Coaxial Cable

If you connect your television set to a cable TV outlet or to a satellite dish, you will use a coaxial cable, which users refer to as simply *coax*. The coaxial cable is so named because the conductor and insulator (as well as the shield) have a common axis.

As shown in Figure 11-3, the coaxial cable has a copper core, across which signals travel, that is surrounded by an insulator, a shield to reduce outside interference from reaching the core, and finally a jacket. The advantage of a coaxial cable is its support for high bandwidth; the disadvantages include cost and its difficulty to work with (the coaxial cable is less pliable than other cable types). Years

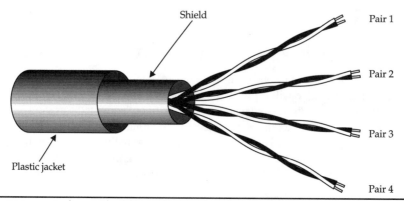

Figure 11.2   Using a jacket to shield twisted-pair cables

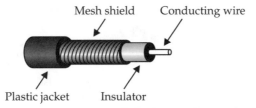

Figure 11.3   Taking a closer look at a coaxial cable

ago, coaxial cables were used extensively in computer networks. Today, however, most networks have replaced the coaxial cable with fiber-optic or twisted-pair cables.

Figure 11-4 illustrates two of the most common coaxial-cable connectors, the F-type connector that you likely use to connect your TV to the cable or satellite, and a BNC connector that provides a rotating collar that lets you attach the cable to a coaxial port.

Users designate coaxial cables by an RG number (a Radio Guide number from the original military specification for cables that defined cables ranging from RG-1 to RG-405 and beyond) that specifies the cable's gauge and impedance. The most commonly used coaxial cable is RG-58, a 50-ohm cable used by 10Base-2 Ethernet.

Understanding Fiber-Optic Cable

As discussed, light travels at 300 million meters per second. A fiber-optic cable transmits and receives signals using pulses of light. Within the fiber-optic cable, the light travels through a glass or plastic strand. An LED (light-emitting diode) or laser generates the light beams that correspond to the signal.

There are two general categories of fiber-optic cable: single-mode and multimode cables. A single-mode fiber-optic cable transmits data in bursts, as shown in Figure 11-5. Telephone companies make extensive use of single-mode cables for long cable connections. Single-mode fiber-optic cables can normally send signals distances up to 3,000 meters.

In contrast, a multimode fiber-optic cable sends multiple streams of light across the fiber at the same time. Within the cable, as shown in Figure 11-6, the various signals travel at different wavelengths,

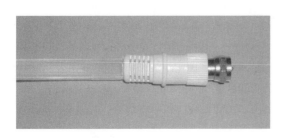

Figure 11.4   The F-type and BNC coaxial cable connectors

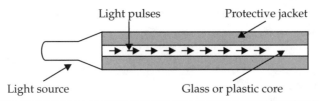

Figure 11.5 A single-mode fiber-optic cable transmits data using bursts of light.

which prevents one signal from interfering with another. As the signals travel within a multimode fiber, the signals may bounce off the sides of the cable (which is not the case for a single-mode cable). As a result, the multimode signals will weaken sooner, and can normally travel distances up to 2,000 meters. The use of multimode fiber-optic cables is common within computer networks, such as a 10Base-FL Ethernet.

As shown in Figure 11-7, the two most widely used connectors for fiber-optic cables are the SC and ST connectors.

Understanding Signal Attenuation

Whether a signal travels through a copper wire or through fiber, the signal will eventually become weaker, as shown in Figure 11-8. Users refer to a signal's weakening over time as *attenuation*. Depending on such factors as the cable type, quality, temperature (signals attenuate faster in heat), and connectors, the speed at which a signal attenuates will differ. As you shop for cables, you may

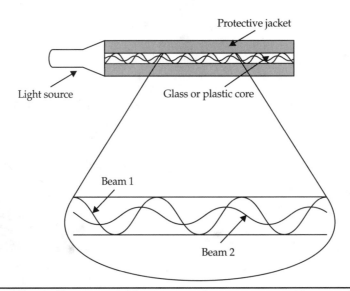

Figure 11.6 A multimode fiber-optic cable transmits data using several beams of light that travel the cable simultaneously at different wavelengths.

SC (subscriber connector)

ST (straight tip connector)

Figure 11.7   The SC and ST fiber-optic cable connectors

find that the cable specifies an attenuation value. The smaller a cable's attenuation, the farther a signal can travel across the cable.

Depending on the distance a signal must travel, you may need to install one or more repeaters throughout the signal's path, which essentially re-amplify the signal, as shown in Figure 11-9.

Understanding Cable Categories

As cables have evolved, the Telecommunication Industries Association (TIA) and the Electronic Industries Association (EIA) have grouped cables into categories based on the cables capabilities and characteristics. Table 11-2 briefly describes the common cable categories.

Taking a Closer Look at Category 5 Cable

Today, most computer networks make extensive use of CAT 5 cable. As shown in Figure 11-10, CAT 5 cables consist of four sets of unshielded twisted-pair (UTP) wires. CAT 5 cables were

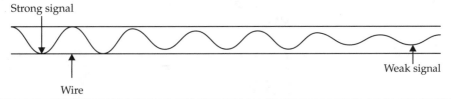

Figure 11.8   As signals travel, they become weaker, or attenuate.

Figure 11.9   Using a repeater to amplify a signal

designed to support bandwidths up to 100 MHz, such as 100Base-TX Ethernet. In fact, some installations successfully run gigabit Ethernets (1000Base-T) using CAT 5 cable. (As it turns out, the gigabit Ethernet achieves much of its high bandwidth through data encoding techniques. As a result, the CAT 5 cable does not have to operate at 1 GHz.) CAT 5 cable can send a signal a distance of 200 meters before a repeater is needed.

The most common connector for a CAT 5 cable is an RJ-45 plug, which looks like a larger and wider version of a standard phone jack.

Making Your Own Cable Connectors

For most network installations, the cost of wiring can make up more than 10 percent of the network's total costs. To reduce wiring costs, many network shops create their own cables and wall outlets. On the Web, you can find many companies that sell cable in bulk, as well as the connectors and wall outlets you will need. In addition, many of the companies also sell wire cutters, crimpers, and devices you can use to quickly attach cable connectors. By creating your own cable connectors and outlets, you may significantly reduce the cost of your cabling.

Category	Description
Category 1	Supports frequencies up to 100 KHz, such as analog telephone connections
Category 2	Supports frequencies up to 4 MHz, such as twisted-pair ArcNet-based networks
Category 3	Supports frequencies up to 20 MHz, such as 10Base-T Ethernet networks
Category 4	Supports frequencies up to 16 MHz, such as UTP Token Ring networks
Category 5	Supports frequencies up to 100 MHz, such as 100Base-TX networks
Category 5E	Supports frequencies up to 100 MHz, but meets TIA/EIA-568-A.5 cabling standards and lower attenuation
Category 6	Supports frequencies up to 250 MHz (proposed standard)
Category 7	Supports frequencies up to 600 MHz (proposed standard)

Table 11.2   Capabilities and Characteristics of Common Cable Categories

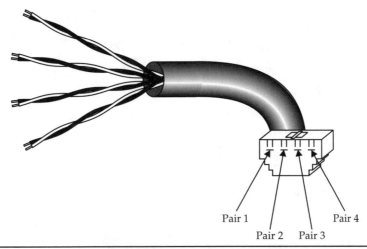

Pair 1   Pair 4

Pair 2   Pair 3

Figure 11.10   The CAT 5 cable consists of four sets of twisted-pair wires.

Making Sense of Ethernet Types

Throughout this chapter and Chapter 16 (as well as other books and magazines that discuss networks), you will encounter terms such as 10Base-T or 100BaseF to describe Ethernet networks. In general, the descriptors specify a network speed (in MHz) and a cable technology, such as twisted-pair or coaxial cable. Table 11-3 describes several terms network administrators often use to describe the speed and cable type for Ethernet networks.

Testing for Broken Cables

USE IT   Depending on the complexity of the cable systems you must support, there is a broad range of tools you can use to troubleshoot various cable problems. At the low end, you can use a continuity tester, as shown in Figure 11-11, to check copper wires (and coaxial cables) for a broken (or "open") wire or short circuit. Many telephone service technicians use a tone generator to place a signal on a wire that generates an audible tone at the other end of the wire if the wire is not broken.

If you are using fiber-optic cables, you can use numerous (expensive) devices to pinpoint locations within the cable system where a damaged cable or poor connector is causing signal loss.

Many testing devices perform "loop back" testing, where you essentially send a signal through the communication channel back to the start. If the signal does not return, you know the wire is damaged or you have a bad connection somewhere within the signal's path. If the signal returns, you can measure the signal's strength to determine the level of attenuation that has occurred across the path.

Descriptor	Type
10Base-2	10 MHz using thin coaxial cable
10Base-T	10 MHz using twisted-pair cable
100Base-TX	100 MHz using CAT 5 or better cable
100Base-T4	100 MHz using CAT 3 cable
100Base-F	100 MHz using a fiber-optic cable
1000Base-T	1 GHz using CAT 5 cable

Table 11.3   Common Ethernet Descriptors

Taking a Close Look at Serial Ports

For years, users made extensive use of the PC's serial ports to connect devices such as modems, mouse devices, joysticks, and even printers (which was a very slow way to print). The serial port is so named because it transmits and receives data one bit at a time over a single wire (serially, one bit after another, unlike the parallel port that sends 8 bits at the same time across 8 different wires). Today, because of the serial port's limited speed (115,200 bits per second), users normally connect devices to other ports, such as USB ports. That said, PCs still ship with one or two serial ports, which may be either 9-pin or 25-pin male connectors. Figure 11-12, for example, shows a 9-pin serial connector.

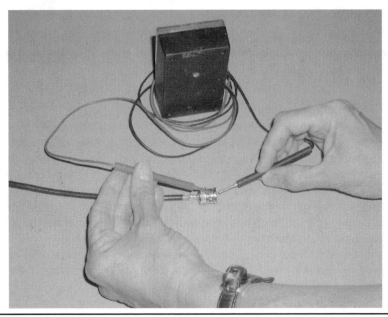

Figure 11.11   Using a continuity tester to test for broken or short-circuited wires

Figure 11.12   Serial ports use either a 9-pin or 25-pin connector.

Table 11-4 briefly describes the purpose of each wire within the serial port connectors.

25-Pin Connector	Purpose	9-Pin Connector	Purpose
1	Not used	1	Data carrier detect
2	Transmit data	2	Receive data
3	Receive data	3	Transmit data
4	Request to send	4	Data terminal ready
5	Clear to send	5	Ground
6	Data set ready	6	Data set ready

Table 11.4   The Purpose of Serial Port Wires

25-Pin Connector	Purpose	9-Pin Connector	Purpose
7	Ground	7	Request to send
8	Data carrier detect	8	Clear to send
9	No used	9	Ring indicator
10	Not used		
11	Not used		
12	Not used		
13	Not used		
14	Not used		
15	Not used		
16	Not used		
17	Not used		
18	Not used		
19	Not used		
20	Data terminal ready		
21	Not used		
22	Ring indicator		
23	Not used		
24	Not used		
25	Not used		

Table 11.4   The Purpose of Serial Port Wires *(continued)*

Because serial ports were first used to let the PC communicate with other serial devices, users refer to the ports as COM ports. In general, the PC supports the use of four COM ports, named COM1, COM2, COM3, and COM4 (however, Windows supports up to 128 ports). Table 11-5 lists the resources (IRQ and port addresses) the PC normally reserves for the COM ports.

If you examine the resources the PC assigns to the COM ports, you will note that the COM1 and COM3 IRQs conflict, as do the COM2 and COM4 IRQs. Normally, most users will not have more than two COM ports (which they use as COM1 and COM2). If you add additional COM ports, you must assign each a unique IRQ.

USE IT   To change a COM port's IRQ settings, perform these steps:

1. Select Start | Settings | Control Panel. Windows will open the Control Panel window.

Port	IRQ	Port Address
COM1	IRQ4	3F8–3FF
COM2	IRQ3	2F8–2FF
COM3	IRQ4	3E8–3EF
COM4	IRQ3	2E8–2EF

Table 11.5   PC Resources Reserved for COM Ports

2. Within the Control Panel, double-click the System icon. Windows will display the System Properties dialog box.

3. Within the System Properties dialog box, click the Device Manager tab. Windows will display the Device Manager sheet.

4. Within the Device Manager, click the plus sign (+) that precedes the Ports entry. The Device Manager will expand the port list.

5. Within the port list, double-click the COM port you want to configure. Windows will display the port's Properties dialog box.

6. Within the Properties dialog box, click the Resources tab. Windows will display the Port Resources sheet, as shown here.

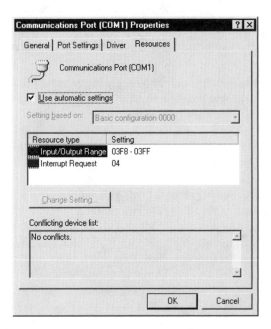

7. Within the Resources sheet, click the Use Automatic Settings check box to remove the check mark. Then, click the IRQ setting and click Change Setting. Windows, in turn, will display a

dialog box within which you can select the new IRQ settings. Enter the IRQ you desire and click OK.

8. Click OK to close the port's Properties dialog box.

Making Sense of Serial Data Communication Parameters

The serial port sends and receives data one bit a time. Within the serial port, a chip called the Universal Asynchronous Receiver Transmitter (UART) collects incoming bits and groups them into a byte value. Likewise, when the serial port sends a byte value, the UART breaks the bytes into its individual bits for transmission. The speed of a serial port is directly related to the speed of the port's UART. Today, most PCs have a 16550 UART capable of 115,200 bits per second. Some newer systems use a 16650 UART capable of speeds up to 460Kb (kilobits) per second.

To communicate with the serial port, a device and the port must agree upon several data communication parameters:

- **Bits per second**   Specifies the speed at which the port and the device will communicate. Normally in the range 110 bits per second to 115,200 bits per second.

- **Data bits**   Specifies the number of data bits the port and the device will use to represent a value. Normally in the range 4 to 8.

- **Parity**   Specifies the type of parity the port and the device will use to detect errors: Even, Odd, or None.

- **Stop bits**   Specifies the number of bits the port and device will place following a data bit. Normally in the range 1 to 2.

- **Flow control**   Specifies how the port or device will control the flow of data (which lets the port or device stop and later resume the transmission to prevent the loss of incoming data). Values are XON/XOFF, hardware, or none.

In general, to receive data, the UART monitors the port's receive wire (line 3 on a 25-pin connector and line 2 on a 9-pin connector). When the UART detects a start bit, the UART will then examine the receive wire's contents at fixed intervals to determine the value of the next data bit. Assuming the device and port communicate at 9600 bits per second, the UART will look for data on the wire about every millisecond (1/9600), as shown in Figure 11-13.

After the UART reads the data bits, the UART will watch for a stop bit and parity bit, if the communication settings are using them. To send data, the UART will generate a start bit and then send the data bits one at a time, in fixed intervals, followed by the optional stop and parity bit.

USE IT   When you attach a device to a serial port, the device will normally have its optimal data communication settings assigned. The manual that accompanies the device will tell you the settings. In some cases, you can use jumpers and switches on the device to change the settings.

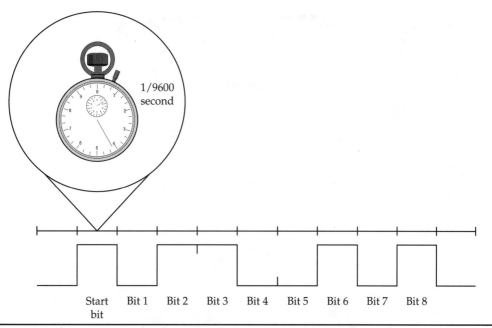

1/9600
second

Start   Bit 1   Bit 2   Bit 3   Bit 4   Bit 5   Bit 6   Bit 7   Bit 8
bit

Figure 11.13   The UART uses the data communication speed to determine when to read the next incoming data bit.

Within Windows, you must assign the matching data communication settings to the serial port to which you connected the device. To assign port settings within Windows, perform these steps:

1. Select Start | Settings | Control Panel. Windows, in turn, will open the Control Panel window.

2. Within the Control Panel, double-click the System icon. Windows will display the System Properties dialog box.

3. Within the System Properties dialog, click the Device Manager tab. Windows will display the Device Manager.

4. Within the Device Manager, click the plus sign (+) that precedes the Ports entry. The Device Manager will expand the port list.

5. Within the port list, double-click the COM port you want to configure. Windows will display the port's Properties dialog box.

6. Within the Properties dialog box, click the Port Settings tab. Windows will display the Port Settings sheet, as shown next.

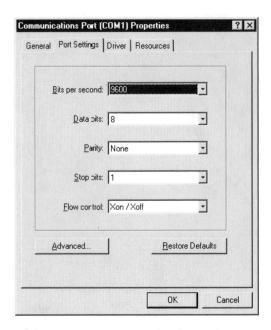

7. Within the Port Settings sheet, assign the data communication settings that match those used by your new device. Click OK to close the dialog box and to put your changes into effect.

If you are not using your PC's serial port, and you do not plan to use the port in the future, you can use the CMOS Setup program, discussed in Chapter 6, to disable the port's use. By doing so, you free up the port's resources (such as the IRQ) for use by other devices.

Using a Null Modem to Connect Computers

As you know, users normally connect computers to networks to exchange files. Unfortunately, many users have notebook computers with which they travel and desktop PCs they use at home on a regular basis. Depending on the files the user must copy between the two PCs, the user can use a floppy disk, or they can possibly e-mail the file across the Internet from one system to the other. To simplify such file exchanges, Windows provides the Direct Cable Connection program that lets two PCs exchange files across the serial port, parallel port, or infrared (IR) connection.

A 25-pin serial port sends data across line 2 and receives data across line 3. To let two computers communicate via their serial ports, you must connect the PCs with a null-modem cable. As shown in Figure 11-14, a null modem cable crosses wires 2 and 3 so that when one PC transmits data, the data arrives on the other PC's receive line, and vice versa.

▶ **NOTE**

To direct connect two PCs using their parallel ports, you must use a bidirectional parallel cable.

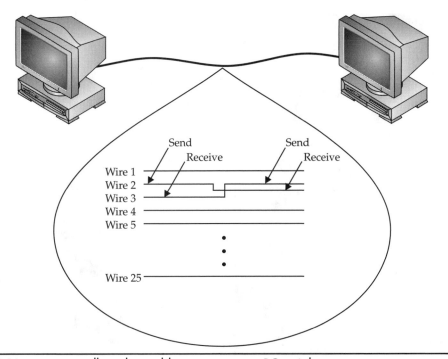

Figure 11.14 Using a null-modem cable to connect two PC serial ports

Taking a Close Look at Parallel Ports

Today, most printers connect to a PC parallel port. The parallel port is so named, because unlike the serial port that sends and receives data one bit at a time over a single wire, the parallel port sends data 8 bits at a time over 8 wires (in other words, the signals for the 8 data bits travel across the parallel cable at the same time, parallel to one another). Because the parallel port's data bits arrive at the same time, the parallel port does not require the data communication parameters the serial port must use to coordinate the bit arrival. All PCs ship with at least one parallel port, which uses a 25-pin female connector, as shown in Figure 11-15.

A standard parallel port can transmit data at 150KB per second. Table 11-6 briefly describes the pins that make up the parallel port.

Because they are normally used to connect printers (formerly referred to as line printers), parallel port names use the letters LPT. Windows supports up to four parallel ports: LPT1, LPT2, LPT3, and LPT4. Normally, Windows reserves resources for LPT1 only.

USE IT To view your parallel port's resource use, perform these steps:

1. Select Start | Settings | Control Panel. Windows, in turn, will open the Control Panel window.

Figure 11.15   The parallel port uses a 25-pin female connector.

Pin	Purpose
1	-Strobe
2	Data bit 0
3	Data bit 1
4	Data bit 2
5	Data bit 3
6	Data bit 4
7	Data bit 5
8	Data bit 6

Table 11.6   The Purpose of Wires in the 25-Pin Parallel Cable

Pin	Purpose
9	Data bit 7
10	-Acknowledge
11	Busy
12	Paper end
13	Select
14	-Auto feed
15	-Error
16	-Initialize printer
17	-Select input
18	Ground
19	Ground
20	Ground
21	Ground
22	Ground
23	Ground
24	Ground
25	Ground

Table 11.6   The Purpose of Wires in the 25-Pin Parallel Cable *(continued)*

2. Within the Control Panel, double-click the System icon. Windows will display the System Properties dialog box.

3. Within the System Properties dialog, click the Device Manager tab. Windows will display the Device Manage.

4. Within the Device Manager, click the plus sign (+) that precedes the Ports entry. The Device Manager will expand the port list.

5. Within the port list, double-click the LPT port you want to configure. Windows will display the port's Properties dialog box.

6. Within the Properties dialog box, click the Resources tab. Windows will display the Resources sheet, as shown in Figure 11-16.

If you are not using your PC's parallel port, and you do not plan to use the port in the future, you can use the CMOS Setup program, discussed in Chapter 6, to disable the port's use. In so doing, you free up the port's resources (such as the IRQ) for use by other devices.

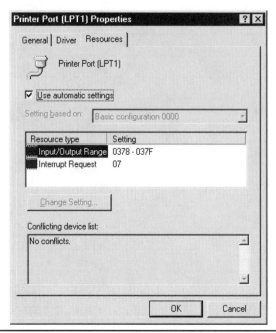

Figure 11.16   Viewing a printer's resource use within the Resources sheet

Improving Parallel Port Performance Using EPP and ECP

A standard parallel port is capable of sending data at 150KB per second, which is considerably faster than a serial port. To meet the demands for faster and more powerful printers, hardware designers created a bidirectional parallel port that can send and receive data. Using a bidirectional port, for example, a printer could tell the operating system when it was out of paper. Likewise, users could attach a Zip drive to the parallel port or use the port for a direct cable connection.

In the early 1990s, several manufacturers developed the enhanced parallel port, or EPP, that was capable of data throughput speeds of up to 2MB per second (more than 10 times faster than the standard parallel port). The EPP improved speeds by providing additional chips to streamline the "handshaking" process the port and printer perform to exchange a byte of data. Using the EPP, users connected disk drives, tape drives, and modems to the fast port. The shortcoming of the EPP is that the CPU must oversee the data transfers, which places considerable overhead on the CPU.

Soon after the EPP arrived on the scene, Microsoft and Hewlett-Packard released the enhanced capabilities port, or ECP, which could achieve data transfer rates of 2MB per second without placing the processing overhead on the CPU. The ECP achieved its high data throughput using a DMA channel.

USE IT   To take advantage of the EPP or ECP capabilities, you must have a 1284 parallel cable (named after the IEEE specification that standardizes advanced bidirectional parallel port operations) and your ports must support the capabilities. In some cases, as discussed in Chapter 6, you may need to use the CMOS Setup program to enable the port capabilities. Normally, when you disable your parallel port's extended capabilities, Windows will automatically update your port settings. To ensure that your printer is using the EPP or ECP port, however, perform these steps:

1. Select Start | Settings | Printer. Windows, in turn, will open the Printers folder.
2. Within the Printers folder, right-click the printer you want to configure. Windows will display a pop-up menu.
3. Within the pop-up menu, select Properties. Windows will display the printer's Properties dialog box.
4. Within the Properties dialog box, click the Details tab. Windows will display the Details sheet.
5. Within the Details sheet, select the ECP or EPP port you desire from the pull-down list labeled Print To The Following Port.
6. Choose OK to close the Properties dialog box and to put your changes into effect.

▶ *NOTE*

Periodically, a system may encounter compatibility problems when you try to use EPP or ECP capabilities. To troubleshoot such problems, disable the port's operations within Windows and, if necessary, within the CMOS Setup program. You may want to try running in Standard or Compatibility mode.

Installing a Parallel or Serial Port

If your system is using an older serial port that does not have a 16650 UART, and you make extensive use of your serial port, you may want to install a newer serial port. Likewise, if you have a high-speed printer that you use on a regular basis, and your system is not using an EPP or ECP parallel port, you should install a new faster port.

Normally, most motherboards implement the serial and parallel ports using a chip. If you want to replace your existing port when you install a new serial or parallel port card, you must disable the motherboard chip by using the CMOS Setup program, as discussed in Chapter 6.

▶ *NOTE*

If you are installing a serial that will serve as COM3 or COM4, you will need to change the port's IRQ settings as discussed in the section "Taking a Close Look at Serial Ports." You may also need to change a jumper or switch on the card itself that specifies the COM port you desire. Likewise, if you are installing a parallel port that will serve as other than as LPT1, you may need to change a switch or jumper on the card to change the card setting.

USE IT To install a serial or parallel card into your system, perform these steps:

1. Shut down and power off your computer.
2. Unplug the system unit and gently remove the system unit cover.
3. Insert and secure the new card into an expansion slot.
4. Replace the system unit and power on your system.
5. If necessary, use the CMOS Setup program to disable the motherboard serial or parallel port.

Normally, Windows will have a driver installed that it can use to communicate with the new port. However, depending on the card type you install, you may have to install a device driver.

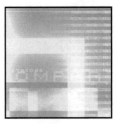

CHAPTER 12

PC Buses

TIPS IN THIS CHAPTER

W ithin a PC, a *bus* is simply a collection of wires that connect two or more chips or devices. As you will learn in this chapter, the PC uses several different bus types, such as the system bus that connects the processor, RAM, BIOS, and other key chips in the chipset, as well as the PCI bus that lets the CPU communicate with cards you install into the motherboard's expansion slots.

This chapter examines the various PC buses in detail. As you will learn, different PC buses operate at different speeds, and the number of wires a bus provides to transfer signals will vary. By the time you finish this chapter, you will understand when, for performance reasons, you may to want use one bus type over another to connect a device to your PC.

Revisiting the System Bus

To perform its processing, the CPU must be able to store and retrieve data and program instructions from RAM. Likewise, each time your system starts, the CPU runs its BIOS-based power-on self-test and uses CMOS system settings. To communicate with RAM and the BIOS (as well as other key chips in the chipset), the CPU uses the system bus, as shown in Figure 12-1. To allow the CPU to communicate with devices that connect to other buses, the system bus uses several special chips users refer to as *bridges* to connect the buses to the system bus.

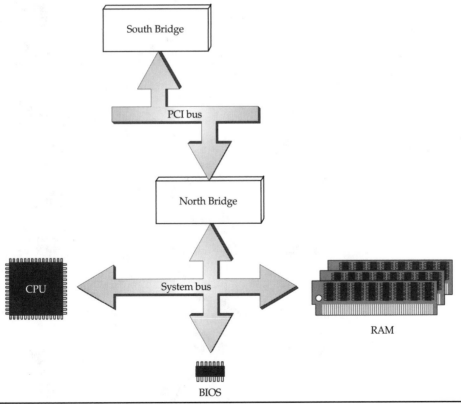

Figure 12.1   The system bus connects the CPU to key components.

The system bus is the fastest bus within the PC. Normally, the system bus operates at a speed that is some fraction of the processor's speed. Users refer to the difference between the processor and system-bus speed as a *multiplier*. Common multipliers range from 2 to 5. The Pentium 4, for example, is capable of speeds of 2 GHz. Its system bus operates at 400 MHz (producing a multiplier of 5).

Understanding Expansion Buses

As you know, within the PC, expansion slots provide users with a way to install hardware cards, such as modem or network interface card, as shown in Figure 12-2. Depending on your PC type (and its age), the number and type of expansion slots your system contains will differ. Today, most PCs use PCI expansion slots that run at 33 MHz or 66 MHz (although most PCI-based cards run at only 33 MHz).

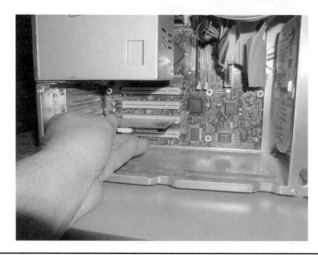

Figure 12.2 Expansion slots are so named because users expand the PC's hardware capabilities by using the slots to install new hardware.

Years ago, the original IBM PC shipped with 8-bit ISA cards, that ran at 4.77 MHz (the speed of the original PC's processor). ISA is an abbreviation for Industry Standard Architecture, an open (published) architecture that let a wide range of hardware manufacturers create cards for the IBM PC. The "open" nature of the ISA bus was one of the keys to the IBM PC's original success. At 4.77 MHz, the 8-bit ISA bus could transfer data at 4.77MB per second. Figure 12-3 illustrates an 8-bit ISA card.

As discussed, a bus is a collection of wires. The 8-bit ISA expansion slot consisted of 62 wires. As shown in Figure 12-4, within the slot, 31 wires connected to the pins on the right side of the card and 31 connected to the card's left side.

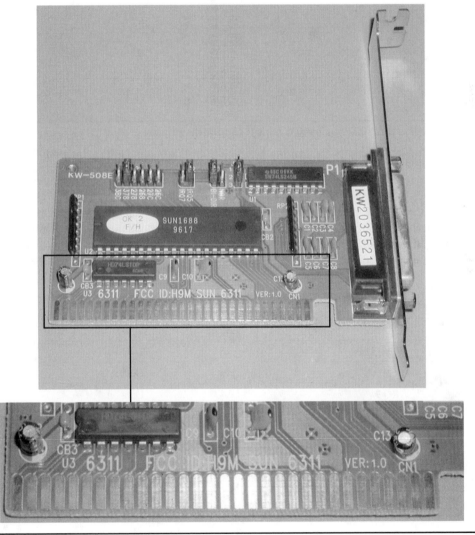

Figure 12.3   An 8-bit ISA card

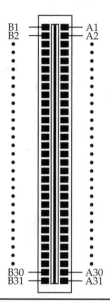

Figure 12.4 The 8-bit ISA bus used 62 wires to transfer signals.

Each pin within the 8-bit ISA bus serves a specific purpose. Table 12-1 briefly summarizes each pin's purpose. By publishing the ISA bus specification, card manufacturers could create a wide range of cards for the IBM PC and PC compatibles. Take time to review the signals each wire within the ISA bus carries. By examining the signals, you will better understand the number of bits the bus can transfer, the number of locations the bus can address, the voltage types (which you can use for troubleshooting), and so on.

Pin	Purpose	Pin	Purpose
B1	Ground	A1	–I/O Channel Check
B2	Reset Drive	A2	Data bit 7
B3	+5V	A3	Data bit 6
B4	IRQ 2	A4	Data bit 4
B5	–5V	A5	Data bit 4
B6	DMA Request 2	A6	Data bit 3
B7	–12V	A7	Data bit 2
B8	Card selected	A8	Data bit 1

Table 12.1 Purpose of Individual Pins Within the 8-Bit ISA Bus

Pin	Purpose	Pin	Purpose
B9	+12V	A9	Data bit 0
B10	Ground	A10	I/O Channel Ready
B11	–System Memory Write	A11	Address Enable
B12	–System Memory Read	A12	Address 19
B13	–I/O Write	A13	Address 18
B14	–I/O Read	A14	Address 17
B15	–DMA Acknowledge 3	A15	Address 16
B16	–DMA Request 3	A16	Address 15
B17	–DMA Acknowledge 1	A17	Address 14
B18	–DMA Request 1	A18	Address 13
B19	–DRAM Refresh	A19	Address 12
B20	Bus Clock	A20	Address 11
B21	IRQ 7	A21	Address 10
B22	IRQ 6	A22	Address 9
B23	IRQ 5	A23	Address 8
B24	IRQ 4	A24	Address 7
B25	IRQ 3	A25	Address 6
B26	–DMA Acknowledge 2	A26	Address 5
B27	Terminal Word Count	A27	Address 4
B28	Address Lines Enabled	A28	Address 3
B29	+5V	A29	Address 2
B30	14.318KHz Oscillator	A30	Address 1
B31	Ground	A31	Address 0

Table 12.1 Purpose of Individual Pins Within the 8-Bit ISA Bus *(continued)*

When the IBM PC/AT released in 1984, it brought with it an 80286 processor and a 16-bit ISA card. As shown in Figure 12-5, the 16-bit ISA card used two connectors, one that matched the original 8-bit ISA slot and a new 36-wire connector.

The 16-bit ISA expansion slot consisted of 98 wires. As shown in Figure 12-6, within the first slot, 31 wires connected to the pins on the right side of the card and 31 connected to the card's left side. Within the card's second slot, 18 wires connected to the right side of the card and 18 to the left.

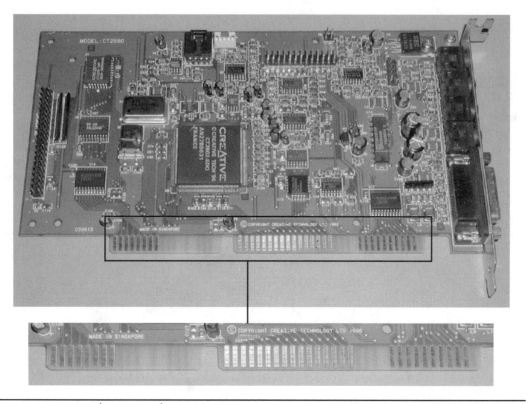

Figure 12.5   A 16-bit ISA card

Because the first slot for 16-bit ISA bus was identical to that of the 8-bit ISA bus, users could insert 8-bit cards into the 16-bit slot (leaving the second slot unused). As discussed, the first 62 wires on the 16-bit ISA bus were identical to those of the 8-bit bus. Table 12-2 describes the purpose of the 36 new wires the 16-bit ISA bus introduced. Initially, the 16-bit ISA bus operated at 6 MHz. Over time, manufacturers increased the bus speed to 8 MHz. At 8 MHz, the 16-bit bus was able to transfer data at 16MB per second.

When the 80386 processor arrived on the scene, it brought with it a 32-bit processor. To match the processor's 32-bit database, hardware manufacturers released a 32-bit version of the ISA bus, which users referred to as the EISA or Extended Industry Standard Architecture. In general, the 32-bit EISA expansion slot looked the same as the 16-bit slot. In fact, users could install and use 16-bit ISA cards within a 32-bit EISA slot. However, as shown in Figure 12-7, the EISA bus doubled the number of connectors on the card and within the slot.

Running at 8.33 MHz, the 32-bit EISA bus could transfer data at 33.3MB per second. Because the EISA bus is used less frequently than other buses, this chapter doesn't present the bus pinouts.

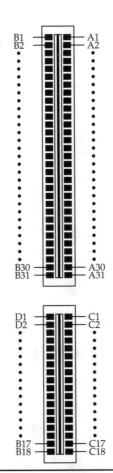

Figure 12.6   The 16-bit ISA bus used 96 wires to transfer signals.

Wire	Purpose	Wire	Purpose
D1	–Memory chip select	C1	–System bus high enable
D2	–Input/Output chip select	C2	Latch address 23
D3	IRQ 10	C3	Latch address 22
D4	IRQ 11	C4	Latch address 21
D5	IRQ 12	C5	Latch address 20
D6	IRQ 15	C6	Latch address 19
D7	IRQ 14	C7	Latch address 18
D8	–DMA Acknowledge 0	C8	Latch address 17

Table 12.2   Purpose of the New 36 Wires Within the 16-Bit ISA Bus

Wire	Purpose	Wire	Purpose
D9	DMA Request 0	C9	–Memory read
D10	–DMA Acknowledge 5	C10	–Memory write
D11	DMA Request 5	C11	Data bit 8
D12	–DMA Acknowledge 6	C12	Data bit 9
D13	DMA Request 6	C13	Data bit 10
D14	–DMA Acknowledge 7	C14	Data bit 11
D15	DMA Request 7	C15	Data bit 12
D16	+5V	C16	Data bit 13
D17	–Master	C17	Data bit 14
D18	Ground	C18	Data bit 15

Table 12.2   Purpose of the New 36 Wires Within the 16-Bit ISA Bus *(continued)*

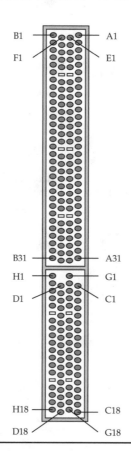

Figure 12.7   A 32-bit EISA card

Understanding the Microchannel Architecture (MCA)

In 1987, IBM released its PS/2 line of computers that replaced the ISA bus with a new bus called the Microchannel bus. The Microchannel bus was a 32-bit bus that operated at 10 MHz (which let the bus achieve data rates of up to 40MB per second). The bus also introduced support for first the Plug and Play devices, by eliminating many of the resource issues (such as IRQs) associated with the ISA bus. Unfortunately, because the Microchannel was expensive and was not compatible with the ISA bus and ISA-based cards, the bus never achieved market acceptance.

Improving Bus Speeds

As you just learned, the maximum throughput of the 32-bit EISA bus was 33MB per second. In the early 1990s, as the Windows environment was gaining popularity, the EISA bus was becoming a bottleneck for graphics operations. To improve video performance, hardware manufacturers created a special "local bus" which connected the video card to the system bus, as shown in Figure 12-8. Users referred to the local video bus as the VESA bus (VESA is an abbreviation for Video Electronics Standards Association).

The VESA bus was a 32-bit bus that operated at the same speed as the system bus. Although the VESA bus was capable of high transfer rates, the problem was that because the system bus speed could differ from one PC to the next, it was difficult for video card manufacturers to build cards that could adjust to the various timing considerations—which lead to compatibility problems.

To eliminate the problems that arose from connecting the video card directly to the system bus, hardware manufacturers created the PCI (Peripheral Component Interconnect) expansion bus, a 32-bit bus that ran at 33 MHz. Figure 12-9 illustrates a PCI-based card.

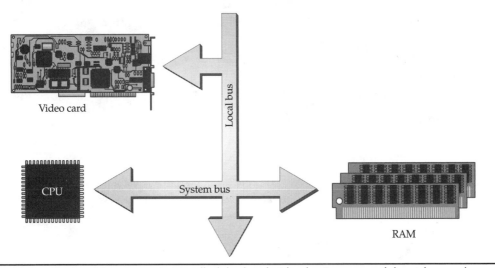

Figure 12.8   The local bus (sometimes called the local video bus) connected the video card to the system bus

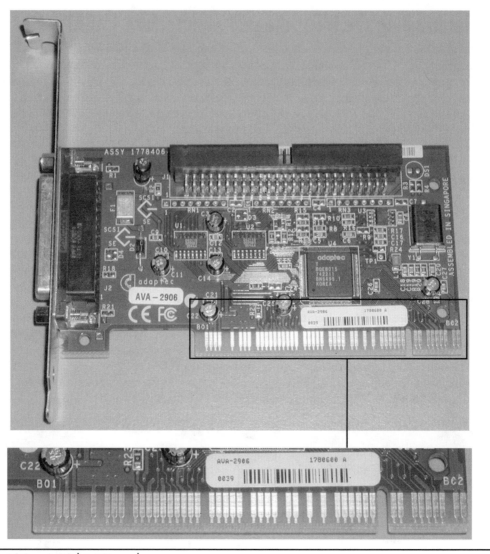

Figure 12.9 A 32-bit PCI card

As shown in Figure 12-10, the PCI bus connects to the system bus via a special set of chips that hardware manufacturers refer to as the North Bridge. To support older hardware cards, some PCs provide a 16-bit ISA or 32-bit EISA slot. Within the motherboard, the slower ISA bus connects to the PCI bus through a set of special chips that hardware manufacturers refer to as the South Bridge. Today, newer PCI buses support 64-bit data transfers at 66 MHz, to produce a data transfer rate of 528MB per second.

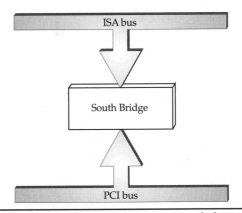

Figure 12.10 The PCI bus connects to the system bus via special chips called the North Bridge and to the slower ISA bus using the South Bridge chips.

The PCI bus uses 94 pins. Table 12-3 briefly describes each pin's purpose for the universal PCI specification normally followed by desktop and tower PCs.

Pin	Purpose	Pin	Purpose	Pin	Purpose	Pin	Purpose
B1	−12V	A1	Test Reset	B48	Address 10	A48	Ground
B2	Test clock	A2	+12V	B49	Ground	A49	Address 9
B3	Ground	A3	Test Mode Select	B50	Ground	A50	Ground
B4	Test Data Output	A4	Test Data Input	B51	Ground	A51	Ground
B5	+5V	A5	+5V	B52	Address 8	A52	Bus Command/ Byte Enable 0
B6	+5V	A6	Interrupt A	B53	Address 7	A53	+3.3V I/O
B7	Interrupt B	A7	Interrupt C	B54	+3.3V	A54	Address 6
B8	Interrupt D	A8	+5V I/O	B55	Address 5	A55	Address 4
B9	Present 1	A9	Reserved	B56	Address 3	A56	Ground
B10	Reserved	A10	+5V	B57	Ground	A57	Address 2
B11	Present 1	A11	Reserved	B58	Address 1	A58	Address 0
B12	Ground	A12	Ground	B59	+5V I/O	A59	+3.3V I/O
B13	Ground	A13	Ground	B60	Acknowledge	A60	Request

Table 12.3 Pins Within the Universal PCI Bus

Pin	Purpose	Pin	Purpose	Pin	Purpose	Pin	Purpose
B14	Reserved	A14	Reserved	B61	+5V	A61	+5V
B15	Ground	A15	Reset	B62	+5V	A62	+5V
B16	Clock	A16	+5V I/O	B63	Reserved	A63	Ground
B17	Ground	A17	Grant	B64	Ground	A64	Bus Command/ Byte Enable 7
B18	Request	A18	Ground	B65	Bus Command/ Byte Enable 6	A65	Bus Command/ Byte Enable 5
B19	+5V I/O	A19	Reserved	B66	Bus Command/ Byte Enable 4	A66	+3.3V I/O
B20	Address 31	A20	Address 30	B67	Ground	A67	Parity
B21	Address 29	A21	+3.3V	B68	Address 63	A68	Address 62
B22	Ground	A22	Address 28	B69	Address 61	A69	Ground
B23	Address 27	A23	Address 26	B70	+3.3V I/O	A70	Address 60
B24	Address 25	A24	Ground	B71	Address 59	A71	Address 58
B25	+3.3V	A25	Address 24	B72	Address 57	A72	Ground
B26	Bus Command/ Byte Enable 3	A26	Initiator Device Selected	B73	Ground	A73	Address 56
B27	Address 23	A27	+3.3V	B74	Address 55	A74	Address 54
B28	Ground	A28	Address 22	B75	Address 53	A75	+3.3V I/O
B29	Address 21	A29	Address 20	B76	Ground	A76	Address 52
B30	Address 19	A30	Ground	B77	Address 51	A77	Address 50
B31	+3.3V	A31	Address 18	B78	Address 49	A78	Ground
B32	Address 17	A32	Address 16	B79	+3.3V I/O	A79	Address 48
B33	Bus Command/ Byte Enable 2	A33	+3.3V	B80	Address 47	A80	Address 46
B34	Ground	A34	Cycle Frame	B81	Address 45	A81	Ground
B35	Initiator Ready	A35	Ground	B82	Ground	A82	Address 44
B36	+3.3V	A36	Target Ready	B83	Address 43	A83	Address 42
B37	Device Select	A37	Ground	B84	Address 41	A84	+3.3V I/O
B38	Ground	A38	Stop	B85	Ground	A85	Address 40
B39	Lock	A39	+3.3V	B86	Address 39	A86	Address 38
B40	Parity Error	A40	Snoop Done	B87	Address 37	A87	Ground

Table 12.3   Pins Within the Universal PCI Bus *(continued)*

Pin	Purpose	Pin	Purpose	Pin	Purpose	Pin	Purpose
B41	+3.3V	A41	Snoop Backoff	B88	+3.3V I/O	A88	Address 36
B42	System Error	A42	Ground	B89	Address 35	A89	Address 34
B43	+3.3V	A43	PAR	B90	Address 33	A90	Ground
B44	Bus Command/ Byte Enable 1	A44	Address 15	B91	Ground	A91	Address 32
B45	Address 14	A45	+3.3V	B92	Reserved	A92	Reserved
B46	Ground	A46	Address 13	B93	Reserved	A93	Ground
B47	Address 12	A47	Address 11	B94	Ground	A94	Reserved

Table 12.3   Pins Within the Universal PCI Bus *(continued)*

Over the past years, video cards have increased the resolution and number of colors a user can view. Today, for example, users often run Windows-based systems using 32-bit colors, which require 4 bytes per pixel. Newer video cards support pixel resolutions of up to 2,048 by 1,536, which, at 4 bytes per pixel, requires about 12MB of data. To support such high-end graphics, hardware manufacturers created the accelerated graphics port (AGP), a 32-bit bus, which normally operates at 66 MHz. Like the PCI bus, the AGP bus connects to the system bus via the North Bridge chips. Figure 12-11 illustrates an AGP bus slot on a motherboard, along with an AGP video card.

Although the AGP bus normally operates at 66 MHz, the AGP 2.0 specification supports various modes of operation that let the AGP bus transfer data two or four times per bus cycle, which effectively increases the bandwidth, as shown in Table 12-4. In the future, we may likely see an 8x mode that supports data transfer rates in excess of 2MB per second.

Because the AGP bus has access to system bus (and hence RAM), AGP-based video cards do not have to have their own video RAM (which may significantly reduce the video card's cost).

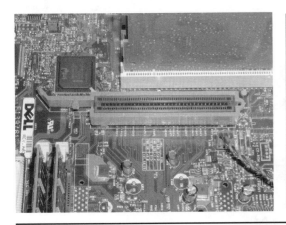

Figure 12.11   The AGP provides support for high-speed graphics operations.

AGP Mode	Transfers per Bus Cycle	Data Transfer Rate
1x	1	266MB per second
2x	2	533MB per second
4x	4	1,066MB per second

Table 12.4   Data Throughput Potential of the AGP

Using the Small Computer System Interface (SCSI) Bus

By the late 1980s, users were making extensive use of a device controller called the Small Computer System Interface (SCSI) bus, to connect several high-speed devices, such as disk drives, tape drives, and CD-ROM drives to the PC. Pronounced "skuzzy," the SCSI bus used a card (the controller card) users installed within an expansion slot. As shown in Figure 12-12, users could connect up to seven devices (originally) to the SCSI controller (today, users can connect up to 15 devices to newer SCSI controllers) in a daisy-chain fashion. Devices connecting to the SCSI chain could be internal (within the PC chassis) or external.

Within the SCSI device chain, each device (including the SCSI controller card) must have a unique ID number (in the range 0 to 7 or 0 to 15, depending on the number of devices the controller supports). Normally, most external devices have a switch similar to that shown in Figure 12-13 that you can use to select the device's ID number. Some devices use DIP switches or jumpers to set the device ID.

Most SCSI devices have two connectors, as shown in Figure 12-14. The first connector attaches the device to the SCSI chain. The second connector either terminates the SCSI bus (if the device is the last device on the bus) or connects another device to the bus.

To successfully send and receive signals across the SCSI bus, the last device in the SCSI chain must terminate the bus. To terminate the SCSI bus, you normally connect a special bus terminator

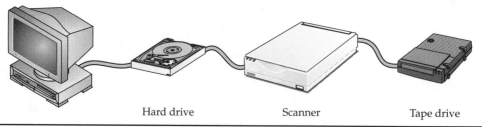

Hard drive   Scanner   Tape drive

Figure 12.12   The SCSI bus connects multiple devices to create a device chain.

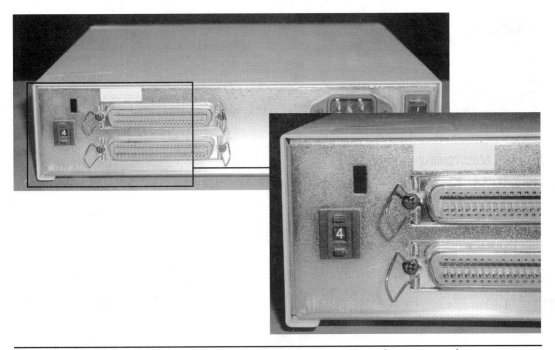

Figure 12.13   Devices in the SCSI device chain must have a unique device ID number.

to the outgoing port of the last device in the SCSI chain, as shown in Figure 12-15. Some devices, however, let you terminate the bus by using switches or jumpers. When you do this, you must later change the switches should you add another device to the SCSI chain.

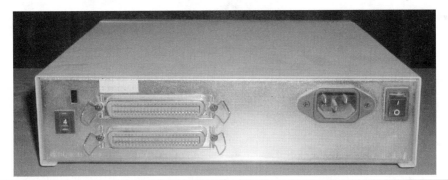

Figure 12.14   Most SCSI-based devices have an incoming and outgoing connector that connects the device to the bus.

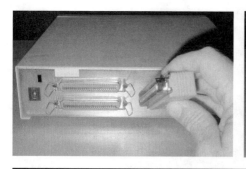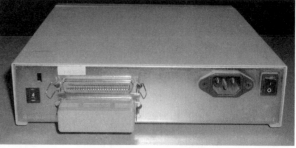

Figure 12.15   Using a terminator to mark the end of the SCSI chain

Understanding the Evolution of SCSI Controllers

Over the years, the SCSI specification has undergone several evolutions. Originally, the SCSI-1 specification used an 8-bit data bus with a speed of 5 MHz, which produced a transfer rate of 5MB per second. Today, the SCSI-3 (also called the Ultra3 SCSI) uses a 16-bit data bus with a 40 MHz bus speed. By transferring data two times per clock cycle, the SCSI-3 interface is capable of transfers of 160MB per second. As the SCSI specification has evolved, so too have the connectors that attach devices to the SCSI device chain. Table 12-5 briefly describes the four most common SCSI connectors.

Illustration	Connector	SCSI Specification
25 1 / 50 26	Low density 50	SCSI 1 and SCSI 2
25 1 / 50 26	High density 50	SCSI 1 and SCSI 2
34 1 / 68 35	High density 68	SCSI 2 and SCSI 3
40 1 / 80 41	80	SCSI 3 (RAID disk arrays)

Table 12.5   The Various SCSI Connectors

Understanding the IDE/ATA Bus

Chapter 16 examines disk operations in detail. As you will learn, disk drives normally connect to the system using an IDE (integrated drive electronics) or SCSI bus. An IDE hard disk, for example, is so named because it contains the controller the PC needs to communicate with the device. In other words, the device's electronics are built (integrated) into the device itself.

An IDE device must eventually connect to the motherboard. Although many users refer to the motherboard connection as the "IDE bus," most PC technical documents refer to the bus as the ATA bus. ATA is an abbreviation for AT Attachment, with corresponds to the fact that the bus first appeared when IBM released the PC/AT in 1984.

Figure 12-16 shows an IDE/ATA cable. The ATA bus is a 40-pin bus, whose pins are a subset of the 96-pin 16-bit ISA bus. Within the motherboard, the IDE/ATA bus connects to the PCI bus via South Bridge controller. Today, using direct memory access (and running in Ultra DMA Mode 5), the IDE/ATA bus can transfer data at 100MB per second.

As shown in Figure 12-16, most IDE cables let you connect two disk drives to the cable. When you connect two drives to the IDE/ADA cable, both drives will see all the signals that move across the wire. However, each drive must respond only to the signals destined for it. To specify which drive the signal is for, the bus uses a drive-select wire. Before the drives will properly respond to the drive-select signal, you must select one drive to act as the bus master and the second drive to act as a slave—which you can do by changing jumpers on each disk drive. Operationally, there is no difference between the master and slave drives other than the fact that when the system starts, the slave will use the Drive Active Slave Present (DASP) to inform the master that it exists. Then both drives will use the drive-select signal to determine which drive is to receive an incoming signal across the bus.

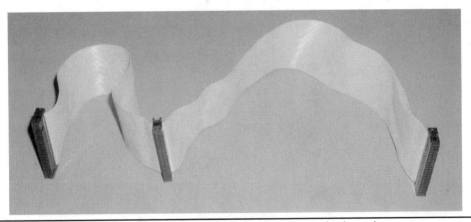

Figure 12.16   An IDE/ATA cable connects a disk drive to the motherboard.

Understanding the Universal Serial Bus (USB)

As you learned in previous chapters, the Plug and Play standard has made it much easier for users to install hardware cards within the PC. Using Plug and Play cards, users have less worries about interrupts and system resources (such as port and base-memory addresses). Over the past few years, a new way to connect devices to the PC, called the Universal Serial Bus (USB) has emerged that eliminates issues such as device interrupts and the need to restart your system when you install or remove a device. Using the USB, a user can connect up to 127 devices to his or her PC. Devices that you can attach to a USB include a mouse, printer, disk drive, network, keyboard, and more.

To start, although the word "serial" appears in the name Universal Serial Bus, the USB has absolutely nothing to do with the PC's serial port. The USB, shown in Figure 12-17, has a unique port and cable connector.

Normally, users connect USB-based devices directly to the USB port. However, if the user has more USB devices than the PC has ports, the user can connect a USB hub to the port and then attach devices (and other hubs) to the hub as shown in Figure 12-18. A unique characteristic of the USB is that users can add or remove devices while the system is active (called "hot swapping") without the need to shut down and later restart the PC.

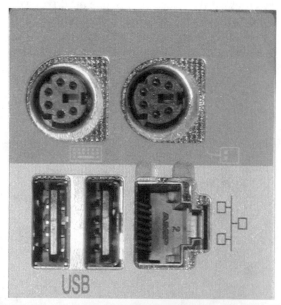

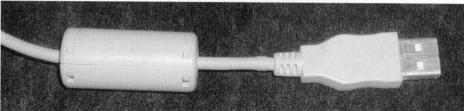

Figure 12.17   A USB port and cable

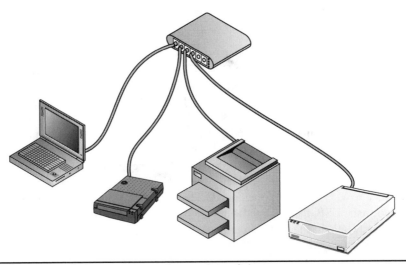

Figure 12.18 Using USB hubs to increase the number of devices users can connect to a USB

The original USB specification (USB 1.1) supported data transfer rates of 1.5MB per second. The USB 2.0 specification is much faster, supporting speeds of up to 60MB per second.

Taking a Closer Look at the USB Wires

The USB uses a simple four-wire cable, as described in Table 12-6. As you can see, the USB provides voltage that devices you connect to the bus can use to power themselves. The USB provides up to 5 volts of power that devices can use as their power source. Devices connected to the USB consume either "low" or "high" power amounts. A device that consumes low power draws 100mA. A high power device can consume up to 500mA. Devices that require more power that the USB can provide, must have their own power source.

How USB-Based Devices Communicate

Across the USB, each device must share the same communication path. Devices communicate across the USB by sending and receiving packets of information (much like networks use message packets to exchange information). Each USB device, therefore, must have a unique address, which the USB controller will assign to the device as the devices come online.

Cable	Purpose
1	+5V
2	–Data
3	+Data
4	Ground

Table 12.6 Wires Within the Universal Serial Bus

Within the message packets, a device sends to the controller is information the USB controller's device driver can use to identify the device.

As shown in Figure 12-19, a USB-based device may send a packet to the USB controller (a card or chip within the PC), which interrupts the CPU. The CPU, in turn, will invoke the USB controller's interrupt service handler. Within the handler, the code will examine the packet to determine which device sent the data. The USB interrupt handler will then hand off the data to the corresponding device driver.

When the operating system needs to send a message to a USB-based device, the operating system interacts with the corresponding device driver, which in turn, sends the data packet using the USB controller. Then each device connected to the bus examines the message to determine if the message is for it.

The USB has a fixed bandwidth, which the device you attach to the bus must share. The more devices you add to the USB, the less bandwidth the bus can allocate to each device. If a device requires more bandwidth than the bus can provide, you may need to move the device to a different controller that has fewer devices attached.

Understanding the FireWire (IEEE-1394) Bus

To support devices that require high bandwidth, such as digital cameras, camcorders, and high-resolution scanners, the Institute of Electrical and Electronics Engineers (IEEE) developed a special high-speed bus called the IEEE-1394. The IEEE modeled the bus after a bus designed by Apple Computer and Texas Instruments called *FireWire*. Sony also came out with their own version of the bus, which they refer to as *i.Link*. To avoid confusion, most books and magazines will refer to the bus as the IEEE-1394 or simply the 1394 bus.

Users connect devices to the bus in a daisy-chain fashion (up to 63 devices), or by first attaching nodes to the bus to which user then connect devices. Like the USB, devices on the 1394 communicate by sending and receiving data packets. Also like the USB, the 1394 bus eliminates issues surrounding

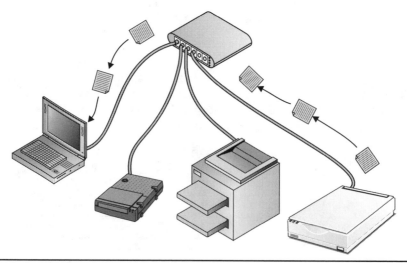

Figure 12.19   USB-based devices communicate by sending and receiving data packets.

device interrupts, and users can "hot swap" devices without having to restart their systems. Further, the bus provides power for devices users connect to the bus. Today, the bus communicates at data transfer rates ranging from 25MB to 50MB per second.

Understanding the PCMCIA Bus

Unlike desktop and tower PCs that have expansion slots within the system chassis, notebook PCs use a special card-based expansion slot called the PCMCIA slot. PCMCIA is an abbreviation for Personal Computer Memory Card International Association—the organization that defines the specification for the expansion slot and the small electronic cards users insert into the slot. Each PCMCIA card provides a specific function, such as support for a modem, network interface card, a SCSI bus adapter, or even a TV receiver.

As shown in Figure 12-20, most notebook PCs provide a PCMCIA slot into which you can insert and later eject a PCMCIA card (which users often refer to as simply a *PC card*). PCMCIA slots exist to provide expansion capabilities to notebook PCs. Most of the cards you can place within the expansions slots of a traditional PC have a PCMCIA counterpart. The PCMCIA bus is a 32-bit bus that operates at 33 MHz. Like the USB and FireWire (IEEE-1394) buses, the PCMCIA bus lets you hot swap cards, meaning, you do not need to shut down and later restart your system when you remove one card and insert another.

Figure 12.20   Inserting a PCMCIA card into a notebook PC

Type	Thickness
Type I	3.3mm
Type II	5mm
Type III	10.5mm

Table 12.7   The Evolution of PCMCIA Cards

The original PCMCIA cards were Type I cards, which, like the cards used today, measured 3.4 by 2.1 inches. Over time, the PCMCIA specification has evolved to support Type II and Type III cards. Table 12-7 briefly describes each PCMCIA card type.

Within Windows, when you use PCMCIA-based devices, the taskbar will normally contain an icon that corresponds to the PCMCIA slot:

PCMCIA slot icon

If you double-click the taskbar's PCMCIA icon, Windows will display the PC Card (PCMCIA) Properties dialog box, as shown in Figure 12-21, which briefly describes the cards currently installed in the slot.

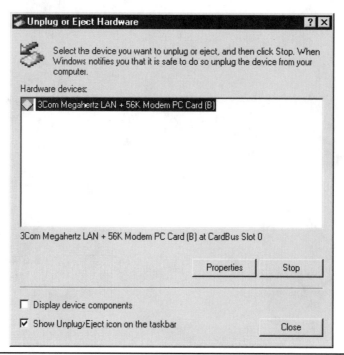

Figure 12.21   Using the PC Card (PCMCIA) Properties dialog box to view the PCMCIA cards in use

Pin	Purpose	Pin	Purpose	Pin	Purpose	Pin	Purpose
1	Ground	18	Programming Voltage (Vpp1)	35	Ground	52	Programming Voltage (Vpp2)
2	Data bit 3	19	Address 16	36	–Card Detect 1	53	Address 22
3	Data bit 4	20	Address 15	37	Data bit 11	54	Address 23
4	Data bit 5	21	Address 12	38	Data bit 12	55	Address 24
5	Data bit 6	22	Address 7	39	Data bit 13	56	Address 25
6	Data bit 7	23	Address 6	40	Data bit 14	57	RFU
7	–Card Enable 1	24	Address 5	41	Data bit 15	58	Reset
8	Address 10	25	Address 4	42	–Card Enable 2	59	–Wait
9	–Output Enable	26	Address 3	43	Refresh	60	–Inpack
10	Address 11	27	Address 2	44	–I/O Read	61	–Register Select
11	Address 9	28	Address 1	45	–I/O Write	62	Battery Voltage Detect 2
12	Address 8	29	Address 0	46	Address 17	63	Battery Voltage Detect 1
13	Address 13	30	Data bit 0	47	Address 18	64	Data 8
14	Address 14	31	Data bit 1	48	Address 19	65	Data 9
15	–Write Enable	32	Data bit 2	49	Address 20	66	Data 10
16	Ready/Busy	33	Write protect	50	Address 21	67	–Card Detect 2
17	+5V	34	Ground	51	+5V	68	Ground

Table 12.8   Pins Within the PCMCIA Bus

As discussed, the PCMCIA bus supports "hot swapping" of cards. Windows, however, prefers that you first stop the device by clicking the device name within the PC Card (PCMCIA) Properties dialog box and then clicking Stop. Windows will then display a message box telling you that it is safe for you to remove the card.

The PCMCIA bus uses 68 pins. Table 12-8 briefly describes each pin's purpose.

Leveraging PCI Shared Interrupts

As you have learned, within the PC, devices must have a unique interrupt that the device uses to signal the CPU. Within the PCI bus, devices can use a set of four special PCI-based interrupts to signal the PCI bus that the bus needs attention. Within the PCI bus, devices can share these

PCI-based interrupts. Beyond the PCI-bus, however, interrupts cannot be shared. As such, the PC (normally the BIOS) maps the PCI-based interrupts to unused ISA interrupts. Users refer to this mapping as *PCI IRQ steering*. Depending on your system BIOS and operating system support for PCI steering, you may have multiple PCI cards mapped to the same ISA interrupt. For example, if you use the System Information Utility to display interrupt information, you may find shared interrupts, as shown in Figure 12-22. By allowing devices to share interrupts in this way, the PCI bus extends the number of interrupts the PC can support.

Within Windows, you can enable or disable PCI IRQ steering using the PCI Bus Properties dialog box shown in Figure 12-23.

USE IT Within the PCI Bus Properties dialog box, you can specify the tables you want Windows to use to resolve PCI interrupt mapping. By default, Windows will use the four tables listed, in the order listed. If, however, you encounter an interrupt conflict with a PCI-based device, you may find that one of the four tables maps the interrupt correctly. In such cases, you can direct Windows to use only that table for mapping. If you use the Device Manager to examine the Computer Properties dialog box, as shown in Figure 12-24, you may find that several interrupts are listed as an "IRQ Holder for PCI Steering." This setting indicates that the PCI bus has programmed the interrupt to handle shared PCI interrupts. When a PCI-based interrupt occurs, the interrupt handler can examine a register within the PCI bus to determine which device is raising the interrupt and then handle the interrupt accordingly.

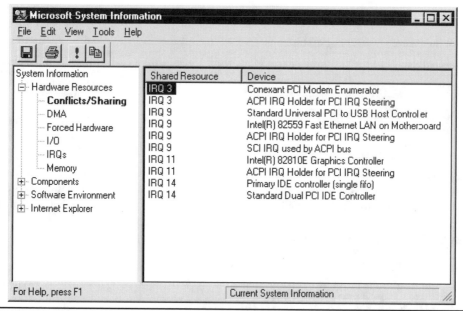

Figure 12.22 PCI-based devices sharing ISA interrupts

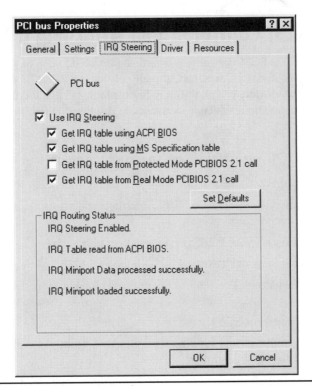

Figure 12.23   The PCI Bus Properties dialog box

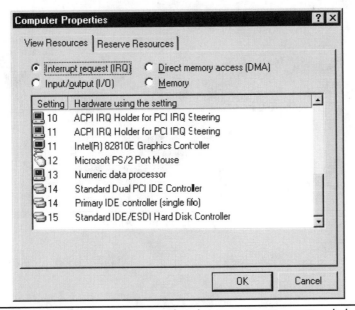

Figure 12.24   Viewing interrupt assignments within the Computer Properties dialog box

Installing a SCSI Controller and Attaching a SCSI Device

As shown in Figure 12-25, a SCSI controller is a card you install into one of your PC's expansion slots. If you are using a notebook PC, you can normally purchase a PCMCIA-based SCSI card. If the card is a Plug and Play device, you may simply be able to install and use the card. Otherwise, you first must determine your system's available interrupts, as discussed in Chapter 4, and then assign an unused interrupt to the card.

USE IT   To install a SCSI controller card into your system, perform these steps:

1. If necessary, identify your system's available interrupts and assign an unused interrupt to the card (using jumpers or switches).
2. Shut down and power off your PC. Unplug the system unit.
3. Gently remove the system unit cover.
4. Locate an unused expansion slot, remove the slot cover, and insert and secure the SCSI controller card.
5. Replace the system unit cover.
6. Plug in, power on, and start your system. After Windows starts, you may need to install a device driver for the SCSI controller.

Figure 12.25   A SCSI controller is a card you install into your PC.

If your system starts successfully, use the Windows Device Manager to view the SCSI controller. If the controller appears, you are ready to attach devices to the controller. To attach your first device to the SCSI controller, perform these steps:

1. Shut down and power off your PC. Unplug the system unit.

2. Determine a unique SCSI ID number (in the case of your first device, one that does not conflict with the SCSI controller) for the new device and assign the number to the device using a switch or jumpers on the device.

3. Use a SCSI cable to attach the device to the controller.

4. Terminate the SCSI device chain by attaching a terminator to the device's outgoing port or by using switches or jumpers on the device.

5. Plug in and power on the device.

6. Plug in, power on, and start your system. After Windows restarts, you likely must install a device driver for the device.

Viewing Your System's SCSI Devices

The two most common conflicts that occur when you attach a device to a SCSI controller are two devices using the same device ID and an improper bus termination. Often, when your system starts, your monitor will display a list of the SCSI devices connected to your PC, along with each device's ID. This SCSI device list appears during the startup process before your system displays the Windows logo.

USE IT   To view devices connected to a SCSI controller from within Windows, you can use the Device Manager, as shown in Figure 12-26. If a device does not appear in the list, make sure the device has a unique SCSI ID number and that you have not terminated the SCSI bus before the device.

To view the SCSI device list using the Device Manager, perform these steps:

1. Select Start | Settings | Control Panel. Windows will open the Control Panel window.

2. Within the Control Panel, double-click the System icon. Windows will open the System Properties dialog box.

3. Within the System Properties dialog box, click the Device Manager tab. Windows will display the Device Manager sheet.

4. Within Device Manager, select View devices by connection. The Device Manager will display a list of controllers to which you can attach devices.

5. Within the controller list, click the plus sign that precedes the entry for your SCSI controller. Device Manager will display a list of the SCSI devices connected to the controller.

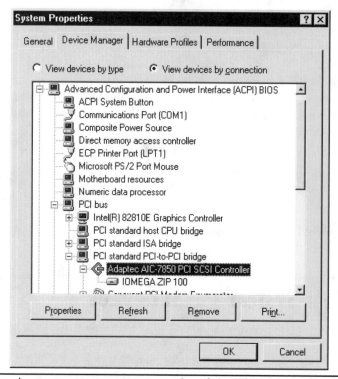

Figure 12.26   Using the Device Manager to view a list of devices connected to the SCSI controller

Connecting a Device to an Existing SCSI Device Chain

To connect a new SCSI device to an existing SCSI chain, you must ensure that you have a unique device ID for the device and that you properly terminate the SCSI bus after you install the device. In addition, you should not "hot swap" SCSI devices, which means that before you install a new device within the SCSI device chain, you should shut down and power off your PC and power off each of the devices within the device chain.

USE IT   Specifically, to install a new SCSI device within an existing SCSI-device chain, perform these steps:

1. Shut down and power off your PC. Unplug the system unit.

2. Power off each device within the SCSI device chain.

3. Determine a unique SCSI ID number for the new device and assign the number to the device using a switch or jumpers on the device. The SCSI controller will treat devices with the higher ID numbers with the higher priority.

4. Determine the location within the SCSI device chain where you want to place the device. If you simply append the device to the chain, you must terminate the device and make sure the device that previously marked the end of the chain is no longer terminated.

5. Plug in and power on the device.

6. Power on other devices within the SCSI device chain.

7. Plug in, power on, and start your system. After Windows restarts, you likely must install a device driver for the device.

Resolving SCSI Bus Termination Problems

 USE IT   As you have learned, before the SCSI bus can successfully communicate, you must terminate the bus using a terminator or jumpers or switches within the last device in the chain. If, when your system starts, your screen does not display a list of SCSI devices, and if you cannot view the devices within the Windows Device Manager, your SCSI bus may not be terminated. Normally, troubleshooting a bus that is not terminated is fairly easy, because the SCSI controller normally will not locate any devices on the bus.

If you append a device to the SCSI bus and later you cannot access the device, the bus may be terminated prior to the device. Some SCSI devices let you terminate the bus using jumpers and switches that may make it difficult to detect that the bus terminates beyond the device.

Positioning SCSI-Based Devices in the Device Chain for Optimal Performance

Depending on your SCSI controller type, the SCSI controller can support between 7 and 15 devices. Each device within the SCSI device chain must have a unique ID number. As you might guess, sometimes two or more devices try to use the SCSI bus at the same time. When such conflicts occur, the SCSI controller will give priority to the device with the lower ID number.

USE IT   Normally, you will assign the device ID number 7 (or 15) to the SCSI controller. Then, you will assign a value in the range 0 to 6 (or 0 to 14 if your controller supports 15 devices) to the device. As you connect devices to the SCSI bus, keep in mind that the controller will first service devices with the lower device ID number. Therefore, you should assign lower device ID numbers to your more important devices. For example, by assigning a disk drive a low ID number, you ensure that the SCSI controller will respond to disk operations quickly. In contrast, your system performance will likely not suffer much if a scanner must wait for an instant before it can use the SCSI bus. As such, you would assign the scanner a high device ID.

Extending the SCSI Cable Length

Normally, as you examine PC buses you will find that the faster the bus, the shorter the bus length. The system bus, for example, which is the PC's fastest bus, is constrained to the section of the motherboard that contains the CPU, RAM, the BIOS, and other key chips in the chipset. In contrast, a SCSI bus is normally 3 to 6 feet in length. If you extend the length of a bus too far, the signal does not have sufficient time to travel across the bus.

USE IT   If, for some reason, you cannot fit the devices you must attach to the SCSI bus within an area with the same proximity, you may be able to use a regenerator or an extender to increase the length of your SCSI bus. (Some articles may refer to these devices as *expanders*.) To start, a regenerator is simply a device you attach to the SCSI bus that boosts the signals strength across a longer cable, much like a repeater. The regenerator does not require a unique ID number and does not appear (to the SCSI controller) as a device on the bus.

An extender is a device that essentially breaks the SCSI bus into two distinct segments—each of which has its own terminator. The extender connects to the SCSI bus and then to a cable, such as a fiber-optic cable that extends the length of the bus. At the far end of the cable is a second extender that connects to another SCSI bus. The extender is transparent to the SCSI controller and devices on the bus. For more information on SCSI extenders and regenerators, visit the Paralan Web site at www.paralan.com.

Installing a USB Controller

Today, most newer PCs and notebook computers have one or more built-in USB ports. If your PC does not have a USB port, you can purchase a USB controller that you insert into an expansion slot. Depending on the type of controller you purchase, the card may provide two or four sockets to which you can attach USB devices.

USE IT   A USB controller should be a Plug and Play device, which means that you should not have to worry about interrupts and port addresses when you install the card. To install a USB controller in your PC, perform these steps:

1. Shut down and power off your PC. Unplug the system unit.

2. Gently remove the system unit cover.

3. Locate an unused expansion slot, remove the slot cover, and insert and secure the USB controller card.

4. Replace the system unit cover.

5. Plug in, power on, and start your system. After Windows starts, you may need to install a device driver for the controller.

If your PC has a USB port, but you have running out of connectors, you can simply purchase a USB hub device to which you can then attach your USB-based devices. Next, remove an existing device from the USB port, plug in the hub, and then plug your devices into the hub. By stringing hubs together in this way, the USB lets you connect up to 127 devices to your PC.

Testing Your System's USB Support

Some older operating systems do not support the USB. One of the easiest ways to determine your system's support for the USB is to run the Intel USB System Check program shown in Figure 12-27. Using the USB System Check program, you can determine if your operating system and PC support USB operations.

USE IT To download and install the Intel USB System Check program, perform these steps:

1. On the Web, several sites (which you can quickly locate by searching for "USBReady" within a search engine) offer the Intel USB System Check program for download. Using your Web browser, connect to the Web site www.usb.org/data/usbready.exe.

2. The Web site, in turn, will display the File Download dialog box you can use to download the program.

3. Within the File Download dialog box, select the folder into which you want to download the program and then click the Save button to begin the download.

4. After the download completes, use Windows Explorer to browse the folder into which you downloaded the program and then double-click the program file to launch the program.

Figure 12.27   Using the Intel USB System Check program to determine USB support

Monitoring the USB's Available Bandwidth

Within a PC, the USB has a fixed amount of bandwidth, which the devices you attach to the USB controller must share. As you attach more devices to the USB, the bus performance will decrease. In some cases, because of limited bandwidth, a device may not function correctly. Most USB-based devices that require large amounts of bandwidth report their needs to the USB controller. Using the Windows Device Manager, you can view the USB controller's bandwidth usage, as shown in Figure 12-28. Depending on the devices you have attached to the controller, sometimes you must move a device to a different USB controller in order to provide the device with sufficient bandwidth.

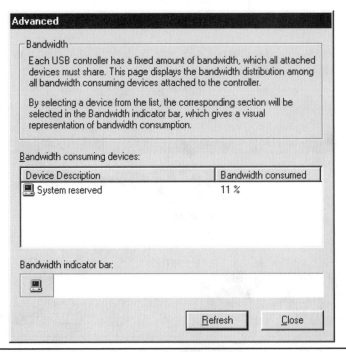

Figure 12.28   Viewing the USB controller's bandwidth use

 To display your USB controller's bandwidth use, perform these steps:

1. Select Start | Settings | Control Panel. Windows, in turn, will open the Control Panel window.

2. Within the Control Panel, double-click the System icon. Windows will open the System Properties dialog box.

3. Within the System Properties dialog box, click the Device Manager tab. Windows will display the Device Manager sheet.

4. Within the Device Manager, click the plus sign (+) that precedes the Universal Serial Bus controllers entry. Windows will expand the list.

5. Within the controller list, double-click the Universal Host Controller entry. Windows will display the Controller's Properties dialog box.

6. Within the Properties dialog box, click the Advanced tab and then click Bandwidth. Windows will display the dialog box shown in Figure 12-28, which you can use to view your USB device's bandwidth use.

Monitoring the USB's Available Power

As you have learned, the Universal Serial Bus provides power (up to 5 volts) that a device connected to the bus can use to power itself. If a device requires more power than the USB can provide, the device must provide its own power source. Using a USB, you can connect up to 127 devices to your PC. As you can guess, the USB would likely run out of power for devices to use somewhere along the line. Using the Windows Device Manager, you can view the USB controller's available power and the amount of power devices consume, as shown in Figure 12-29. Depending on the devices you have attached to the controller, sometimes you must move a device to a different USB controller in order to provide the device with sufficient power. Also, you may be able to find a USB hub that provides power to the devices that you connect to the hub.

USE IT To display your USB controller's bandwidth use, perform these steps:

1. Select Start | Settings | Control Panel. Windows, in turn, will open the Control Panel window.

2. Within the Control Panel, double-click the System icon. Windows will open the System Properties dialog box.

3. Within the System Properties dialog box, click the Device Manager tab. Windows will display the Device Manager sheet.

4. Within the Device Manager, click the plus sign (+) that precedes the USB controller's entry. Windows will expand the list.

5. Within the controller list, double-click entry that corresponds to the USB hub. Windows will display the hub's Properties dialog box.

6. Within the Properties dialog box, click the Power tab and then click Power Properties. Windows will display the Power dialog box shown in Figure 12-29, which you can use to view your USB device's power use.

Installing IEEE-1394 Support

To support users who manipulate large multimedia files, such as large scanned images, digital photographs, and digital camcorder video, many newer systems provide an IEEE-1394 (or FireWire) port. If your system does not have a 1394 bus, you can install a 1394 controller card within one of your PC's expansion ports.

USE IT A 1394 controller should be a Plug and Play device, which means you should not have to worry about interrupts and port addresses when you install the card. To install the controller card in your PC, perform these steps:

1. Shut down and power off your PC. Unplug the system unit.

2. Gently remove the system unit cover.

3. Locate an unused expansion slot, remove the slot cover, and insert and secure the 1394 controller card.

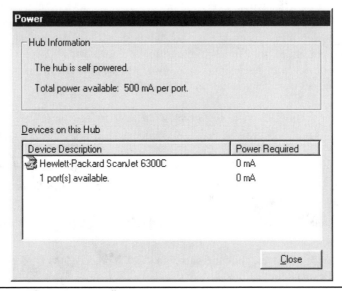

Figure 12.29   Viewing the USB controller's power use

4. Replace the system unit cover.

5. Plug in, power on, and start your system. After Windows starts, you may
   need to install a device driver for the controller.

After you successfully install the 1394 controller card, the Windows Device Manager should
display an entry for the controller. Most 1394 adapter cards will provide two connectors to which
you can connect devices. As discussed, the 1394 bus lets you daisy chain devices much like you
would SCSI-based devices. If you require more devices, you can attach a 1394 hub to the connector,
to which you can connect up to a number of devices (many PC-based hubs support up to 6 devices;
however, some larger hubs let you connect up to 16 devices).

Common System Components

Throughout this book, most of the chapters focus on a specific PC component, such as the CPU, BIOS, motherboard, or RAM. This chapter, in contrast, examines several components that either do not fit well into a different chapter or do not offer sufficient content to merit a chapter of their own. To start, you will examine the keyboard and mouse, and operations you can perform to improve the user's keyboard and mouse performance. Then you will examine the PC's sound card and audio capabilities. Finally, you will examine the steps you must perform to add a video camera or TV receiver to your PC.

Understanding the Keyboard

The three most commonly used parts of the PC are the keyboard, monitor, and mouse. Most users normally do not give the keyboard a second thought, until either a key sticks or stops working. Depending on the age of your PC, your keyboard will either use a large or small connector to attach to the system unit, as shown in Figure 13-1.

Depending on the connector type your keyboard uses, the connector will contain five to six pins, whose signals will differ, as Table 13-1 briefly describes.

Figure 13.1   Connecting a keyboard to the PC system unit

Pin	Large Connector	Small Connector
1	Keyboard clock	Keyboard data
2	Keyboard data	Not used
3	Reserved	Ground
4	Ground	+5V
5	+5V	Keyboard clock
6	Not present	Not used

Table 13.1 Cables Within the Keyboard Connector

Users normally refer to PC keyboards as QWERTY keyboards due to the first six keys on the keyboard's top row of character keys:

Taking a Closer Look at the Keyboard Controller

Built into the keyboard is a chip called the *keyboard controller*. The chip's purpose is to convert the keys the user presses into scan-code values the keyboard sends to the PC. For example, when the user presses the A key, the keyboard controller will generate the scan-code value 31. When Windows (actually the keyboard's device driver) reads input from the keyboard, software receives the scan-code values, as opposed an ASCII character that corresponds to the key pressed.

Actually, as it turns out, when you press a key, the keyboard controller generates a scan-code value. When you release the key, the keyboard controller generates a break code (which is equivalent to the original scan code value plus 128). By watching for the break-code value, the BIOS can determine when it should start repeating a keystroke when a user leaves a key pressed.

Each time your system starts, the power-on self-test (POST) interacts with the keyboard controller to ensure that the keyboard is working properly. If the keyboard controller returns an error status, the POST will display a keyboard-related error message, and the system will not start.

Different Ways to Connect a Keyboard to the PC

In addition to using a standard cable to connect a keyboard to a PC, some newer keyboards support Universal Serial Bus (USB) connections. The advantage of connecting a keyboard to a USB port is that you free up the interrupt request (IRQ) the standard keyboard cable requires.

Some PCs provide support for an infrared (IR) keyboard connection that eliminates the keyboard cable from the user's desk. The IR-based keyboard, much like a TV remote control, requires a clear line of sight between the keyboard and the IR receiver. An IR-based keyboard is very well suited for a PC/monitor combination that bundles the system unit, disk drives, and monitor into the same package, as shown in Figure 13-2.

If your PC does not provide built-in support for an IR-based keyboard, you can purchase an IR-based keyboard upgrade that provides an infrared keyboard and receiver. Normally, you will connect the receiver to the USB port.

Figure 13.2   Using an IR-based keyboard connection

Figure 13.3 An ergonomic keyboard and a flat keyboard

Ergonomic and Windows Keyboards

For over 20 years, most PCs have used traditional flat PC keyboards. In response to users complaining about sore hands and wrists (and due to lawsuits related to carpal tunnel syndrome), many manufacturers now offer an ergonomic keyboard that curves the keyboard surface and provides a better "resting place" for the wrist, as shown in Figure 13-3. The shape of the ergonomic keyboard is designed to reduce strain on the user's wrist and hands.

USE IT   If you do not have an ergonomic keyboard, you may want to use a small wrist pad, similar to that shown in Figure 13-4, that slightly elevates your wrist to reduce strain. As you shop for a wrist pad, you may find a pad that also offers an antistatic pad you can touch to discharge static before you touch your PC, keyboard, or mouse.

Today, many manufacturers sell "Windows keyboards," so named because the keyboard provides special buttons you can use to interact with your system, as shown in Figure 13-5. One button, for example, might launch your e-mail program. A second button may launch your Web browser. The goal of Windows keyboard is let you perform common operations that normally require a mouse click directly from your keyboard, so you do not have to move your hand between the keyboard and mouse.

Figure 13.4 Using a wrist pad with a keyboard to reduce wrist strain

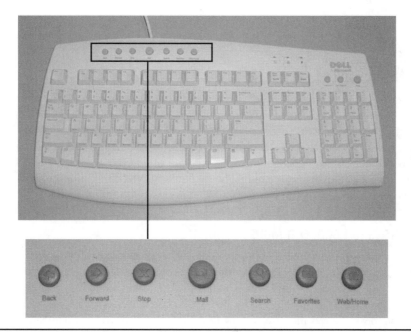

Figure 13.5   A "Windows keyboard" includes buttons that launch common Windows-based operations.

Understanding the Mouse

Depending on the type, your mouse will normally connect to either a serial port or to a bus connector, as shown in Figure 13-6 (although USB-based mice exist).

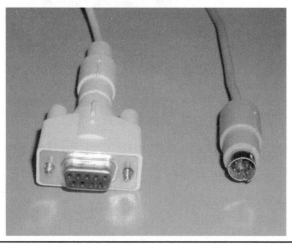

Figure 13.6   Connecting a mouse to the PC system unit

Today, most mouse devices connect to a bus-mouse port (as opposed to a serial port or USB port). Table 13-2 briefly describes the pins within bus-mouse cable.

Taking a Closer Look at the Mouse Controller

Built into the mouse is electronics collectively called the *mouse controller*. The electronics' primary purpose is to convert the mechanical movement of the mouse rollers into values Windows can use to move the mouse pointer across the screen and to signal mouse-click operations that Windows can process. The mouse controller sends its signals across the mouse cable to the connector at the back of the PC. Within the PC, the mouse controllers generate an interrupt to which the CPU responds by executing the interrupt handler built into the mouse device driver. Each time you move your mouse, the mouse generates an interrupt to which the CPU must respond.

Different Ways to Connect a Mouse to the PC

In addition to using a standard serial or bus cable to connect a mouse to a PC, some newer mouse devices support USB connections. The advantage of connecting a mouse to a USB port is that you free up the IRQ the serial port or bus mouse requires. Also, just as some PCs provide support for an IR keyboard connection, the same is true for infrared mouse devices—which eliminate the mouse cable from your desk. As was the case with an IR-based keyboard, you can purchase an IR-based mouse and receiver. Again, the IR receiver normally connects to the USB.

Other Mouse Considerations

Earlier in this chapter, you examined ergonomic keyboards and keyboard wrist pads. To reduce wrist strain, some users purchase mouse pads that provide wrist support. Also, many users find that using a large trackball, as opposed to a mouse, relieves strain on their wrists.

Depending on the size and resolution of a user's monitor, as well as the current screen contents, some users may have trouble locating the mouse pointer on the screen. To make the mouse pointer easier to see on the screen, some users will use the Mouse Properties dialog box to enable mouse trails. As shown in Figure 13-7, they essentially display a chain of mouse pointers that appear to chase the primary mouse pointer across the screen as the user moves the mouse.

Pin	Purpose
1	Mouse data
2	Not used
3	Ground
4	+5V
5	Clock
6	Not used

Table 13.2 Pins Within the Bus-Mouse Cable

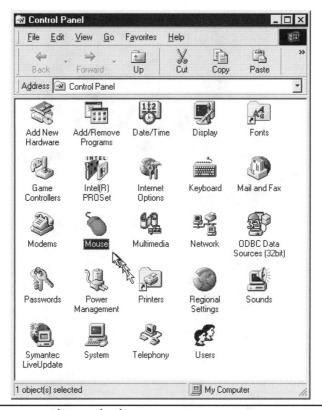

Figure 13.7   Using mouse trails to make the mouse pointer easier to see

Today, to simplify scrolling through a document or Web page, many mouse devices provide a scrolling roller, similar to that shown in Figure 13-8. To scroll using the roller, you simply click your mouse within the document and move the roller with your finger to move up or down within the document.

If you travel with a notebook PC that you use for presentations, you may want to purchase a wireless (handheld) mouse-clicker. Using the handheld clicker device, you can stand several feet away from your PC and use the device to simulate right or left mouse-click operations, which in turn, will let you move forward or backward within a presentation program, such as PowerPoint. The mouse clicker device requires that you connect a small receiver to your notebook, normally to a serial or USB port.

Understanding the Sound Card

Due to the popularity of multimedia applications, all PCs sold today include a sound card to which you can connect speakers and a microphone, and often, a MIDI (Musical Instrument Device Interface) device, such as an electronic keyboard. Normally, to help you connect the correct devices to the

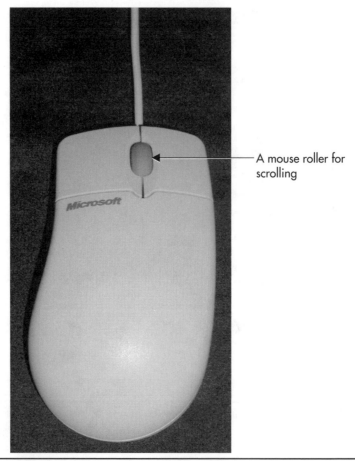

A mouse roller for scrolling

Figure 13.8   A mouse with a roller between the right and left buttons for scrolling

sound card ports, the sound card will display small icons that correspond to the correct device near each port, as shown in Figure 13-9. Also, some cards may color code the ports.

Depending on your preferences, the speakers you connect to a sound card can run the gamut from the traditional low-end (inexpensive) battery-powered speaker to high-end expensive Bose speakers, complete with tweeters and woofers similar to those you might normally attach to a stereo system. Some sound cards provide ports for left and right speakers, and some high-end cards support four speaker connections.

Built into the sound card is a music synthesizer that lets the card create the sounds that correspond to a specific musical instrument. Depending on the sound card's capabilities, the number of instruments the card can synthesize will differ. High-end sound cards, for example, provide support for up to 128 different instruments.

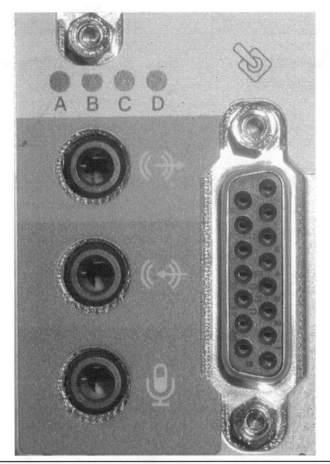

Figure 13.9 Using icons to identify sound card ports

If you are using battery-powered PC speakers, you should purchase an inexpensive AC power adapter (which you can find at any electronics store) to provide your speakers with constant power. Also, the headphones you attach to a stereo system use a larger plug than what will fit into a sound card. However, most electronics stores provide plug converters into which you can insert your existing headphone plugs so that you can then plug the headphones into the sound card.

With Digital Sound, the Number of Bits Dictates Quality

As you may recall from your school days, sound travels through the air (or other objects such as water) in a wavelike pattern, hence the term *sound waves*. As shown in Figure 13-10, different sounds will create a different pattern of waves.

Figure 13.10   Displaying different sound patterns using the Windows Sound Recorder

To represent sounds using ones and zeros, the PC must assign a value that represents the sound's amplitude (the wave's height) at a specific time. An 8-bit sound card, for example, uses values in the range 0 to 255 to represent sound levels, as shown in Figure 13-11. A 16-bit card, in contrast, uses values in the range 0 to 65,535.

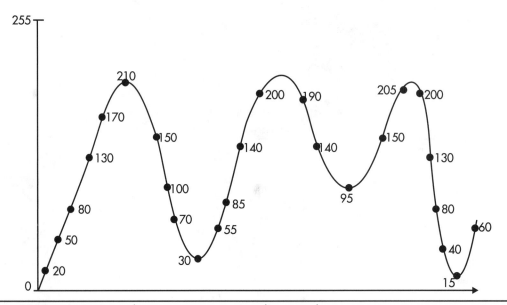

Figure 13.11   Assigning values to represent a signal's strength

Bit Depth	11 KHz	22 KHz	44 KHz	48 KHz
8-bit	337,920 bytes	675,840 bytes	1,351,680 bytes	1,474,560 bytes
16-bit	675,840 bytes	1,351,680 bytes	2,703,360 bytes	2,949,120 bytes
20-bit	844,800 bytes	1,689,600 bytes	3,379,200 bytes	3,686,400 bytes
32-bit	1,351,680 bytes	2,703,360 bytes	5,406,720 bytes	5,898,240 bytes

Table 13.3   File Sizes Created by a Sound for a 30-Second Recording at Different Sampling Rates and Bit Sizes

Because the 16-bit card has more values to work with, the card can more accurately represent slight variations within the sound wave, which produces a higher-quality digital representation of the sound. The cost of this increased quality is twice the data size, which means, for example, that using a 16-bit card to record a sound will generate a file twice as large as the file of a sound recorded on an 8-bit card.

Today, many sound cards use 20 bits to represent sounds, which provides values in the range 0 to 1,048,575. In addition, some high-end cards use 32 bits to represent sounds using values in the range 0 to 4,294,967,295. The more values the sound card can use to represent a signal, the higher the sound quality. However, as the number of bits the sound card uses increases, so too does the size of resulting audio files.

Understanding Sound Card Sampling Rates

Sound cards create digital representations of analog sound waves by measuring the sound wave's amplitude at specific times and then, depending on the number of bits the card uses to represent sounds, assigns a value that represents the signal's strength. The frequency at which the card examines the signal is the *sampling rate*. The more frequently the card samples the signal, the better the card can represent the corresponding sound. Common sampling rates include 11 KHz (11,264 samples per second), 22 KHz, 44 KHz, and 48 KHz. Audio cards provide the different sampling rates to let you trade quality for file size. Table 13-3 lists the file sizes a sound card will create for a 30-second recording using 8-, 16-, 20-, and 32-bit cards at different sample rates.

Video Cameras

With the growing popularity of Internet-based chat programs and the availability of low-cost high-speed Internet connections, such as DSL, many users are attaching small video cameras to their PCs, similar to that shown in Figure 13-12. In fact, some PCs now ship with such cameras built in. Although most video cameras today are black and white, color cameras exist.

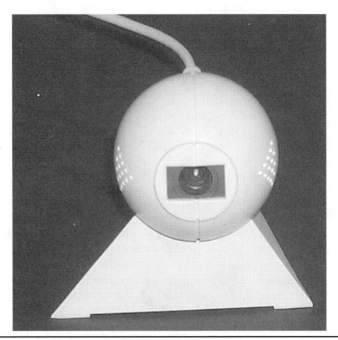

Figure 13.12 Connecting a video camera to a PC

Normally, the video cameras connect to the USB, which provides the camera with the amount of power the camera needs to operate. Depending on the speed of each user's Internet connection, the quality of the video users can exchange across the Internet will vary. Full-motion video, such as a movie on a DVD, plays at 30 frames per second. Across the Internet, most users will consider a frame rate of a few frames per second acceptable. To increase the frame rate video cameras can achieve, many cameras and video players support video compression, which reduces the amount of data that PCs must transmit across the Internet to represent the video image. Figure 13-13 illustrates a video image produced by a PC-based video camera.

Using a TV Tuner

Depending on the information you must have to perform your job, or if you simply want to take a break from the long hours you spend at your PC, you may find that installing a TV tuner within your PC lets you keep abreast with current news and information. Figure 13-14, for example, illustrates a PC displaying a TV channel within a window.

Figure 13.13 Using a PC-based camera to generate a video image

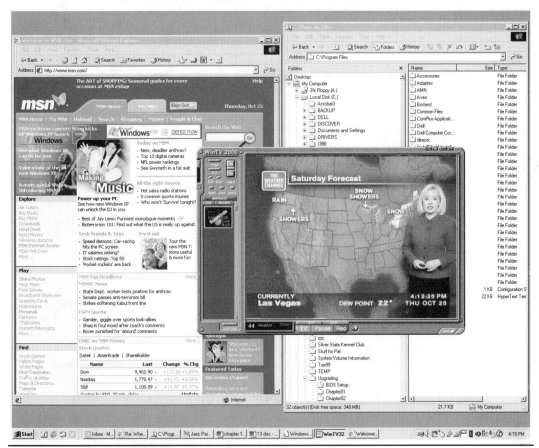

Figure 13.14 Viewing a TV program within a window on the PC screen

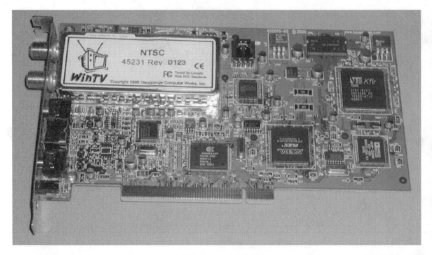

Figure 13.15 TV tuners can be internal or external.

USE IT   For around $100, you can install an internal or external TV tuner on your PC. Most external tuners connect to the USB. Likewise, the internal tuners install within a PCI expansion slot. After you connect the TV tuner to your PC, you can then connect the tuner to your cable TV or satellite cable, or you can attach a small antenna to the tuner to receive your local channels. Figure 13-15 illustrates an internal and an external TV tuner. Then you can view TV programs within a window on your screen or using your monitor's full screen.

Most TV tuner cards come with video capture software you can use to digitize video data. If you have a video camera, for example, that does not connect to an IEEE-1394 (FireWire) port, or if your PC does not have such a port, you can connect your VCR directly to the TV tuner card to capture and digitize your videos.

Cleaning the Keyboard

Over time, if you are like most users, your keyboard will accumulate dust, cookie crumbs, fuzz, and more. Some users will use a vacuum to clean their keyboard. However, doing so, if you are not careful, can put your keyboard's electronics at risk of the static electricity the vacuum generates. In Chapter 18, you will learn that many users vacuum spilled ink toner and paper fragments from their printer by attaching a straw to the end of the vacuum to create an extension that reduces the risk of shock and which creates a powerful suction. In the case of a keyboard, attaching a straw to a vacuum in this way may also prevent you from inadvertently vacuuming a loose key from the keyboard. In addition, many users, as shown in Figure 13-16, will use an aerosol blower to blow dust and other items from within the keyboard.

USE IT   If you should spill soda or some other drink on your keyboard, immediately shut down your system and disconnect the keyboard from your PC, which will turn off power to the

Figure 13.16   Using an aerosol blower to clean a keyboard

keyboard's electronics. Then, using a screwdriver, you can normally open your keyboard to expose the electronics, as shown in Figure 13-17.

If the keyboard is still wet, use a paper towel or napkin to absorb the spill. You may want to let the keyboard sit and dry or use an aerosol blower to blow off any condensation that remains. If your keyboard is sticky, it will be more likely to attract and hold dust in the future. You have a choice. First, you may want to reassemble your keyboard and see if it still works. If it does, you may not want to do any more cleaning, because by trying to clean off the "stickiness" you may damage the

Figure 13.17   Viewing a keyboard's electronics

keyboard's electronic components. If you want to clean your keyboard, use rubbing alcohol and a cotton swab. Do not use tap water because it may contain minerals that remain on the electronics after the water evaporates. Some keyboards use small springs within each key, which you can easily misplace and which can be difficult to put properly back in place. The fewer keys you must remove from your keyboard the better. As you remove keys, you may want to align the keys on your table to simplify your installation process when you are ready to place the keys back onto the keyboard.

Using a System Without a Keyboard

By default, each time the PC starts, the POST will interact with the keyboard controller to ensure that the keyboard is working correctly. If the keyboard controller returns an error, the POST will display an error message and the system will not start. If you have one or more servers within your office, you may want to make it more difficult for users to access the server by removing the server PC's keyboard. However, if you simply remove the keyboard, the server will not successfully restart in the future because the POST will not receive a status value from the keyboard.

 Fortunately, many newer CMOS startup programs let you disable the keyboard, as shown in Figure 13-18. After you disable the keyboard within the CMOS setup, the POST will not perform its keyboard tests, which lets the system start without an attached keyboard.

Extending a Keyboard or Mouse Cable

 Most keyboards and mouse devices come with a six-foot cable you can use to attach the device to the PC. Depending on where your PC sits in relation to your desk, sometimes your keyboard or mouse simply can't reach the PC. In such cases, you purchase a PC or mouse cable

```
                                SETUP
  Main    Advanced    Security    Boot      Exit

  Peripheral Configuration                        Configure the
                                                  keyboard.


  Serial Port A          [Auto]

  Parallel Port          [Auto]

    Mode                 [Bi-directional]



  Keyboard               [Enabled]

  Mouse                  [Enabled]               <- -> Select Menu
                                                 ↑  ↓ Select Item
                                                 Tab    Select Field
                                                 Enter Select Sub-Menu
                                                 F9     Setup Defaults
                                                 F10    Save and Exit
                                                 ESC    Exit
```

Figure 13.18   Using the CMOS setup program to disable the keyboard

extender, which are normally also six feet in length, which should give you ample cable length to position your keyboard and mouse as you require. Extending the keyboard and mouse cable by an additional six feet will not introduce hardware problems.

Improving Keyboard and Mouse Responsiveness

Each time you press a key on your keyboard, the keyboard controller sends the PC a scan code that corresponds to the key. When you later release the key, the keyboard controller sends the PC a break code that corresponds to the key. As you know, when you hold down a key, the PC will repeat the key you press. To determine whether you are holding down the key, Windows waits to receive the break code. If you do not release the key within a fixed interval of time, the BIOS (not your keyboard) will begin to repeat the key.

Within Windows, the keyboard *repeat delay* specifies the interval of time Windows will wait for the break code to occur before it begins to repeat the key that is currently pressed. The keyboard *repeat rate*, in turn, specifies how fast Windows will repeat the key.

USE IT To make your keyboard more responsive to the user, you should specify a minimum repeat delay value (so that your system will start repeating the key sooner), and a fast repeat rate (which causes the system to repeat the key faster). To change your keyboard settings within Windows, perform these steps:

1. Select Start | Settings | Control Panel. Windows, in turn, will open the Control Panel window.

2. Within the Control Panel, double-click the Keyboard icon. Windows will display the Keyboard Properties dialog box, as shown here.

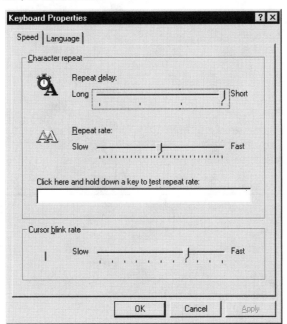

3. Within the Keyboard Properties dialog box, use the two sliders to select a short repeat delay and a fast repeat rate.

4. Click OK to close the Keyboard Properties dialog box and to put your settings into effect.

Just as you can use the Control Panel to improve your keyboard responsiveness, you can also use it to fine-tune your mouse responsiveness. Within Windows, you can use the Mouse Properties dialog box shown in Figure 13-19 to change your mouse pointer speed and the double-click speed. Depending on the version of Windows you are using and your mouse type, the options that appear may differ.

The mouse pointer speed controls how fast Windows moves the mouse pointer across the screen as you move your mouse across your desk. The double-click speed controls how fast you must click your mouse two times in succession for Windows to treat the operation as a double-click. Although experienced users may want to decrease the double-click time, first-time users may find Windows easier to manipulate if you increase the double-click time (so they can click their mouse twice at a slower speed and Windows will still recognize the operation as a double-click).

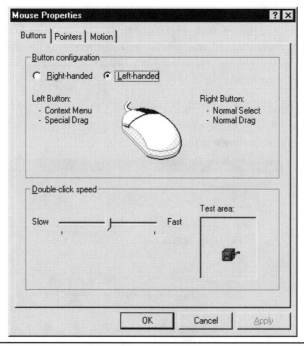

Figure 13.19 The Mouse Properties dialog box

USE IT   To change you system's mouse responsiveness, perform these steps:

1. Select Start | Settings | Control Panel. Windows will open the Control Panel window.

2. Within the Control Panel, double-click the Mouse icon. Windows, in turn, will display the Mouse Properties dialog box, shown Figure 13-19.

3. Within the Mouse Properties dialog box (which may differ in appearance, depending on your Windows version and mouse type), use the Pointer speed slider to increase or decrease the mouse pointer speed. (Depending on your mouse driver, the number of tabs that appear within the Properties dialog box may differ. You may need to select various tabs before you locate the Pointer speed slider.) As you move the slider, Windows will immediately increase or decrease the speed of your mouse pointer.

4. Next, depending on your Mouse Properties dialog box, the steps you must perform to change your mouse double-click speed will vary. In some systems, you may use a slider to increase or decrease the speed. In other systems, you may simply double-click a button at the speed you want to perform your future double-click operations.

5. Click OK to close the Mouse Properties dialog box and put your settings into effect.

Cleaning a Mouse

USE IT   If, when you move your mouse across your desk, your mouse does not seem as responsive as it once was, your mouse ball or rollers are likely dirty. To start, shut down your system and then disconnect your mouse from your PC, to turn off power to the mouse electronics. Then turn your mouse over, and you will find that you can open it to remove the ball and gain access to the rollers, as shown in Figure 13-20.

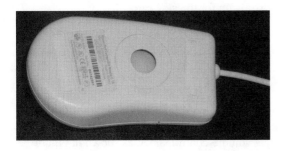
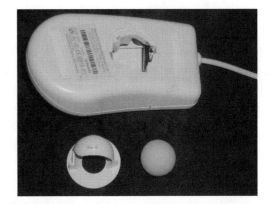

Figure 13.20   Opening the mouse for cleaning

After you remove the mouse ball, you may want to use an aerosol blower to clean dust from within the mouse. Next, using a cotton swab and rubbing alcohol, clean the rollers within the mouse. Then wash and dry the mouse ball. After you are sure the mouse ball and rollers are dry, put the ball in place, close the mouse, and reconnect the mouse to the PC.

Upgrading Your Sound Card

As you have learned, sound cards can differ by the number of bits they use to represent sounds, the number of instruments they can simulate, the number of speaker ports, and more. Upgrading a sound card is actually quite easy; you simply replace your existing card with the new card. Most newer sound cards are Plug and Play devices, which means that you normally do not need to worry about IRQ and other resource settings.

Today, many PCs implement sound card capabilities using a chip on the motherboard. If your system does not use a sound card, but instead uses a chip, you must use the CMOS Setup program, as discussed in Chapter 6, to disable the chip's use before you can use a new sound card.

USE IT Specifically, to upgrade your sound card, perform these steps:

1. Shut down your system and unplug your system unit from the power outlet.

2. Remove your speaker and microphone cables from your existing sound card.

3. Gently open your system unit, and if you are using a sound card (as opposed to a chip on the motherboard), remove your existing sound card.

4. Insert and secure your new sound card within an expansion slot.

5. Cover your system unit and then plug in and power on your system.

6. After Windows starts, install the device driver software for the new card.

Adjusting the Sound Card Volume

USE IT When you use a sound card and speakers, you can control the volume in one of three ways. To start, the Windows taskbar will normally contain a small speaker icon. If you click the taskbar speaker icon, Windows will display a volume-control slider, as shown in Figure 13-21. If the volume-control slider does not appear on your taskbar, you can use the Control Panel's Multimedia Properties dialog box to control your volume and to place the volume-control slider's icon on the taskbar.

Second, as shown in Figure 13-22, most PC speakers provide volume-control knobs you can use to adjust the volume. Finally, some sound cards themselves have a volume-control knob.

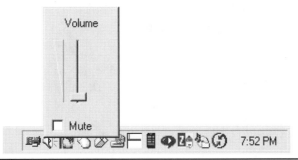

Figure 13.21   Controlling volume using the Windows taskbar volume-control slider

Unfortunately, because the sound card's volume-control knob is on the back of the sound card, which is at the back of your PC (which is likely under your desk), getting to the sound card's volume control can be difficult.

Because the Windows volume-control slider is the easiest to access, most users use it to adjust the volume. To start, you may want to place the volume-control slider at its middle setting and then use either the speaker's volume-control knobs or the sound card's volume-control knob to fine-tune the volume for the midlevel volume. After that, you can use the Windows volume-control slider to increase or decrease the volume, based on your current speaker and sound card setting.

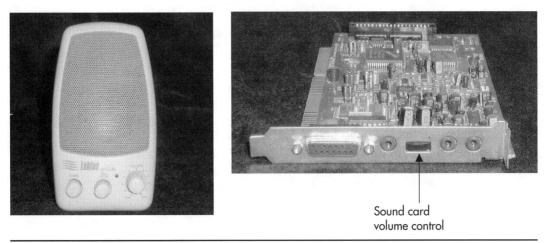

Sound card
volume control

Figure 13.22   Using speaker and sound card volume control knobs

Troubleshooting a Sound Card

If your system has a sound card but does not generate any sounds, first perform the following steps to troubleshoot the problem. Note that as you perform these steps, you may want to use a program such as the Windows Media Player to play back a sound (or MIDI music file) that you should be able to hear if your sound card and speakers are working.

USE IT   To use the Media Player to play a song, perform these steps:

1. Select Start | Programs | Accessories. Windows will display the Accessories submenu.
2. Within the Accessories submenu, select Media Player (if the option appears) or select Entertainment | Media Player. Windows will open the Media Player window.
3. Within the Media Player, select File | Open. The Media Player will display the Open dialog box.
4. Within the Open dialog box, double-click a media file. You can then click the Media Player Play button to play the sound file as you troubleshoot your sound card problem.

Next, to troubleshoot your sound card, perform these steps:

1. Click the Windows taskbar speaker icon and make sure the volume control slider is not in a low-volume position.
2. Check your speaker volume-control knob to make sure it is not in a low-volume position.
3. Check your sound card to see if it provides a volume control; if so, make sure the volume control knob is not in a low-volume position.
4. Select Start | Settings | Control Panel. Windows, in turn, will open the Control Panel window. Within the Control Panel, double-click the Multimedia icon. Windows will open the Multimedia Properties dialog box, as shown next. Within the Multimedia Properties dialog box, make sure the current playback device corresponds to your sound card. If not, use the pull-down list to select your sound card. Next, again within the Multimedia Properties dialog box, click the speaker icon. Windows, in turn, will display a Properties dialog box specific to your device. Within the dialog box, make sure the Use Audio Features On This Device radio button is selected.

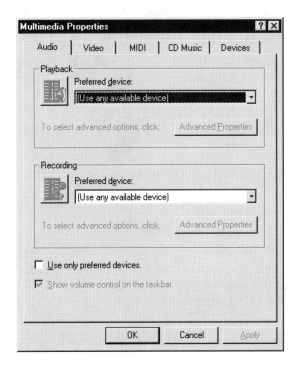

5. If your sound card is still not working, you may have a device-driver conflict. Using the Windows Device Manager, remove the sound card and direct Windows to delete the device driver. Then reinstall the device driver that accompanied your card.

6. If your card is still not working, you may have an IRQ conflict. Use the Windows Device Manager to determine your system's current IRQ and resource settings. Refer to the documentation that accompanied your card to determine how to change your card's settings.

▶ **NOTE**

Using your Web browser, visit the Web site http://windowsmedia.com/radiotuner/default.asp, where you can reach a wide range of Internet-based radio stations that you can listen to using your PC sound card and speakers.

Using Windows to Fine-Tune Audio Performance

Depending on your sound card type, Windows may let you fine-tune several settings that improve the card's performance, using the card's Advanced Audio Properties dialog box Performance sheet, as shown in Figure 13-23.

USE IT To display the Advanced Audio Performance dialog box, perform these steps:

1. Select Start | Settings | Control Panel. Windows will open Control Panel window.
2. Within the Control Panel, double-click the Multimedia icon. Windows will open the Multimedia Properties dialog box.
3. Within the Multimedia Properties Audio sheet, click Advanced Properties. Windows will display the Advanced Audio Properties dialog box.
4. Within the Advanced Audio Properties dialog box, click the Performance tab. Windows will display the Performance sheet, shown in Figure 13-23. Within the Performance sheet, use the fields to fine-tune the settings your device supports.

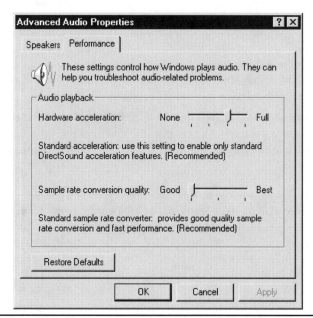

Figure 13.23 The Advanced Audio Properties dialog box Performance sheet

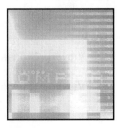

CHAPTER 14

Modem Operations

TIPS IN THIS CHAPTER

ach day, hundreds of millions of users connect to the Internet to send and receive e-mail, to "surf" the Web, to participate in chat sessions, and more. The vast majority of these users will connect to the Net using a modem. Many users will connect using a dial-up account and a 56 Kbs (56 kilobits per second) modem. Other users will connect using a faster cable modem or DSL (digital subscriber line) connection. Still others will gain access using a wireless (cellular-based) modem or satellite connection. Finally, others will connect to the Net using a high-speed connection, such as T1 or T3 line.

This chapter examines modem operations in detail. To start, the chapter examines the modem's basic operations. Next, the chapter examines the various ways you can use a modem to connect to the Net. Finally, the tips section examines ways you can benchmark and improve modem performance.

Understanding Modulation and Demodulation

A modem is an internal or external hardware device that sends and receives data over traditional phone lines (or other communication channels, such as a television cable). Modems are so named because to send a signal over a transmission line, a modem must modulate a digital signal within the PC (which the PC represents using ones and zeros) into an analog waveform suitable for transmission. Then, the receiving modem must demodulate the analog signal back into a digital format suitable for use by the receiving PC. Figure 14-1 illustrates the process of modulating and demodulating signals.

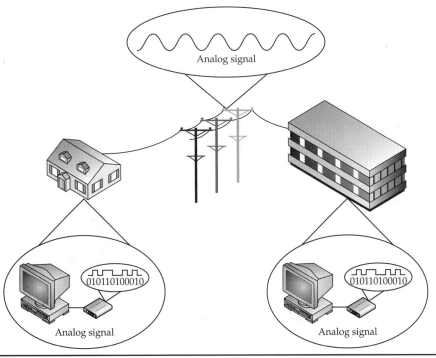

Figure 14.1   The sending modem modulates a digital signal into analog while the receiving modem demodulates the analog signal back to a digital form.

Traditional PC modems send data one bit at a time over phone lines. Within the modem is a special chip called a Universal Asynchronous Receiver Transmitter (UART).When a modem sends data, the UART oversees much of the communication process, breaking a byte value into its individual bits for transmission. In contrast, to receive data, the UART bundles incoming bits back into bytes.

Before two modems can communicate, the modems must agree on several data-communication parameters, such as the speed at which the modems will send data across the wire. In addition, the modems must agree on several settings that correspond to how the modems will represent data.

Many books and articles refer to modem communications as *asynchronous communications*, because the sender and receiver do not synchronize when a transmission will occur. Instead, a modem simply listens to the communication channel. The sending modem will first send a *start bit*, which essentially "wakes up" the receiving modem and prepares it to receive incoming data.

Across the transmission lines, the data communication speed (often called the *baud rate*) controls how fast the bits will travel. Data communication speed is expressed in terms of bits per second, not bytes per second. A 56K modem, for example, can send and receive 56K bits per second, or 56 Kbs. After the receiving modem receives the start bit, the modem knows, based on the communication speed, when each data bit will arrive. For example, at 9,600 bits per second, a data bit will arrive (after the start bit occurs) every 1/9,600 of a second (or roughly every tenth of a millisecond). To receive the incoming data, the UART will examine the data communication wire at intervals that correspond to the communication speed, as shown in Figure 14-2.

Normally, modems will represent data using eight bits. But, most data communication programs provide the ability to represent a data message using four to eight bits. The number of bits a modem uses to represent data defines the message's *data bits*. Behind the scenes, as the sending modem's UART sends data bits and the receiving UART repackages the data into bytes, the UARTs will package the data they send and receive based on the number of data bits specified.

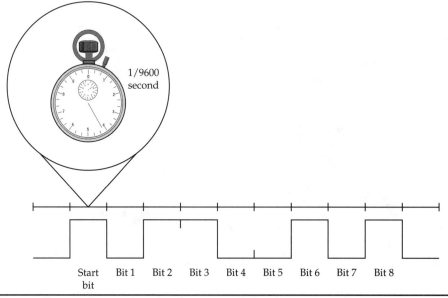

Figure 14.2   Following the start bit, data bits arrive at fixed time intervals.

As a signal travels across the transmission medium, errors can occur. To help modems recognize simple errors (errors that may convert one bit from a one to a zero, or vice versa), data communication software often direct the UART to place a *parity* bit following the last data bit.

Depending on the data communication settings, a parity bit will either make the total number of bits whose value is 1 an even number or an odd number. For example, in the data bits 00000111 are three bits that are one, meaning an odd number of bits. If the data communication settings are using *odd parity*, the parity bit would be 0, so that when you count the number of bits set to 1, the total will remain odd. In contrast, if the data communication settings are using even parity, the parity bit would be set to 1, so when you add up the number of data bits that are set to 1 (three), and you add the parity bit, you would get an even value (four). The following table illustrates the parity bit value to maintain an odd parity:

Data Bits	Parity Setting	Total Bits	Result
00000000	1	1	Odd
00000001	0	1	Odd
00000011	1	3	Odd
01010101	1	5	Odd

Likewise, the following table illustrates the parity bit value to maintain even parity:

Data Bits	Parity Setting	Total Bits	Result
00000000	0	0	Even
00000001	1	2	Even
00000011	0	2	Even
01010101	0	4	Even

The parity bit's purpose is to help the data communication hardware (or software) to determine when an error occurs during the data transmission. For example, assume that odd parity is being used. The sender will send a data word and parity setting that contains an odd number of bits, such as 00001100 and 1. If the receiver receives an even number of bits 00000100 and 1, the receiver knows that somewhere in the data a bit error occurred. As such, the receiver can notify the sender that the data was bad so that the sender can resend it. The following table illustrates how parity can detect a bit error when odd parity is in use (meaning the number of one bits in the data bits and the parity bit should be odd):

Data Bits	Parity Setting	Total Bits	Result
00000000	1	1	Correct
00000001	1	2	Error
00000011	0	2	Error
01010101	1	5	Correct

Whether the data communication settings use an odd or even parity does not matter. They simply need to use the same setting. Because parity can detect only a one-bit error, sometimes the data communications will not use a parity bit (meaning, they will set the settings to none), and then rely on a stronger error-detection protocol to detect errors.

Finally, depending on the communication parameters, the UART may place a *stop bit* after the parity bit. The stop bit is optional. Figure 14-3 illustrates how a modem may package data for transmission across a phone wire.

How Baud Rate Differs from Data Bits per Second

When discussing data communication speeds, users will often refer to the term *baud rate*. In general, the baud rate specifies the number of bits (total bits, not simply data bits) the sender and receiver will exchange per second. Common baud rates include 28.8 Kbs and 56 Kbs. Assume, for example, that the baud rate is 28.8 Kbs (or 28.8×1024 bits per second, roughly 29,492 bits per second). As you have learned, bits are not all data bits. Some of the bits correspond to start bits, stop bits, parity bits, and so on. As such, the number of data bits the connection can send per second will depend on the other bit settings. Assuming, for example, that the data communication is using 1 start bit, 8 data bits, 1 parity bit, and 1 stop bit (11 bits total), the 28.8 Kbs connection's maximum data throughput would become roughly 2,682 bytes per second (29,492÷11, or roughly 2KB per second).

By calculating the number of bytes per second in this way, you can approximate the download times for various file sizes, as shown here:

File Size	28.8 Kbs (roughly 2Kb per second)	56.6 Kbs (roughly 4Kb per second)
30KB	15 seconds	7.5 seconds
100KB	50 seconds	25 seconds
500KB	2 minutes, 10 seconds	1 minute, 5 seconds
1MB	4 minutes	2 minutes

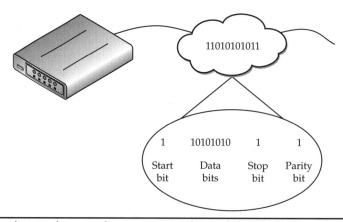

Figure 14.3   To exchange data, modems use a start bit and data bits, as well as an optional parity bit and optional stop bit.

These download times are simply rough approximations, because they do not take into account that modems can often compress data to improve throughput.

Modems Use Compression to Improve Performance

As you have learned, modems send data over a phone line as a series of ones and zeros. To increase the amount of data a modem can send during a period of time, modems often compress data. For example, assume that the modem must send the data that represents a Web-page graphic. Within the image file are long repeating sequences that might, for example, correspond to the image's background color:

```
11110000111100001111000011110000111100001111000011110000
```

In this case, rather than sending the individual bits, the modem can send a message that tells the receiver that the series 11110000 repeats six times, which significantly reduces the number of bits the UARTs must exchange.

Just as two modems must agree on the data communication speed and the number of start, data, parity, and stop bits, the modems must agree on the compression scheme the sender will use to compress the data and the receiver will later use to decompress it. As you know, when two modems connect, the modems exchange audible tones. In addition, the modems exchange several initialization packets. Using the tones and packets, the modems negotiate their initial settings, which includes determining the compression schemes they will use. Users refer to the modem's initialization as a *handshaking process*. Common compression schemes include Microcom Network Protocol (MNP) version 5 (MNP 5) and V.42bis (the letters *bis* are French for encore, which many international protocols use to represent the first revision of a protocol).

Understanding Error Correcting Protocols

As discussed, as a signal travels across a phone line, errors may occur that change the corresponding data. Parity checking provides a first-line defense against simple errors (one-bit errors). Unfortunately, if an error causes two bits, for example, to change their values, a parity check will not detect the error:

Original Value	Parity Setting	Ending Value	Parity Setting	Status
00000000	0	00000011	0	Parity remains even, error not detected
10000001	0	00000011	0	Parity remains even, error not detected
11000011	0	00000011	0	Parity remains even, error not detected
11111111	0	00000000	0	Parity remains even, error not detected

Because parity has limited error-detection capability, many systems will disable parity and rely on a more complex error-detection technique. Some of the error-handling techniques, called *error-correcting codes*, not only detect errors, they can determine which bit or bits have changed and then correct the data so the modems do not have to retransmit the errant data. To use error-correcting codes, the modems must send additional bits with each word that the error-correcting software can use to detect and, if necessary, correct bit changes. As such, the use of error-correcting codes consumes bits (bandwidth) that could otherwise have been used to send data. However, because they eliminate the need to retransmit errant data, most modems employ error-correcting codes during their transmissions. Common error correcting codes include the Microcom Networking Protocol (MNP) versions 1 through 4 and V.42.

Understanding Issues Surrounding the 56 Kbs Communication Speed

Throughout this chapter, you will read about modem technologies such as ISDN and DSL that deliver high-speed bandwidth over phone connections. However, traditional dial-up modems appear to have stalled at 56 Kb per second. The 56 Kb per second "limit" on data communication speed corresponds to limitations within older analog-based telephone switching equipment. In many locations, the telephone equipment may limit the data speeds you can achieve to 35 Kb per second. Then, depending on the quality of your phone lines, the speed may become even lower.

If your phone company has fast-switching equipment available, and your connection manages to travel only through similar fast-switching components, your dial-up connection, in the best case, will achieve speeds of up to 53 Kb per second. Because speeds beyond 53 Kb per second consume more electricity, the Federal Communication Commission (FCC) currently limits dial-up connections to a maximum of 53KB per second.

To achieve 56 Kbs modems, manufacturers implemented several different protocols, the two most common being x2 and K56flex. Normally, when a user purchases a modem, the modem support one of these two standards. The problem with the two standards is that to take advantage of the technologies, Internet service providers had to support both modem types (meaning they had to purchase and install both types of modems). Then, depending on the user's modem type, the user had to dial into a specific number to connect to the corresponding modem type. To standardize the protocols, manufacturers released the V.90 and V.92 protocols. Unfortunately, the new standards do not help users who own older modems.

Understanding Integrated Services Digital Network (ISDN) Modems

One of the first higher-speed alternatives the phone company offered to online users was the Integrated Services Digital Network (ISDN). Using ISDN connections, a user could achieve data throughput speeds of 128 Kbs. Companies (or wealthy users) willing to make a substantial monthly investment in ISDN lines could achieve data throughput as high as 1.5 Mbs!

To use an ISDN connection, users first must sign up with the phone company for an ISDN connection. Although ISDN uses standard phone lines, the phone company imposes distance requirements on ISDN connections that restrict access to locations that reside within a specific distance from a phone-company station.

The "digital" in Integrated Digital Services Network corresponds to the fact that ISDN does not convert signals to analog for transmission. Although most users refer to the ISDN hardware as a "modem," the device actually does not modulate or demodulate signals. Instead, all signals that travel across an ISDN connection are digital. Many books and magazines refer to the ISDN device as an *adapter*.

A unique aspect of ISDN is that a user can attach a PC, phone, and even a fax machine to the same connection. In fact, a user can even use two ISDN-based devices at the same time.

Standard ISDN divides the connection into three channels. Two of the channels, called *bearer* (or *B*) *channels*, send and receive data (or voice or fax data) at 64 Kbs. The third channel, the *delta* (or *D*) *channel*, transmits the ISDN control signals that oversee the communication.

If a user needs only data support (meaning a phone or fax call is not in progress), ISDN will allocate both channels to the data communication, providing data throughput at 128 Kbs. If, however, the user must place a call or send or receive a fax, while the user is online, ISDN will use one channel for data and the second channel for the phone or fax call. After the call completes, ISDN will resume using two channels for data. Best, ISDN will perform the channel allocations without the need for user intervention. The user simply makes a call or sends a fax. Behind the scenes, ISDN will allocate channels as necessary.

Users (and the telephone company) refer to the two-bearer channel ISDN as the basic rate interface ISDN, or BRI ISDN. In contrast, the primary rate interface ISDN, or PRI ISDN, lets businesses use up to 23 channels operating at 64 Kbs. Using the 23 channels, BRI ISDN supports data speeds up to 1.5 Mbs.

Understanding Cable Modem Connections

Across the world, three industries run cables to most homes: the power, telephone, and cable TV industries. Today, most users connect to the Net using a standard, ISDN, or DSL (discussed later in this chapter) connection from the phone company. As the Internet's growth exploded, cable TV companies didn't take long before realizing they were sitting on some very valuable bandwidth.

A *cable modem* is a device that connects a PC to the cable that normally sends signals to your television. To attach a PC to a cable system requires that you first establish an Internet account with your cable provider. Your provider, in turn, will give you a box, the cable modem that connects to the cable TV wall outlet. The box, in turn, connects to an Ethernet network interface card (NIC) you install within your PC, as shown in Figure 14-4. When you use a cable modem to connect to the Net, you essentially create a network that consists of your PC and the cable TV company.

The cable TV company sends data down the cable at different frequencies. Each channel you view on your TV occupies a specific frequency range. As you change channels, your TV "tunes in" the corresponding frequency, and hence the term *TV tuner*. To provide support for data communication, the cable company normally allocates one frequency range for outgoing data and one for incoming data. The cable company shares these frequency ranges between you and others in your neighborhood. The cable modem tunes in the frequencies it needs to send and receive data.

Using a cable modem connection, you can achieve data transmission rates as high as 1.5 Mbs, depending on the monthly fees you are willing to pay. Because cable modem signals take advantage of an existing cable infrastructure, cable TV companies can offer high-performance connections for a relatively low price.

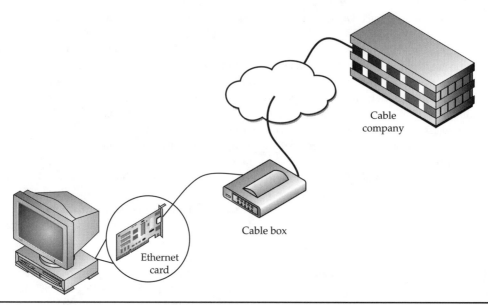

Figure 14.4   Connecting a PC to a cable modem

Understanding Digital Subscriber Line (DSL) Connections

DSL is an Internet communication service offered by phone companies that provides users and businesses a range of speed and cost alternatives. To describe their DSL offerings, many phone companies precede the letters *DSL* with a letter that corresponds to a specific DSL type or speed. For example, ADSL stands for *asymmetrical DSL*, an offering that offers a faster download speed than upload speed. In contrast, SDSL, or *symmetrical DSL*, offers the same upload and download speeds. Table 14-1 briefly describes the common DSL offerings.

DSL Type	Description	Download Speed	Upload Speed
ISDL	ISDN DSL	144 Kbs	144 Kbs
HDSL	High bit-rate DSL	1.5 Mbs	1.5 Mbs
SDSL	Symmetric DSL	1.5 Mbs	1.5 Mbs
ADSL	Asymmetric DSL	Based on distance, up to 9 Mbs	Based on distance, down to 384 Kbs
RADSL	Rate Adaptive DSL	Varies	Varies
VDSL	Very high bit-rate DSL	Up to 25 Mbs	Up to 3 Mbs

Table 14.1   Common DSL Offerings

To connect your PC to a DSL connection, you must first sign up for DSL service from the phone company. Then, you must establish an account with an Internet service provider (which may again be the phone company). The Internet service provider, in turn, will establish an Internet address (an IP address) for your PC. If you are using DSL to connect an office-full of computers to the Internet, the Internet service provider will reserve a range of Internet addresses for your use. Then, as shown in Figure 14-5, you connect a DSL modem to the incoming phone lines. If you are attaching one PC, you will use a Category 5 cable to connect the modem to an Ethernet NIC that resides within the PC. If you are attaching a network, you will connect the DSL modem to a network hub.

Using a Satellite Connection

The major problem with ISDN, cable, and DSL connections is that the services aren't available in many geographic regions. Although one would expect such holes in the coverage area to appear in rural areas, the services are often not available just outside of most major cities. For users who find themselves in locations such technologies cannot service, a satellite-based receiver (one quite similar to the one that receives television signals) may provide a good option—at least with respect to download operations.

Like a TV cable modem, a satellite connection will allocate a range within its transmission frequency spectrum that it uses to send data. Unlike a cable modem's two-way connection, many existing satellite connections provide a one-way data communication. To send data across the Internet, such as e-mail or even the mouse-click operations you perform to select hyperlinks on the Web, you must have a dial-up connection that works in conjunction with the satellite downlink. In other words,

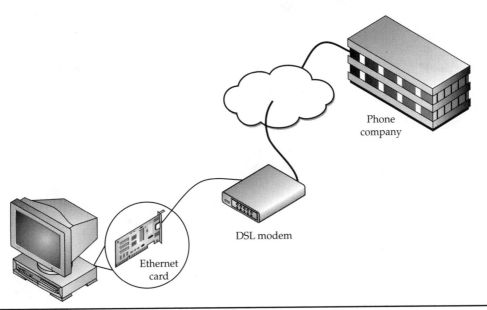

Figure 14.5 Connecting a PC or network to a DSL connection

the satellite sends all incoming data to your PC, as shown in Figure 14-6. The phone-based dial-up connection sends outgoing data. To keep the input and output operations coordinated, you must dial into a computer that resides within the satellite provider's facilities. Recently, companies have begun offering two-way satellite communications that use satellite antennae to receive and send data. These early systems use asymmetric communication, meaning the download speed is substantially faster than the upload speed. For more information on two-way satellite communication, visit www.starband.com and www.direcpc.com.

If you spend considerable time "surfing" the Web, a satellite connection can give you download speeds up to 500 Kb per second (upload speeds for phone-based systems depend on the speed of your modem connection, and for two-way satellite-based systems, are in the 40Kb to 60Kb per second range). If you must send large amounts of data across the Net, the dial-up-based output connection will restrict your system's performance. To connect your PC to a satellite system, you connect the satellite receiver to a PCI- or USB-based modem.

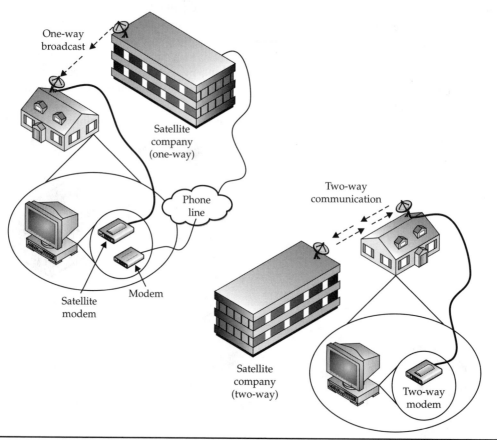

Figure 14.6   Connecting a PC to a satellite-based connection

> **FACT**

Users refer to connections that have unequal upload and download speeds as asymmetric communications.

Understanding Wireless Modems

If you travel with a notebook PC, you likely understand how challenging it can be to find a phone outlet to which you can connect your PC modem. Many "road warriors" travel with an acoustic coupler they can use to connect the PC modem to a payphone. Others may connect their modems to cellular phones, as shown in Figure 14-7.

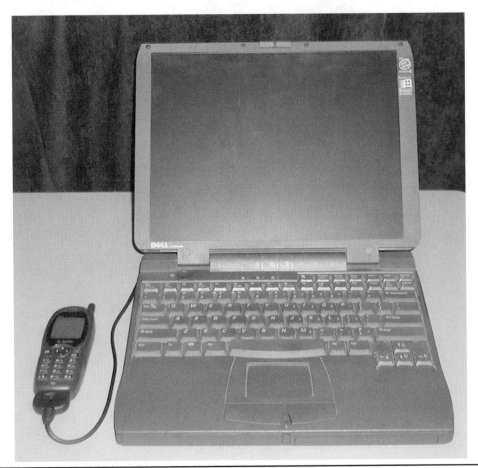

Figure 14.7   Connecting a notebook modem to a cellular phone

To simplify the connection process, many manufacturers now offer a PCMCIA-based wireless modem, similar to that shown in Figure 14-8. The wireless modem operates much like a cellular phone—which means that the modem coverage will differ. Most major cities provide coverage for wireless modems. Unfortunately, wireless modems, like cellular phones, frequently have difficulty communicating deep within a building. Further, the wireless modems are still restricted to the slow cellular speeds, which may fall in the range 9600 bps to 14.4 Kbs. Some companies do offer high-speed

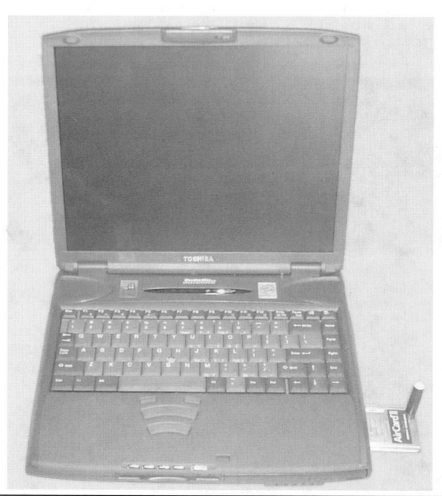

Figure 14.8 Using a PCMCIA-based wireless modem

wireless connections with speeds up to 128 Kbs and better reception capabilities. However, such services are expensive and are normally available only in large metropolitan areas.

Understanding Leased-Line Connections

To achieve very high data throughput speeds, many businesses and schools turn to *leased lines*, which provide a collection of channels, each running at 64 Kbs. A T1 leased line, for example, which consists of two pair of wires, provides the throughput of 24 channels (multiplexed frequencies on the wires) running at 64 Kbs, which provides speeds up to 1.5 Mbs. Such high data rates do not come cheap. On average, the monthly fees for a T1 line will exceed $1,000. In contrast, a T3 line provides the speed of 28 T1 lines (using only two pair of wires!) to produce a data throughput speeds up to 45 Mbs, which, depending on your location, may cost five to ten times T1. Beyond T3 are optical-carrier networks (whose standards are called OC-1, OC-3, and so on) that offer speeds in the gigabits per second range.

► *FACT*

The OC-192 standard provides support for data throughput speeds approaching 10 gigabits per second.

Upgrading Your Modem

Depending on the connection type you choose, such as a dial-up, DSL, cable-based, or satellite-based connection, your choice of modem will differ. For example, when you use a DSL or cable-based connection, you will actually use a NIC, as opposed to a modem, to make your connection. In some cases, the cable-modem or DSL provider you select may provide a service technician to provide the installation for you.

If you are using a dial-up connection, you must choose between an internal and external modem. The advantage of an external modem is that you can easily move the modem to a different PC, and you can use the modem's light to assist you in troubleshooting. Fast external modems normally connect to a USB port or to a bidirectional parallel port. Most internal modems fully support Plug and Play operations, which simplifies their installation. After you install a modem, you must install device driver software that lets Windows interact with the modem.

USE IT   Should you experience problems connecting to your modem, the Windows help facility provides an excellent troubleshooter that will walk you step-by-step through the process of identifying the common connection problems. Rather than waste pages repeating the steps here, you should use the Windows help facility to troubleshoot your modem connection by performing these steps:

1. Select Start | Help. Windows will open the Windows Help window.
2. Within the Index tab, search for "modems troubleshooting" and then click Display. The Windows Help will display a link you can use to launch the Modem Troubleshooter. Click the link to begin the troubleshooting process.

Interpreting Modem Lights

USE IT   If you are using an external modem to connect to a standard phone line, your modem will normally have a series of LED lights similar to those shown in Figure 14-9. By examining the lights, you can understand your modem's current operations, and you can potentially troubleshoot modem problems. Table 14-2 briefly describes the lights that may appear on an external modem.

If you do not have an external modem, you may want to download and install a shareware program such as Modemsta, shown in Figure 14-10, that you can download at www.webattack.com/shareware/com/swdialup.shtml, which displays a window containing lights that correspond to the current modem operations.

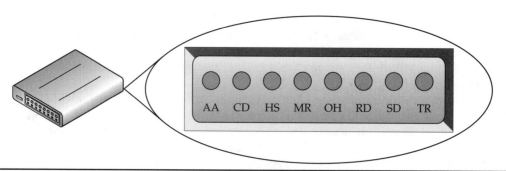

Figure 14.9   Modem lights indicate the modem's current operations.

Light	Description	Meaning
AA	Auto Answer	When lit, the modem will answer an incoming call.
CD	Carrier Detect	When lit, two modems have successfully established a connection.
HS	High Speed	When lit, the modem is transmitting at its highest possible speed.
MR	Modem Ready	When lit, the modem is on and operational.
OH	Off Hook	When lit, the modem has a dial tone and is ready for use.
RD	Receive Data	When flashing, the modem is receiving data.
SD	Send Data	When flashing, the modem is sending data.
TR	Terminal Ready	When lit, this normally indicates that the data-communications program is running.

Table 14.2   The Meaning of Modem Lights

Establishing a Provider Connection

USE IT   Before you can connect to an Internet service provider, you must create a dial-up connection for the provider. To simplify the steps you must perform, Windows provides a wizard that walks you though the process. To start the Make a New Connection Wizard, perform these steps:

1. Select Start | Programs | Accessories. Windows will display the Accessories submenu.

2. Within the Accessories submenu, select Communications | Dial-Up Networking. Windows will display the Dial-Up Networking window.

3. Within the Dial-Up Networking window, double-click the Make New Connection icon. Windows will start the wizard that will prompt you for the name and phone number you want to use for the provider.

Figure 14.10   Using the Modemsta program to simulate an external modem's lights

After the wizard is done processing, it will place an icon in the Dial-Up Networking window, which you can use to connect the provider.

Next, you will likely want to make your new connection the default service for applications such as your browser or e-mail. To select your new connection as the Windows default, perform these steps:

1. Select Start | Settings | Control Panel. Windows will open the Control Panel window.

2. Within the Control Panel, double-click the Internet Options icon. Windows will open the Internet Properties dialog box.

3. Within the Internet Properties dialog box, click the Connections tab. Windows will display the Connections sheet, as shown here.

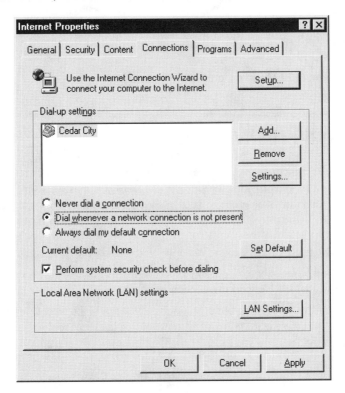

4. Within the Connections sheet Dial-Up Settings list, select the connection you desire and then click Set Default. Click OK to put your change into effect and to close the dialog box.

▶ *NOTE*

Before you can assign a connection as the default, you must assign the phone number you want the connection to dial.

Establishing Your Modem's Data Communication Settings

Before two modems can communicate, the modems must agree on the communications speed and the following data-communication parameters:

Parameter	Description
Bits per second	Specifies the speed at which the port and the device will communicate. Normally in the range 110 bytes to 115,200 bits per second.
Data bits	Specifies the number of data bits the port and the device will use to represent a value. Normally in the range 4 to 8.
Parity	Specifies the type of parity the port and the device will use to detect errors: Even, Odd, or None.
Stop bits	Specifies the number of bits the port and device will place following a data bit. Normally in the range 1 to 2.
Flow control	Specifies how the port or device will control the flow of data (which lets the port or device stop and later resume the transmission to prevent the loss of incoming data). Values include XON/XOFF, hardware, and none.

When you use an Internet service provider to gain access to the Net, the provider will tell you the setting values you should assign.

USE IT To assign data-communication parameters, perform these steps:

1. Select Start | Programs | Accessories. Windows will display the Accessories submenu.

2. Within the Accessories submenu, select Communications | Dial-Up Networking. Windows will display the Dial-Up Networking folder. Right-click the icon that corresponds to the connection you want to configure. Windows will display a pop-up menu.

3. Within the pop-up menu, choose Properties. Windows will display the connection's Properties dialog box, as shown here.

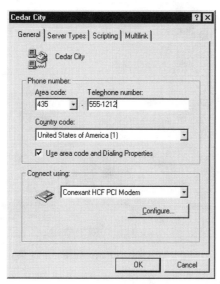

4. Within the Properties dialog box, click Configure. Windows, in turn, will display the modem's Properties dialog box.

5. Within the General sheet of the modem's Properties dialog box, use the Maximum Speed box to choose 115200. (This connection specifies the maximum speed the connection can support, which is likely not the speed you will achieve. By selecting 115200, you will not limit the potential speed.)

6. Click the Connection tab. Windows will display the Connection sheet, as shown in Figure 14-11. Within the sheet, assign the data-bit, parity, and stop-bit settings your provider specified and click OK. Click OK to close the connection's dialog box.

Maximizing the UART Buffer Sizes for Faster Performance

As you have learned, a special chip within the modem called the UART oversees much of the communication. Specifically, within the sending modem, the UART breaks apart a byte value into its corresponding bits for transmission across the wire. Likewise, within the receiving modem, the UART packages in the incoming bits back into a byte value.

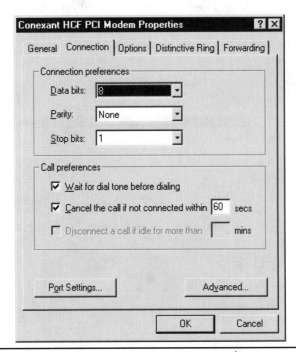

Figure 14.11   Assigning data-communication parameters using the Connection sheet

USE IT To send data, a modem flows the outgoing data into the UART for transmission. If the UART cannot hold any more data, the modem must temporarily suspend the data flow. In contrast, within the receiving modem, the UART packages bits into bytes that the modem then processes. If the modem is busy, the UART will buffer the bytes. Should the UART's buffers fill, the UART must suspend the flow of data across the wire.

To maximize data communication performance, you should increase the number of buffers the UART can use for incoming and outgoing data by performing these steps:

1. Select Start | Settings | Control Panel. Windows will display the Control Panel window.

2. Within the Control Panel, double-click the Modem icon. Windows will display the Modems Properties dialog box.

3. Within the Modems Properties dialog box, select the Modem you want to configure and then click Properties. Windows will display the modem's Properties dialog box.

4. Within the Properties dialog box, click the Connections tab. Windows will display the Connections sheet.

5. Within the Connections sheet, click Port Settings. Windows will display the Advanced Port Settings dialog box, as shown here.

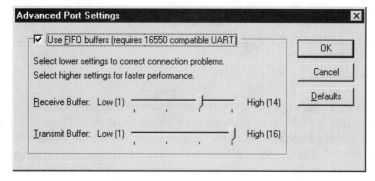

6. Within the Advanced Port Settings dialog box, click the Use FIFO Buffers check box, placing a check mark in the box. Then use the sliders to select the maximum number of input and output UART buffers. Click OK to put your changes into effect. Then click OK to close the Properties dialog box. Finally, click Close to close the Modems Properties dialog box.

Using the Modem Properties Dialog Box to Troubleshoot a Modem

If you are experiencing modem errors, you may gain insight into the error by letting Windows query the modem using the Modems Properties dialog box. When you direct Windows to query a modem, Windows will send the modem several different AT modem commands and then analyze the modem's response. Windows will display the results of its test within the More Info dialog box shown in Figure 14-12.

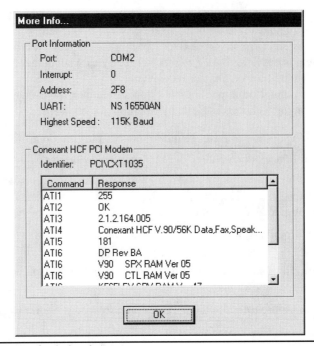

Figure 14.12 The More Info dialog box

Behind the scenes, to dial a number and to establish various data communication settings, modems respond to a wide range of commands (called *AT commands* because they typically follow the letters AT, which get the modem's attention) they receive from software programs. Users often refer to these commands as "Hayes Modem Commands" because many of the commands originated with Hayes modems, which held the majority of the modem market share during the 1980s. For example, the following AT command directs a modem to dial the number 800-555-1212:

```
ATD800-555-1212 <Enter>
```

Many data communication programs let you specify an initialization string the software sends to the modem before the modem dials a number. The initialization string consists of a series of AT commands. For a detailed listing of the AT modem commands, visit www.modems.com.

USE IT To run modem diagnostics within Windows, perform these steps:

1. Select Start | Settings | Control Panel. Windows will display the Control Panel window.

2. Within the Control Panel, double-click the Modem icon. Windows will display the Modems Properties dialog box.

3. Within the Modems Properties dialog box, click the Diagnostics tab. Windows will display the Diagnostics sheet, as shown here.

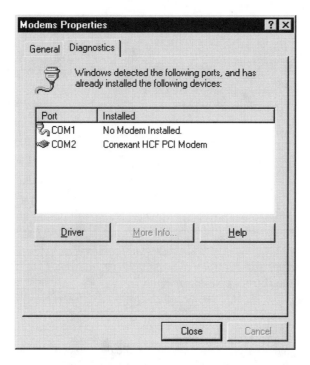

4. Within the Diagnostics sheet, click the port you desire and then click More Info. Windows will display the More Info dialog box, as shown in Figure 14-12.

Viewing Your Connection Speed

If you use a dial-up connection, the speed at which you establish a connection may not always be the same. Factors that influence the connection speed include: modem type, line quality, compression, error checking and error processing, other devices connected to the phone line (such as a fax or answering machine), as well as Windows settings. Depending on the task you must perform, such as downloading a large file, sometimes you may want to establish a new and potentially faster connection.

USE IT To view your current connection speed, double-click the dial-up connection icon that Windows displays in the taskbar. Windows, in turn, will display a dialog box similar to the one shown in Figure 14-13 that shows your current connection speed.

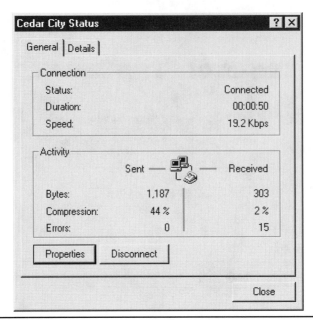

Figure 14.13   Viewing the current connection speed

Also, if you simply hold your mouse pointer above the dial-up connection icon, Windows will display a pop-up that shows your connection speed, as shown here.

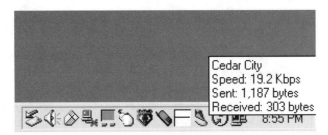

On the Web, you can visit several sites, such as www.bandwidthplace.com/speedtest, to test the speed of your DSL or cable-modem connection.

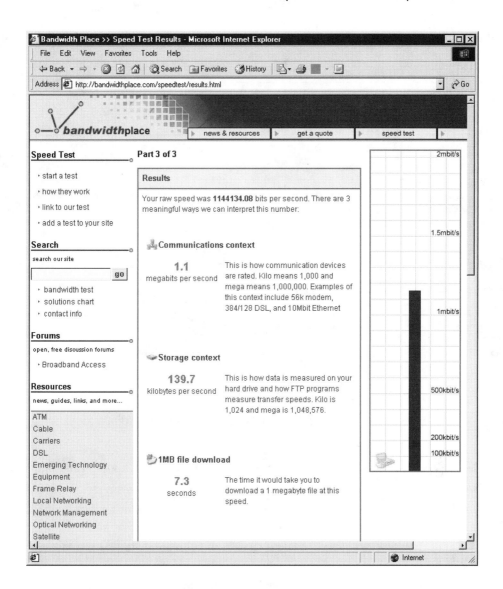

Monitoring a Dial-Up Connection

To maximize the speed of a dial-up connection, you may need to "tweak" several modem settings. As you apply your changes, use the Windows System Monitor, as shown in Figure 14-14, to determine if the setting change is making a positive or negative performance impact.

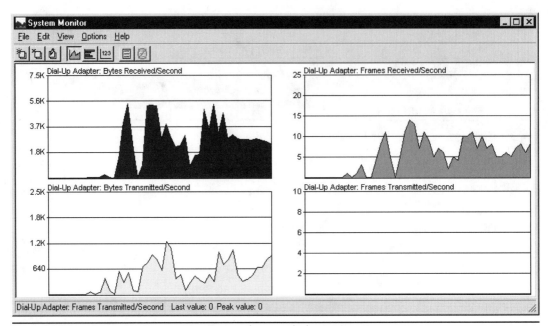

Figure 14.14 Using the System Monitor to observe dial-up operations

USE IT   To view your dial-up settings within the System Monitor, perform these steps:

1. Select Start | Programs | Accessories. Windows will display the Accessories submenu.
2. Within the Accessories submenu, select System Tools | System Monitor.
3. Within the System Monitor, select Edit | Add Menu. The System Monitor will display the Add Item dialog box.
4. Within the Add Item dialog box, click the Dial-Up Adapter entry. The System Monitor will display a list of dial-up settings you can monitor.
5. Within the settings list, click the entry you want to monitor and then click OK. The System Monitor, in turn, will begin monitoring the settings.

Within the System Monitor, you can use the Explain button to briefly describe each of the dial-up settings you can monitor. If you find that changing a setting, such as changing the UART buffer size, introduces a larger number of errors, you will also normally find that your overall performance will drop as well. By monitoring the various fields and recording their average values, you can better analyze how your changes impact your dial-up performance.

Avoiding Call-Waiting Disconnects

If your phone supports call waiting, your phone will generate an audible beep as you talk to let you know you have an incoming call. To put the current caller on hold, so that you can respond to the call, you simply press the flash button (the hangup button). Then to resume your original call you simply again press the flash button. Unfortunately, call waiting is not always compatible with dial-up network connections. When an incoming call occurs, many modems will disconnect the current connection, which is frustrating and difficult to troubleshoot.

USE IT If your phone line supports call waiting, you should disable the feature each time you place a modem call. When you later end your modem connection, the call-waiting feature will resume its normal operations. To configure your system to disable call waiting when a modem places a call, perform these steps:

1. Select Start | Settings | Control Panel. Windows will display the Control Panel window.
2. Within the Control Panel, double-click the Modem icon. Windows will display the Modems Properties dialog box.
3. Within the Modems Properties dialog box, click Dialing Properties. Windows will display the Dialing Properties dialog box, as shown here.

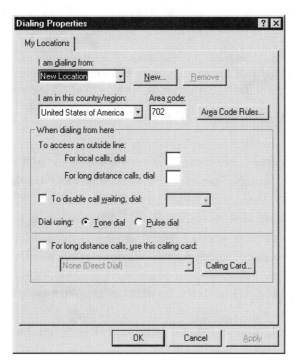

4. Within the Dialing Properties dialog box, click the To Disable Call Waiting, Dial check box, placing a check mark in the box. Then use the pull-down list to select the sequence that disables call waiting for your phone (which is normally *70, but you can ask your phone company). Click OK to put your change into effect.

> **NOTE**

*In addition to using these steps to disable call waiting, you can also simply precede the phone number the modem is to dial with the characters specific to your phone system, such as "*70,555-555-1212."*

Doubling Your Connection Speed Using a Multilink Connection

If you live in an area that does not offer high-speed connections, you may want to consider adding a second modem connection to your PC with which you can create a multilink connection. After you create a multilink connection, your provider will let your system send and receive packages across both modem lines at the same time. Depending on the number of modems and phone lines you have available (as well as the number of connections your provider will let you make), Windows will let you use multiple modems at the same time, however, most Internet service providers will limit you to two modem connections.

Before you can establish a multilink connection, your PC must have two modems, each modem must have its own phone line, and your Internet service provider must support multilink connections. The modems you use to create a multilink connection do not have to be the same type or the same speed.

USE IT To create a multilink connection, perform these steps:

1. Select Start | Programs | Accessories. Windows will display the Accessories submenu.

2. Within the Accessories submenu, select Communications | Dial-Up Networking. Windows, in turn, will open the Dial-Up Networking window.

3. Within the Dial-Up Networking window, right-click the connection for which you want to use two modems. Windows will display a pop-up menu.

4. Within the pop-up menu, choose Properties. Windows will display the connection's Properties dialog box.

5. Within the Properties dialog box, click the Multilink tab. Windows will display the Multilink sheet.

6. Within the Multilink sheet, click the Use Additional Devices radio button. Then click the second modem you want to use and click Add.

7. Repeat step 6 for each modem you want to use.

8. Click OK to close the dialog box and to apply your changes.

Dealing with International Phone Systems

If you travel internationally, you are aware that countries around the globe use different electrical currents and use different outlet types. In addition, many countries use a dial to which a US-based modem cannot detect. Before you can plug your modem into a wall outlet, you will likely need a cable converter specific to the country you are visiting.

 USE IT Before you travel, you should visit your modem manufacturer's Web site and determine whether your modem can recognize international dial tones. Often, if the modem cannot recognize a dial tone, the modem will not dial. In some cases, you may be able to convince your modem to dial without first waiting for a dial tone, by performing these steps:

1. Select Start | Programs | Accessories. Windows will display the Accessories submenu.

2. Within the Accessories submenu, select Communications | Dial-Up Networking. Windows will display the Dial-Up Networking folder. Right-click the icon that corresponds to the connection you want to configure. Windows will display a pop-up menu.

3. Within the pop-up menu, choose Properties. Windows will display the connection's Properties dialog box.

4. Within the Properties dialog box, click Configure. Windows will display the modem's Properties dialog box.

5. Within the modem's Properties dialog box, click the Connection tab. Windows will display the Connection sheet, as shown here.

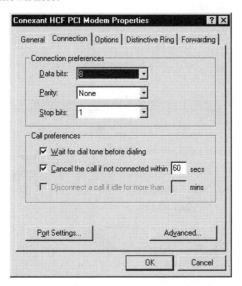

6. Within the Connection sheet, remove the check mark from the Wait For Dial Tone Before Dialing check box and click OK.

Depending on your data communication needs while you travel, as well as your length of stay or frequency of travel, you may want to buy a modem when you arrive at your destination.

If you use a larger Internet service provider, such as AOL, MSN, or Earthlink, your provider likely has connection points around the globe to which you connect with your modem as you travel. By using the local connection points, you eliminate the long-distance charges that would apply if you dial into your provider's US-based number. Before you travel, visit your provider's Web site and print the connection numbers available in the places you plan to visit.

Controlling Modem Tones

When you use your modem to connect to a remote host, the modem will normally generate a sequence of tones. The modem uses these tones, along with a series of initialization packets to configure modem settings, such as the compression scheme the modems will use as they send and receive data. If your modem normally successfully establishes a connection, you may want to turn down your modem's speaker volume so that you and others do not have to listen to the tones. However, if you are experiencing connection problems, you may want to listen to the tones to verify that a modem is answering and responding to the call.

USE IT   To control your modem's speaker volume, perform these steps:

1. Select Start | Programs | Accessories. Windows will display the Accessories submenu.

2. Within the Accessories submenu, select Communications | Dial-Up Networking. Windows will display the Dial-Up Networking folder. Right-click the icon that corresponds to the connection you want to configure. Windows will display a pop-up menu.

3. Within the pop-up menu, choose Properties. Windows will display the connection's Properties dialog box.

4. Within the Properties dialog box, click Connection. Windows will display the modem's Properties box, as shown here.

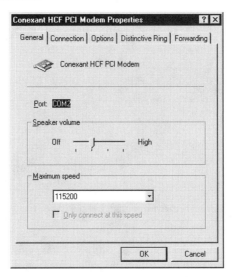

5. Within the Properties dialog box, use the Speaker Volume slider to increase or decrease the volume and then click OK to put your change into effect.

Powering On Your System in Response to an Incoming Phone Call

USE IT   Today, most PC power supplies provide a constant voltage to the motherboard, even when the PC is powered off. If you have a NIC installed in your PC, the card may illuminate small LED lights, even when your PC is off.

As shown in Figure 14-15, most newer CMOS Setup programs let you configure your system so it will power itself on in response to an incoming phone call. For example, assume that you travel with notebook PC and that you have a desktop PC at home. Using the CMOS Setup, you can configure your system so that you could later, if necessary, call the phone number that corresponds to the modem line. If your system is not powered on, your system will start when it detects the incoming call. Then, as discussed in Chapter 9, you can configure your system so that it automatically runs a data communication program when it starts that you can use to connect to your system. If you connect to your system using a program such as pcAnywhere, you can then access files or e-mail messages the system contains via your modem connection.

```
                                   SETUP
 Main    Advanced        Security      Boot       Exit
 Quiet Boot                  [Enabled]                    Allows you to set the
 Quick Boot                  [Enabled]                    system to power on
                                                          if a modem ring is
                                                          detected
 Restore on AC/Power Loss  [Last state]
 On LAN                      [Power On]
 On Modem                    [Power On]
 Auto Power On               [Disabled]

 1st Boot Device           [ATAPI-CDROM]
 2nd Boot Device           [ARMD-FDD]
 3rd Boot Device           [IDE-HDD]
 4th Boot Device           [Disabled]               <- -> Select Menu
                                                    ↑  ↓ Select Item
                                                    Tab    Select Field
                                                    Enter  Select Sub-Menu
                                                    F9     Setup Defaults
                                                    F10    Save and Exit
                                                    ESC    Exit
```

Figure 14.15   Using the CMOS Setup program to configure the PC to power on when an incoming call occurs

Tweaking the TCP/IP Max Transfer Unit Setting for a Dial-Up Connection

If you connect your PC to the Internet using a dial-up connection, you may be able to tweak key TCP/IP settings that improve your performance. To begin, many TCP/IP protocols define the maximum transfer unit (MTU) as the maximum number of bytes a packet can contain. Several protocols define the MTU value as 576. Often, Windows will initialize the value to 1500. To send a packet 1500 bytes in length across a network connection that supports an MTU of 576 will cause the remote connection to break the 1500 byte packet into three smaller packets. The first two packets will normally contain 576 bytes, and the remaining third packet will contain 348 bytes of data and 228 bytes of wasted space. To avoid such wasted space, you can configure Windows to use a MTU setting of 576.

▶ **NOTE**

Before you make changes to an entry within the Windows Registry, you should write down the entry's original value so you can later restore it should your change create an error or reduce your system performance.

 To change the MTU setting, perform these steps:

1. Select Start | Run. Windows, in turn, will display the Run dialog box.
2. Within the Run dialog box, type **regedit** and press ENTER. Windows will run the Registry Editor.
3. Within the Registry Editor, select Edit | Find. The Registry Editor will display the Find dialog box.
4. Within the Find dialog box, type **MaxMTU** and click OK. The Registry Editor will search for the corresponding entry and display its results, as shown next. (If you are using Windows 98, you may not have a MaxMTU setting, but, rather, you will have a IPMTU setting, as discussed in step 6.)

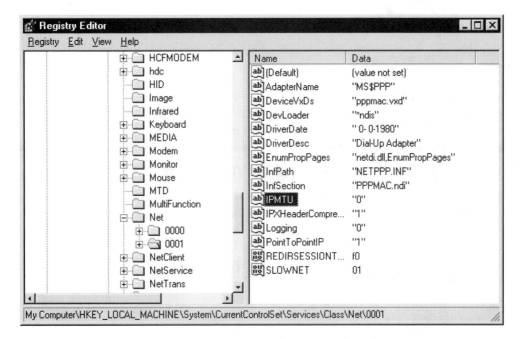

5. Select Edit | Modify. The Registry will display the Edit String dialog box within which you can type the setting's new value. Type **576** and click OK.

6. Repeat steps 3 through 5 to assign the value 576 to the IPMTU entry (Windows 98 refers to the entry as IPMTU).

If you are using Windows 98, you may also be able to change the IPMTU setting by performing these steps:

1. Select Start | Settings | Control Panel. Windows will open the Control Panel window.

2. Within the Control Panel, double-click the Network icon. Windows will display the Network Properties dialog box.

3. Within the Network Properties dialog, click the Dial-Up Adapter and then click Properties. Windows will display the Dial-Up Adapter Properties dialog box.

4. Within the Dial-Up Adapter Properties dialog box, click the Advanced tab. Windows will display the Advanced sheet.

5. Within the Advanced sheet Property field, click the IP Packet Size entry. Then, within the pull-down list, choose Small. Click OK to close the dialog box.

After you make your changes, you must restart your system for the changes to take effect. Use the System Monitor to determine how your changes are affecting your data transfer rates, errors, and so on.

▶ *NOTE*

You may want to check with your Internet service provider to see if it has a setting recommendation that best suits your system and its network configuration.

Tweaking the Windows Receive Buffer Size

Within Windows, the default receive window specifies the buffer into which Windows stores all incoming packets. To improve your downloading performance, you may want to increase the window size. The window size should be a multiple of the maximum segment size, whose value should be 40 less than the value you assign to the MaxMTU or IPMTU settings. For example, if you set MaxMTU and IPMTU to 576 (which may be optimal for a dial-up connection), your max segment size is 40 less (536). You should then assign a multiple of that value (536, 1072, 2144, 4288. . .65392).

▶ *NOTE*

Before you make changes to an entry within the Windows Registry, you should write down the entry's original value so you can later restore the value should your change create an error or reduce your system performance.

 Depending on your Windows version, you may be able to change the size of the Windows default receive window, perform these steps:

1. Select Start | Run. Windows, in turn, will display the Run dialog box.

2. Within the Run dialog box, type **regedit** and press ENTER. Windows will run the Registry Editor.

3. Within the Registry Editor, select Edit | Find. The Registry Editor will display the Find dialog box.

4. Within the Find dialog box, type **DefRecieveWindow** and click OK. The Registry Editor will search for the corresponding entry.

5. Select Edit | Modify. The Registry will display the Edit DWORD dialog box within which you can type the setting's new value.

6. Within the Edit DWORD dialog box, click the Decimal radio button, type in the window size you desire, and click OK.

After you change the setting, you must restart your system for the change to take effect. Use the System Monitor to determine how your changes are affecting your data transfer rates, errors, and so on.

NOTE

You may want to check with your Internet service provider to see if it has a setting recommendation that best suits your system and its network configuration. If you are using an Ethernet-based network, as opposed to a dial-up, your max segment size will normally be 1460, of which your receive window size should be a multiple.

Tweaking the Packet Time to Live Setting (TTL)

As packets make their way across the Internet, the packet will often move from one system to another (packet switching) in order to reach its destination. To prevent a packet from traveling the Internet lost forever, each packet has a time to live setting that corresponds to the number of sites the packet can visit before it should be considered lost and destroyed. When a packet does not reach its destination, the sender will eventually resend the packet. Many Windows systems assign the value 32 (meaning a packet can make 32 hops on its way to its destination). As the Internet becomes larger and more complex, many network programmers recommend that users should increase the setting to 128.

 Depending on your Windows version, you may be able to change the size of the Windows default receive window. Here are the steps:

1. Select Start | Run. Windows, in turn, will display the Run dialog box.
2. Within the Run dialog box, type **regedit** and press ENTER. Windows will run the Registry Editor.
3. Within the Registry Editor, select Edit | Find. The Registry Editor will display the Find dialog box.
4. Within the Find dialog box, type **DefaultTTL** and click OK. The Registry Editor will search for the corresponding entry.
5. Select Edit | Modify. The Registry, in turn, will display the Edit String dialog box within which you can type the setting's new value.
6. Within the Edit String dialog box, type the value you desire, such as 128, and click OK. After you make your change, you must restart your system for your change to take effect.

Viewing Modem Resources within the System Information Utility

As you troubleshoot modem problems, you will need to know the hardware and software resources the modem uses, such at the IRQ and memory settings, as well as the modem device drivers. To quickly gather the modem information, you can use the System Information utility, as shown in Figure 14-16.

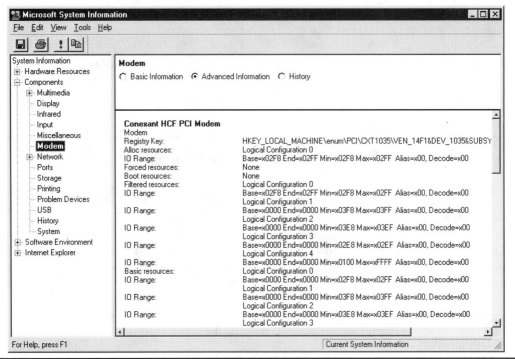

Figure 14.16 Viewing modem resources within the System Information utility

USE IT To display modem information within the System Information utility, perform these steps:

1. Select Start | Programs | Accessories. Windows will display the Accessories submenu.

2. Within the Accessories submenu, select System Tools | System Information. Windows will open the System Information utility.

3. Within the System Information utility, click the plus sign (+) that precedes the Components entry. The System Information utility will expand the list of your system's hardware components.

4. Within the component list, click the Modem entry. Then, click the Advanced Information radio button. The System Information utility, in turn, will display your modem's resource use, as shown in Figure 14-16.

If you are using a DSL or cable modem connection, you can perform these steps to view the resources your modem has in use:

1. Select Start | Programs | Accessories. Windows will display the Accessories submenu.

2. Within the Accessories submenu, select System Tools | System Information. Windows will open the System Information utility.

3. Within the System Information utility, click the plus sign (+) that precedes the Components entry. The System Information utility will expand the list of your system's hardware components.

4. Within the component list, click the Network entry. Then, click the Advanced Information radio button. The System Information utility, in turn, will display your network card's resource use.

Viewing the Modem's Communication Log

To help you troubleshoot modem operations, Windows logs information about the current modem session. By examining the log's contents, you can determine the connection speed, whether the modem is performing error checking or data compression, and so on. Figure 14-17 shows the contents of the modem log within the Windows Notepad.

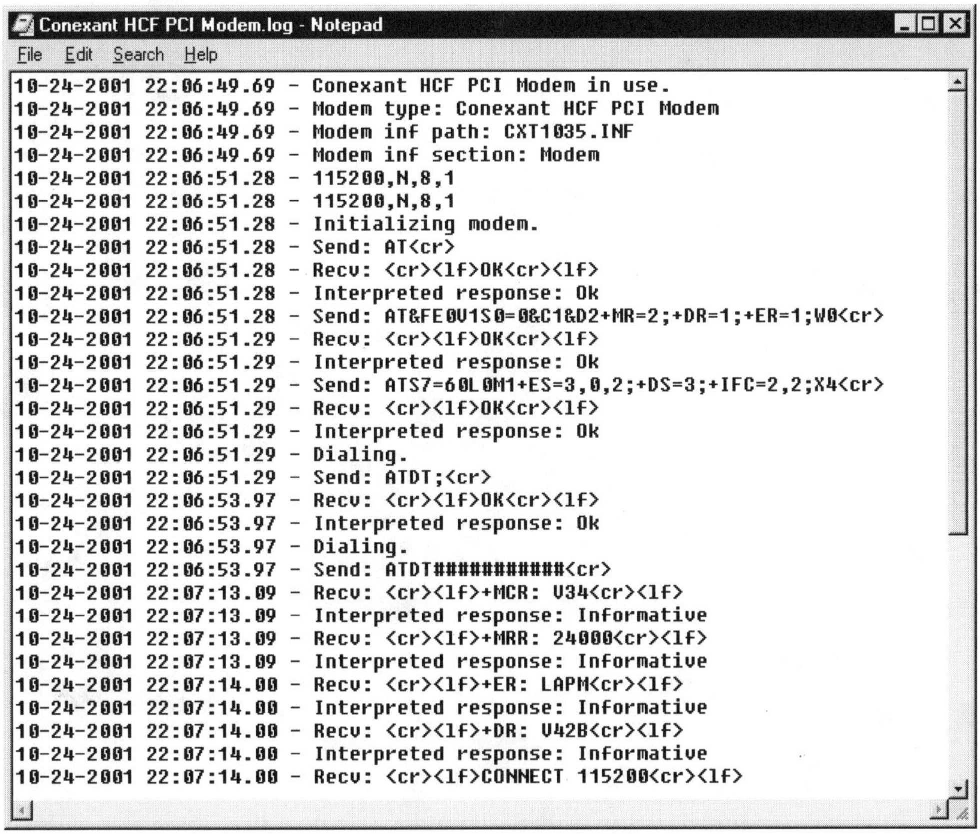

```
Conexant HCF PCI Modem.log - Notepad                          _ □ ✕
File  Edit  Search  Help
10-24-2001 22:06:49.69 - Conexant HCF PCI Modem in use.
10-24-2001 22:06:49.69 - Modem type: Conexant HCF PCI Modem
10-24-2001 22:06:49.69 - Modem inf path: CXT1035.INF
10-24-2001 22:06:49.69 - Modem inf section: Modem
10-24-2001 22:06:51.28 - 115200,N,8,1
10-24-2001 22:06:51.28 - 115200,N,8,1
10-24-2001 22:06:51.28 - Initializing modem.
10-24-2001 22:06:51.28 - Send: AT<cr>
10-24-2001 22:06:51.28 - Recv: <cr><lf>OK<cr><lf>
10-24-2001 22:06:51.28 - Interpreted response: Ok
10-24-2001 22:06:51.28 - Send: AT&FE0V1S0=0&C1&D2+MR=2;+DR=1;+ER=1;W0<cr>
10-24-2001 22:06:51.29 - Recv: <cr><lf>OK<cr><lf>
10-24-2001 22:06:51.29 - Interpreted response: Ok
10-24-2001 22:06:51.29 - Send: ATS7=60L0M1+ES=3,0,2;+DS=3;+IFC=2,2;X4<cr>
10-24-2001 22:06:51.29 - Recv: <cr><lf>OK<cr><lf>
10-24-2001 22:06:51.29 - Interpreted response: Ok
10-24-2001 22:06:51.29 - Dialing.
10-24-2001 22:06:51.29 - Send: ATDT;<cr>
10-24-2001 22:06:53.97 - Recv: <cr><lf>OK<cr><lf>
10-24-2001 22:06:53.97 - Interpreted response: Ok
10-24-2001 22:06:53.97 - Dialing.
10-24-2001 22:06:53.97 - Send: ATDT###########<cr>
10-24-2001 22:07:13.09 - Recv: <cr><lf>+MCR: V34<cr><lf>
10-24-2001 22:07:13.09 - Interpreted response: Informative
10-24-2001 22:07:13.09 - Recv: <cr><lf>+MRR: 24000<cr><lf>
10-24-2001 22:07:13.09 - Interpreted response: Informative
10-24-2001 22:07:14.00 - Recv: <cr><lf>+ER: LAPM<cr><lf>
10-24-2001 22:07:14.00 - Interpreted response: Informative
10-24-2001 22:07:14.00 - Recv: <cr><lf>+DR: V42B<cr><lf>
10-24-2001 22:07:14.00 - Interpreted response: Informative
10-24-2001 22:07:14.00 - Recv: <cr><lf>CONNECT 115200<cr><lf>
```

Figure 14.17   Using the Windows Notepad to view the modem's communication log

USE IT   To display modem log, perform these steps:

1. Select Start | Settings | Control Panel. Windows will display the Control Panel window.

2. Within the Control Panel, double-click the Modem icon. Windows will display the Modems Properties dialog box.

3. Within the Modems Properties dialog box, click the modem you desire and then click Properties. Windows will display the modem's Properties dialog box.

4. Within the Properties dialog box, click the Connection tab. Windows will display the Connections sheet.

5. Within the Connections sheet, click Advanced. Windows will display the Advanced Connection Settings dialog box.

6. Within the Advanced Connection Settings dialog box, click View Log. Windows will open the modem log within Notepad, as shown in Figure 14-17.

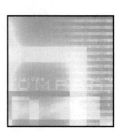

CHAPTER 15

Network Operations

TIPS IN THIS CHAPTER

Over the past decade, the use of computer networks has experienced explosive growth. Within businesses, users connect PCs to computer networks to share resources such as files, disk space, and printers, to exchange e-mail messages, and more. Within homes, users create computer networks when they access the Internet using a DSL or cable-modem connection. Further, other users create networks to share resources, which may include a high-speed network connection.

This chapter examines computer networks in detail. You will learn how network architects design and implement networks and ways in which network administrators improve network performance. With the advent of low-cost wireless networks, many homes and small offices will find that connecting computers to a simple network provides tremendous flexibility.

Understanding Resource Sharing

For many users, computer networks provide a means of Internet access, which means access to electronic mail and to the vast unlimited information that is the World Wide Web. Less than a decade has past since the Internet began its explosive worldwide growth. In the1980s and early 1990s, computer networks existed to provide users with the ability to share resources, such as printers, databases, and other files, as shown in Figure 15-1. Often, within many networks, e-mail was available, but it was not the network's most widely used application, as is the case today.

In general, a computer network consists of the cables, hardware cards, and software that connect two or more computers together. In the simplest network, a cable connects two PCs, as shown in Figure 15-2.

Network administrators refer to simple computer networks, within which no computer plays a special role, as a *peer-to-peer* network. In contrast, a *client/server* network, as shown in Figure 15-3, relies on a special high-performance computer, called a *server*, which offers various services to client computers. The World Wide Web makes extensive use of client/server relationships. When you browse the Web, for example, your browser is a *client program* that requests a Web server to provide it with HTML-based Web pages. After the server satisfies your browser's request, the server services other browsers.

Within a client-server network, one server may provide clients with access to database files, while a second server responds to Web requests, while yet a third server handles e-mail operations. The number of servers a network uses depends on the network's purpose and the number of users (clients) it must support.

Users categorize computer networks as either local-area networks (LANs) or wide-area networks (WANs) based on the proximity of the computers that connect the network, as shown in Figure 15-4. Computers within a LAN normally reside in the same office space (or adjoining offices). In contrast, computers within a WAN are dispersed across a large geographic area, such as a large city, state, or even across the globe. Many large corporations, for example, use WANs to tie together LANs that reside in corporate offices worldwide.

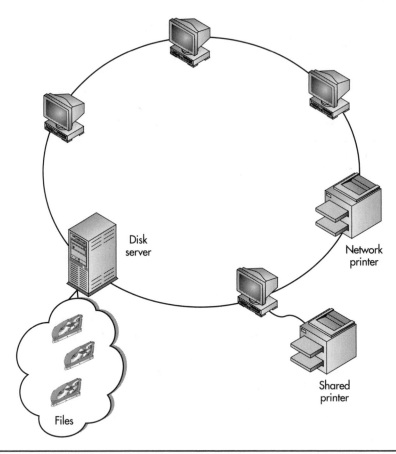

Figure 15.1   Computer networks let users share resources such as printers, disks, and files.

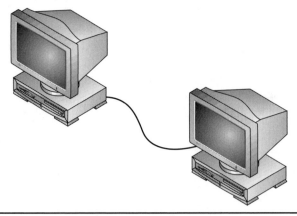

Figure 15.2   A simple computer network consisting of two PCs

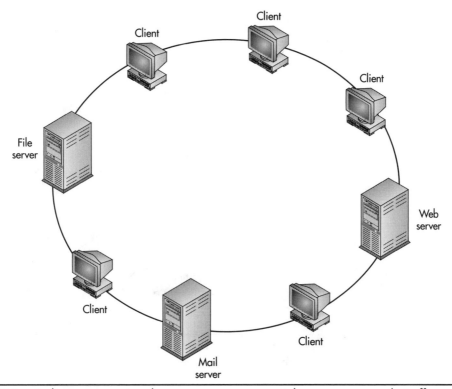

Figure 15.3   A client-server network uses one or more special purpose servers that offer services to client computers.

Piecing Together a Network

Within a network, computers exchange signals (electronic messages, which network administrators refer to as *packets*) to communicate. As shown in Figure 15-5, most networks exchange such message over network cables, however, recently, the number of wireless networks (which eliminates the need to physically connect systems), have experienced rapid growth. Such wireless networks eliminate the cost and challenge of running cables throughout offices and homes.

As shown in Figure 15-6, to connect a PC to a network, the PC must contain a network interface card (NIC). Because of the pervasive use of networks, many newer PC provide network support on a motherboard chip.

Revisiting Network Cables

Chapter 11 examines cables and connectors in detail. To connect PCs within a network environment, network administrators use a wide range of cables, the most common being twisted-pair, coaxial, and fiber-optic. The majority of computer networks use Category 5 (or simply Cat 5) twisted-pair cabling.

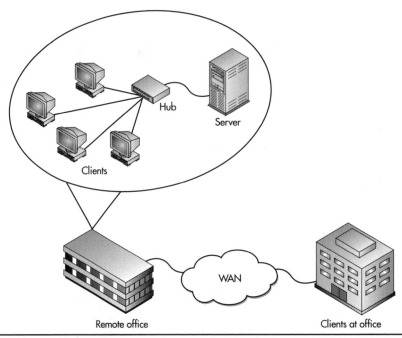

Figure 15.4   LANs connect computers in close proximity, whereas a WAN connects computers (or networks) that are geographically dispersed.

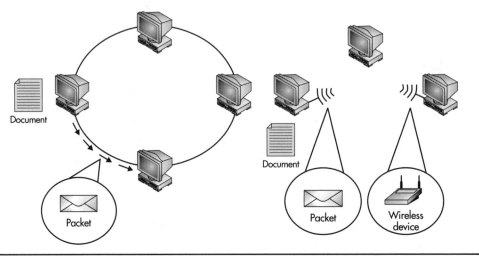

Figure 15.5   Connecting computers via cables and through wireless connections

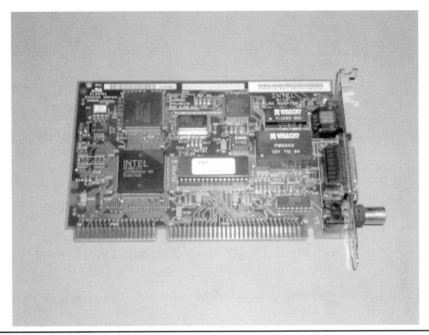

Figure 15.6   PCs connect to a network using a NIC.

As discussed in Chapter 11, the cable type and quality can have a very significant influence on network performance.

Understanding Network Topologies

To create a network, administrators must connect the PCs and other network devices (such as network printers) to one another using a cable or wireless connection. Figure 15-7 shows the three most commonly used topologies administrators use to build networks: the bus, star, and ring networks.

Each network topology provides different benefits and disadvantages. Within ring and bus networks, for example, network administrators connect PCs in a chain-like fashion, connecting one PC to the next. The primary advantage of the ring and bus topologies is simplicity. The disadvantage of the ring and bus topologies is that should one PC, network card, or cable link fail, the entire network will fail.

Within a star network, PCs connect to a central hub. The advantage of the star topology is that should a PC, network card, or cable link fail, the rest of the network is unaffected. The disadvantage, however, is should the hub fail, the entire network will fail.

Within a bus network, the network administrators must terminate both ends of the bus, following the last PC on the bus. Normally, terminating the bus simply requires that the administrator connect a special terminator (a connector) to the NIC, as shown in Figure 15-8.

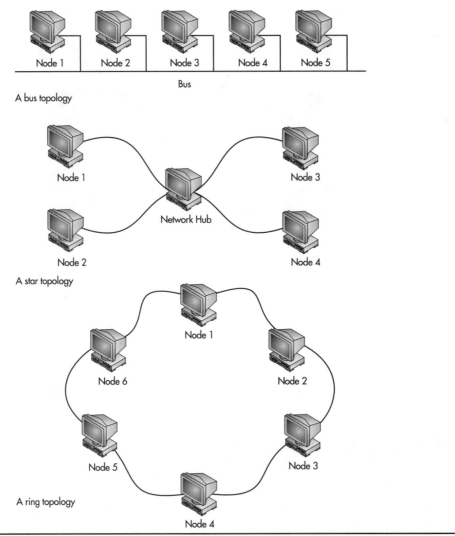

Figure 15.7   The bus, star, and ring network topologies

Understanding Network Technologies

As you have learned, a computer network consists of cables, network cards, network hubs, and other hardware. Within a network, the computers must use compatible cards, cables, speeds, and communication protocols. Network administrators refer to a network's compatible hardware as the network's *technology*. The common "general" network technology is Ethernet. Depending on the underlying cables and NICs, network administrators further classify Ethernet networks as twisted-pair Ethernet, fiber-optic Ethernet, thin-wire Ethernet, and so on. Further, as shown in Table 15-1, network administrators also

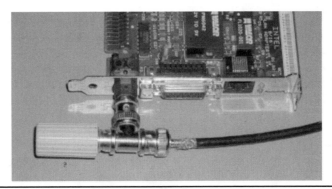

Figure 15.8   Terminating a NIC within a bus network

classify Ethernet networks based on speed. Common network speeds include 10Mb per second (10 Mbs), 100Mb per second (100 Mbs), and 1000Mb per second (1000 Mbs, or gigabit Ethernet).

Understanding Network Protocols

To communicate across a network, computers must agree on a variety of issues, such as the speed at which they will transmit and receive messages, the size and format of each message, how the receiver will acknowledge to the sender the messages it successfully receives, and how it will report errant messages. A *network protocol* describes a set of rules and procedures. Within a network, a protocol specifies the rules the computers must follow to ensure successful communication. Across computer networks, as well as across the Internet, the Transport Control Protocol/Internet Protocol (TCP/IP) is the most widely used protocol.

Understanding the ISO/OSI Network Model

Network designers build networks using layers of hardware and software, each of which performs a specific task. The lowest network layer, for example, transfers data over cables, fiber, or wireless

Ethernet Descriptor	Characteristic
10Base-2	10 MHz using thin coaxial cable
10Base-T	10 MHz using twisted-pair cable
100Base-TX	100 MHz using Category 5 or better cable
100Base-T4	100 MHz using Category 3 cable
100Base-F	100 MHz using a fiber-optic cable
1000Base-T	1 GHz using Category 5 cable

Table 15.1   Common Ethernet Types

connection. The next layer may perform error detection and possibly correction. Further, the next layer may be responsible for determining the route data will travel to reach its destination. To maximize your network performance, you need knowledge of the basic services network layers perform.

The *ISO/OSI network model* provides a framework network developers can use to design networks. The Internet's TCP/IP suite, for example, follows the ISO/OSI design guide. To define the operations a network performs, the ISO/OSI model stacks task modules into layers. Each layer, in turn, performs a specific function in the task of sending or receiving data. To allow data to move up and down through the layers, each layer provides specific services to its adjacent layers. Further, each layer hides its implementation details from the other layers, forcing the adjacent layers to interact with the layer's servers. As information flows up and down the network layers, the information cannot bypass a layer. As a result, each layer cares only about its adjacent layers. Figure 15-9 shows the layers in the ISO/OSI network model. Assuming that no errors occur, the data travels across the channel and up through the network layers of the target computer. If errors occur, the network software performs operations, as specified by the protocol, to resolve the error.

Taking a Closer Look at the Physical Layer

The physical layer consists of the network's physical elements, such as the cables and connectors. At a lower level, the physical layer defines the network's control signals, timing, and voltages. The physical layer specifies, for example, the number of wires within a network connection and the type of cable that connects systems, as well as other cable properties, such as bandwidth. The physical layer dictates the network's technology, such as Ethernet. The physical layer transmits binary data across the network's communications channel. All messages that a network sends or receives travel through a communications channel controlled by the physical layer.

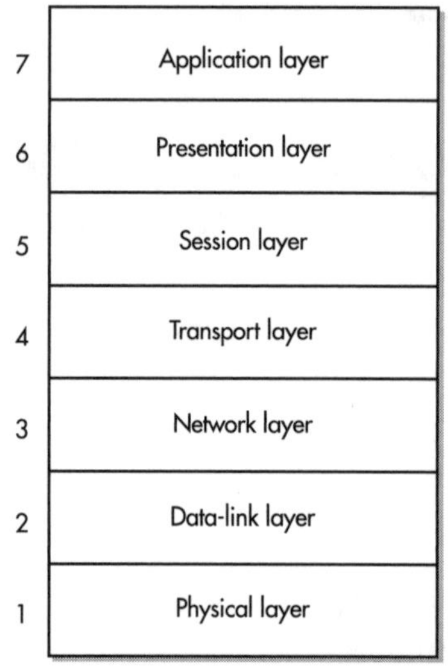

7	Application layer
6	Presentation layer
5	Session layer
4	Transport layer
3	Network layer
2	Data-link layer
1	Physical layer

Figure 15.9 The seven layers of the ISO/OSI network model

Taking a Closer Look at the Data-Link Layer

Immediately above the physical layer is the data-link layer, whose purpose is to transfer data between the physical layer and the network layer. Within a PC, the NIC implements the data-link layer. When receiving data entering the network, the data-link layer combines the bits it receives from the physical layer into *frames*, which it transfers to the network layer. Likewise, to transmit data, the data-link layer breaks the frames it receives from the network layer into bits for transmission by the physical layer.

To connect a PC to a network, the PC must have a NIC that matches the network's technology. This means that if you are using a 10 Mbs Ethernet (the physical layer), the PC must use a 10 Mbs Ethernet NIC.

To detect transmission errors that may occur across the physical layer, the sending and receiving data-link layers use a *cyclic-redundancy-check* (CRC) value (sometimes called a *checksum*). Before the sending PC sends a packet, its data-link layer calculates the CRC value based on the data's contents, which it then appends to the data frame. When the receiving PC gets the incoming message, its data-link layer performs the same calculation on the data to determine the CRC, which it then compares to the sender's CRC. If no transmission errors occurred, the two CRC values will be the same. If the CRCs differ, the receiver can discard the frame and notify the sender of the error.

Taking a Closer Look at the Network Layer

Before the physical layer can send data across the network to a remote PC, the network layer must specify the path that the packet will follow to reach its destination. To determine the optimal path to the destination PC, the network layer relies on a *routing table* to determine the potential paths. Next, the network layer considers network traffic to determine the optimal path. Most networks use dynamic routing tables whose contents the network software automatically updates based on information it learns from the paths traveled by incoming packets. As computers communicate across a network, it is not uncommon for one computer to send data faster than another can receive it. In such cases, network software relies on *flow control* protocols to control the data rates. The network layer relies on flow control to manage data rates between computers.

Taking a Closer Look at the Transport Layer

As discussed, the network layer determines the path packets will follow to move between computers. In other words, the network layer is concerned about computer-to-computer communication. Above the network layer is the transport layer, whose purpose is to deliver messages between applications running on the two communicating computers. After the network layer delivers data to the correct computer, the transport layer delivers data to the correct application within that computer. For example, the transport layer will deliver a message from a Web browser running on a client system to a Web server running on the remote system.

Taking a Closer Look at the Session Layer

Above the transport layer, the session layer provides an application's interface to a network. The session layer handles issues such as security, ensuring that users provide correct usernames and passwords. Before two PCs can establish a network connection, the computers negotiate various communication settings, such as data-transfer rates, error control, and compression techniques. The session layer must manage requests for changes to a negotiated option. Network designers often refer to the process of setting up a network session as a *binding*.

As you will learn, the TCP/IP protocol that drives the Internet does not use a session layer. Instead, applications ensure network authorization and the transport layer implements many session-layer operations.

Taking a Closer Look at the Presentation and Application Layers

Above the session layer, the presentation layer contains network-based programs, such as your Web browser or e-mail program. In addition, the presentation layer defines how the network presents itself to the programmers who create the network applications. From a programmer's perspective, the presentation layer provides services that programs can use to perform network-file operations, data encryption, and more. As you will learn, TCP/IP, the protocol that drives the Internet, does not contain a presentation layer, per se.

Understanding the Internet's TCP/IP

Across the Internet, two protocols, the Transport Control Protocol (TCP) and the Internet Protocol (IP), connect millions of networks in the world. Collectively, TCP and IP (TCP/IP) define several protocols that have become the standard for communication across the Internet. In contrast to the ISO/OSI seven-layer network model, TCP/IP uses only five layers, as shown in Figure 15-10.

As data moves through the layers of the TCP/IP stack, the network software formats (packages) the data for use by the next level. In other words, as data moves down through the TCP/IP protocol, each layer adds information to the previous layer's message packet. For example, The transport layer formats the data into a TCP segment that includes the application data and the TCP header. Within each TCP segment are two 16-bit addresses that identify the *ports* of the sending and receiving applications. A port is simply the address of a program within a specific computer.

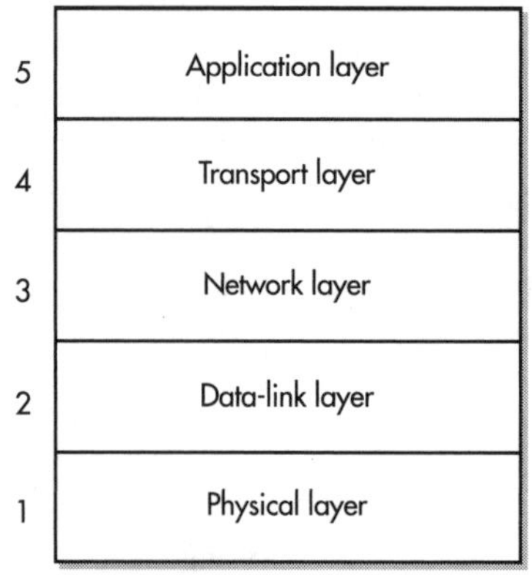

5	Application layer
4	Transport layer
3	Network layer
2	Data-link layer
1	Physical layer

Figure 15.10   The five layers within TCP/IP

As the data passes through the network layer's IP module, the network software formats the segment into an IP datagram (or packet). To send information across the network, the network software breaks the data apart into packets. To reach the correct destination, the packets must contain address information. As packets leave the IP (network) layer, the IP packets contain a 32-bit (dotted-decimal) IP address. Finally, in the data-link layer, the Ethernet driver formats the IP datagram into an Ethernet frame.

Understanding Routers, Bridges, Proxy Servers, and Firewalls

In Chapter 11, you examined cables and cable operations in detail. As you learned, as a signal travels across a cable, resistance within the cable will cause the signal to become weaker the further the signal travels. Users refer to the weakening of a signal as it travels as *attenuation*.

As a signal travels across a network, signal attenuation can result in data-transmission errors. To reduce attenuation, networks often employ *repeaters*, a hardware box whose purpose is simply to amplify the incoming signal strength, as shown in Figure 15-11. Chapter 11 briefly describes the distance signals can travel over different cable types. If you are designing a network or upgrading a network with cable distances that exceed the cable's "rated" length, you should plan to integrate one or more repeaters into your network design.

If you are designing a network or planning to upgrade an existing network, you may find that is cost-effective to break your network into two or more subnets, one that operates at high speed (at either gigabit or 100 Mbs speed) and a second that uses slower technologies. Or, for security reasons, you may choose to base your subnets around operational considerations, possibly placing your sales and marketing staff on one subnet and your research and development staff on a second, for example. If your network uses two or more subnets, you must use a device called a bridge to connect the subnets, as shown in Figure 15-12.

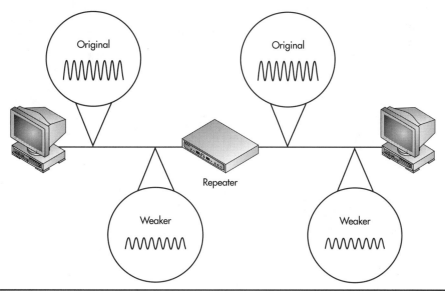

Figure 15.11 A repeater amplifies a signal's strength as the signal travels a network connection.

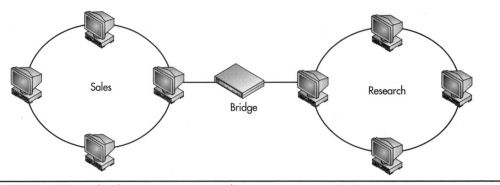

Figure 15.12   Using a bridge to connect two subnets

To reduce network traffic and server operations, networks often use one or more servers, called *proxy servers*, in front of the network (or primary server) to perform operations on the server's behalf. A proxy server, for example, might authenticate incoming requests on behalf of the primary server, allowing only "authorized users" to request specific resources. Offloading specific operations to a proxy server in this way often improves network security and performance.

To protect networks from attacks by hackers, network administrators often place a firewall between the network and the Internet, as shown in Figure 15-13. A firewall can be either a hardware device or a program running on a PC.

In general, a firewall examines (filters) the packets coming into the network. Depending on the firewall's configuration, the firewall might, for example, allow only packets containing HTTP requests to enter the network, and discard other packets. By restricting the packets that can enter the network, the firewall not only protects the network from potential intruders, but it also reduces the network traffic, to which the network's servers must respond, which, in turn, may improve the network's performance.

USE IT   On the Web, many companies sell firewall devices and software that is well suited for business use. Recently, however, many personal firewall products have emerged that provide firewall support to home computer users. To get a better feel of how your own PC may be

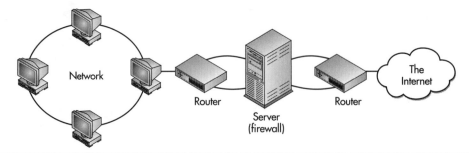

Figure 15.13   Network administrators place firewall technology (hardware and/or software) between a network and the Internet.

at risk, you should take time to run the ShieldsUp!!, shown in Figure 15-14, which you can run from within your browser at the Gibson Research Web site at www.grc.com.

Understanding the Microsoft Network Client Software

Within the Windows environment, the Microsoft Network Client software lets your computer share files and printers with other users. For example, when you view computers within the Network Neighborhood, as shown in Figure 15-15, the Microsoft Network Client software provides your ability to view and connect to other systems.

The Microsoft Network Client software essentially sits on top of your network software. If your network is running TCP/IP, the Microsoft Network Client will use TCP/IP to communicate with other systems. If you are not using TCP/IP, the Microsoft Network Client will use the NetBIOS to perform network communication. Within the Microsoft Network Client software, unlike a TCP/IP network that requires domain names or dotted-decimal IP addresses, you can refer to computers

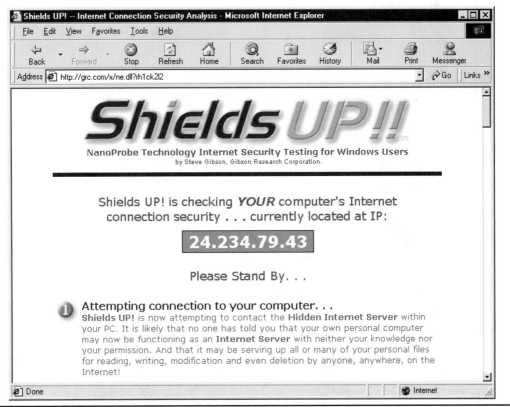

Figure 15.14   Using the ShieldsUp!! analyzer to detect potential security holes in your network connection

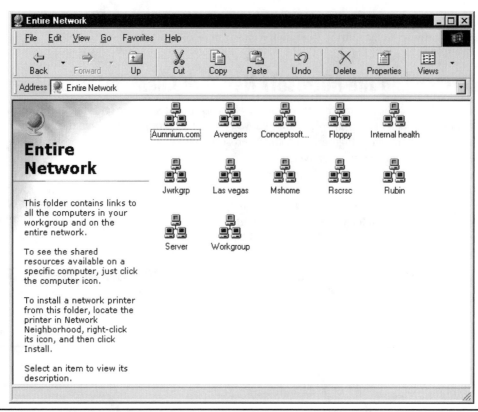

Figure 15.15   Viewing network computers within the Network Neighborhood

within the network using the computer's workstation ID, which the user assigns within the Network Properties dialog box Identification sheet, shown in Figure 15-16.

Running Network Benchmarks

USE IT   In Chapter 1, you learned that one of the fastest ways to identify bottlenecks within your PC is to run benchmark programs. In a similar way, one of the best way to identify bottlenecks within your network is to run network benchmarks. On the Web, you can find a range of programs that perform network benchmarks, such as the wsttcp program shown in Figure 15-17, which you can download from www.pcausa.com/Utilities/pcattcp.htm. Using the network benchmark programs, you can monitor your system's network transfer rate.

In addition, Table 15-2 lists several network benchmark programs you can download from the Web.

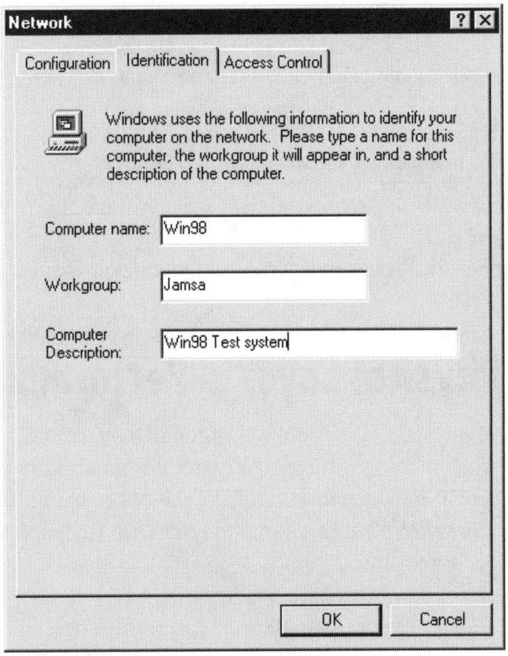

Figure 15.16   Within Microsoft Network Client software

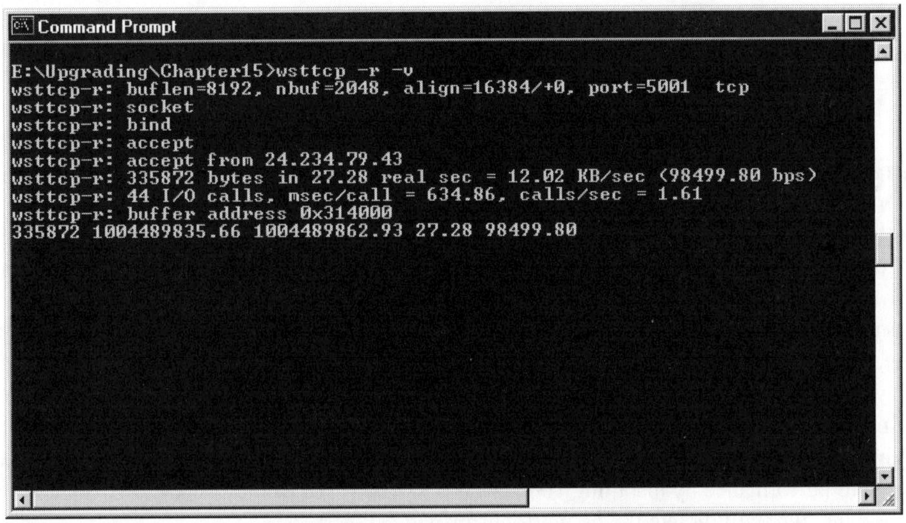

Figure 15.17   Using the wsttcp program to measure network benchmarks

Program	Web Site
NetBench	http://etestinglabs.com/benchmarks/netbench/netbench.asp
tdiq	http://www.pcausa.com/tdisamp/tdiq.htm
IPerf	http://ncne.nlanr.net/software/tools/tcp.html
VisualProfile	http://www.visualware.com/products/index.html

Table 15.2 Network Benchmark Programs You Can Download from the Web

Improving the Physical Layer's Performance

Within a network model, the physical layer consists of the cables, connectors, hubs, routers, and other hardware across which network messages travel. Network administrators estimate that 10 percent or more of a network's cost corresponds to cables. Despite the costs, using high-quality cables and connectors leads to fewer network errors, less signal attenuation (the signal remains stronger for greater distances), and hence, higher throughput.

USE IT If you are planning a network installation, you should budget for the cost of high-quality cables. If you have an existing network whose performance is less than you desire, you may want to establish a plan that lets you upgrade your higher network traffic areas with high-quality cables and connectors. To separate the high-quality systems from the rest of the network, you can install one or more bridges, which essentially lets you create subnetworks, as shown in Figure 15-18.

Next, you can upgrade your primary network to faster hubs and NICs (by improving the data-link layer). You might, for example, upgrade a 10 Mbs network to a 100 Mbs network, which, if you limit the network size, you can do for a reasonable cost.

Improving the Data-Link Layer's Performance

Within the network layers, the data-link layer, which resides immediately above the physical layer, exchanges error-free transmission packets between physical layer and network layer. Within a network, the data-link layer actually corresponds to the NIC that resides within your PC. Normally, the NIC supports a specific network technology, such as 10 Mb per second twisted-pair Ethernet or a thin-wire Ethernet. Some NICs support more than one technology.

Today, you can purchase low-speed (10 Mbs) NICs for about $20. The NIC will dictate the speed at which a PC can send and receive data. However, the card's capabilities must match that of the underlying network, which means that if your network uses hubs that operate at 10 Mbs, you will not improve your performance by installing 100 Mbs NICs. The speed of the slowest network component, in this case the hub, will dictate the network performance.

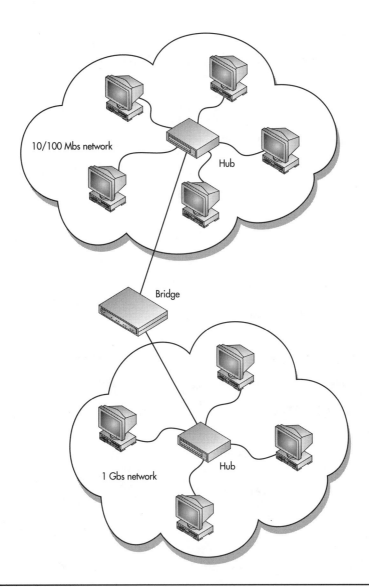

Figure 15.18   Using subnets to upgrade a network in stages

If you are building a new network, you should budget for higher performance cards and hubs. If you have an existing network, you may want to identify key network components (your high-traffic areas or high-salary employees) and create one or more subnetworks by upgrading one network to faster NICs and hubs. For a minimum investment, you can upgrade part of your network from 10 Mbs to 100 Mbs hardware.

▶ **NOTE**

Many network manufacturers offer cards and hubs that will operate at 100 Mbs or 10 Mbs on a per-connection basis. Depending on your network size, you may find that installing a 100/10Mbs hub gives you an easier upgrade path than developing two or more subnets.

USE IT Many PCs now provide network support on a motherboard chip. Before you can install and use a different network card, you must use the CMOS Setup program discussed in Chapter 6 to disable the motherboard-based network. Then you can install a faster NIC by performing these steps:

1. Shut down, power off, and unplug your system.

2. Gently remove your system-unit cover.

3. Locate an unused expansion slot and insert and secure the card.

4. Gently restore and secure your system-unit cover.

5. Plug in, power on, and start your system. After Windows starts, you must install the device driver that accompanied your NIC.

Improving the Network and Transport Layer Performance

In previous tips, you have learned that you can improve the performance of your network's physical layer by upgrading your cables and connectors. Likewise, to improve the performance of your data-link layer, you can upgrade to faster NICs and routers. To upgrade the network and transport layers, however, you must rely on software upgrades—often operating-system or device-driver upgrades.

Within the Windows environment, the system uses software called the Windows socket (Winsock) interface to interact with TCP/IP. To display the current Winsock version, you can use the System Interface utility, as shown in Figure 15-19.

USE IT To display the Winsock information using the System Information utility, perform these steps:

1. Select Start | Programs | Accessories. Windows will display the Accessories submenu.

2. Within the Accessories submenu, select System Tools | System Information. Windows will run the System Information utility.

3. Within the System Information utility, click the plus sign (+) that precedes the Components option. The System Information utility will display a list of your system components.

4. Within the component list, click Networks and then click the Winsock. The System Information utility will display your Winsock version number, as shown in Figure 15-19.

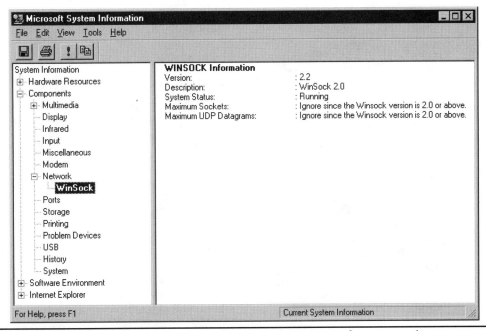

Figure 15.19   Viewing Winsock version number using the System Information utility

Monitoring Microsoft Network Client Operations

Throughout this book, you have used the Windows System Monitor to display various hardware and software settings. If you are using the Microsoft Network, you can use the System Monitor to monitor the number of network connections you have open, the number of files you have open across the network, as well as network communication statistics, as shown in Figure 15-20. The System Monitor's Microsoft Networks settings will not monitor a dial-up session. To view dial-up statistics, you must use the System Monitor's dial-up settings.

USE IT   To use the System Monitor to watch Microsoft Network operations, perform these steps:

1. Select Start | Programs | Accessories. Windows will display the Accessories submenu.

2. Within the Accessories submenu, select System Tools | System Monitor. Windows will display the System Monitor.

3. Within the System Monitor, select Edit | Add Item. The System Monitor will display the Add Item dialog box.

4. Within the Add Item dialog box, click the Microsoft Network Client option. The System Monitor will display a list of items you can monitor.

5. Within the list of items, click the item you want to monitor and then click OK.

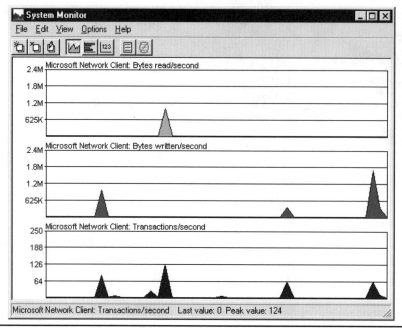

Figure 15.20 Using the System Monitor to examine Microsoft Network operations

Monitoring Network Packets

USE IT One of the best way to understand network operations is to examine the various messages that various network protocols (TCP, IP, HTTP, and so on) exchange. You can download and install several packet monitoring programs, such as the CommView program you can find at www.WebAttack.com\get\commview.shtml. Figure 15-21 shows TCP packets within the CommView application.

▶ **NOTE**

If you are using a Windows 2000 server, you can use the Network Monitor to capture and decode network packets.

Monitoring a Server

Computer networks use a wide range of programs, each of which performs a specific task. For example, a network server may run software that lets users send and receive e-mail, different software that responds to requests for Web pages, and other software that supports network operations. To fine-tune your network operations, you must recognize when a network application is becoming a bottleneck. Then

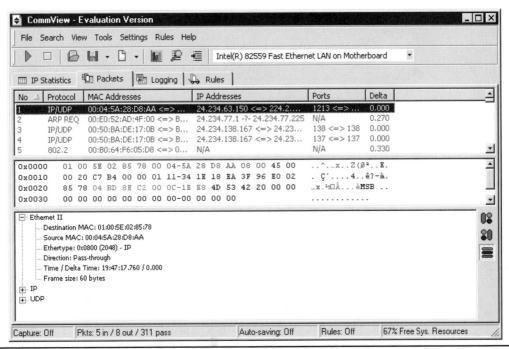

Figure 15.21   Using the CommView program to monitor network packets

you may decide to move the program to a new server or possibly to use multiple servers to perform the task.

USE IT   A simple, yet effective way to monitor program network tasks on a server is to use the Windows 2000 Task Manager, shown in Figure 15-22, to display information about each program's CPU use.

To monitor applications using the Windows 2000 Task Manager, perform these steps:

1. Right-click on an unused area of the taskbar. Windows will display a pop-up menu.

2. Within the pop-up menu, select Task Manager. Windows will display the Task Manager dialog box, within which you can view each application's CPU and memory use.

Blame Network Performance on the Internet

USE IT   Most users understand that the Internet consists of millions of networks that span the globe. If you administer a network, there are likely times when you would like to blame your network's poor performance on the Internet. Unfortunately, until now, getting your users to

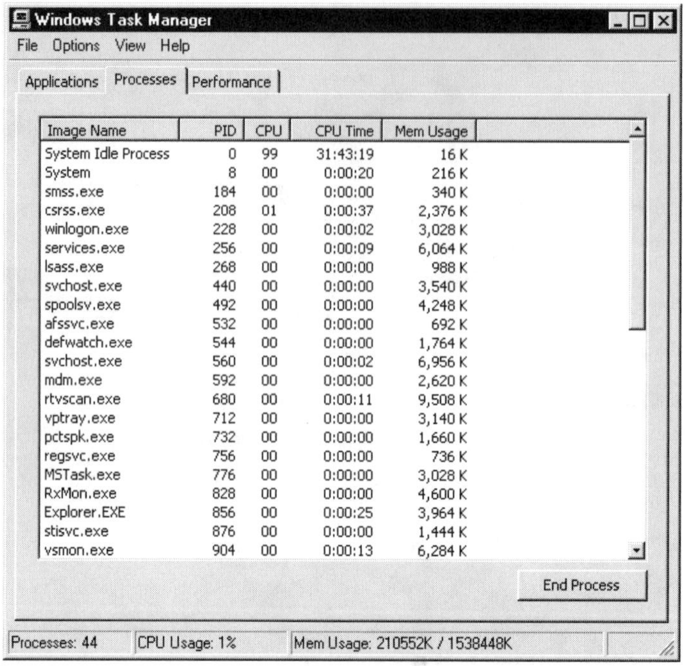

Figure 15.22   Using the Windows 2000 Task Manager to monitor application CPU use

believe you was likely difficult. Fortunately, by using the Internet Traffic Report Web site at www.internettrafficreport.com (see Figure 15-23), you can actually show users current traffic levels on the Internet. If your network operations become slow, you may be able to point to bottlenecks across the network. Okay, so it might work once. That said, it is still interesting to use the site to watch Internet traffic at different times of the day and before, during, and after various events, such as Presidential address.

Monitoring Network Operations Within Windows 2000

Throughout this book you have used the System Monitor to observe key system operations. If you are using Windows 2000, the System Monitor lets you monitor a wide range of network settings, as shown in Figure 15-24.

USE IT   To use the System Monitor to track network settings within Windows 2000, perform these steps:

1. Select Start | Settings | Control Panel. Windows will open the Control Panel window.

2. Within the Control Panel, double-click the Administrative Tools icon. Windows will display the Administrative Tools window.

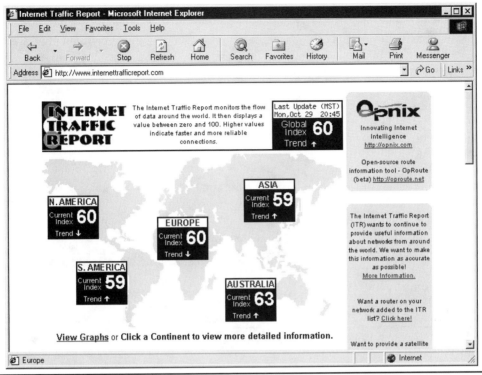

Figure 15.23   Monitoring Internet traffic at the Internet Traffic Report Web site

3. Within the Administrative Tools window, double-click Performance. Windows will display the Performance Monitor.

4. Within the Performance Monitor, click the Add button (+). The Performance Monitor will display the Add Counters dialog box.

5. Within the Add Counters dialog box, use the Performance Object pull-down menu to select Network. The Performance Monitor will display a list of counters you can monitor.

6. Within the counter list, select the counters you want to display and then click Add.

Viewing Your IP Settings

As you perform different network operations, there may be times when you must know your system's dotted-decimal IP address. For example, if you are experiencing network problems, you can examine your system's IP address to verify that your system is correctly configured for network operations (which means that your Internet service provider or network's DHCP server assigned your system a

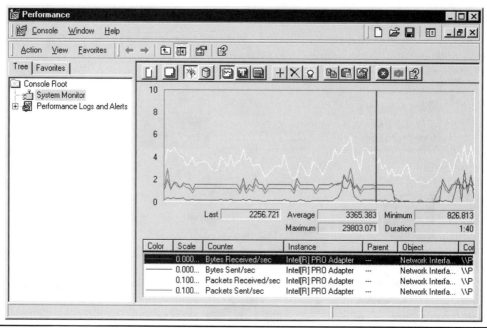

Figure 15.24 Using the Windows 2000 System Monitor to observe network operations

valid IP address). Also, several network-based programs, such as the Personal Web Server (which lets you configure your PC to act as a Web server capable of downloading HTML-based Web pages to other users), will require that others who want to connect to your Web site (assuming you don't have your own domain name) will need to use your PC's IP address.

USE IT To determine your PC's IP address, you can issue the **ipconfig** command from the system prompt within an MS-DOS window, as shown here:

```
C:\> ipconfig  <Enter>

Windows 98 IP Configuration

0 Ethernet adapter :
      IP Address. . . . . . . . . : 199.174.0.79
      Subnet Mask . . . . . . . . : 255.255.255.0
      Default Gateway . . . . . . : 199.174.0.79
```

In addition to using the **ipconfig** command to display your IP address, depending on your Windows version, you may also be able to run the **winipcfg** command, as shown in Figure 15-25.

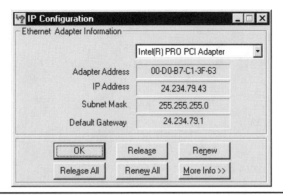

Figure 15.25   Using the winipcfg command to display a PC's IP address

To run the **winipcfg** command, perform these steps:

1. Select Start | Run. Windows will display the Run dialog box.

2. Within the Run dialog box, type **winipcfg** and press ENTER. Windows will run the **winipcfg** command, as shown in Figure 15-25.

Within the winipcfg window, click More Info to display additional information about your network configuration, as shown in Figure 15-26.

Using ping to Troubleshoot Network Problems

As you surf the Web, there may be times when you cannot connect to a specific site. In some cases, you cannot reach the site because the site is down, or because the domain name server that converts domain names you work with, such as www.osborne.com, into the dotted-decimal addresses Internet-based programs use (such as 198.45.24.130), or because your own network is experiencing problems. At other times, you may feel a site is responding slower to your requests than normal. In such cases, you can use the **ping** command, as shown in Figure 15-27, to determine whether the remote site is working.

The **ping** command is so named, because like the sonar signal a submarine sends out, the **ping** command sends a message (or series of messages) to a remote site. The **ping** command, like the submarine, then sits and waits for a response. You can use it to determine if a remote site is up and running or if your domain name server is working correctly. You can also use it to monitor the connection speed between your system and the remote computer.

 Before you can use the ping command, you must open an MS-DOS window by performing these steps:

1. Select Start | Run. Windows will display the Run dialog box.

2. Within the Run dialog box, type **command** and press ENTER. Windows will open an MS-DOS window.

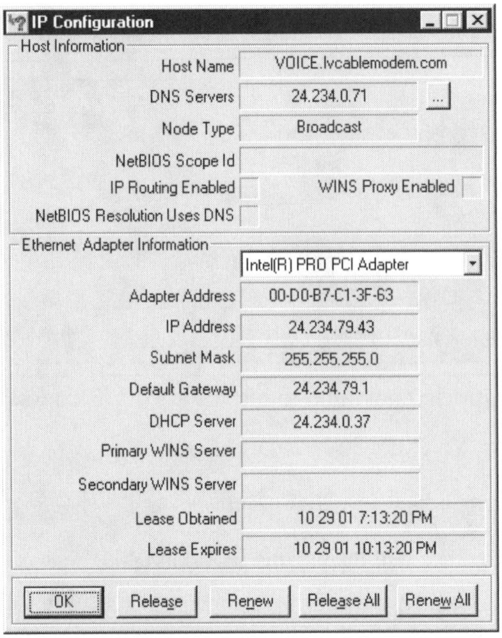

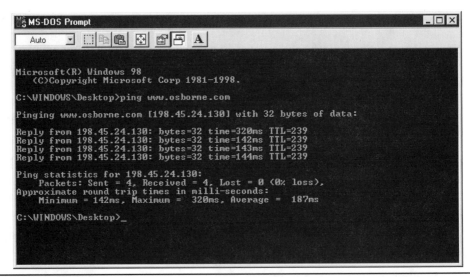

Figure 15.26   Expanding the winipcfg window to display additional network settings

Figure 15.27   Using the ping command to connect to www.osborne.com

To use the **ping** command to determine whether a remote site is operational, type **ping** at the system prompt, followed by the site's domain name. For example, to **ping** the Yahoo site, you would issue the **ping** command, as shown here:

```
C:\>ping yahoo.com  <Enter>

Pinging yahoo.com [216.115.108.245] with 32 bytes of data:

Reply from 216.115.108.245: bytes=32 time=248ms TTL=244
Reply from 216.115.108.245: bytes=32 time=237ms TTL=244
Reply from 216.115.108.245: bytes=32 time=235ms TTL=244
Reply from 216.115.108.245: bytes=32 time=235ms TTL=244

Ping statistics for 216.115.108.245:
    Packets: Sent = 4, Received = 4, Lost = 0 (0% loss),
Approximate round trip times in milli-seconds:
    Minimum = 235ms, Maximum =  248ms, Average =  238ms
```

When a site is operational, the **ping** command will send several messages for which it will receive responses. By tracking the amount of time between the message and the reply, **ping** can monitor the network's response time. If the remote system is not up and operational, the **ping** command will display a timeout error message similar to that shown here:

```
C:\ >ping somesite.com  <Enter>

Pinging somesite.com [217.66.167.102] with 32 bytes of data:
Request timed out.
Request timed out.
Request timed out.
Request timed out.

Ping statistics for 217.66.167.102:
    Packets: Sent = 4, Received = 0, Lost = 4 (100% loss),
Approximate round trip times in milli-seconds:
    Minimum = 0ms, Maximum =  0ms, Average =  0ms
```

In some cases, you may not be able to connect to a remote computer because of an error in the domain name server that converts a domain name to the dotted-decimal IP address that network programs use to address a remote system. When your domain name server is not working, the **ping** command will display an unknown host error message, as shown here:

```
C:\ >ping somesite.com  <Enter>
Unknown host somesite.com
```

When you encounter such an error, you should contact your network administrator or Internet service provider to see whether they are aware of a domain name server error. In some cases, you may be able to configure your system to use a different domain name server using the TCP/IP Settings dialog box, shown in Figure 15-28.

Using tracert to Monitor Network Connections

As you have learned, to send information across the network, TCP/IP breaks the information into small data packets. To travel to remote computer, a packet may travel may several intermediate hops, moving from one computer to the next. As discussed, within the TCP/IP stack, the network layer determines the route a packet will travel. As the packet makes its way across the Net, a router may choose to change the packet's route based on current network conditions or traffic. To monitor the path the network is using to send packets to a remote computer, you can run the **tracert** command.

 Before you can use the **tracert** command, you must open an MS-DOS window by performing these steps:

1. Select Start | Run. Windows will display the Run dialog box.
2. Within the Run dialog box, type **command** and press ENTER. Windows will open an MS-DOS window.

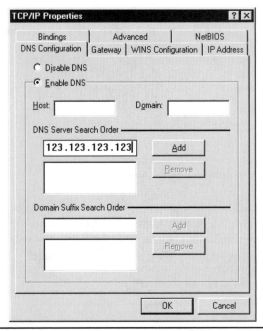

Figure 15.28   Using the TCP/IP Settings dialog box to specify a domain name server

To use **tracert** to examine the path your computer will use to send packets to yahoo.com, for example, issue **tracert** as follows:

```
C:\> tracert  yahoo.com  <Enter>
Tracing route to yahoo.com [216.115.108.245]

over a maximum of 30 hops:
 1  164ms  200ms  199ms  arc-3b.hou.mindspring.net [207.69.219.82]
 2  220ms  260ms  199ms  cisco-f0-1-0.hou.mindspring.net [207.69.219.65]
 3  176ms  200ms  200ms  206.181.103.185
 4  190ms  200ms  200ms  iah2-core1-s3-2.atlas.icix.net [165.117.63.222]
 5  164ms  160ms  168ms  dfw3-core3-pos4-3.atlas.icix.net [165.117.50.85]
 6  458ms  210ms  227ms  165.117.52.198
 7  237ms  199ms  199ms  so-4-1-0.mp2.Dallas1.Level3.net [209.247.10.109]
 8  236ms  209ms  239ms  so-3-0-0.mp2.SanJose1.Level3.net [64.159.1.130]
 9  239ms  209ms  239ms  giga10-2.ipcolo4.SanJose1.Level3.net [64.159.2.170]
10    *       *       *       Request timed out.
11  233ms  226ms  203ms  ge-3-3-0.msr1.pao.yahoo.com [216.115.101.42]
12  212ms  240ms  250ms  vl20.bas1.snv.yahoo.com [216.115.100.225]
13  211ms  210ms  240ms  yahoo.com [216.115.108.245]

Trace complete.
```

By examining **tracert**'s output, you can view not only the path the packet took to reach the remote site, but also the intermediate delays. When you feel that a remote network is responding slowly, you can use to **tracert** to learn more about the network traffic that exists between your system and the remote site.

CHAPTER 16

Disk Drives

TIPS IN THIS CHAPTER

ithin the PC, the programs that you run and the documents that you store reside on files on your disk. Disk drives exist to provide you with long-term storage capabilities. Unlike most PC components, a disk drive contains moving parts, which make the drive slower than its electronic components. This chapter examines disk drives in detail. You will learn how the disk stores information, as well as the factors that influence a disk's speed and storage capacity. This chapter also examines steps you can take to improve your disk performance. Finally, you will examine CD-ROM and DVD technologies and how you can use each to retrieve and store large amounts of data.

Taking a Closer Look at the Hard Drive

Within the PC, the hard drive is enclosed within a case, as shown in Figure 16-1. The drive connects to a power cable from the power supply and to a ribbon cable that connects the drive to a disk controller that normally resides on the motherboard.

If you could look into the drive's case (you should never open the case of a working hard drive, however), you would find that the drive contains several storage platters (often referred to as the disk's *surface*), as shown in Figure 16-2. Each platter has its own read/write head that reads and records data that resides on the disk's surface. Within the drive, the platters spin rapidly past the read/write heads. Older disk drives spin the disk platters at 3,600 revolutions per minute (RPM). Newer drives spin at 10,000 RPM.

Understanding Tracks and Sectors

To organize the data it stores on a disk, the disk drive first organizes the disk surface into circular tracks. Then, as shown in Figure 16-3, the drive divides each track into fixed-size (normally 512-byte) sectors.

As discussed, a hard drive may consist of multiple platters, each of which has two read/write heads (one for each side of the platter). When you examine low-level disk settings, you will often

Figure 16.1   A hard drive resides within an enclosed case.

Figure 16.2 Within a disk's case are multiple platters and read/write heads.

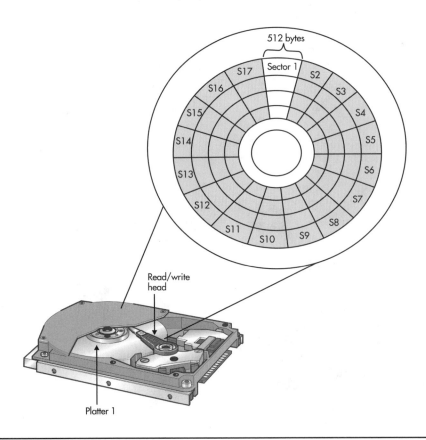

Figure 16.3 Disk drives organize information using tracks and sectors.

encounter values for heads and cylinders. The heads value corresponds to the number of read/write head the drive uses. In general, a cylinder corresponds to same track on several different disk platters. To determine a disk's storage capacity, you can use the following equation:

```
Number of Heads × Tracks per Platter × Sectors per Track × Sector Size
```

For example, given a disk with 10 heads, 1024 trackers per platter, and 64 sectors per track, you can calculate the disk's storage capacity as follows:

```
Number of Heads × Tracks per Platter × Sectors per Track × Sector Size
10 × 1024 × 64 × 512
335,544,320 bytes
```

Understanding How a Disk Stores Data

Within the disk drive, the hard disk platter is normally made from aluminum, the surface of which is coated with a thin film (or metal oxide on older disks) that can store magnetic charges. If you could take a close look at a track on the platter, you would find that each track contains thousands of *domains*, each of which the disk drive is capable of magnetizing to represent a one or a zero. For simplicity, assume, as shown in Figure 16-4, that the disk magnetizes domains with the value 1 such that they point north and domains with the value 0 such that they point south.

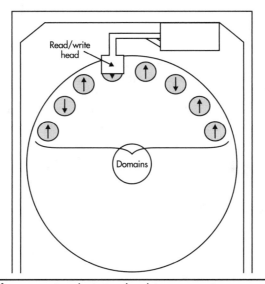

Figure 16.4   The disk surface contains domains the drive magnetizes to represent a zero or a one.

▶ *FACT*

Disk density refers to the number of bits the disk can store in a fixed amount of space. In general, disk density increases by 60 percent per year, quadrupling disk storage capacity every three years.

Understanding Disk Drive Types

Disk drives—whether hard drives, floppy drives, CD-ROM, or DVD drives—can be internal or external devices. Before your PC can store or retrieve information on a drive, you must first connect the drive to the PC. Most internal hard drives are IDE (Integrated Drive Electronics) drives that provide their own built-in disk controller. Using a ribbon cable, you connect an IDE drive to an IDE controller that resides on the motherboard. External hard drives, in contrast, normally connect to SCSI controllers (some internal drive also connect to SCSI controllers). However, recently external drives have come on the market that connect to FireWire 1394 buses, as well as to parallel port connectors.

Within the PC, a floppy disk connects to a floppy-disk controller. If you have an internal Zip drive, the drive will connect to an IDE controller (the controller you normally use to connect a hard drive). External Zip drives can connect to SCSI, USB, or parallel port interfaces. Finally, internal CD-ROM and DVD drives can connect to either an IDE or SCSI controller, whereas external CD-ROM and DVD drives may connect to SCSI, USB, or FireWire 1394 interfaces.

Understanding the Disk Controller

Within the disk drive, special electronics called the *disk controller* oversee all read and write operations. When the first hard drives became available for PCs, the disk controller actually resided on a card users installed into a PC expansion slot. Over time, these drives were replaced by IDE drives that contained their own controller electronics. Today, IDE and SCSI drives contain the electronics that let the drive perform read and write operations.

Normally, when you install an IDE drive in your PC, you will use a ribbon cable to connect the drive to the motherboard. Most IDE cables, as shown in Figure 16-5, let you connect two drives to an IDE controller that resides on the motherboard. The IDE controller simply coordinates the exchange of signals that travel the ribbon cable (IDE bus). The IDE controller does not perform or influence disk drive operations. It simply serves as an intermediary between the disk drive and the operating system.

Figure 16.5   Connecting a disk drive to an IDE controller on the motherboard

Understanding Disk Performance

A disk drive is a mechanical device. Within the drive, the disk platters spin past the read/write heads. Depending on the track that contains the data the drive is to read or write, the disk must move the read/write head in or out to the corresponding location. Then the drive must wait for the corresponding sector to spin past the drive's read/write head. Unfortunately, the disk's moving parts make the drive much slower than the PC's electronic components, such as RAM or the CPU.

Users normally measure disk performance in terms of *average access time*, which corresponds to the disk's average seek time and average latency. The *average seek time* corresponds to the average amount of time the drive requires to move the read/write head to the desired track. The *average latency*, in turn, corresponds to the average amount of time the drive must then wait for the desired sector to spin past the read/write head. Often, the average latency is equal to the amount of time it takes the drive to spin one-half revolution. In the case of a disk spinning at 10,000 RPM, the average latency becomes the following:

```
1 revolution = 1/10,000 of a minute
             = 0.006 seconds (6 ms)

½ revolution = 0.003 seconds (3 ms)
```

The average access time is the sum of the average seek time and the average latency:

```
Average Access Time = Average Seek Time + Average Latency
```

Common disk access times include 8.5 ms to 9.5 ms for IDE drives and 4.9 ms to 5.4 ms for SCSI drives. (At the high end, you may find SCSI drives that operate at 15,000 RPM to reduce the access time to 3.6 ms.)

▶ *FACT*

Because disk access speed is limited by the disk's mechanical (moving) parts, disk access speeds have increased only by about 33 percent over the past decade.

Understanding CMOS Disk Settings

To start your system, the BIOS must read and load the disk's boot sector into RAM. To provide the BIOS with information about the disk, the PC's CMOS settings contain specifics about the disk, which users refer to as the disk's *geometry*, such as the number of heads, sectors per track, sector size, and so on. For years, when users installed a new hard drive, the user had to use the CMOS Setup program to specify the drive's attributes.

To simplify the CMOS configuration process, disk manufacturers use a list of standard disk types. Within the CMOS Setup program, for example, the type 1 disk has the following geometry:

```
Type: 1
Capacity: 10MB
```

```
Heads: 4
Cylinders: 306
Sectors: 17
```

Today, most disk drives will automatically specify their type to the BIOS. Within the CMOS Setup program, you specify the disk type as auto or automatic.

Understanding Disk Drive Partitions

Before you can use a disk drive to store information, you must first partition the drive into one or more logical disks. In other words, when you install a drive, the operating system lets you divide the drive into separate logical drives. Users refer to drives as logical drives because the drives do not physically exist as separate drives on your system. Instead, however, the users can access the logical drives using a drive letter, just as if the drives did exist. For example, assume that you have a 10GB drive. Rather than create one large drive that used the entire disk space, you can partition the disk into smaller drives, each of which you assign its own drive letter. You might for example, partition the drive into two 5GB partitions, to which you assign the drive letters C and D. Figure 16-6 illustrates different ways you can partition a 10GB drive. Within an extended partition, you can divide it into 23 logical drives.

Partitioning a Disk Drive

To partition a disk, you use a special software program. For years, MS-DOS users and Windows users have partitioned disks by using the FDISK program, shown in Figure 16-7. Using FDISK, you first define the size of the partition. Then, you assign a logical drive (a drive letter) to the partition. To divide your disk into multiple drives, you would use FDISK to first create a primary partition to which you assign a logical drive. Then, you would create an extended partition that you can divide up and assign to up 23 logical drives.

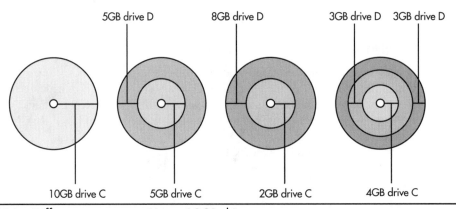

Figure 16.6   Different ways to partition a 10GB drive

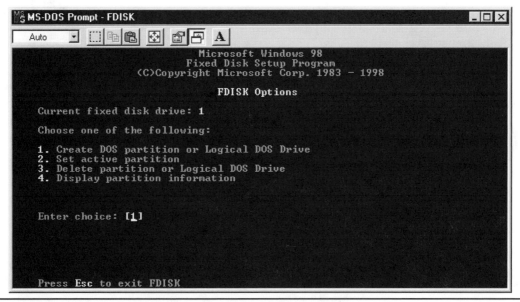

Figure 16.7   Using the FDISK utility to partition a drive

Within Windows 2000, you use the Disk Management function of the Computer Management Administrative utility, as shown in Figure 16-8, to partition a disk.

▶ *CAUTION*

Never change the partition information for a disk that contains information you need. When you change a partition's attributes, you will lose the disk's current contents.

Understanding the Master Boot Record

Chapter 9 examines the system startup process in detail. As you learned, each time your system starts, the PC loads the operating system's boot record from the boot drive. When your disk contains multiple partitions, the PC must first determine which partition it should boot. The PC determines the boot partition by reading the *master boot record*, which resides in the hard drive's first sector. The master boot record contains a small program that reads the partition table information (which a program such as FDISK records within the master boot record) to determine the bootable partition and then loads that partition's boot record. Figure 16-9 briefly describes how the PC uses the master boot record to start the system.

Formatting a Drive

After you partition a disk and create a logical drive for the disk, you must then format the disk for use by a specific operating system. In general, the format process prepares the disk for use by a specific

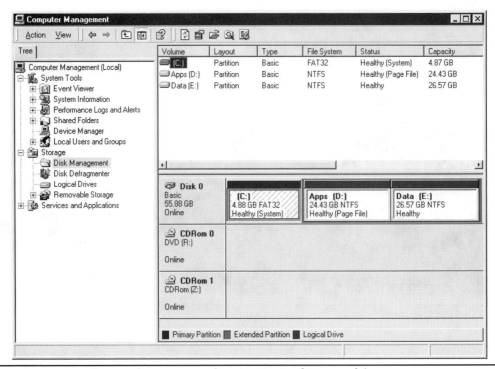

Figure 16.8 Using the Windows 2000 Disk Management function of the Computer Management Administrative utility to partition a disk

file system. The file system is the operating-system software that tracks where each file resides on disk. The file system also creates and manages the directories (folders) that you use to organize files. Within the MS-DOS and Windows 9*x* environments, users format disks by using the **FORMAT** command.

Assume, for example, that you must replace your previous hard drive, which has gone bad. To prepare your hard disk for use, you will need a bootable floppy disk that contains the following:

- System files to boot the PC (which will reside on a bootable floppy disk)
- **FDISK** command, which you will use to partition the disk
- **FORMAT** command, which you will use to prepare the disk to store files

After you install your hard drive (as discussed later, in the tips section of this chapter), you must then boot your system using the floppy disk. When your system starts, it will display a command line prompt. From the command line, you first use the FDISK command to format your drive:

```
A:\> FDISK  <Enter>
```

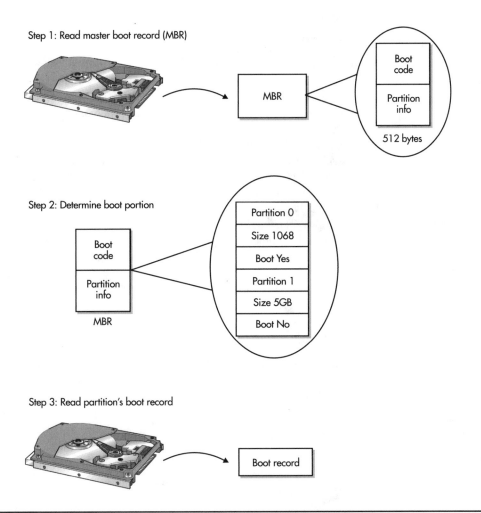

Step 1: Read master boot record (MBR)

MBR

Boot
code

Partition
info

512 bytes

Step 2: Determine boot portion

Boot
code

Partition
info

MBR

Partition 0

Size 1068

Boot Yes

Partition 1

Size 5GB

Boot No

Step 3: Read partition's boot record

Boot record

Figure 16.9   How the PC uses the master boot record to locate the bootable partition

FDISK, as previously discussed, will provide a menu you can use to first create a disk partition and then to assign a logical drive to the partition. After the FDISK command is completed, you must then format the disk as a bootable system disk, by using the FORMAT command, as follows:

```
A:\> FORMAT  C:  /S  <Enter>
```

The /S switch that appears in the FORMAT command directs FORMAT to create a boot record on the drive from which your system can start and to transfer to the disk the necessary files to start the system. After the FORMAT command completes, your hard disk is ready for use. You would then need to install Windows onto your disk.

Understanding Low-Level Formatting

One confusing aspect of disk operations is that there are actually two types of disk format procedures. A *high-level* format is an operation a user performs to prepare a disk for use by a specific operating system. In contrast, the disk manufacturer performs a *low-level* format before it ships the disk.

As you have learned, the disk organizes information using tracks and sectors. Before a disk drive leaves the factory, the disk manufacturer performs a low-level format of the disk that creates the tracks and sectors on the disk's magnetic surface, as shown in Figure 16-10.

In addition to creating the tracks and sectors, the low-level format also examines the disk's surface for locations that are unable to store data. The low-level format operation also marks the locations of any damaged sectors to prevent the disk from later trying to use the bad sectors to store information.

For simplicity, most books normally present disks as having the same number of sectors per track. Today, however, most disk drives vary the number of sectors per track. The tracks on the disk's outer (largest) tracks have more sectors than the inner (smaller) tracks. In general, to handle varying number of sectors per track, the disk drive divides its tracks into *zones*. As shown in Figure 16-11, within each zone, the tracks have the same number of sectors. The outer zones, however, have more sectors per track than the inner sectors. Users refer to the technology that lets disks vary the number of sectors per track as *zone bit recording*.

Understanding Sector Interleaving

Within a drive, the disk spins past the read/write heads at speeds up to 10,000 revolutions per minute. When the disk drive must read or write information, the drive waits for the corresponding sector to spin up to the read/write head and then it begins the operation. Years ago, because of the speed at which the drive spun, the drives did not have time to prepare to read or write the next sector before the sector had spun past the head. To better match the speed at which the disk spins to the speed of

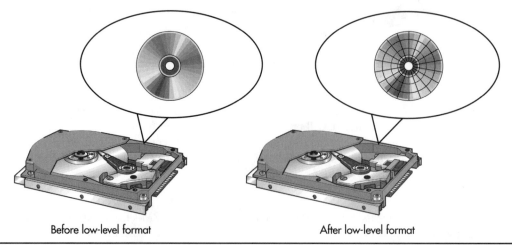

Before low-level format   After low-level format

Figure 16.10   The disk manufacturer performs a low-level format to identify a disk's tracks and sectors.

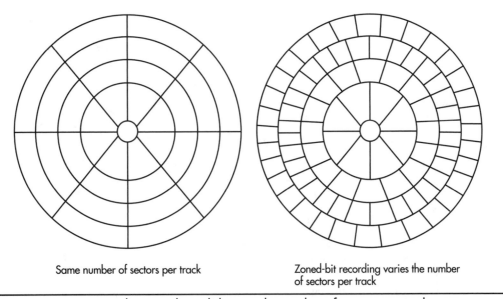

Same number of sectors per track | Zoned-bit recording varies the number of sectors per track

Figure 16.11 Using zone bit recording, disks vary the number of sectors per track

the disk, many disk drives interleave sectors, by spacing successive logical sectors apart on the drive. For example, Figure 16-12 shows three disks. The first uses no interleaving, placing the successive sectors side by side. The second figure separates successive sectors by placing them two sectors locations apart, creating what users refer to as 2:1 interleaving. The third figure separates the sectors using 4:1 interleaving. Today, however, disk drive electronics can easily keep up with the speed at which the drive spins, which means that to maximize disk performance, today's disk drives do not interleave sectors (which some documents refer to as 1:1 interleaving).

Understanding Data Encoding and Error-Correcting Codes (ECC)

For simplicity, most users assume that the disk drive stores ones and zeros that represent data. However, behind the scenes, the disk drive encodes the ones and zeros into a more compact form, in order to increase the disk's storage capacity and performance. Users refer to the compaction scheme the disk employs as the disk's *encoding mechanism*.

A disk stores binary information: ones and zeros. Within the information a disk stores are frequently long series of zeros. Rather than record all the zeros on the disk's surface, the drive encodes a special value that lets it replace the zeros with a special code and a count of the corresponding number of zeros. Assume, for example, that you must write an e-mail message to a friend that contains 256 consecutive zeros. Rather type all the zeros, assume that you instead use a special code you and your friend have agreed on to represent it, such as the pound sign (#) followed by a count, such as #256. By encoding the zeros in this way, you reduce the size of your e-mail, and you may also complete your message faster. The disk drive's encoding scheme works in a similar way.

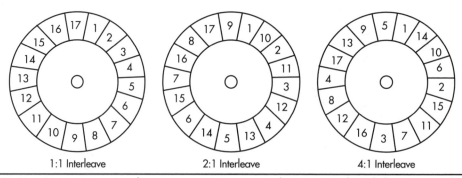

Figure 16.12 Using sector interleaving to optimize sector locations with a disk's rotational speed

Originally, most disk drives used modified frequency modulation (MFM) encoding to represent data. The MFM encoding scheme (which floppy disk drives still use) represents data but does not compress the data.

Today, most disk drives use run length limited (RLL) encoding, which limits the number of successive zeros that can appear within the disk's data. Using RLL encoding, the disk can store data in a more compact manner, which greatly increases the disk's storage capacity.

Although disk drives have become very reliable, they will periodically encounter errors. To reduce (and often to automatically detect and correct) errors, most disk drives make extensive use of error-correcting codes (ECCs). Throughout this book, you have seen the use of error-correcting codes with RAM, modem communications, and networks. By recording error-correcting codes on disk, the disk controller can detect and often correct disk errors, without placing additional overhead on the system.

Understanding Landing Zones

Within a disk drive, the read/write head floats less than 1/10,000 of an inch above the disk surface, so that it can magnetize or read the polarity of the domains that represent data. If the read/write head comes in contact with the disk surface (which may be spinning at 10,000 or more revolutions per minute), a *disk crash* occurs that normally scrapes and then splatters the metal oxide that coats the surface of the disk, which further damages the disk's surface. To give you a better understanding of just how close the read/write resides above the disk surface, Figure 16-13 compares the read/write head's separation distance with several small objects.

To prevent a disk crash, you should never move your PC while the disk drive is active. Should you jar or bump the PC, you risk the read/write head crashing into the disk's surface. When you power off a disk, most drives will actually land the read/write head on a special area on the drive's surface, called the *landing zone*. After the read/write is safely in place, the PC is safe to move.

Understanding File Systems

A disk stores data on disk within fixed-size sectors. To organize information on disk, the operating system tracks the disk locations where each file resides, which means that the operating system must

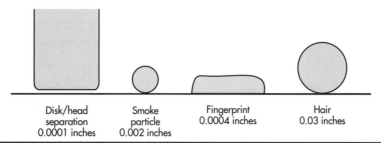

Disk/head
separation
0.0001 inches

Smoke
particle
0.002 inches

Fingerprint
0.0004 inches

Hair
0.03 inches

Figure 16.13   Comparing the disk/head separation distance to common objects

track each file's sectors. Within the operating system, special software called the *file system* oversees the process of storing and later retrieving data to or from disk. The file system, for example, lets the operating system and the programs you run create, open, and save files. Further, the operating system lets you create and manage folders as well as the files each folder contains.

Each time you create a file, the file system allocates a fixed number of sectors to store the file, called a *disk cluster*. For larger disks, file systems use as many as 64 sectors per cluster. Therefore, each file you create—even if you store only one byte of data within the file—consumes a minimum of 64×512 bytes (or 32,768) bytes. If, for example, a file contains only one byte, 32,767 bytes within the cluster will be unused. However, allocating a large number of sectors per cluster is one way that file systems support large disks. Further, as the file's size grows, the use of many sectors within a cluster reduces file fragmentation.

When you create a file on disk, the file system creates an entry in the directory within which you stored the file. The directory entry contains information such as the filename, extension, and attributes, such as whether the file is read-only or if the file has been changed since the last backup operation. Further, the file's directory entry contains the starting location of the file's first cluster.

To track each of the file's storage locations on disk, the file system uses a special table called the *file allocation table* (FAT). In general, the FAT tracks each file's cluster locations. Assume, for example, that a file resides in clusters 4, 5, 8, and 10. The file's directory entry will contain the file's starting cluster number, which in this case is 4. To locate the file's cluster, the file system looks up cluster 4 in the FAT. As shown in Figure 16-14, cluster 4 points to cluster 5. Likewise, cluster 5 points to cluster 8, which in turn points to cluster 10. Cluster 10, in turn, contains the hexadecimal value FFFF that indicates the cluster in the chain.

The file system stores the FAT at the start of the disk (actually, the file system places two copies of the FAT on the disk to prevent a disk error within one FAT from rendering the disk unusable). When you create, grow, or delete a file, the file system updates the FAT entries accordingly.

Understanding Disk Size Barriers

As disk technology improved over the years, the disk's storage capacity has grown rapidly, in some cases, outgrowing the size the BIOS, IDE controller, or the file system can support. If, for example, you are installing a drive larger than 528MB, you must ensure that your BIOS implements either "extended

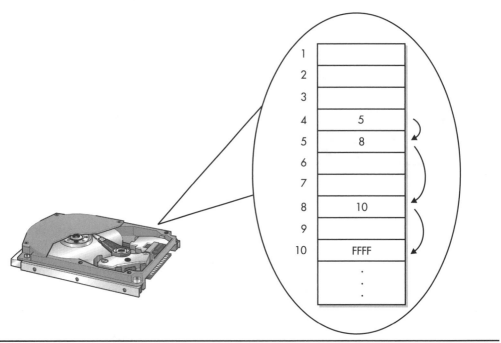

Figure 16.14   The FAT tracks a file's cluster locations on disk.

Int 13H support" or logical block addressing (LBA). Within some older systems, the BIOS interrupt 13H, which interacts with the IDE disk controller, does not support disks larger than 528MB. Normally, however, as discussed in Chapter 6, you can download a BIOS upgrade from your PC manufacturer's Web site to upgrade your flash BIOS.

   If you are installing a disk larger than 2GB, you must first determine if your BIOS supports the disk size (some BIOS systems have disk size limitations of 2.1GB or 3.7GB). Next, the FAT16 file system limits partition sizes to 2GB. If you want a partition size larger than 2GB, you must use the FAT32 file system (or the NTFS file system). The FAT32 file system supports partition sizes up to 2TB (2 terabytes). The NTFS, however, can support huge disks up to 16EB (16 exabytes, which is 2^{64} bytes, or 1,024 terabytes).

Using a Disk Cache to Improve Performance

The disk drive's mechanical components make the drive much slower than the computer's electronic components. To improve system performance, the operating system tries to reduce the number of slow disk operations the PC must perform. When a program reads information on disk, the smallest unit of information the operating system can transfer from disk is a sector. As such, should a program need only the first 10 bytes of a file, the operating system must read the sector that contains the first 10 bytes. The operating system, as shown in Figure 16-15, reads information from disk into buffers

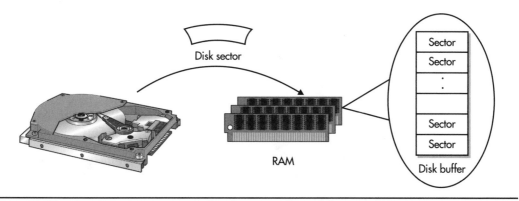

Disk sector

RAM

Sector
Sector
.
.
Sector
Sector

Disk buffer

Figure 16.15 The operating system reads information from disk into RAM.

that reside in RAM. Assume, for example, that a program reads a file's contents one character at a time. When the program performs its first read operation, the operating system will read the file's first sector from disk into RAM. As the program performs the next 511 one-byte read operations, the operating system can provide the data to the program using its RAM-based buffer, which eliminates the need for slow disk operations.

As you have learned, the CPU uses cache memory to reduce the slow number of RAM-based operations the PC must perform. In a similar way, the operating system, as shown in Figure 16-16, uses a RAM-based disk cache to reduce disk operations. In general, a disk cache takes advantage of the fact that when a program reads information from disk, the program will likely read information from nearby disk sectors. Using a disk cache, the operating system can direct the disk to read the sectors the program requires as well as several adjacent sectors into RAM. Because the disk drive can load data into RAM using direct memory access (DMA), loading the additional sectors adds little system overhead. Should the program later ask the operating system to read the data that resides in the additional sectors, the operating system can provide the data from the RAM-based cache, which eliminates the need for the slow disk-read operation.

Within the MS-DOS operating system, users could install the SMARTDRV.SYS device driver to create a disk cache. Windows, in contrast, provides its own built-in cache. As you will learn in the "Maximizing Windows File System Performance Settings" tip later in this chapter, you can increase the size of the Windows disk cache to improve your system performance.

Years ago, when applications stored information on disks, the applications would have to wait for the drive to physically record the data—which, in comparison to the CPU's fast execution speed, was a slow process. Using a disk cache for disk-write operations, in contrast, a program could write its data, which the operating system wrote to the cache. After the operating system placed the data in the cache, the program could resume its processing. Later, the operating system could write data from cache to the disk. The problem with the disk-write cache is that for a brief period, the application believes it has recorded the information on disk—which is not the case until the operating system later writes the disk cache contents to disk. Should the PC's power fail before the operating system records the disk cache contents, the program's updates will be lost.

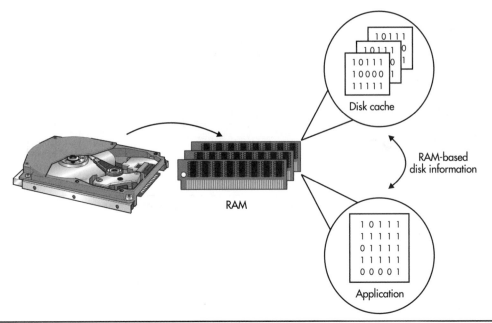

Figure 16.16 Using a disk cache to reduce slow disk operations

Understanding RAID Systems

To meet the high storage requirements of high-end Web servers and network servers, disk manufacturers developed a multiple drive device called a *redundant array of independent disks* (RAID). (Many users also refer to RAID systems as a *redundant array of inexpensive disks*.) A RAID system combines multiple disks into a single device that provides large storage capacity. However, the RAID system's primary goal is to protect the data on each of the drives should one disk fail.

The simplest RAID system that offers data protection, which users refer to as *RAID level 1*, uses two disks. Each disk stores an identical copy of the same data. If one disk fails, the second disk contains a "mirror copy" of the first, so no data is lost.

Advanced RAID systems use a technique called *data striping*, which divides the storage space on each drive into fixed-size units called *stripes*. The size of the stripe may be as small as a sector or several MB in length. The RAID controller interleaves the stripes across the drives, which means that the first stripe will reside on the first disk, the second stripe on the second disk, and so on. When you store a large file on a RAID system, the file will reside in stripes spread across each disk.

The "magic" or power of RAID systems—in addition to its capability of storing data—is that each disk stores "RAID parity" information (advanced error-correcting data). If one of the disks in the RAID system should fail, the RAID controller can use the error-correcting data to rebuild the failed disk's data on the fly. RAID systems that provide the ability to rebuild a failed disk in this way are *RAID level 5* systems.

Behind the scenes, the error-correcting information a RAID disk must store consumes space on each drive. To determine the disk-space utilization of your system, use the following expression:

```
Disk utilization = (Number of disks - 1) ÷ Number of disks × 100
```

For example, if you are using two disks in a RAID system, your storage utilization becomes the following:

```
Disk utilization = (Number of disks - 1) ÷ Number of disks × 100
                 = (2 - 1) ÷ 2 × 100
                 = 50%
```

Likewise, if you are using five disks, your storage utilization becomes the following:

```
Disk utilization = (Number of disks - 1) ÷ Number of disks × 100
                 = (5 - 1) ÷ 5 × 100
                 = 80%
```

Understanding CD-ROM Drives

With the advent of multimedia, and as programs became larger and more complex, the CD-ROM became a primary means of distributing large amounts of data. The CD-ROM (which stands for Compact Disc-Read Only Memory) is so named because a user can only read the disc's contents. Unlike a magnetic disk, the user cannot store information on a standard CD-ROM. Later in this chapter, you will examine disks called CD-Recordable (CD-R), as well as CD-Rewriteable (CD-RW) that let you store information. Note, however, that these discs, which let you record information, do not contain the letters *ROM* or words "Read Only Memory" in their names.

A CD-ROM can store up to 650MB of data. CD-ROM discs store information on only one side of the disk (the side opposite of the label). CD-ROMs represent binary data through the presence or absence of small pits on the disks surface. To read the CD-ROM's contents, the drive uses a laser to bounce a beam of light of the disc's surface. The pits on the disc, however, do not reflect the laser beam's light, which lets the drive distinguish between the representation of ones and zeros on the disc's surface, as shown in Figure 16-17. As you can imagine, if you scratch the disc's surface, you may change the disc's reflective capabilities, which, in turn, introduces errors when the drive tries to read the disc.

Understanding CD-ROM Drive Speeds

Users refer to CD-ROM drive speeds using terms such as 12X, 24X, 36X, and so on. The speeds are in reference to the original CD-ROM speed, which could transfer data at 150KB per second. A 2X CD-ROM drive, for example, transfers data at 2×150KB per second, or 300KB per second. Likewise, a 36X CD-ROM drive transfers data at 36×150KB per second, or 5.4MB per second.

Understanding the CDFS File System

To organize the information a CD-ROM stores, the CD-ROM uses a file system, just like a disk drive does. Using the file system's interface, the operating system can locate and access folders and files on

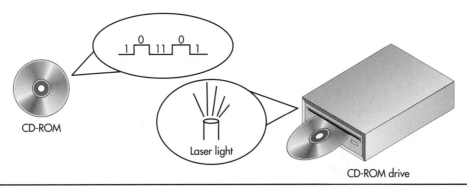

Figure 16.17 CD-ROMs represent ones and zeros through the presence or absences of pits on the surface that cause the disk to absorb or reflect light.

the CD. Today, CD-ROMs use a file system known as a CDFS (for compact disc file system). The file system—which users refer to as ISO-9660 or the High Sierra format (so named because CD-ROM manufacturers got together at Lake Tahoe, in the High Sierra mountains) to standardize the interface—is based on a standard from the International Standards Organization (ISO).

When you purchase a program that ships on a CD-ROM, the CD will use the CDFS to organize the program's files. The CDFS format differs from the format used by audio CDs to store music (which users refer to CD-DA for compact disc-digital audio). The Windows operating system, however, supports the CDFS and CD-DA formats, which lets Windows read the files a CDFS CD contains or play the songs on a CD-DA music CD.

Some CDs, called *multimode CDs*, store information using the CDFS and CD-DA formats. Within the multimode CD, track one stores information using the CDFS format. The remaining tracks are in the CD-DA format (which contain music tracks).

Understanding Recordable CD-ROM Drives

With the ability to store up to 650MB of data (some writers can create 700MB discs), users wanted the ability to create their own CDs, on which they could store large files, multimedia data, or system backups. As discussed, CD-ROMs store information through pits on the disk surface whose presence or absence a laser within the drive can detect. After the pits exists on a CD-ROM disc, the pits cannot be changed.

To allow users to store information on a CD, hardware manufacturers developed a technology that placed a die within a film-like surface on the CD. By heating the die at high temperatures at precise locations, a *CD writer* (a hardware device, also called a *CD burner*) could change the dye's reflective characteristics to create a pit-like area on the surface of the disc. Hardware manufacturers referred to the writeable CDs as a CD-R (compact disc-recordable).

Originally, the CD writers were large devices. Over time, hardware manufacturers were able to reduce the electronics so that the burner looks nearly identical to a standard CD-ROM drive. Users often refer to CD-R discs as *WORM discs*, meaning that you could write the disc's contents one time (the *WO* in WORM stands for *write once*), but you could read the discs contents many times (the *RM* in WORD stands for *read many*).

When manufacturers combined the CD-ROM drive and burner into one device, they would normally specify two speeds for the device. The first speed corresponded to how fast the drive could read data (such as 36X), and the second speed corresponded to how fast the burner could record data (such as 4X).

Although you cannot change information on a CD-R after you burn the disc, most CD-R drives let you create multiple sessions on the drive. Using multiple sessions, you can add more information to your disk at different times. You might for example, use a CD-R disc to store one week's backups of your hard disk. Using multiple sessions, you can record a backup to the drive on each day of the week.

Understanding Rewriteable CDs

As discussed, the CD-R discs were write-once discs. After you record information onto a CD-R disc, you cannot later change the disc's contents. Today, most CD writers support the rewriteable CD format that lets you overwrite information you have previously recorded on a CD. Using a CD-RW disc, you can rewrite the disk's contents hundreds if not thousands of times.

The difference between a CD-R and CD-RW disc is that unlike the CD-R, which uses a reflective dye whose state the burner changes, the CD-RW uses a surface chemical (which normally consists of silver, indium, antimony, and tellurium) whose reflective properties the CD writer can change and later restore using different temperatures. To reuse a CD-RW disc, the burner reformats the disc's contents, realigning the surface chemicals to their default (reflective) state.

Understanding DVD Drives

Today, when most users think of DVDs, their first thought is of renting movies at a video store. DVD is an acronym for Digital Versatile Disc. Depending on the DVD's storage format, it can store between 1.4GB and 17GB. The DVD achieves its tremendous storage capacity through a slightly larger surface area and the use of smaller pits.

Like CD-ROM drives, users express speeds for DVD drives using the format 2X, 4X, and so on. The original DVD speed was 1.385MB per second. A 16X DVD drive, therefore, can transfer data at 16×1.385MB per second or 22.16MB per second.

DVDs use the Universal Disk Format (UDF) to store data, video, audio, or a mix of all three. The DVDs that play movies on your television, for example, use the UDF physical-file format. Likewise, to store files, DVDs use UDF to manage the files and folders you use to manage the data you store on the disc. Like CDs, the DVD technology supports recordable DVDs (DVD-R), as well as rewriteable DVDs (DVD-RW). Today, however, the DVD writers and the DVD discs are significantly more expensive than their CD counterparts.

Cleaning a CD-ROM or DVD Disc

To store information, CD-ROM and DVD disks create pits on the drive's surface that do not reflect the light beam the drive's laser shines against the drive. However, fingerprints or dust on the disk's surface may prevent the drive from successfully reading the disc.

USE IT To clean the surface of a CD-ROM, you can normally simply use a soft cloth to gently remove the smudges. If the smudges persist, you may want to dampen the cloth with a little rubbing alcohol. If your disc is dusty, you can simply clean the disc's surface using an aerosol blower.

Running Disk Drive Benchmarks

USE IT In Chapter 1, you learned that to monitor your system's performance and to identify potential bottlenecks, you should run benchmarks. On the Web, you may find several different disk drive benchmarks, such as the HWiNFO32 shown in Figure 16-18, which you can download from www.hwinfo.com. Using the HWiNFO32 benchmark, you can gain insight into your disk's access time and burst read rate. Table 16-1 provides a list of disk benchmarks and the Web sites from which you can download them.

Monitoring Disk Operations

Throughout this book, you have used the System Monitor to monitor key hardware devices. Using the System Monitor, you can view your system's disk drive activities. If your system makes extensive use of your hard drive, you may think that you should install a faster drive to improve your system performance. However, by monitoring the operations the disk drive is performing, you may discover that your system's performance problem is not due to your disk drive, but rather, your disk drive is being overused because your system has insufficient RAM. Figure 16-19 illustrates the System Monitor settings you view regarding your disk drive. Within the System Monitor, you do not specifically monitor disk operations, but rather, you monitor disk-cache and file-system settings. Using the System Monitor, you should perform "before and after" analysis of your disks after you apply the performance improvements this chapter presents.

USE IT To use the Windows System Monitor to observe memory operations, perform these steps:

1. Select Start | Programs | Accessories. Windows will display the Accessories submenu.
2. Within the Accessories submenu, select System Tools | System Monitor. Windows will display the System Monitor window.

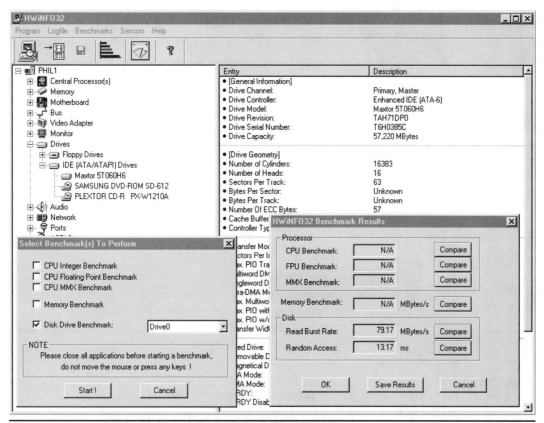

Figure 16.18   Using the HWiNFO32 benchmark to analyze your system's memory bandwidth

3. Within the System Monitor, select Edit | Add Item. The System Monitor will display the Add Item dialog box.

4. Within the Add Item dialog box, click the Disk Cache entry. The System Monitor will display a list of cache-related items you can monitor.

Benchmark	Web Site
WinBench 99	www.etestinglabs.com/benchmarks/winbench/winbench.asp
Iometer	http://developer.intel.com/design/servers/devtools/iometer/
HD Tach	www.tcdlabs.com/hdtach.htm
ThreadMark	www.acnc.com/benchmarks.html

Table 16.1   Disk Benchmark Programs You Can Download from the Web

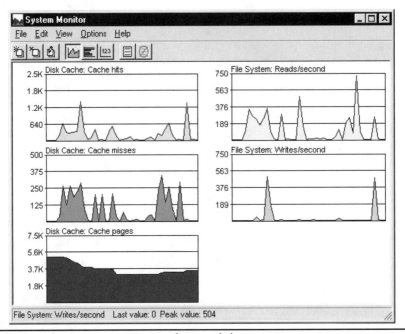

Figure 16.19   Using the System Monitor to observe disk operations

5. Within the item list, select the items you want to monitor and then click OK.

6. Again select Edit | Add Item. The System Monitor will display the Add Item dialog box.

7. Within the Add Item dialog box, click the File System entry. The System Monitor will display a list of file-system items you can monitor.

8. Within the item list, select the items you want to monitor and then click OK.

To monitor memory operations within Windows 2000, perform these steps:

1. Select Start | Settings | Control Panel. Windows will open the Control Panel window.

2. Within the Control Panel, double-click the Administrative Tools icon. Windows will display the Administrative Tools window

3. Within the Administrative Tools window, double-click Performance. Windows will display the Performance Monitor.

4. Within the Performance Monitor, click the Add button (+). The Performance Monitor will display the Add Counters dialog box.

5. Within the Add Counters dialog box, use the Performance Object pull-down menu to select Physical Disk. The Performance Monitor will display a list of counters you can monitor.

6. Within the counters list, select the counters you want to display and then click Add. The Performance Monitor will display your settings, as shown in Figure 16-20.

Maximizing Windows File System Performance Settings

Before you perform other disk-tuning operations, you should take a quick moment to fine-tune the Windows file-system settings for maximum performance by using the File System Properties dialog box Hard Disk sheet, shown in Figure 16-21. By fine-tuning the file-system settings, you can increase the number of RAM-based buffers Windows can use for file and disk operations. The more buffers Windows has in RAM, the fewer slow mechanical disk operations Windows must perform, which, in turn, improves your system performance.

USE IT   To fine-tune the Windows file-system settings, perform these steps:

1. Select Start | Settings | Control Panel. Windows will open the Control Panel window.

2. Within the Control Panel, double-click the System icon. Windows will display the System Properties dialog box.

3. Within the System Properties dialog box, click the Performance tab. Windows will display the Performance sheet.

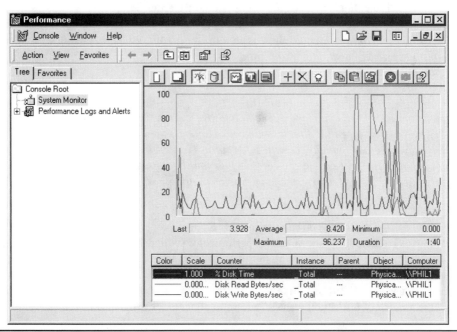

Figure 16.20   Using the Windows 2000 Performance Monitor to observe disk operations

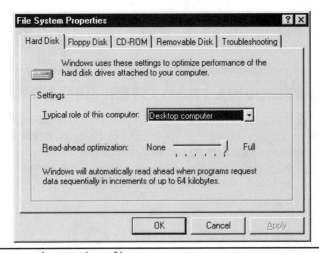

Figure 16.21   Fine-tuning the Windows file-system settings

4. Within the Performance sheet, click File System. Windows, in turn, will display the File System Properties dialog box.

5. Within the File System Properties dialog box, use the pull-down list to select the system type that best describes your computer. Then use the slider to set Read-Ahead Optimization to Full. Select OK. Then click Close to close the System Properties dialog box. Windows will display a dialog box asking you if you want to restart your system to put your changes into effect. Depending on your preference (and possibly the programs you have running), you can either restart your system now or at a later time.

▶ *NOTE*

If you have sufficient RAM, you may be able to improve your system's performance by selecting the Network Server system type that directs Windows to allocate the largest number of disk buffers. The tradeoff, however, is that you may allocate RAM for use as disk buffers that your system does not use. To best understand the proper settings for your PC, you should monitor your system's disk cache and file performance before and after you change various settings.

If your PC has a CD-ROM, you can use the File System Properties dialog box CD-ROM sheet shown in Figure 16-22 to fine-tune Windows performance settings for the drive. Using the performance settings, you can again trade off the amount of RAM Windows allocates to use for device buffers, which reduces the number of slow CD-ROM operations your system must perform. Depending on how often you use your CD-ROM drive (and whether you use it to retrieve text versus multimedia content), the amount of RAM you want Windows to allocate for drive buffers may vary.

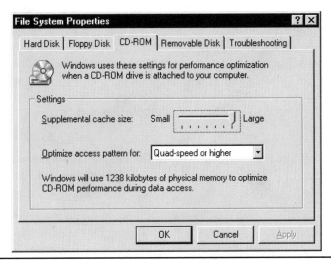

Figure 16.22   Fine-tuning Windows CD-ROM drive performance settings

To fine-tune the Windows CD-ROM drive performance settings, perform these steps:

1. Select Start | Settings | Control Panel. Windows will open the Control Panel window.
2. Within the Control Panel, double-click the System icon. Windows will display the System Properties dialog box.
3. Within the System Properties dialog box, click the Performance tab. Windows will display the Performance sheet.
4. Within the Performance sheet, click File System. Windows, in turn, will display the File System Properties dialog box.
5. Within the File System Properties dialog box, click the CD-ROM tab. Windows will display the CD-ROM sheet.
6. Within the CD-ROM sheet, use the slider to select a large cache size. Then, use the pull-down Optimize Access Pattern for the CD-ROM drive that matches your drive's speed. Click OK. Then click Close to close the System Properties dialog box. Windows will display a dialog box asking you if you want to restart your system to put your changes into effect. Depending on your preference (and possibly the programs you have running), you can either restart your system now or at a later time.

Cleaning Up Your Drive Using the Disk Cleanup Utility

Regardless of disk drive storage capacity, most users can quickly consume available space on their drives. Unfortunately, as the amount of available disk space becomes low, system performance can degrade quickly. Normally, most users can clean up their disk drives by performing a few simple operations, which in turn, normally frees up considerable disk space. The easiest way to quickly clean up your disk drive is to run the Windows Disk Cleanup utility, as shown in Figure 16-23. Using the Disk Cleanup utility, you can quickly delete files that often accumulate and consume disk space unnecessarily.

USE IT   To run the Windows Disk Cleanup utility, perform these steps:

1. Select Start | Programs | Accessories. Windows will display the Accessories submenu.

2. Within the Accessories submenu, select System Tools | Disk Cleanup. Windows will display the Select Drive dialog box.

3. Within the Select Drive dialog box, use the pull-down Drives list to select the disk you want to clean up and then click OK. Windows will then display the Disk Cleanup dialog box, as shown in Figure 16-23.

4. Within the Disk Cleanup utility, click the check box, placing a check mark in the box that corresponds to the item whose files you want to delete. The Disk Cleanup utility displays the amount of disk space you will regain by deleting the files. Then click OK. The Disk Cleanup utility will display a dialog box asking you to confirm that you want to delete the files; click Yes.

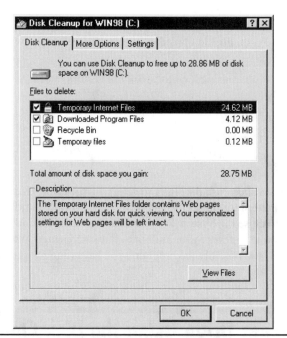

Figure 16.23   Using the Windows Disk Cleanup Utility to delete unnecessary files quickly

In addition to letting you delete unnecessary files, the Disk Cleanup utility also lets you remove Windows programs or other applications that you are no longer using. When users install applications, the setup programs normally install the applications on the same drive that contains Windows (which is normally the boot drive). Often, when programs must create temporary files, they will use the drive upon which they were installed (better behaved programs will use the TEMP environment entry to determine where they should place temporary files). If your disk drive contains applications you no longer use, you should remove the applications to free up the disk space for other uses. When you use the Disk Cleanup utility to delete unused programs, Disk Cleanup will launch the Windows Add/Remove Programs dialog box, within which you can select the programs you want to remove.

Update Your Disk Drive and Disk Controller Device Drivers

To communicate with your disk drive, the operating system interacts with the disk controller's device driver, as well as the disk drive's device driver. Because most users make extensive use of their disks, users should make sure they are running the most recent device driver for a controller or drive. Using the Windows Device Manager, checking for and installing a device driver update is very easy.

USE IT To check for and to upgrade to a new device driver for your disk drive, perform these steps:

1. Select Start | Settings | Control Panel. Windows will open the Control Panel window.
2. Within the Control Panel, double-click the System icon. Windows will display the System Properties dialog box.
3. Within the System Properties dialog box, click the Device Manager tab. Windows will display the Device Manager.
4. Within the Device Manager, click the plus sign that precedes the Disk drives entry. The Device Manager will display a list of your hard drives.
5. Within the hard drive list, click the drive you desire and then click Properties. The Device Manager will display the drive's Properties dialog box.
6. Within the Properties dialog box, click the Driver tab. The Device Manager will display the Driver sheet.
7. Within the Driver sheet, click Update Driver. Windows will launch the Update Device Driver Wizard, which will walk you through the driver upgrade process. Within the wizard, select the Windows Update option to direct the wizard to examine the Microsoft Web site for driver updates.

To update the device driver for your disk controller, repeat the same steps, but in step 4, click the plus sign that precedes the Hard Disk Controller entry and then select the disk controller you desire.

Managing Your E-Mail Files to Conserve Disk Space

Today, users consume a tremendous amount of disk space with e-mail messages. The worst disk-space consumers within a user's e-mail are the Inbox, Deleted Items, and Sent Items folders. Many users receive dozens if not hundreds of e-mail messages each day. Most users delete the messages they no longer need. Unfortunately, when you delete an e-mail message, you do not remove the message from your disk. Instead, your e-mail software simply moves the message into a Deleted Items folder. Likewise, each time you send a message, your e-mail software places a copy of the message into your Sent Messages folder. Over time, these e-mail folders can consume a considerable amount of disk space. If you are using Microsoft Outlook, you can view the amount of disk space a folder consumes within the Folder Size dialog box, as shown in Figure 16-24.

USE IT To view a folder's disk space consumption within Microsoft Outlook, perform these steps:

1. Within Outlook, right-click the folder you desire. Outlook will display a pop-up menu.
2. Within the pop-up menu, select Properties. Outlook will display the folder's Properties dialog box.
3. Within the Properties dialog box, click the Folder Size button. Outlook will display the Folder Size dialog box shown in Figure 16-24.

Within Outlook, you can perform several steps to reduce the amount of space your messages contain. Before you simply delete messages, you may first want to make a copy of the messages you may need in the future. Some users prefer to print a hardcopy of their important messages that they then file. Other users prefer to create an electronic copy by exporting or archiving their messages (two different processes).

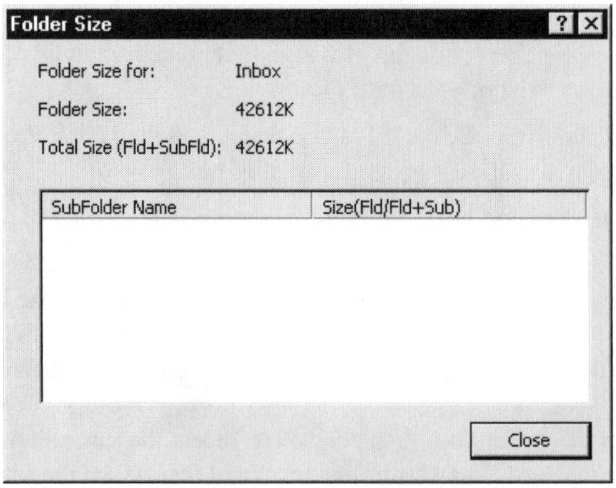

Figure 16.24   Viewing the disk space consumed by an e-mail folder

When you export copies of your e-mail messages, Outlook will make a copy of your messages to a file on disk, leaving your messages within your e-mail folders. Ideally, you will then move your exported file copy to a backup disk for storage. Then, you can delete the messages you no longer need. Remember, when you delete messages, Outlook will move the messages into your Deleted Items folder. After you delete your messages, you should clean up your Deleted Items by permanently deleting the messages.

USE IT   To empty your Deleted Items folder, perform these steps:

1. Right-click the Deleted Items folder. Outlook will display a pop-up menu.
2. Within the pop-up menu, select the Empty Deleted Items Folder option.

When you instead archive your messages, Outlook will move your messages from your e-mail folders into an archive file that resides on your disk. Unfortunately, by moving files to the archive file, you do not reduce disk space (you are simply moving files from Outlook to your disk). However, you may improve Outlook's performance because it has less data to manage. Within Outlook, you can archive mail folders manually or you can direct Outlook to auto-archive your folders after specific periods of time. Should you ever need to restore a message, you can use Outlook to open the archive file. For specifics on archiving e-mail folders, refer to the Outlook online help. By better managing e-mail folders, most users can regain significant amounts of disk space.

Scanning Your Disk for Errors

As you have learned, a disk stores information by magnetizing data onto the disk's surface. Although disk operations are quite reliable, errors can periodically occur, often when a PC (that does not have the support of an uninterruptible power supply) loses power before Windows can complete disk operations it has in progress. To test your disk drive for errors, you should use the Windows ScanDisk utility, shown in Figure 16-25. Using the ScanDisk utility, you can test your disks for data that has become lost on your disk (data that is no longer associated with a file), files that have been cross-linked in such a way that both files believe some data belongs to each of them, and for damaged locations on the disk's surface that are no longer capable of storing information (a time-consuming test).

USE IT   To run the ScanDisk utility, perform these steps:

1. Before you run the ScanDisk program, close your other programs. Otherwise, one of the programs may write to the disk as ScanDisk performs its analysis, which causes ScanDisk to restart its operations.
2. Select Start | Programs | Accessories. Windows will display the Accessories submenu.
3. Within the Accessories submenu, select System Tools | ScanDisk. Windows will open the ScanDisk window, as shown in Figure 16-25.

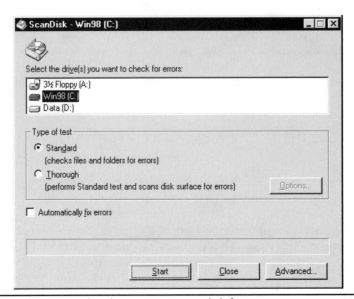

Figure 16.25   Using the ScanDisk utility to examine a disk for errors

4. Within the ScanDisk window, select the drive you want to examine and then choose the test you want ScanDisk to perform. Normally, unless you have been experiencing disk read or write errors, you will want to run a Standard test, which examines the disk's file system. (If you have been encountering disk errors, you should run the Thorough test, which examines your disk's surface for potential problems. The Thorough test normally takes several hours to complete.) Click Start to begin the test.

If ScanDisk encounters an error as it examines your disk, it will display a dialog box similar to that shown in Figure 16-26, which you can use to direct ScanDisk to repair the damaged file, delete the damaged file, or simply ignore the error.

Within the ScanDisk dialog box, note the name of the damaged file. If the file is a Word or Excel document, whose contents you can easily edit, you may want to let ScanDisk try to correct the error. Often, you will lose data during the ScanDisk file-recovery process. However, being able to recover some of the data may be helpful to you. If, however, the damaged program is a program file (a file with the .EXE or .COM file extension), you should normally direct ScanDisk simply to delete the corresponding file (running a program file that may now be missing program instructions may damage more files on your disk). When ScanDisk recovers a file, it will create one or more files in your disk's root directory whose names are in the form File0001.chk, File0002.chk, and so on. Using an editor, you can view the file's contents to determine if the recovered file contains usable information. If you recognize the file's contents, you should rename the file and then open the file using the correct operation. If, however, you do not recognize any meaningful data within the file, you can simply delete the .CHK file.

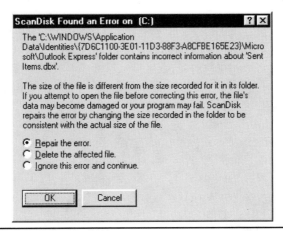

Figure 16.26   Responding to a ScanDisk file error

As a rule, to ensure that your disk and file system are in working order, you should run the ScanDisk program at least once a week and immediately following a loss of power or unexpected system shutdown.

Defragmenting Your Drive

Disks store files on disks within sectors. When you create a file, Windows allocates several sectors (users refer to the group of sectors as a *cluster*). As you change and grow a file, it is not uncommon for a file to wind up with information stored in several clusters. When a file's cluster resides in consecutive clusters, the file is said to be *contiguous*. In contrast, as shown in Figure 16-27, when a file resides in clusters dispersed about the disk, the file is fragmented.

The problem with fragmented files is that they take the disk drive longer to read, either because the disk drive must move its read/write head in or out to move to the next cluster, or the drive must wait for the next cluster to spin past the read/write head. When programs or files seem to take longer to load than they have in the past, it is possible that the disk has become fragmented. If a disk becomes badly fragmented (meaning many files are fragmented), you can often hear the disk drive's read/write head move in and out. Because the disk drive's mechanical parts are much slower than your computer's electronic components, fragmented files, which introduce more mechanical movements, significantly slow down your system performance.

Fragmented files are a natural occurrence of creating, editing, and saving files. For example, assume that you create a file named School, within which you log all your homework and tests. Windows will allocate clusters to store the file. Next, assume that you create a second file called Work, within which you record the hours you work and your schedule. Windows will allocate clusters to hold the file's contents. Finally, assume you later add more information to the School file that increases the file's size. Windows will allocate additional clusters for the file. As shown in Figure 16-28, the file now is likely fragmented.

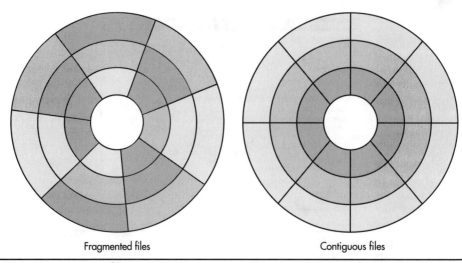

Fragmented files   Contiguous files

Figure 16.27   Contiguous files reside in consecutive clusters, whereas a fragmented file resides in a clusters that are dispersed about the disk.

In general, you cannot prevent file fragmentation. Instead, after it occurs, you simply must correct the fragmentation. Fortunately, Windows provides the Disk Defragmenter utility that you can run to defragment your disk, as shown in Figure 16-29.

USE IT   To defragment a disk, perform these steps:

1. Close any programs you are running. (If an active program writes to the disk while the Disk Defragmenter is running, the Disk Defragmenter will likely have to restart its processing.)
2. Select Start | Programs | Accessories. Windows will display the Accessories submenu.
3. Within the Accessories submenu, select System Tools | Disk Defragmenter. Windows will display the Select Drive dialog box.

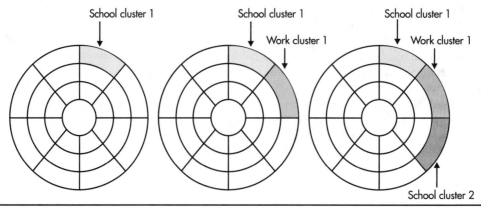

Figure 16.28   How a file becomes fragmented

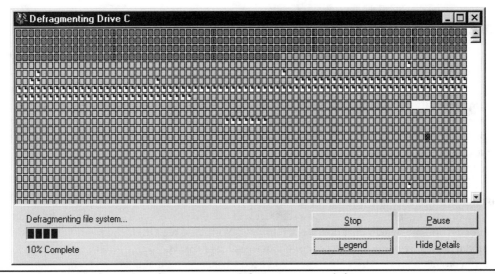

Figure 16.29   Using the Disk Defragmenter to defragment your disk

4. Within the Select Drive dialog box, select the drive you want to defragment and then click OK.

5. The Disk Defragmenter will begin its processing. To view a chart of your disk's current file layout, click Show Details. The Disk Defragmenter will display the disk's layout, as shown in Figure 16-29.

Users often ask how often they should defragment their disks. In general, if your programs or files load more slowly than usual, it's probably time to defragment. Likewise, if you can hear your disk drive when it reads a file's contents, your disk is likely defragmented. If you create and change a large number of files on a regular basis, you should defragment your disk as often as once a week. Normally, there are many times when you are not using your PC when you can run the Disk Defragmenter. The more frequently you run the Disk Defragmenter, the faster the Disk Defragmenter can complete its processing.

▶ *NOTE*

If you are using Windows 98, the Disk Defragmenter uses log files that reside in a hidden subfolder within the Windows folder named Windows/applog to track which applications you run on a regular basis. Using the contents of the log files, the Disk Defragmenter tries to move the applications you use on a regular basis to more optimal locations on your disk drive. In Chapter 10 you learned that to reduce overhead when you run programs, you may want to disable such application logging. If you disable the logging, the Disk Defragmenter cannot optimize the disk location of the programs you most frequently use, which may cause the programs to load slightly slower. However, by disabling the logging, you reduce overhead each time your program runs, which may slightly improve your performance.

Doubling Your Disk's Storage Capacity

If you are running low on disk space and you are not using the FAT32 file system, you can use the Windows DriveSpace utility to compress all or a part of your disk. Using the DriveSpace utility, you can compress a hard or floppy drive. When you use the DriveSpace utility to expand your disk, the DriveSpace utility will store your disk's contents in a compressed format, which is known as a compressed volume file (or CVF). When you convert a drive, the DriveSpace utility actually creates two drives, one which it compresses and one which it leaves uncompressed (which users refer to as *host drive*). If you run a program such as the Windows Explorer, both drives will appear in the Explorer's drive list.

Assume, for example, that you use the DriveSpace utility to compress your boot disk. The DriveSpace utility, in turn, will leave part of the drive's contents uncompressed, which Windows will use to boot your system. After Windows starts, it will use the DriveSpace device driver to mount the compressed volume, which then operates as drive C. Normally, the DriveSpace software will then mount the host drive using a different drive letter, such as drive H.

Before you compress a drive, however, you need to understand that although compressing a drive lets you increase your disk's storage capacity, you must understand that the compressed drive will be slower than its uncompressed counterpart because the DriveSpace software must decompress (or compress) data each time a program reads (or writes) a file. If you are concerned primarily with performance, you should not compress your drive. If you are short on disk space, however, you may simply want to compress part of your hard drive and then use the compressed drive to store the data you do not need to access on a regular basis.

USE IT To compress a drive using DriveSpace, perform these steps:

1. Select Start | Programs | Accessories. Windows will display the Accessories submenu.

2. Within the Accessories submenu, select System Tools | DriveSpace. Windows will display the DriveSpace 3 window.

3. Within the DriveSpace 3 window, select the drive you want to compress. Then, select Drive | Compress. DriveSpace will display the Compress A Drive dialog box, which shows you the amount of disk space you will have after you compress the drive.

4. Within the Compress a Drive dialog box, click Start. Windows will display a dialog box suggesting that you create a bootable floppy disk. Then DriveSpace will display a dialog box that gives you a chance to back up your drive before you compress it. If you do not have a current backup, you should back up your files before you continue with the disk compression.

5. Click Compress Now. DriveSpace will begin the compression process, which, depending on your disk's contents, may take several hours. After the compression is complete, DriveSpace will display a dialog box telling you that you must restart your system before you can use the compressed drive. Click Yes to restart your system.

Changing Your File System to FAT32

If you are running Windows 98, and you have not upgraded your system to the FAT 32 file system, you should consider the upgrade in order to improve your system performance (programs will run faster) and to regain several megabytes of disk space. However, after you convert a drive to the FAT32 format, you cannot later convert the drive back to a FAT16 file system. Also, if you are using disk compression to increase your drive's storage capacity, you may not be able to convert your drive into the FAT32 format until you decompress your drive. The FAT 32 file system uses 32-bit FAT which lets it track a greater number of clusters, which lets Windows uses a smaller cluster size, which often results in less wasted disk space for small files.

USE IT To convert your disk to the FAT32 file system, perform these steps:

1. Select Start | Programs | Accessories. Windows will display the Accessories submenu.
2. Within the Accessories submenu, select System Tools | Drive Converter (FAT 32).

Windows will run the Drive Converter (FAT 32) Wizard, as shown in Figure 16-30, which will walk you through the conversion process.

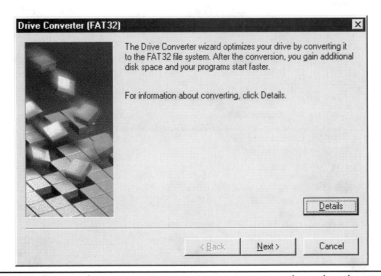

Figure 16.30   Using the Windows Drive Converter (FAT 32) Wizard to select the FAT 32 file system

Displaying Disk Drive Information and Benchmarking Your Disks Using Sandra

Throughout this book, several tips have taken advantage of the SiSoftware Sandra (**System ANalyser, Diagnostic, and Reporting Assistant**) program, which you can use to provide low-level device information and to run various benchmarks. Using Sandra, you can display a wealth of high-level information (such as available space) and low-level specifics (such as sector and cluster information) regarding your disk drives, as shown in Figure 16-31.

USE IT To download the Sandra program, visit the SiSoftware Web site at www.sisoftware.demon. co.uk. After you install and run the Sandra software, double-click the Drives Information icon to display your disk drive settings. Using Sandra, you can also run a disk benchmark program, as shown in Figure 16-32. To run the benchmark program, click the Drives Benchmark icon.

You can also benchmark your CD-ROM drive. To run the CD-ROM benchmark, double-click the CD-ROM Benchmark icon. The benchmark, in turn, will display information on how your drive compares to other CD-ROM or DVD drives.

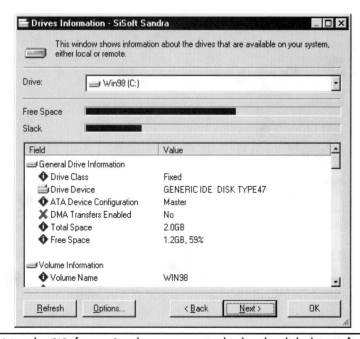

Figure 16.31 Using the SiSoftware Sandra program to display the disk-drive information

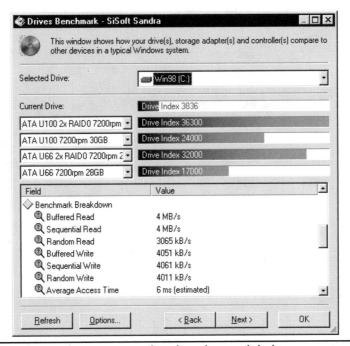

Figure 16.32   Using the Sandra program to benchmark your disk drives

Managing Your Hard Drive's Power Consumption

To keep your hard drive spinning, your PC can consume a considerable amount of power. If you are using a notebook PC, you may be able to conserve your battery life by directing Windows to "spin down" your hard drive when it is not in use by using the Power Management Properties dialog box, as shown in Figure 16-33. By spinning down your drive, your system will consume less power, which, in turn, extends your battery life. However, if you continue to use your disk on a regular basis, you will experience considerable performance delays because Windows must "spin up" your disk each time you must read or write to the drive.

To control the drive's spin-down time, perform these steps:

1. Select Start | Settings | Control Panel. Windows will open the Control Panel window.

2. Within the Control Panel, double-click the Power Management icon. Windows will display the Power Management Properties dialog box, shown in Figure 16-33.

3. Within the Power Management Properties dialog box, use the Turn Off Hard Disk pull-down list to select the minimum time delay. Then click OK to put your change into effect.

Later, when you are ready to use your PC under normal conditions, perform these steps and increase the drive's shutoff time.

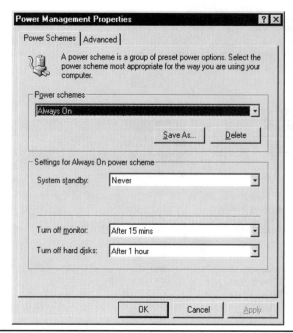

Figure 16.33   Using power management to control disk drive spin-down

Using the Device Manager to Change a Drive Letter

Within a system, Windows assigns drive letters to each disk and CD-ROM drive. Normally, Windows assigns drive letters based on how you connect the drive to the controller. Depending on your system configuration, there may be times when you need to change a drive's letter. For example, some programs store information in the Windows Registry that tells the program the CD-ROM drive from which they were installed (so that the program can later locate its data on the CD). If you later remove a disk, your system may rename drives, which causes the Registry entry to point to the wrong disk.

USE IT   Using the Device Manager, you may be able to change the drive's letter to a permanent setting by performing these steps:

1. Select Start | Settings | Control Panel. Windows will open the Control Panel window.

2. Within the Control Panel, double-click the System icon. Windows will display the System Properties dialog box.

3. Within the System Properties dialog box, click the Device Manager tab. Windows will display the Device Manger.

4. Within the Device Manager, expand the Disk Drives or CD Drives list and click the drive whose letter you want to change. Then click Properties. Windows will display the drive's Properties dialog box.

5. Within the Properties dialog box, click the Setting tab. Windows will display the Settings sheet, as shown here.

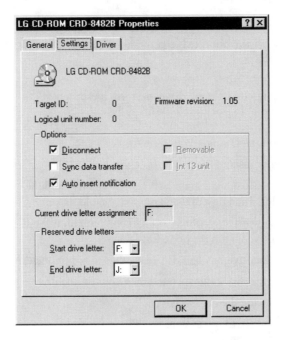

6. Within the Settings sheet, use the Reserved Drive Letters field to assign the drive letters you want Windows to assign to the drive. (If the Reserved Drive Letters field is not available, Windows will not let you change the drive's letter.) Click OK.

Upgrading a Floppy Disk Drive

Years ago, users often upgraded 5 1/4-inch floppy drives to 3 1/2-inch drives, or they added a second floppy drive. To connect a floppy drive to the PC, you use a ribbon cable to attach the drive to a floppy-disk controller, which normally resides on the motherboard (older PCs used a floppy-disk controller that resided in an expansion slot).

As shown in Figure 16-34, the floppy disk ribbon cable contains two connectors. The first connector corresponds to the drive the operating system will treat as drive A. The second connector, in turn, corresponds to drive B.

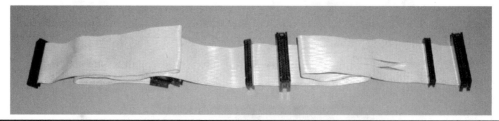

Figure 16.34 The floppy drive ribbon cable provides a connector for drive A and a connector for drive B.

USE IT To install or upgrade a floppy drive, perform these steps:

1. Shut down, power off, and unplug your system.
2. Gently remove your chassis cover.
3. If you are replacing a drive, unplug the drive's power cable and the cable that connects the drive to the controller. Then unscrew and remove the old drive.
4. If you are adding a new drive, you may need to purchase and install drive rails within which you will install the drive within the drive bay.
5. Slide the drive into the drive bay and use the screws to secure the drive in place.
6. Connect the drive to the disk controller and then connect the drive's power cable.
7. Gently replace and secure the chassis cover.
8. Plug in, power on, and start your system.
9. As your system starts, enter the CMOS Setup program as discussed in Chapter 7. Within the CMOS setup, set the drive's size attribute. Save your change and exit the setup program.

Upgrading or Installing a Zip Drive

Years ago, users regularly exchanged files using floppy disks. Today users normally exchange small documents (1MB and less) by using e-mail. As such, few users today can readily find a floppy disk. For larger files, users often use a Zip drive, which uses a floppy-like disk (only larger) that is capable of storing 100MB (or more). Figure 16-35 illustrates an external Zip drive. Depending on the Zip drive's type, you may connect the drive to a SCSI adapter, Universal Serial Bus, or even a parallel port.

USE IT To install a Zip drive, perform these steps:

1. If you are connecting a SCSI drive, select and assign a unique SCSI ID to the drive.
2. If you are connecting a drive to a Universal Serial Bus or to a FireWire 1394 bus, you can "hot connect" the device to the bus without shutting down your system.

Figure 16.35   Zip drives provide users with a convenient way to exchange large files.

3. If you are connecting the drive to a SCSI adapter or to a parallel port connector, shut down, power off, and unplug your system. Then connect the drive (and, if necessary, terminate the SCSI bus). Plug in and power on the drive.

4. If you previously shut down your system, plug in and power on your system.

5. After your system starts, depending on your drive type, you may need to install a device driver, which will accompany your drive on a floppy disk or CD-ROM.

Upgrading Your Hard Drive

When you install a hard drive, the steps you must perform will differ slightly, depending on whether you are installing an internal or external drive, as well as the controller-type (such as an IDE or SCSI) to which you connect the drive. Normally, when users install an internal drive, the users will connect the drive to an IDE controller that resides on the motherboard. In some cases, users will connect internal drives to a SCSI controller.

▶ NOTE

Depending on the size of the disk you are installing, you may need to update your system BIOS (discussed in Chapter 6) before your system can support the drive.

USE IT   To install an internal hard drive, perform these steps:

1. Shut down, power off, and unplug your system.

2. Gently remove your chassis cover.

3. If you are installing a SCSI drive, select and assign a unique SCSI identifier to the drive. If you are connecting two drives to an IDE controller, you must change one of the drive's bus master settings using jumpers or switches on the new drive, as briefly discussed in Chapter 11.

4. If you are replacing a drive, unplug the drive's power cable and the cable that connects the drive to the controller. Then unscrew and remove the old drive.

5. If you are adding a new drive, you may need to purchase and install drive rails within which you will install the drive within the drive bay.

6. Slide the drive into the drive bay and use the screws to secure the drive in place.

7. Connect the drive to the disk controller and then connect the drive's power cable.

8. Gently replace and secure the chassis cover.

9. Plug in, power on, and start your system.

10. If you are installing an IDE drive, enter the CMOS Setup program, as discussed in Chapter 7. Within the CMOS setup, set the drive's type to Auto or Automatic. Save your change and exit the setup program.

11. After your system starts, you must partition and then format the drive for use by your operating system. Within the Windows 9x environment, you will use the FDISK command to partition your drive and the FORMAT command to format the drive for use. Within Windows 2000, you will use the Disk Management function of the Computer Management Administrative utility to partition and format your drive.

To install an external drive, perform these steps:

1. If you are connecting a SCSI drive, select and assign a unique SCSI ID to the drive.

2. If you are connecting a drive to a Universal Serial Bus or to a FireWire 1394 bus, you can "hot connect" the device to the bus without shutting down your system.

3. If you are connecting the drive to a SCSI adapter or to a parallel port connector, shut down, power off, and unplug your system. Then connect the drive (and, if necessary, terminate the SCSI bus). Plug in and power on the drive.

4. If you previously shut down your system, plug in and power on your system.

5. After your system starts, depending on your drive type, you may need to install a device driver, which will accompany your drive on a floppy disk or CD-ROM.

6. Finally, you must partition and then format the drive for use by your operating system. Within the Windows 9x environment, you will use the FDISK command to partition your drive and the FORMAT command to format the drive for use. Within Windows 2000, you will use the Disk Management function of the Computer Management Administrative utility to partition and format your drive.

CHAPTER 17

Video Cards and Monitors

TIPS IN THIS CHAPTER

W ithin the PC, a video card (or in some cases, one or more video chips that reside on the motherboard) produces the images that appear on your monitor's screen. In this chapter, you will examine video cards and monitors in detail. As you will learn, your choice of video cards impacts not only the speed at which your PC can display images (which is very important for users who run multimedia programs or interactive computer games), but the video card also controls the image resolution (sharpness) and the number of colors the monitor displays.

How Monitors Display an Image

As you know, the monitor displays text and graphics created by the programs the PC is running. A monitor has two connections. The first is simply a standard AC power cord that provides the monitor with electricity. The monitor also connects to a video adapter within the PC. The video adapter is often a card that resides within an expansion slot. However, a PC may implement the video adapter using one or more chips that reside on the motherboard.

Many users refer to the video monitor as a *cathode ray tube* (CRT). As shown in Figure 17-1, the CRT is a triangular component that houses the screen. At one end of the screen is an electronic component called a *cathode* that houses the "electron guns" that illuminate the screen to create an image. The CRT is much like a light bulb; it maintains a vacuum between the screen and the cathode.

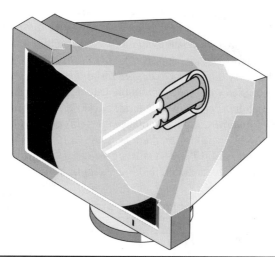

Figure 17.1 The cathode is a vacuum that contains the electron guns that illuminate the screens.

When the monitor is on, the cathode receives energy that it uses to release (to shoot) electrons at specific coordinates on the screen. At this same time, the monitor applies a positive charge to the face of screen that attracts the negatively charged electrons the cathode releases. The electrons, in turn, travel through an inert gas contained within the CRT's vacuum that strike red, green, and blue phosphor elements that reside on the inside of the monitor screen. The phosphor elements, in turn, heated by the electrons, begin to glow in their corresponding colors.

Understanding Pixels, RGB Phosphors, and Dot Pitch

A monitor essentially consists of hundreds of thousands (possibly millions) of small picture elements (pixels) which the monitor illuminates to display text and graphics. The term *screen resolution* describes the number of pixels the monitor is using to display text and images. When users discuss resolution, they specify the number of pixels across the screen followed by the number of pixels from the top to the bottom of the screen, as shown in Figure 17-2.

You express a screen resolution, such as 800×600 using the term *800 by 600*. The higher a screen's resolution, the more pixels the screen will use to represent text and images and often, the sharper the screen's contents will appear. Table 17-1 lists several common screen resolutions and the number of pixel elements each requires.

Each pixel element on the screen actually consists of a red, green, and blue phosphor element. The phosphor elements are unique in that when the element is heated, the element glows in a specific color. The greater the heat, the brighter the color's intensity. The three phosphor elements, together, form a pixel. By varying the intensity (the heat applied to each phosphor element), the monitor can cause the pixel element to take on a wide range of colors. For example, when the monitor does not apply heat to any of the elements, the pixel appears black. Likewise, if only the blue phosphor is heated, the pixel appears blue. By heating the red, green, and blue pixels at different intensities to a high intensity, the monitor creates white. Most monitors can apply 256 different intensity levels to each phosphor element, which lets the monitor generate 2^{24}, or 16 million different colors.

As you shop for monitors, a term you will encounter that indicates a monitor's quality is *dot pitch*. The dot pitch, which is measured in millimeters, tells you the distance between successive phosphors of the same color, as shown in Figure 17-3. The smaller the dot pitch, the sharper the images will appear on the screen. As you shop, you should look for monitors with a dot pitch of 0.28mm or less.

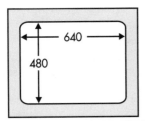 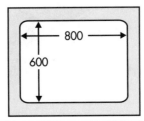 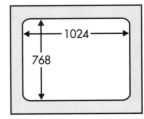

Figure 17.2 Common screen resolutions

Resolution	Number of Pixels
640×480	307,200
800×600	480,000
1024×768	786,432
1280×1024	1,310,720

Table 17.1   Pixels Displayed by Common Video Resolutions

Making Sense of Monitor Sizes

As you shop for monitors, you will encounter a myriad of sizes, from 13- to 21-inch and beyond. The important fact to know when you discuss monitor size is that the size measurement corresponds to the diagonal length of the monitor's screen, as shown in Figure 17-4. Today, larger monitors have become much more affordable than they were even just a few years ago. If you spend hours in front of your monitor each day, to reduce eye strain you should select at least 15-inch monitor and ideally, a 17-inch. Fortunately, monitors tend to hold their value longer than their PC counterparts and are less frequently made obsolete by a new technology. That said, because they consume much less desk space, many users may upgrade in the near future to flat-panel monitors.

Understanding Monitor Frequencies

To display a complete screen image, the monitor must illuminate all the screen's pixels at various intensities. To illuminate the pixels, the monitor targets its electron beams from left to right across the screen from top to bottom, as shown in Figure 17-5.

When the electron beam reaches the right edge of the screen, the monitor turns off the beam temporarily as it targets the beam at the first pixel element at the start of the next row. Later, when the beams reach the lower-rightmost pixel, the monitor again turns off the beams while it targets them at the upper-leftmost pixel.

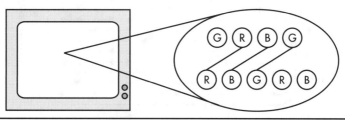

Figure 17.3   A monitor's dot pitch tells you the distance between similarly colored pixels.

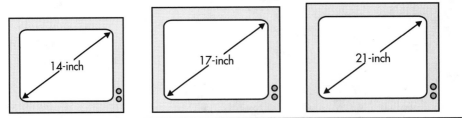

Figure 17.4 Monitor sizes correspond to the diagonal length of the screen.

Users refer to the speed at which the monitor moves from left to right across the screen as the monitor's *horizontal scan rate*, and the speed at which the monitor moves from the top to the bottom of the screen as the monitor's *vertical scan rate*. The faster a monitor's scan rates, the less wavelike an image appears on the screen.

Horizontal scan rates are normally expressed in kilohertz (KHz) or thousands of circles per second. A monitor with a horizontal scan rate of 48.8 KHz, for example, can refresh approximately 50,000 rows of pixels per second.

Depending on the monitor's resolution (the number of rows it must refresh) and its horizontal scan rate, as well as the speed at which the monitor can refresh the entire screen, the vertical scan rate will differ. Vertical scan rates are normally expressed in hertz (cycles per second). To minimize screen flicker, which in turn, reduces eye strain, a monitor should perform at least 72 or more vertical

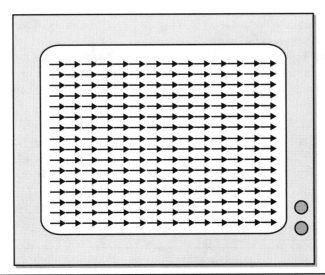

Figure 17.5 A monitor must continually refresh the phosphors that illuminate to produce the screen image.

refresh operations per second. In other words, to reduce flicker, the monitor must refresh the screen contents at a rate faster than our eyes can detect.

Most monitors sold today are *multi-sync monitors*, meaning that they support a range of refresh frequencies. Normally, you will change the refresh rate by changing a video card setting. Your monitor, in turn, will sync itself to the new rate. As you shop for monitors, you will find that many monitors advertise specific frequency rates. What you must determine is the monitor's refresh frequency at higher resolutions. For example, a monitor that can refresh a 640×480 screen at 75 Hz may not provide flicker-free updates if you are running the screen at 1024×768. Also, you should look for *non-interlaced* frequencies, and you should avoid monitors that use interlacing. To increase their refresh frequency, interlaced monitors will refresh every other row of pixels during a vertical refresh operation, as shown in Figure 17-6. By skipping rows of pixels, the monitor can complete the operation at a fast rate. However, because the interlaced monitor only refreshes every other row of pixels with each pass, it often creates a wavelike result, which can be very distracting.

▶ **NOTE**

Many software programs, including Windows, may let you select a refresh rate that your monitor cannot support, which may damage it. Before you assign a refresh rate to your monitor, refer to your monitor documentation to verify that it supports the rate.

USE IT   Depending on the capabilities your video card provides, you may be able to use Windows to change your monitor's refresh rate (remember, the video card must provide data at a rate that matches the refresh operations). As discussed, when you change the refresh rate the video

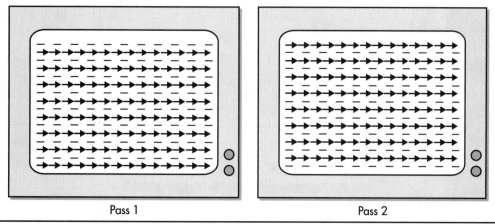

Pass 1   Pass 2

Figure 17.6   Avoid interlaced monitors that refresh every other row of pixels during a vertical refresh.

card is using, your monitor will sync itself to the new rate. To change the refresh rate using Windows, perform these steps:

1. Right-click on an unused location on the desktop. Windows will display a pop-up menu.

2. Within the pop-up menu, select Properties. Windows will open the Display Properties dialog box.

3. Within the Display Properties dialog box, click the Settings tab. Windows will display the Settings sheet.

4. Within the Settings sheet, click Advanced. Windows will display the video card's Properties dialog box.

5. Within the Properties dialog box, select the Adapter tab. Windows will display the Adapter sheet, as shown in Figure 17-7.

6. Within the Adapter sheet, use the pull-down Refresh Rate list to select the refresh rate you desire. Click OK to put your change into effect.

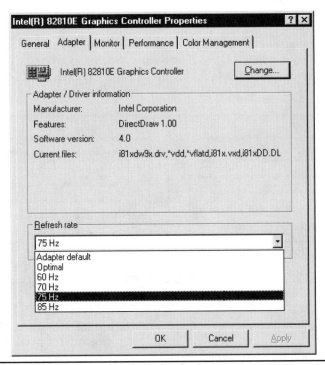

Figure 17.7   Assigning a specific monitor vertical refresh rate

How the Monitor Targets the Electron Guns

As you have learned, to display an image, the monitor rapidly aims an electron gun at phosphor elements on the screen display. The monitor doesn't have any moving parts that aim the electron guns. Instead, the monitor uses two magnets to focus the electron beam. The first magnet controls the beam's horizontal projection, and the second the beam's vertical projection. To further focus the beam, monitors place a screen-like shield between the electron guns and the phosphors, called a *shadow mask*. The screen's purpose is to prevent errant electrons from reaching and illuminating the screen's phosphors.

The Video Adapter Card Provides the Image the Monitor Displays

As discussed, you connect the monitor to a video adapter card that resides within the PC. The video adapter, in turn, controls the monitor's operations, by overseeing the horizontal and vertical refresh operations and by specifying the red, green, and blue intensity levels the monitor uses to illuminate each pixel element.

In general, the video adapter, as shown in Figure 17-8, consists of video RAM that contains the color information for every pixel on the screen, a video BIOS that contains instructions programs can use to create the text and images that appear on the screen, and a digital-to-analog converter that converts the color values from digital values to analog signals that drive the monitor's electron guns.

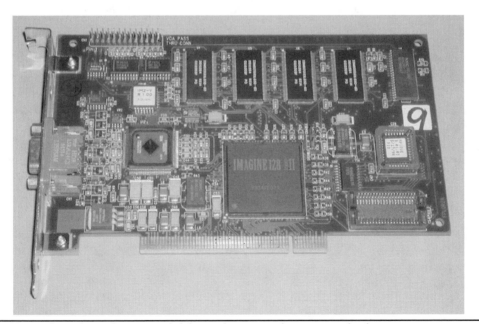

Figure 17.8   The video adapter card delivers the image the monitor displays.

Understanding Video RAM

Before a monitor can display an image, the monitor must know the color intensity values for each screen pixel. The monitor gets the pixel-color information from the video adapter. Specifically, the pixel-color values reside within the video adapter's RAM.

Within its video RAM, the video adapter color values might correspond to text or graphics. To the video adapter, whether a pixel is part of a text character or graphics image does not matter. Instead, the video RAM stores three byte values that correspond to the intensity level for the pixel's red, green, and blue color elements.

The amount of video RAM within the video adapter controls the number of colors and the resolutions the card supports. Most video cards, for example, support 256 color intensities for each of the red, green, and blue color components. To represent 256 color values requires one byte. Therefore, to represent a pixel's red, green, and blue intensity levels requires three bytes. Table 17-1 previously listed the number of pixels the screen displays at various resolutions. To display a resolution of 800×600, for example, requires 480,000 pixels. To support the display of 16 million colors, each pixel requires three bytes, which means that the video card must have over 1.4MB of RAM, as shown here:

```
Video RAM = (number of pixels) × (bytes per pixel)
          = (800x600) × (3)
          = (480,000) × (3)
          = 1,440,000 bytes
```

Table 17-2 lists the video-adapter RAM requirements for various resolutions and color requirements. Today, most high-end video cards ship with at least 4MB and often, 8MB of RAM.

Video RAM is Key to Video Performance

Chapter 8 examines RAM in detail. In Chapter 8, you learned that to improve video performance, many video card manufacturers migrated to a fast video RAM (VRAM) that improved performance by providing two ports. The VRAM's first port provided support for video-memory write operations

Resolution	256	65,536	16,777,216
640×480	307,200	614,400	1,228,800
800×600	480,000	960,00	1,920,000
1024×768	786,432	1,572,864	3,145,728
1280×1024	1,310,720	2,621,440	5,242,880

Table 17.2 Video RAM Requirements at Different Color Settings

(which let the CPU or a controller chip on the video card update the memory contents). The VRAM's second port provided support for read operations, which let the card's digital-to-analog converter read the memory contents, which it would send to the monitor for display. Today, most video cards use Synchronous Dynamic RAM (SDRAM), which is designed to support bus speeds of up to 200 MHz.

The Evolution of Video Adapter Types

When the IBM PC was first released in 1981, the PC came with a monochrome (black and white) monitor. Over the years, the monitor and video adapter cards have evolved to support larger numbers of colors and higher resolutions. Table 17-3 briefly describes the evolution of PC video adapter types.

Table 17-4 summarizes the pinouts used by the various video adapters.

Using Monitor Controls

Most monitors provide several controls (knobs or buttons) you can use to configure various monitor settings, such as the brightness, contrast, and image orientation. Often, the controls will appear on the front of the monitor, as shown in Figure 17-9. In other cases, you may have to open a plastic cover that hides the controls. Rather than providing a range of different controls, many newer monitors simply display a menu of options you can use the controls to select and perform.

Video Adapter	Description
MDA	Monochrome display adapter. Released with the original IBM PC. 25 rows of 80 column text. No graphics. One color.
CGA	Color graphics adapter. First monitor to support color and graphics operations. Supported 16 colors at 160×200, 4 colors at 320×200, and 2 colors at 640×200.
EGA	Enhanced graphics adapter. Expanded on the CGA to provide support 16 colors in each video mode and provided a 640×350 mode.
VGA	Video graphics array. Provided 640×480 resolution in 16 colors and 320×240 at 256 colors.
SuperVGA (SVGA)	Super video graphics array. Colors and resolutions are dependent on the amount of onboard RAM the video card contains.

Table 17.3 Common Video Adapter Types

Video Adapter	Pin Settings
MDA	Pin 1 Ground Pin 2 Ground Pin 3 not used Pin 4 not used Pin 5 not used Pin 6 Intensity Pin 7 Video Pin 8 Horizontal sync Pin 9 Vertical sync
CGA	Pin 1 Ground Pin 2 Ground Pin 3 Red Pin 4 Green Pin 5 Blue Pin 6 Intensity Pin 7 not used Pin 8 Horizontal sync Pin 9 Vertical sync
EGA	Pin 1 Ground Pin 2 Red intensity Pin 3 Red Pin 4 Green Pin 5 Blue Pin 6 Green intensity Pin 7 Blue intensity Pin 8 Horizontal sync Pin 9 Vertical sync
VGA/SuperVGA (SVA)	Pin 1 Red Pin 2 Green Pin 3 Blue Pin 4 Ground Pin 5 Ground Pin 6 Red intensity Pin 7 Green intensity Pin 8 Blue intensity Pin 9 not used Pin 10 Ground Pin 11 Ground Pin 12 not used Pin 13 Horizontal sync Pin 14 Vertical sync Pin 15 not used

Table 17.4   Pinouts for Common Video Adapter Cards

Figure 17.9   Monitor controls let you fine-tune the monitor's display.

Using the monitor controls (or monitor menu options), you can normally stretch the monitor image so that the image fills the entire viewing area, and you can move an image up or down or left or right to align it on the monitor screen. If you are traveling with a notebook computer, you may want to use the notebook's monitor controls to decrease the screen's intensity so that you consume less battery power.

Understanding the Video ROM BIOS

Within a video adapter is a ROM BIOS chip that provides built-in instructions that programs (specifically the operating system) can use to interact with the video card. Using instructions that reside within the video ROM, the operating system, for example, can configure the screen resolution and the number of colors the screen displays, and it can also display text or pixels at specific screen locations. The instructions that reside within the card's video ROM, essentially define the card's capabilities. Many newer video cards provide a flash-based BIOS that you can update by downloading and running a video-BIOS upgrade program, much like you would update a flash-based PC BIOS, as discussed in Chapter 6.

Understanding the Video Adapter's Device Driver

As you know, a device driver is a special software program the operating system uses to interact with a device. When you purchase a new video card, you will receive a floppy disk or CD-ROM that contains the card's device driver software. Before Windows, for example, can display text on the screen, it must interact with the video card's device driver to place the text on the screen at the correct locations. The device driver, in turn, will likely rely on instructions that reside within the card's video ROM to place the corresponding values for the text's pixel within the video RAM, as shown in Figure 17-10.

In Chapter 10, you learned that you should update the device drivers that correspond to the devices you use most often. Your video card and monitor definitely fall into that category. Fortunately, Windows makes it very easy for you to check if new drivers are available for your video card and monitor. Before you upgrade your drivers, however, you should save the current driver files in a safe location, in case you must restore them should the new driver create incompatibility programs.

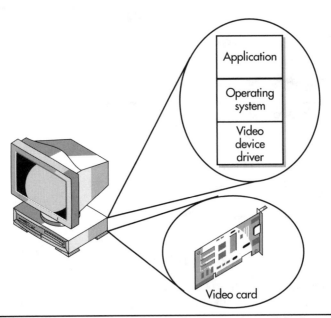

Figure 17.10   Windows interacts with the video card's device driver, which in turn, interacts with the video card.

USE IT   To determine which device driver files your video card is using, perform these steps:

1. Select Start | Settings | Control Panel. Windows will open the Control Panel window.

2. Within the Control Panel, double-click the System icon. Windows will open the System Properties dialog box.

3. Within the System Properties dialog box, click the Device Manager tab. Windows will display the Device Manager.

4. Within the Device Manager, click the plus sign (+) that precedes the Display Adapters entry. Windows will expand the list of your system's video adapters.

5. Within the video adapter list, click your video adapter entry and then click Properties. Windows will display your video card's Properties dialog box.

6. Within the Properties dialog box, click the Driver tab. Windows will display the Driver sheet. Then click Driver File Details. Windows will display your card's device driver files, as shown here.

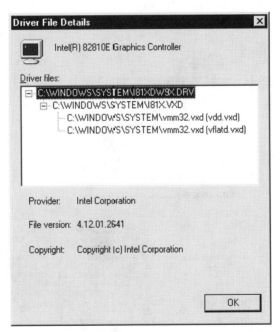

7. Using the Explorer, copy the device driver files into a folder (you may want to create a subfolder within the Windows\System folder that you call VideoDrivers).

8. After you successfully copy the files, close the dialog box that lists the driver files and then click Update Driver within your video card's Properties dialog box. Windows, in turn, will start the Update Device Driver Wizard that will walk you through the update process. When the Wizard displays a page prompting you to select the device driver location, select the Microsoft Windows Update option that directs the wizard to search the Microsoft Web site for driver updates.

Using similar steps, you can record and then update your monitor's device driver as well. In steps 4 and 5, rather than selecting your video adapter within the Device Manager, you select your monitor instead.

USE IT In addition to using the Device Manager to display video adapter and monitor device drivers, you can use the System Information utility, as shown in Figure 17-11.

To display video adapter and monitor information using the System Information utility, perform these steps:

1. Select Start | Programs | Accessories. Windows will display the Accessories submenu.

2. Within the Accessories submenu, select System Tools | System Information. Windows will display the System Information utility.

3. Within the System Information utility, click the plus sign (+) that precedes the Components entry. The System Information utility, in turn, will display a list of your system's hardware components.

4. Within the Component list, click the Display option and then choose the Advanced radio button. The System Information utility will display your video adapter and monitor specifics, as shown in Figure 17-11.

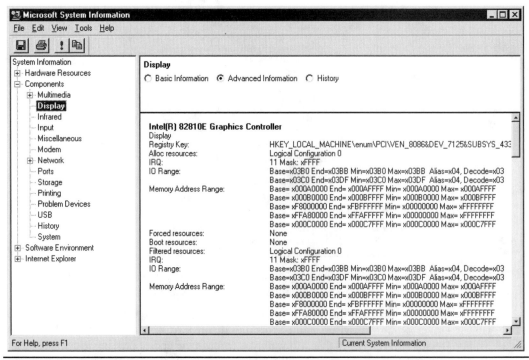

Figure 17.11 Using the System Monitor to display video adapter and monitor device driver information

Speeding Data to the Video RAM

Before the monitor can display an image, the image's pixel color values must reside within the video card's RAM. As you have learned, a screen displaying a resolution of 800×600 at 16-million colors requires roughly 1.4MB of pixel data.

Assume, for example, that you are using your PC to watch a DVD-based movie, full-screen on your monitor. To avoid flicker during screen updates, movies update the screen 30 times per second. Using the 800×600 screen at 24 colors, that would mean the PC must place over 30MB of data into the video RAM every second! As you might guess, to maintain the flow of data to the video adapter card can consume considerable bus bandwidth.

Today, most graphics cards reside in either a PCI or Accelerated Graphics Port (AGP) expansion slot. Chapter 12 examines the PCI and AGP buses in detail. Although strong debate exists among users as to true performance gains an AGP-based card will achieve over a PCI-based card, most users with high-end graphics applications are turning to the AGP. In Chapter 12, you learned that the AGP provides an expansion-card slot on the motherboard that lets a card (via the North Bridge controller) access the system bus. Figure 17-12 illustrates an AGP slot on a motherboard. Originally designed to operate at 264MB per second transfer rates, many systems now support the 2X AGP mode that operates at 533MB per second or the 4X AGP mode that offers 1066MB per second transfer rates. As the complexity of graphics applications (primarily high-end 3-D games) increases, the AGP will play a key role in the PCs ability to display high-speed, high-quality images.

Figure 17.12   An AGP slot on the motherboard

Understanding Liquid Crystal Display (LCD) Monitors

Notebook PCs and some flat-screen monitors do not use phosphor-based screens. Instead, they use liquid crystal display (LCD) screens. The LCD screens are so named because they rely on small liquid crystal cells, one for each pixel color, to control the amount of red, green, and blue light that reaches the screen.

The crystals themselves do not illuminate. Instead, they filter (restrict or permit) the light to reach the screen at different intensities. By applying an electrical charge to each crystal, the monitor controls the crystal's alignment, which, in turn, controls the amount of light that reaches the screen.

LCD screens use either an active- or passive-matrix of transistors to apply a signal to each crystal. Within an active-matrix display, each pixel has its own transistor, which applies a specific charge to the corresponding crystals. In an 800×600 screen, for example, the display would use 480,000 transistors. In contrast, in a passive-matrix display, each row and column have a transistor that assigns the charge to crystals in the matrix. A passive-matrix screen at 800×600 would use 1,400 transistors (800 for the columns and 600 for the rows). Because the active-matrix screen (which costs more) uses individual transistors to charge each crystal, the active-matrix crystals have finer alignment that results in a sharper image.

Understanding 32-Bit and 3D Video Adapter Cards

Many Windows users currently run their monitors using 24-bit pixel colors, which provides support for over 16 million colors (2^{24}). Over the past year, 32-bit video cards have emerged that advertise "true color." In general, the 32-bit cards still use 8 bits to describe the red-color intensity, 8 bits for green, and 8 for blue, which yields support for 2^{24} or 16 million colors. However, the 32-bit cards also provide each pixel with an alpha channel value (in the range 0 to 255) that programs can set to influence the pixel's transparency. High-end video applications that display water, glass, or other transparent objects can use the alpha setting to produce a more realistic image.

▶ *FACT*

The human eye can distinguish between close to six million colors.

Further, many new video cards provide support for 3-D applications (primarily high-end video games), such as memory buffers for surface textures, z-buffer support that lets programs express a pixel's depth within an image, as well as coprocessors and accelerators that perform the complex operations required to render a 3-D image. In addition, most 3-D cards contain large amounts of video RAM to store the complex images.

Changing Video Settings Within Windows

Within Windows, you can change your video resolution, as well as the number of colors your monitor is using to display images by using the Display Properties dialog box, as shown in Figure 17-13. As

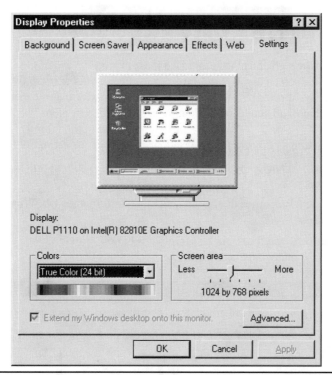

Figure 17.13   Using the Display Properties dialog box Settings sheet to change system colors or resolution

previously discussed, the number of colors and resolutions you can select are dependent on your video card type and the amount of RAM it contains.

To change your system's resolution or colors within Windows, perform these steps:

1. Right-click an unused location on the desktop. Windows, in turn, will display a pop-up menu.

2. Within the pop-up-menu, select Properties. Windows will display the Display Properties dialog box.

3. Within the Properties dialog box, click the Settings tab. Windows will display the Settings sheet, as shown in Figure 17-13.

4. Within the Settings sheet, use the Screen Area slider to select the screen resolution you desire.

5. Using the pull-down Colors list, select the number of colors you want Windows to display.

6. Click OK to put your changes into effect. Depending on your Windows version, Windows may first display a dialog box asking you to confirm your selection. Click OK to put your changes into effect.

Maximize Windows Video Acceleration

USE IT The Windows graphical user interface makes extensive use of the video adapter to manage the screen display. Before you run benchmarks or try to tweak other settings, first make sure that you have directed Windows to maximize any performance capabilities it can achieve by maximizing graphics hardware acceleration, by performing these steps:

1. Select Start | Settings | Control Panel. Windows will display the Control Panel window.

2. Within the Control Panel, double-click the System icon. Windows will display the System Properties dialog box.

3. Within the System Properties dialog box, click the Performance tab. Windows will display the Performance sheet.

4. Within the Performance sheet, click the Graphics button. Windows will display the Advanced Graphics Settings dialog box, as shown here.

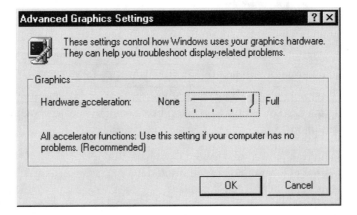

5. Within the Advanced Graphics Settings dialog box, use the slider to select Full Acceleration. Click OK to put your changes into effect. Then click OK to close the System Properties dialog box.

▶ **NOTE**

Some older video cards may encounter problems when you direct Windows to use full graphics acceleration. If you change the acceleration setting and you experience immediate or intermittent video errors, you may need to decrease the setting until the errors stop.

Improving Multimedia Device Performance and Capabilities Using DirectX

Microsoft DirectX is a tool built into Windows that programmers use to access low-level hardware features (such as high-performance graphics operations) without having to write hardware-specific code. Since Microsoft introduced DirectX in 1995, it has become a programming standard for developing multimedia applications for Windows. In general, DirectX gives programmers a set of routines they can use within their programs to create multimedia applications that run on any Windows-based PC, regardless of hardware.

Behind the scenes, DirectX takes advantage of any advanced settings the multimedia hardware provides, such as accelerator chips. Programmers, in turn, can use DirectX to write a single program without worrying about the various hardware devices and configurations in existence.

USE IT Depending on the programs you run, your system may make extension use of DirectX. In fact, many video benchmarks will require that you upgrade DirectX to a recent version before you run them. To view your current DirectX capabilities, you can use the DirectX Diagnostic Tool, shown in Figure 17-14.

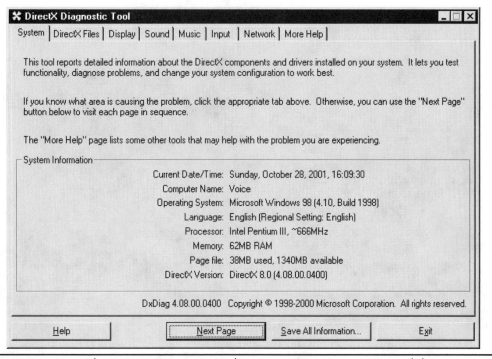

Figure 17.14   Using the DirectX Diagnostic Tool to view a system's DirectX capabilities

To run the DirectX Diagnostic Tool, perform these steps:

1. Select Start | Programs | Accessories. Windows will display the Accessories submenu.

2. Within the Accessories submenu, select System Tools | System Information. Windows will run the System Information utility.

3. Within the System Information utility, select Tools | DirectX Diagnostic Tool. Windows will run the DirectX Diagnostic Tool shown in Figure 17-14.

Like most Windows-based programs, Microsoft periodically releases updates to DirectX that you can download from the Microsoft DirectX homepage at www.microsoft.com/directx. To maximize your system performance, you should install and use the most recent version of DirectX.

Running Video Benchmarks

In Chapter 1 you learned that a good way to identify bottlenecks are to run benchmark programs. On the Web, you can find several very good video benchmark programs, such as the XL-R8R benchmark shown in Figure 17-15, which you can download from www.MadOnion.com. Most video benchmark programs exercise a card's data transfer rates, DirectX support, 3-D capabilities, and more.

Figure 17.15   Running the XL-R8R video benchmark program

Program	Web Site
3D WinBench	www.etestinglabs.com/benchmarks/3dwinbench/3dwinbench.asp
WinTune	www.rocketdownload.com/Details/Util/wintune.htm
VidPerf	www.clear-simple.com/benchmark.shtml
PerformanceTest	www.passmark.com/

Table 17.5 Video Benchmark Programs Available on the World Wide Web

Table 17-5 lists several benchmark programs you can download from the Web.

Upgrading Your Video Card

Throughout this chapter, the text has referred to the video adapter as a card. Many systems, however, implement the video adapter by using motherboard chips. If you upgrade your video adapter, you will need to use the CMOS Setup program discussed in Chapter 6 to disable the motherboard's video chip, as shown in Figure 17-16.

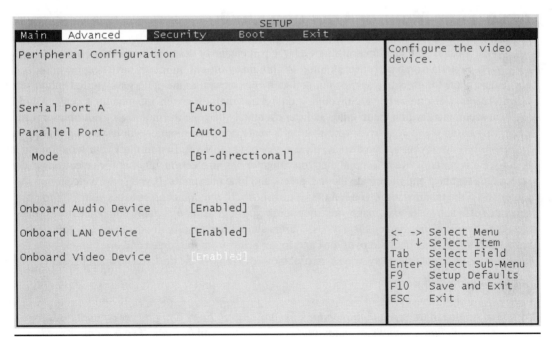

Figure 17.16 Using the CMOS Setup program to disable the motherboard video

If you are shopping for a video card, you need to consider how you will use the card. If you make extensive use of high-end graphics editing programs and 3-D drawing packages, or if you develop or play video games, you should consider a high-end graphics card that supports 32-bit color and 3-D operations. Otherwise, look for an AGP-based video card that contains sufficient RAM to run at the resolutions you require. Refer to Table 17-2 to see the RAM amounts required for various screen resolutions.

USE IT   Most newer video cards will fully support Plug and Play operations, which will simplify your installation process. To install a new video card, perform these steps:

1. Shut down, power off, and unplug your system.

2. Next, gently remove your system-unit cover.

3. If you are installing an AGP-based video card, locate the AGP-slot on your motherboard and insert the card. If you are using a PCI-based card, locate an unused slot and insert and secure the card.

4. Gently restore and secure your system-unit cover.

5. Plug in, power on, and start your system. After Windows starts, you must install the device driver that accompanied your video card.

Keep Your Monitor Cool and Clean

USE IT   Because the monitor consumes a large percentage of desk space, many users stack materials on top of their monitor. Within many offices, monitors have become a convenient place for users to stack incoming documents, as well as the gallery for stuffed animals and other artifacts. Unfortunately, placing objects on top of a monitor covers the monitor's vents, which lets heat accumulate within the monitor and can eventually damage the monitor's electronics or cause a fire. Do not place any items over your monitor's vents, and your monitor will last a long time.

Before you clean your screen display, always make sure that you first turn off your monitor and let it sit for a few minutes. Keep in mind that your monitor has an electron gun that fires electrons at the screen area that heat and illuminate the red, green, and blue phosphors. If you spray a cleaner on the screen while the monitor is on, you run the risk of shock. If you do not electrocute yourself, you may generate sufficient static to damage your monitor or your PC. Although many computer stores sell cleaning chemicals for a screen display, most users should find that lightly dampening a soft cloth with a little rubbing alcohol removes dust and finger prints from the screen and dries quickly. If your monitor's vents are dusty, use an aerosol blower to remove the dust, as shown in Figure 17-17.

▶ *CAUTION*

Most users should never open their monitor—for any reason. Even if you power off and unplug your monitor, the monitor is capable of maintaining a charge that can be fatal. If your monitor needs service, let a trained technician perform the work for you.

Figure 17.17 Clean a monitor screen using a soft cloth and ensure that the monitor vents are clear.

Degauss Your Monitor

 USE IT To display an image, a monitor uses electron guns to heat phosphors that reside on the monitor screen. As the monitor shoots negatively charged electrons at the phosphors, the monitor also applies a positive charge to the screen that attracts the charges. Over time, magnetic interference may disrupt the appearance of part of an image on your screen. The interference may be caused by the physical presence of a magnet too close to monitor or via natural forces. In such cases, you can *degauss* your monitor to eliminate the impact of the magnetic interference. Normally, when you power on your monitor, the monitor's hardware will degauss the screen by using a special coil within the monitor to remove any magnetic buildup within the monitor. In addition, many monitors provide a button or menu option you can select to manually degauss the monitor. Normally, when you degauss your monitor, the monitor's image will flicker for a few seconds and your monitor may even generate a tone you can hear as it performs the degaussing operation.

Reduce the Monitor's Power Consumption by Using Power Management

In Chapter 3, you examined PC power in detail. Of the various PC components, the monitor consumes a large amount of power (up to 100 watts). Using the Windows power-management capabilities, you can direct Windows to turn off the monitor after a period of no use. By directing Windows to turn off the monitor when it is not in use, you not only reduce your system's power consumption, you may also prevent damage to your monitor, called *phosphor burn in*. This occurs when the same image appears unchanged on the screen for an extended period of time. As you have learned, to display an image, a monitor uses an electron gun to heat and illuminate phosphors on the screen display. In older monitors, it was possible for phosphors to become damaged after extended use, such that the phosphors appeared to be illuminated even when they were off—creating ghost-like images on the screen.

USE IT   Although most newer monitors are less susceptible to burn in, you should still use the Windows power-management capabilities to prevent possible burn in by performing these steps:

1. Right-click on an unused area on the desktop. Windows will display a pop-up menu.

2. Within the pop-up menu, select Properties. Windows will display the Display Properties window.

3. Within the Display Properties window, click the Screen Saver tab. Windows will display the Screen Saver sheet.

4. Within the Screen Saver sheet, click Energy Star Settings. Windows will display the Power Management Properties dialog box, as shown here.

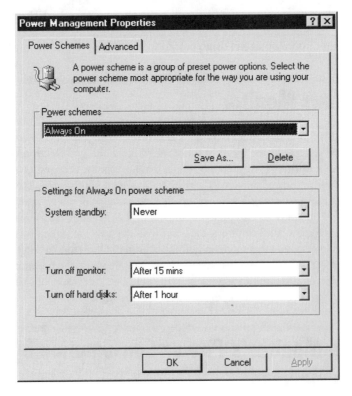

5. Within the Power Management Properties dialog box, use the pull-down list labeled Turn Off Monitor to select the length of idle time you want Windows to wait before it turns off your monitor. Most users will select 15 minutes. Click OK to put your changes into effect.

When you later need to use your system, simply move your mouse or press a keyboard key. Windows, in turn, will automatically turn your monitor back on.

Connecting Multiple Monitors to Your PC

If you have spent time in a larger electronics store, you have likely seen a display that combines several television sets to display one large image. As it turns out, if you are using PCI- or AGP-based video cards, Windows lets you configure your PC to use multiple monitors.

USE IT   To use multiple monitors with your PC, perform these steps:

1. Shut down, power off, and unplug your PC.

2. Gently remove your PC system-unit cover.

3. Install a video card for each monitor you want to use. The video cards must be PCI or AGP cards. Most newer video cards are Plug and Play cards, which will simplify your installation process.

4. Gently replace and secure your system-unit cover.

5. Restart your system. You may need to install device drivers for each video card. Then, you may again need to restart your system.

6. After Windows restarts, right-click on an unused location on the desktop. Windows will display a pop-up menu.

7. Within the pop-up menu, select Properties. Windows will display the Display Properties dialog box.

8. Within the Display Properties dialog box, click the Settings tab. Windows will display the Settings sheet.

9. Within the Settings sheet, drag the monitor icons onto the corresponding screens where you want the item to appear.

10. Click OK to put your changes into effect.

Calibrating Monitor Colors

If you place 10 identical PCs and monitors side by side, you will initially have a difficult time distinguishing differences between the images each displays. However, if you let 10 users work with the systems for a month and then you repeat the exercise, you will likely find that changes users have made to the monitor's brightness and contrast produce significant differences.

For most users, calibrating the monitor means picking a brightness and contrast that works well within the user's work environment (some users must compete with glare from windows, others must compensate for low light). For graphics artists, monitor calibration is very important. Often, many novice graphics artists are surprised when the colors of pieces they have professionally printed do not match the colors they previewed on their screen displays. Although many factors, such as the paper type and ink density may change the appearance of printed colors, the problem may have originated with the artist's monitor.

Calibrating a monitor for graphics arts work normally requires that you purchase high-end software that comes with color swatches you can use to fine-tune your monitor settings. Some programs, such as Photoshop, provide software such as Adobe Gamma, that you can use to get your monitor settings reasonably accurate. Using such software, you can normally fine-tune the following monitor settings:

- **Gamma**   Relates the strength of a monitor's input voltage to the brightness of the screen image
- **White point**   Normally specifies a temperature in degrees Kelvin that yields a bright white
- **Ambient light**   Lets you adjust the monitor settings to compensate for the level of light in the work environment

USE IT   After you calibrate your monitor, you can use the Windows Color Management tools to select a color profile your screen uses to display images that may better reflect the printed output you desire. To use the Windows Color Management features, perform these steps:

1. Right-click on an unused location on the desktop. Windows will display a pop-up menu.
2. Within the pop-up menu, select Properties. Windows will open the Display Properties dialog box.
3. Within the Display Properties dialog box, click the Settings tab. Windows will display the Settings sheet.
4. Within the Settings sheet, click Advanced. Windows will display the video card's Properties dialog box.
5. Within the Properties dialog box, select the Color Management tab. Windows will display the Color Management sheet, as shown in Figure 17-18.
6. Within the Color Management sheet, you can add color profiles (that Windows and other graphics arts programs provide) to the list of available profiles, and you can select a profile Windows will place into use.

Displaying Video System Information Using Sandra

Throughout this book, several tips have taken advantage of the SiSoftware Sandra (System **AN**alyser, **D**iagnostic and **R**eporting **A**ssistant) program, which you can use to provide low-level device information and to run various benchmarks. Using Sandra, you can display specifics about your video adapter and monitor, as shown in Figure 17-19.

USE IT   To download the Sandra program, visit the SiSoftware Web site at www.sisoftware.demon.co.uk. After you install and run the Sandra software, double-click the Video System Information icon to display your video card and monitor settings.

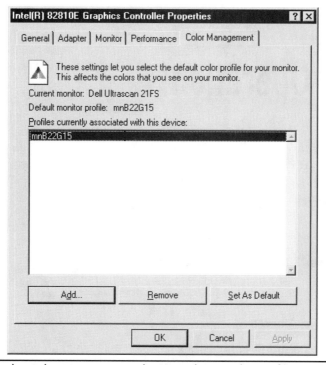

Figure 17.18   Using the Color Management sheet to select a color profile

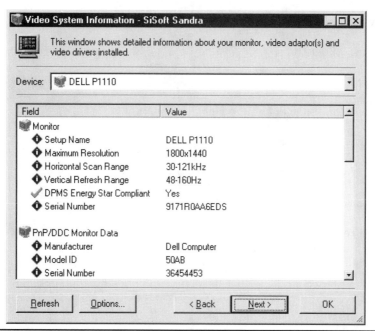

Figure 17.19   Using the SiSoftware Sandra program to display the video system information

CHAPTER 18

Printer Operations

TIPS IN THIS CHAPTER

Regardless of the programs users run, from word processors to spreadsheets to database applications, the final step is often to print output. This chapter examines printer operations in detail and presents steps you can take to improve your printer's performance. You will also learn how connecting a printer that supports different ports (such as a parallel port, Universal Serial Bus [USB] port, or network interface card [NIC]) can impact performance. Also, you will examine operations you can perform within the operating system (and your applications) to change printer settings that have a direct impact on speed and quality. Finally, this chapter examines how you can maintain your printer to ensure high-quality output.

Understanding the Printing Process

To print data, such as a word-processing document, graphic, or the contents of a Web page, applications rely on the operating system to interact with the printer, as shown in Figure 18-1.

Within the operating system is "generic" printer code that uses a device driver to interact with the printer. When a user connects a printer to his or her PC, the user must first install a *device driver* specific to the printer before the operating system can use the printer. Likewise, before a user can print to a printer that resides on a network, the PC must have a device driver installed that is specific to the network printer type.

Windows Uses the Spooler to Manage Printer Jobs

Years ago, within the MS-DOS operating system, users could run only one program at a time. If an application printed data, the application would normally finish printing before the application could end and a second program could run. Within the Windows environment, in contrast, users often run multiple programs at the same time. In fact, most users frequently switch between Windows applications, possibly printing data within one program and then switching to a second program to print other data.

Windows applications gain access to the printer on a first-come, first-served basis. Unlike the MS-DOS environment—where an application often had to finish printing before it could perform another task—after a Windows application starts a print job, the application can quickly begin other tasks while the data prints.

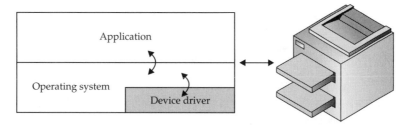

Figure 18.1 The operating system provides software applications used to send data to the printer.

As it turns out, when a Windows application prints data, Windows itself does not interact directly with the printer. Instead, Windows places the data within a file on your hard disk that a special program, called the *spooler*, manages in order to print the data. As shown in Figure 18-2, each time any Windows application prints data, Windows places the data within the spool file on disk. The spooler, in turn, will print the data in the spool file one file at a time, based on the order in which the applications printed their data.

One of the primary advantages of spooling print jobs to disk is that an application can quickly resume its work. The printer is much slower than a disk drive. By letting the application send its data to the disk, as opposed to waiting on the slow printer, the application can quickly resume other processing, while the spooler oversees the printing.

When you print a file within Windows, your Taskbar will display a smaller printer icon as shown:

 ←——— Printer icon

If you double-click the Taskbar printer icon, Windows will display a dialog box—whose name corresponds with the printer, as shown in Figure 18-3—that lists the print jobs you have spooled to the printer, as well as the order the spooler will use to print the jobs.

Within the printer dialog box, you can cancel a print job by clicking the job and then pressing DELETE or by selecting Document | Cancel Printing. You can also change the order the spooler will use to print jobs by dragging a file up or down in the list of jobs to print.

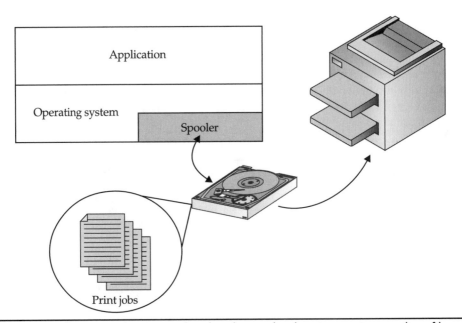

Figure 18.2 Windows "spools" printer data by placing the data into an intermediate file on disk, which the spooler program manages to print data.

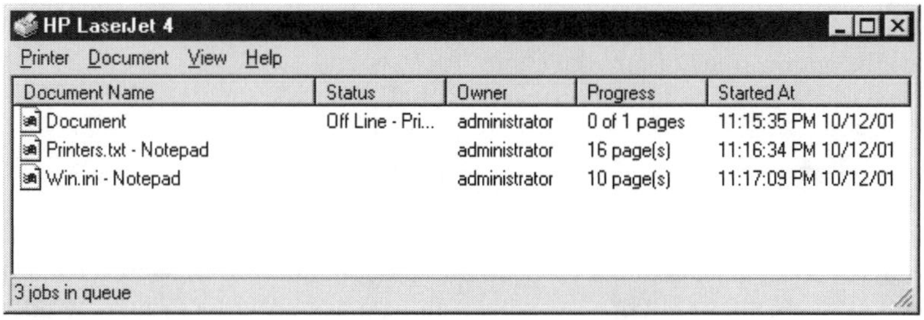
HP LaserJet 4
Printer Document View Help
Document Name | Status | Owner | Progress | Started At
Document | Off Line - Pri... | administrator | 0 of 1 pages | 11:15:35 PM 10/12/01
Printers.txt - Notepad | administrator | 16 page(s) | 11:16:34 PM 10/12/01
Win.ini - Notepad | administrator | 10 page(s) | 11:17:09 PM 10/12/01
3 jobs in queue

Figure 18.3 Using the printer dialog box to monitor your print jobs

Changing Printer Settings Within a Windows Application

Within Windows applications, users normally print to the default printer by clicking the printer icon that appears within the application's toolbar.

Print to default printer
100%

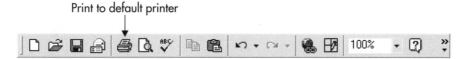

In addition to using the toolbar printer icon to print a document, users can select File | Print. Most applications, in turn, will display a Print dialog box, similar to that shown in Figure 18-4.

Using the pull-down printer Name list in the Print dialog box, you can select the printer to which you want the application to print the document. In addition, as you will learn later in this chapter, you can use the Properties button to display the printer's Properties dialog box that you can use to select

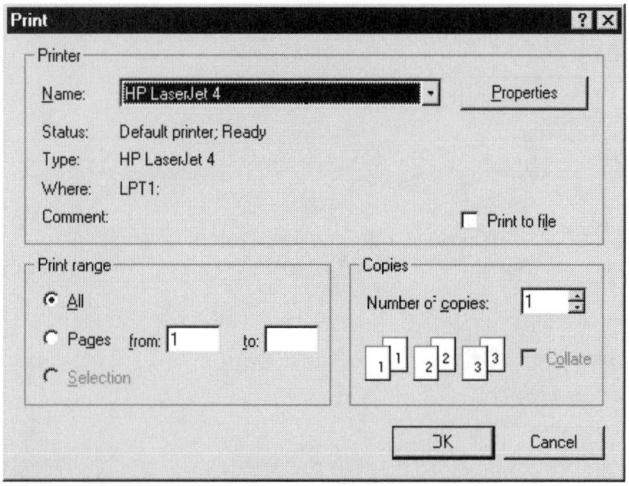
Print
Printer
Name: HP LaserJet 4
Properties
Status: Default printer; Ready
Type: HP LaserJet 4
Where: LPT1:
Comment:
Print to file
Print range
All
Pages from: 1 to:
Selection
Copies
Number of copies: 1
Collate
OK
Cancel

Figure 18.4 Printing a document using the Print dialog box

the document's quality (such as draft or high-quality), the number of copies you want to print, whether or not the application collates the copies for you, and more.

Viewing Printers Installed on Your System

Before you can use a printer connected to your PC or a printer that resides on a network, your PC must have a device driver installed that is specific to the printer type. To view a list of the printers for which device drivers are installed on your system, you can open the Printers window, as shown in Figure 18-5. Note that the Printers window does not list icons for printers physically connected to your PC, but rather, the window lists icons for printer device drivers installed on your system. To open the Printers window, select Start | Settings | Printers.

Understanding Printer Performance

In general, users measure a printer's performance in terms of the printer's page-per-minute output. A typical laser printer, for example, can print at 12 pages per minute. A faster (more expensive) printer may reach speeds of up to 20 pages per minute. Several factors influence a printer's page-per-minute output, such as how you connect the printer to a PC. An EPP, for example, will normally provide

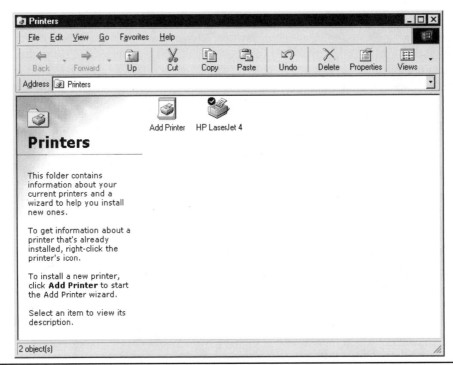

Figure 18.5   Viewing printer device drivers installed on your system

faster data throughput than a standard parallel port. Likewise, a USB connection will outperform an EPP. Further, a direct network connection to a printer will normally provide the highest data throughput. Also, the amount of RAM the printer contains can impact the printer's speed as well.

The page-per-minute metric can be a little misleading. Before a printer can print a page, the printer must convert the page's text and graphics into the dots that represent the page's contents. Depending on the page's complexity, the processing the printer must perform can consume a considerable amount of time—up to several minutes for complex pages. After the printer converts the data to dots, the printer can then print copies of the complex page at its page-per-minute rate. To benchmark a printer, therefore, you must take into account the speed of the printer's raster image processor (the chip that converts the printer output to dots).

Understanding Printer Resolution

To display text and graphics, printers (much like monitors) make extensive use of dots. The printer, unlike a typewriter, does not have specific keys that create letters, numbers, and punctuation symbols. Instead, as shown in Figure 18-6, the characters and graphics the printer displays are composed of dots.

A printer's *resolution* specifies the number of dots the printer uses (normally within a one-inch square region) to present an image. Older printers use resolutions of 300 dots per inch (300 dpi). Newer printers, in contrast, can print images at 1,200 dpi. The higher a printer's resolution, the sharper the text and graphics appear on the page. Normally, the printers that print books use a resolution better than 2,500 dpi. Figure 18-7 illustrates the same image at different resolutions.

To render a page at a higher resolution requires that the printer perform considerably more processing than rendering a page at a low-resolution image. For text-based output, detecting a difference between high- and low-resolution output is often difficult. Therefore, to improve printer performance, you should normally direct your printer to use lower resolution for text output, which you can do using the Printer Properties dialog box, as shown in Figure 18-8.

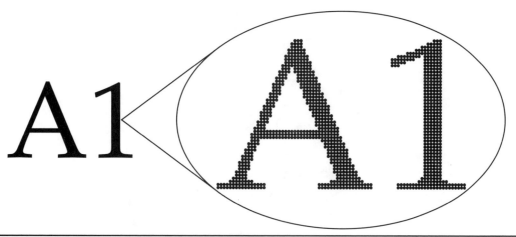

Figure 18.6   Printers represent text and images using dots.

Figure 18.7 The same image at two different printer resolutions

Understanding How Dot-Matrix Printers Print

Unlike a typewriter that has individual keys for each letter, number, and punctuation symbol, a *dot-matrix* printer has a print head that contains a set of pins the printer can extend, as necessary, to press an ink ribbon against a sheet of paper. In other words, to represent a letter, number, or punctuation symbol, the dot matrix printer prints specific dots.

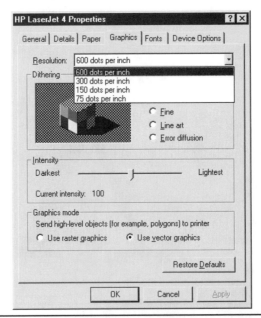

Figure 18.8 Using the Printer Properties dialog box to change the printer resolution

The dot-matrix printer is so named because the printer's head organizes its pins using a matrix of rows and columns. To print different characters, the dot-matrix printer extends the pins that correspond to the character's dot pattern. As you might guess, because of the mechanical movements the printer must perform, the dot-matrix printer is slow and noisy. Over time, the ribbon within a dot matrix printer will run out of ink. To replace the printer ribbon, you normally simply remove the ribbon cartridge and replace it with a new cartridge, sliding the ribbon into a slot near the printer's print head.

Understanding How Ink-Jet Printers Print

An *ink-jet* printer is similar to a dot-matrix printer in that it uses a pattern of dots to represent characters. Unlike the mechanical printing process the dot-matrix printer performs, the ink-jet printer creates the pattern of dots by a spraying a fast-drying ink onto the sheet of paper. Within the printer ink-cartridge head are several openings (a matrix of jet streams) that the printer aims at each dot location.

Depending on the number of colors the ink-jet printer supports, the printer will use a single (black) ink cartridge, or the printer will use four ink cartridges, which contain magenta (red), green, cyan (blue), and black ink. By using combinations of the cyan, magenta, yellow, and black ink, the ink-jet printer can represent colors throughout the color spectrum. Users often refer to the colors cyan, magenta, yellow, and black using the initials CMYK. Although it is possible to create black using cyan, magenta, and yellow ink, doing so would consume a considerable amount of three inks, which is why color printers provide the black ink cartridge. Over time, the ink-jet printer's cartridges will run out of ink. To replace a cartridge, you simply remove the empty cartridge and insert a new cartridge, as shown in Figure 18-9.

Understanding How Laser Printers Print

A *laser* printer, like an ink-jet printer, represents text and graphics using dots. Normally, laser printers use at least 300 dpi. A high-resolution laser printer will print at 1200 dpi. To print a page, the laser (the light beam within the printer), never actually comes in contact with the paper. Instead, within the printer is a cylindrical drum, upon the surface of which the printer places a negative electronic charge.

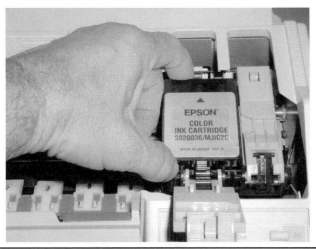

Figure 18.9   Replacing an ink-jet cartridge

The laser, in turn, removes the charge from the areas of the drum that correspond to the portions of the page to which the printer will apply toner. Next, as shown in Figure 18-10, the charged drum then

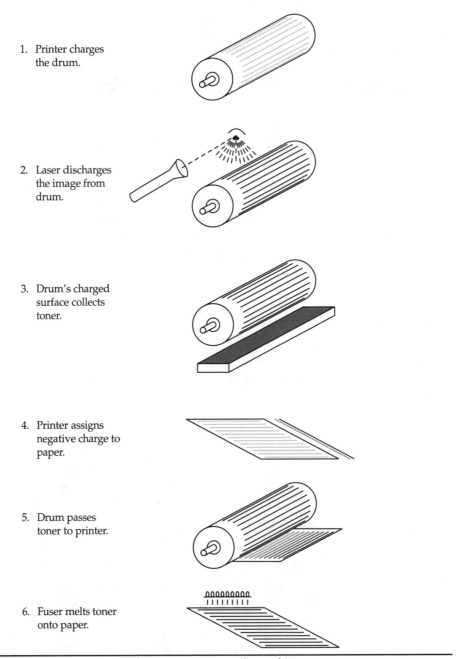

1. Printer charges the drum.

2. Laser discharges the image from drum.

3. Drum's charged surface collects toner.

4. Printer assigns negative charge to paper.

5. Drum passes toner to printer.

6. Fuser melts toner onto paper.

Figure 18.10   How a laser printer transfers an image to a sheet of paper

passes by the toner cartridge at which time the charged regions of the drum attract toner. Then the printer assigns a negative charge more powerful than that of the drum to the sheet of paper that is about to come in contact with the drum. The paper's charge causes the toner to move from the drum onto the page. Next, the paper moves through a heated "fuser" that melts the toner onto the paper.

Over time, the printer cartridge will run out of toner. To replace the cartridge, power off, unplug the printer, and then open the printer. Remove the existing toner cartridge, as shown in Figure 18-11. Next, before you insert the new cartridge, you must normally remove a cover (that resides within the cartridge that you cannot see) that holds the toner in place while the cartridge is shelved for use. Normally, you remove the toner cover by pulling a tab that tears the cover free from within the cartridge. Then simply insert the new cartridge into the printer, close the printer's cover, and plug in and power the printer back on.

Understanding How Color Printers Print

Over the past few years, low-cost, quality color ink-jet printers have made color printers readily available to the masses. As briefly discussed, color ink-jet printers create colors by combining cyan, magenta, yellow, and black inks. For a few hundred dollars, you can purchase a quality color ink-jet printer that can produce results that are suitable for most business applications. The only shortcoming of color ink-jet printers is their speed. A complex image can take considerable time to print.

Color laser printers are faster than ink-jet printers, but they are still quite expensive. A quality color laser printer still costs several thousand dollars for a high-quality printer. Like the ink-jet printer, the color laser printer creates images using cyan, yellow, magenta, and black inks. Normally, you will purchase and install a toner cartridge specific to each color.

At the high-end of the cost and quality spectrum are dyesublimation printers, which produce images as close to photo quality as a computer printer can create. The printers use a special paper and chemical process to produce the image, which results in an average cost of a few dollars per image.

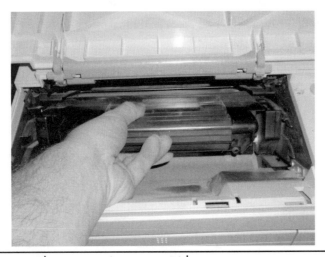

Figure 18.11   Changing a laser printer's toner cartridge

Making Sense of PCL, PDL, and Postscript

As you shop for printers, or as you search the Web for printer device drivers, you will encounter terms such as PDL, PCL, and PostScript. In general, these terms describe languages that device drivers use to send the printer information about the page the printer is going to print. For example, to print text a printer must not only display characters, numbers, and symbols on a page, but the printer must also respond to carriage-return and line feed characters that advance the output to the start of the next line and the form feed character that directs the printer to eject the current page and to continue its output on a new page. Users refer to such characters that control the printer's processing as *control codes*. Different printers support different control codes.

PDL is an abbreviation for page-descriptor language. In general, a PDL contains codes that tell the printer how to lay out a page for printing. Within the PC environment, the two most common page-descriptor languages are PCL and PostScript.

PCL is an abbreviation for Printer Control Language. In general, PCL, which was developed by Hewlett-Packard to support its laser printers, specifies a set of codes the device driver sends to the printer to control the printer's processing of a page. Using PCL codes, for example, the device driver can tell the printer to use a specific font, to position a graphic at a specific location on a page, to change colors (in the case of a color printer), and so on.

Since the first PC-based laser printer released in the early 1980s, Hewlett-Packard has upgraded PCL to provide greater support for fonts, graphics, colors, and even the display of two or more pages on the same sheet of paper. As you shop for printers, you will find that different printers support different levels (versions) of PCL. To use the features a specific version of PCL provides, you must first install a device driver on your system that supports the PCL version. Table 18-1 briefly describes the evolution of PCL versions.

PCL Level	Functionality
PCL 1	Introduced in the early 1980s, provided basic printing and spacing functionality
PCL 2	Also introduced in the early 1980s, provided support for printer transactions and multiuser environments
PCL 3	Introduced in 1984, provided support needed by the word processors and provided limited capabilities for bitmapped fonts and graphics
PCL 4	Introduced in 1985, provided new page formatting capabilities and greater support for bitmapped fonts and graphics
PCL 5	Introduced in 1990, provided greater support desktop publishing applications, such as scalable fonts
PCL 5 ECL	Introduced in the 1990s, provided support for bidirectional communication and more support for fonts
PCL Color	Introduced in the late 1990s, provided support to select colors
PCL 6	Introduced in the late 1990s, provided increased network support, faster processing, and support for higher resolutions

Table 18.1   The Evolution of PCL

PostScript was created by Adobe, and like PCL, it is a language that applications use to describe the layout of a page. Unlike PCL, which defines page layout in terms of control codes a Hewlett-Packard printer understands, PostScript is more generic. In fact, PostScript appears quite similar to a traditional programming language, such as C++. Printers that support the PostScript page description language have a processor that converts the PostScript statements that represent the page into the individual dots the printer will print. Because of its generic nature, the same PostScript data should print on a wide range of printers that support PostScript processing. Because of its portability, PostScript is widely used by the graphics arts community. Like PCL, Postscript has evolved since its release in the 1980s. Today, the standard most newer printers support is PostScript level 3. Figure 18-12 illustrates the processing that occurs when an application prints data.

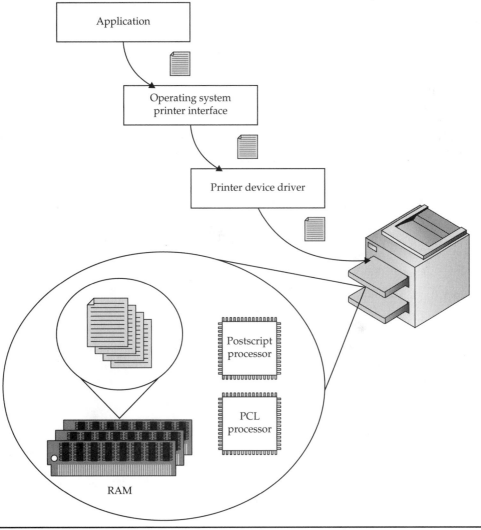

Figure 18.12   Tracing the flow of data from an application to printed output

Understanding Network Printers

By placing a printer on to a network, you let users on the network share the printer. As shown in Figure 18-13, you can make a printer available to network users in two ways. First, a user who has a printer connected to his or her PC can choose to let users access the printer. Second, the printer can have its own NIC that lets the printer itself connect to directly to the network.

Although letting network users access a printer connected to a PC lets users share the printer, the problem is that each document (print job) a remote user sends to the printer creates overhead on the corresponding PC, which decreases the PC's system performance. The ideal way to connect a printer to the network is to use a printer that has its own NIC.

In either case, before a user can print to a remote printer, the user must have a device driver for the remote printer type installed on his or her system. Then, to print to the remote printer, the user simply selects the network printer from Print dialog box printer list.

Installing a New Printer

After you connect a printer to your PC, or before you can use a network printer, you must install a device driver for the printer before you can print to it. The Windows CD-ROM you used to install Windows on your PC contains device drivers for many common printers. Likewise, when you purchase a new printer, you will receive a CD-ROM that contains the printer's device driver. Or you can locate and download a printer device driver from the Web. To locate the device driver on the Web, you can simply use a search engine to search for your printer name and model and the words "device driver."

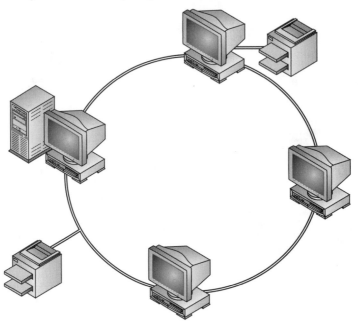

Figure 18.13   Connecting printers to a local-area network

The search engine will usually connect you to a page on your printer manufacturer's Web site from which you can download a device driver specific to your operating system. Normally, the CD-ROM you receive with your printer or the device driver file you download from the Web will contain an installation program you can run that will walk you though the installation process.

If you do not have a program you can execute to install the printer device driver, you can take advantage of the Add Printer Wizard, a special software program Windows provides that will walk you through the installation process. To start the wizard, perform these steps:

1. Select Start | Settings | Printers. Windows, in turn, will display the Printers window.

2. Within the Printers window, double-click the Add Printer icon. Windows will start the Add Printer Wizard, shown next, that will walk you through the installation process.

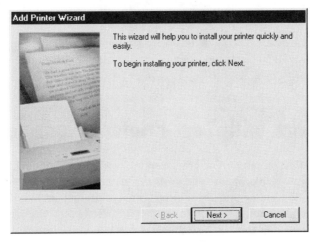

3. Within the Add Printer Wizard, you must specify if you are connecting to a local or network printer. Next, the wizard will ask you to select the printer from a list of printers for which Windows provides device drivers, as shown here.

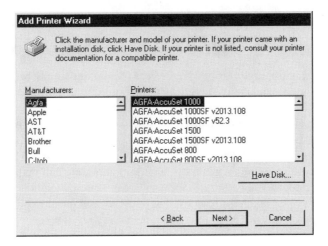

4. If your printer appears in the list, select the printer and choose Next. Windows may prompt you to enter the Windows CD-ROM from which the wizard can install the device driver software.

5. If your printer does not appear in the list, you must specify the disk that contains the device driver file (which you may have downloaded from the Web or received on a CD-ROM that accompanied your printer).

After the Add Printer Wizard completes the installation, you can select the printer for use from within the Print dialog box, or you can select the printer as your default printer from within the Printers window.

If your system has multiple printers attached, or if you have multiple printers available on a network, you may want to choose one of the printers as the default by performing these steps:

1. Select Start | Settings | Printers. Windows will display the Printers dialog box.

2. Within the Printers dialog box, click the printer icon of the printer you want to use as the default. Windows will highlight the icon.

3. Select File | Set as Default.

Getting Familiar with Your Printer's Console Menu

USE IT   If you have a laser printer that provides a built-in console window, you should take time to learn which printer features you can access from the console menu. As shown in Figure 18-14, the console window provides a menu with options you can use to perform a range of printer operations, such as selecting the port the printer will use to communicate with the PC (such as a parallel port, universal serial bus, or NIC); printing printer status data, which contains such information as the amount of RAM the printer contains; or selecting the network protocols the printer will use to communicate via a direct network connection. Depending on your printer type, the operations you can perform from the menu will vary. However, your successful use of the menu is the key to maximizing your printer use.

Adding Memory to Your Printer to Improve Performance

Although most users think of printers as passive devices (the printer simply prints the data it receives from the PC), quite the opposite is true. Within the printer are several processing chips the printer uses to download data from the PC and to format the page of output.

Before a printer prints a page, it must convert the text and images that will appear on the page to the dots the printer will use to represent the page contents. As the printer builds the page for output, the printer stores the page for output, and the printer stores the image within RAM that resides within the printer. Assuming you are printing at 300 dpi, an 8 ½×11-inch page of output will require over 8 million dots. Because a dot is either on or off, the printer can represent eight dots using one byte of data, which means the printer requires about 1MB of RAM to hold the page's dots. In a similar way, to convert a 1,200 dpi page (about 135 million dots), the printer needs roughly 16MB of RAM.

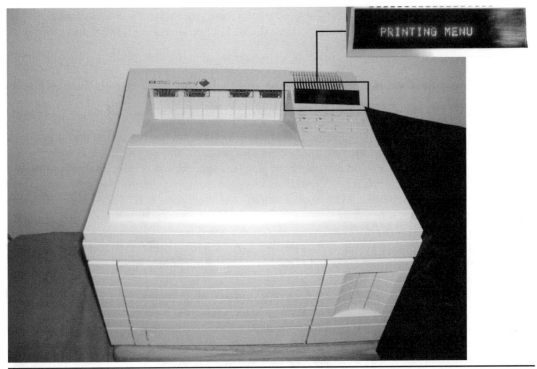

Figure 18.14   Using the printer's console menu to control printer operations

As the printer processes the page, the printer may download and store different fonts within its RAM. If the printer has limited RAM, the printer may need to move one font from RAM before it can load another font, which decreases printer performance.

Further, as the printer processes one page, the printer often receives and buffers subsequent pages from the PC that it will later process. Normally, the printer buffers the pages it receives from the PC within RAM (although some high-end network printers have built-in hard disk drives to which the printer can buffer data and fonts). The more RAM the printer contains, the more pages it can buffer, which lets the spooler complete its download operation quicker.

USE IT   To determine the amount of RAM your printer contains, you can print a printer status page, which will list the amount of memory within the printer. Depending on your printer type, the steps you must perform will differ. Most laser printers, for example, let you print a status page using the printer's console menu. Other printers, will print a status page when you hold down a specific printer button (such as the form feed button) when you power on the printer. Refer to your printer documentation to determine the specific steps you must perform.

If you make extensive use of your printer, and you often find yourself waiting for your printer to produce output, your printer may be a good candidate for improving performance through additional RAM. Depending on your printer type, the amount of RAM (and the specific type of RAM) you can install in your printer will very. Again, refer to your printer documentation for more information. On the Web, you can find many sites that offer printer RAM. Most printers use SIMM memory chips similar to PC RAM.

Working with Printer Fonts

When a program displays text, numbers, and punctuation symbols on the screen, or a printer prints a text document, both use a specific font to represent the characters and symbols. A font specifies a typeface (which defines how each character will appear) at a specific size. Figure 18-15 illustrates several different fonts within Microsoft Word. Font sizes are specified in terms of points, such as an 8-point, 10-point, or 36-point font. With respect to font sizes, each point is 1/72 of each—meaning there are 72 points in one inch.

To print a page, the printer must convert text into the dots the printer will use to represent the page's contents. Within the printer, a processor uses the font definition to convert text to corresponding dots the printer will print, using a process called *rasterizing*. The font definition must reside within the printer before the processor can convert the text to dots.

To simplify (and to speed up) the conversion of text to dots, most printers have built-in sets of fonts that include commonly-used fonts. Years ago, to increase the number of fonts a printer could use, users would insert a font cartridge (which may have contained many different fonts) into the cartridge slot on the front of the printer. Today, most printers have several common fonts built into ROM-based chips. When a printer does not have a specific font, most programs will download the fonts to the printer as they print documents, which means that the user's PC must contain the corresponding fonts. Otherwise, depending on the application that is printing the document, the application will either display an error message and cancel the print operation, or the application will substitute a different font.

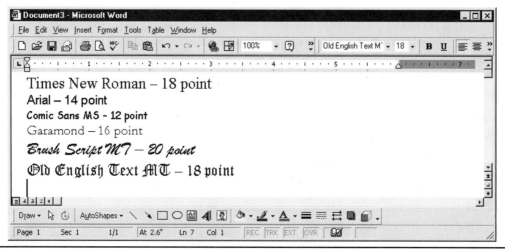

Figure 18.15   Using fonts to specify the appearance of characters, numbers, and symbols

To view the fonts on your system, you can open the Font window, as shown in Figure 18-16, by performing these steps:

1. Select Start | Settings | Control Panel. Windows will open the Control Panel.
2. Within the Control Panel, double-click your mouse on the Fonts icon. Windows will open the Fonts window.

As you can see, most of the fonts within the Fonts window have the letters *TT* on their icons, which indicates that the font is a TrueType font. TrueType fonts are a family of fonts supported by Windows and the Mac that provide an efficient scalable font. TrueType fonts reside in a file with the TTF file extension. Windows and the Mac contain special rasterizer software that converts the font into pixels for display on the screen or for printing.

Within the Fonts window, you can double-click a font icon to display the corresponding font's typeface. For example, if you double-click the Comic Sans font, Windows will display the Comic Sans window, shown in Figure 18-17. Within the window, you can click Print to print a copy of the font.

As discussed, before you can print or display a font, your PC must have the font installed on the system. Within the Fonts window, you can install a new font on your system by selecting File | Install New Font. Windows, in turn, will display the Add Fonts dialog box, which you can use to copy a font from a floppy disk or network disk to your system.

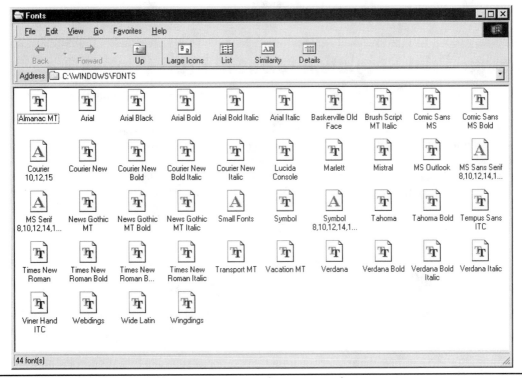

Figure 18.16   Displaying the fonts on a PC using the Fonts window

Figure 18.17   Displaying the Comic Sans typeface

Reduce Print Resolution to Speed Draft Printing

USE IT   Most users often print and review their documents several times before they print their final copy. Depending on the document's size and content, you may be able to print a lower-resolution copy of the document's contents, which prints faster and consumes less toner or ink. Using the Print dialog box, you can normally select a Properties button that directs Windows to display the printer's Properties dialog box, similar to that shown in Figure 18-18. Within the Properties dialog box, you can often reduce the resolution at which the printer will print the document. Later, when you are ready to print the final copy of your work, you can use the Properties dialog box to select a higher resolution. As a general rule, by printing most documents at a lower resolution, you will extend the life of your printer resources (namely toner and ink).

Choosing Whether to Collate a Document

USE IT   When you print large quantities of a complex document (one that contains high-resolution graphics and a number of fonts), you have two choices. First, you can let your application print one complete copy of the document at a time (which means you will not have to later collate the document), or you can have the application print the copies one page at a time. Before the printer can print a page, the printer must convert the page's text and graphics into the dots the printer will use to represent the page. Depending on the complexity of the page contents, the amount of the time the printer

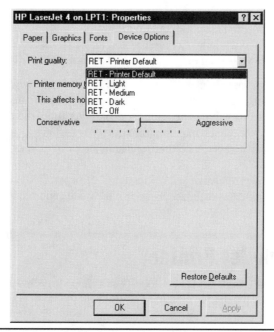

Figure 18.18 Using the Properties dialog box to change the print job's resolution

requires to build the output page can vary. Assume, for example, that it takes the printer 30 seconds to build a complex page that appears within a 3-page document, and that you need 120 copies of the document. If you print the documents one copy at a time, the printer will need to build the complex page each time the document prints. In this case, rebuilding the page 120 times at 30 seconds per page would consume one hour. If you instead print the copies of the pages individually, the printer can build the page one time (which takes 30 seconds) and then use that page to print 120 copies (which the printer can do at its standard pages-per-minute rate). In the case of a 12-page-per-minute printer, the document would require about 10 minutes to print. However, you must then collate the pages by hand.

So, when you must print a complex document in quantity, you should determine whether it will be faster for you to let the printer print and collate pages or for you to print pages individually and then to collate the pages by hand.

Using Better Paper to Improve Your Printer's Output Quality

If you are using a color printer, the paper you select can have a significant visible impact on the quality of your printer output. If you use traditional copier or printer paper within a color ink-jet printer, the paper will absorb the ink the printer sprays onto the page, much like a paper towel. What should appear on the page as a small dot (and images and text are comprised of such dots) may grow as the paper absorbs the dot's ink—which users refer to as *dot gain*—the result of which is fuzzy text and blurry images. In contrast, paper that is designed for use by color printers absorbs less ink, which lets the ink dry on the paper's surface, to create a sharper output.

If you are using a black and white ink-jet printer, you may find that by changing the paper you use (specifically when you print your final output), your text and graphics will become much clearer.

USE IT   If you are using a laser printer, you may use the least expensive paper you can find to print your draft output. Although the paper's quality should be more than sufficient for your needs, one of the side effects of inexpensive paper is more dust. Over time, the dust from the paper may accumulate within your printer, which may in turn reduce your printer's quality and lifespan. If you choose to use a less- expensive paper, take time to clean your printer on a regular basis, as discussed in the tips that follow.

You can find plenty of Web sites that sell a wide range of paper, from coated stocks for color printing, labels, and even ink-jet transfer sheets upon which you can print an image and then use an iron to transfer the image onto a T-shirt.

Cleaning an Ink-Jet Printer

As you know, to print output, an ink-jet printer's cartridges spray ink onto a page as the sheet of paper passes by the jet. Over time, the ink may begin to accumulate on the cartridge, which creates small streaks on the paper or which may interfere with the cartridge's ability to print the stream ink correctly.

USE IT   Today, most ink-jet cartridges have a built-in heads (nozzles that spray the ink). The easiest way to clean an ink-jet printer is to periodically run a special cleaning sheet through the printer that cleans the jets as the sheet moves through the printer. In addition, as shown in Figure 18-19, you can remove the cartridges and clean off the ink using a Q-tip and rubbing alcohol.

Also, depending on the quality of the paper you are using, your printer may accumulate paper dust. In such cases, open your printer and use an aerosol blower to clean the dust from within the printer.

If your printer uses cartridges that do not contain a built-in head, but rather the head mechanism is part of your printer, you can again likely clean the head using a Q-tip and alcohol (make sure you first unplug the printer). In addition, you may want to use a cleaning cartridge that contains chemicals that clean the hoses and nozzles.

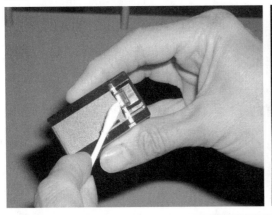 

Figure 18.19   Cleaning an ink-jet cartridge and removing dust from a printer

Cleaning a Laser Printer

Over time, a laser printer will accumulate dust from the paper that passes through it as well as pieces small pieces of paper that may have torn from sheets. When you change your printer's toner cartridge, you should inspect the inside of your laser printer and use an aerosol blower to remove any dust or paper. To reduce the risk of shock to yourself and your printer's electronics, you should unplug your printer before you open and replace the cartridge.

 USE IT If you spill toner within your printer as you install a toner cartridge, your best solution is to vacuum the toner from the within the printer. Try to keep the vacuum itself as far from the printer as possible. The vacuum's motor can possibly generate static electricity that could damage the PC's sensitive electronic components. If you have a vacuum cleaner with a hose attachment, you may want to tape a drinking straw to the vacuum, as shown in Figure 18-20 to create a smaller, more powerful extension that you can use to get into the printer's cracks and crevices as you clean out the toner.

Saving Money Through Refurbished Ink and Toners

Depending on how often you use your printer, you may consume a significant amount of toner or ink. To reduce costs (often as much as 50 percent), many users purchase refurbished toner and ink cartridges. In fact, analysts project that by the year 2004, users will purchase over $1 billion worth of refurbished toner and ink cartridges per year. When you purchase a toner cartridge, the box may contain shipping instructions you can use to return your old cartridge to the manufacturer for free. Although the manufacturers present your return of the cartridge as being environmentally responsible, getting the cartridge back lets the manufacturer refurbish the cartridge for resale.

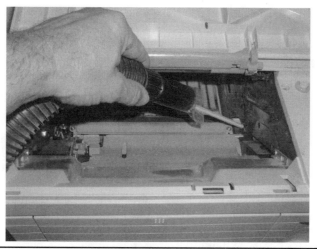

Figure 18.20   Using a vacuum to clean toner from within a laser printer

In addition to being less expensive, refurbished cartridges often contain more toner than standard toners, which increases the cartridge's life. Further, many refurbished cartridges come with a warranty equivalent to that of a standard toner.

If you shop for a refurbished laser toner cartridge, look for the word "refurbished" as opposed to "refilled." When manufacturers refurbish a printer, they replace the cartridge's drum, as opposed to simply adding toner to the cartridge. Although the refurbished cartridge will be more expensive than the refilled cartridge, the new toner drum will insure a higher-quality output. On the Web, you can find many companies that sell refurbished toner cartridges.

In addition to purchasing refurbished ink-jet printers, many users will purchase ink in bulk that they use to refill the ink cartridges themselves. (Some users also refill their laser toner cartridges, but most users will find the process more difficult than the cost savings is worth.) You can find Web sites that offer ink for a wide range of printers and the supplies you need to refill the cartridge.

USE IT   Most lasers printers will show a "low toner" message on their display when the cartridge gets low on ink. In such cases, you may be able to extend the life of your cartridge by simply removing the cartridge and shaking it from right to left several times to distribute the toner that remains, as shown in Figure 18-21.

Extending a Printer Ribbon's Lifetime

If you are using a printer that employs a ribbon, you may have noticed that when the ribbon runs out of the ink, the middle of the ribbon, the area where the printer's pins strike the ribbon, becomes quite light, and the remainder of the ribbon maintains ink that you cannot use. Rather than simply discarding the printer ribbon, you may want to lightly spray the ribbon with a substance such as WD-40, which causes the ribbon's unused ink to run, filling in the print area. By rewinding the ribbon as you spray, you may extend a second use from the ribbon.

Figure 18.21   Extending the life of a printer cartridge by shaking the cartridge to distribute the remaining toner

Providing PostScript Support for a Non-PostScript Printer

PostScript is a language application used to describe the layout of items on a page or how the printer should print a specific object on a page. Graphics artists often store the images they create using a PostScript file called an Encapsulated PostScript, or EPS file. The EPS file is so named because the file contains (encapsulates) all the information the printer needs to print the object. The graphics artist can then simply place the EPS file within a document, such as a Word document, much as they would for any image file. When the graphics artist later prints the document, the application will simply send the PostScript data to the printer, which in turn will process the instructions to print the object.

 There may be times when you receive a document from another user that contains an EPS object. Unfortunately, if your printer does not support PostScript processing, it cannot print the object. Should you need to print PostScript objects, and you do not have a PostScript printer, you can download a special program called Ghostscript, which processes the PostScript statements and converts them to PCL statements or escape codes that your printer supports. On the Web, you can download Ghostscript and related utilities from www.cs.wisc.edu/~ghost, as shown in Figure 18-22.

After you install Ghostscript, you can use the program to open your document that contains the PostScript and then to print the contents of the file to a non-PostScript printer.

If you have a PostScript printer, there still may be times when you will want to take advantage of Ghostscript, depending on the complexity of PostScript pages you must print and the speed of your PC. Normally, when you print PostScript data, a processor within the printer must then convert the PostScript into the dots that represent the page. If your PC has a very fast processor and you are printing a complex page, you may find it faster to let your PC convert the PostScript into PCL commands your printer understands, as opposed to using the printer's slower processor to convert the PostScript.

Take Advantage of an Enhanced Parallel Port

As you have learned, PCs ship with a set of standard ports, such as a serial port, mouse, and keyboard ports, as well as a parallel port. Although some printers connect to serial ports, networks, and even USB ports, most users connect their printers to a parallel port. You need to understand, however, that not all parallel ports are created equal.

Older parallel ports, for example, only output data. In contrast, since the early 1990s, most parallel ports support bidirectional communication, which lets the printer send data back through the port (perhaps, for example, to notify the operating system that the printer needs paper). Today, most newer parallel ports are either ECPs (extended capabilities ports) or EPPs (enhanced parallel ports). By configuring your system to use the capabilities this ports provide, you may increase your printer performance by as much as a factor of 10.

Both ECPs and EPPs are bidirectional ports. Also, an ECP may use direct memory access (DMA) to speed communication. In addition to providing fast printer output, EPPs often connect other peripheral devices, such as scanners. To the system, the EPP appears as a bus to which you can daisy chain multiple devices.

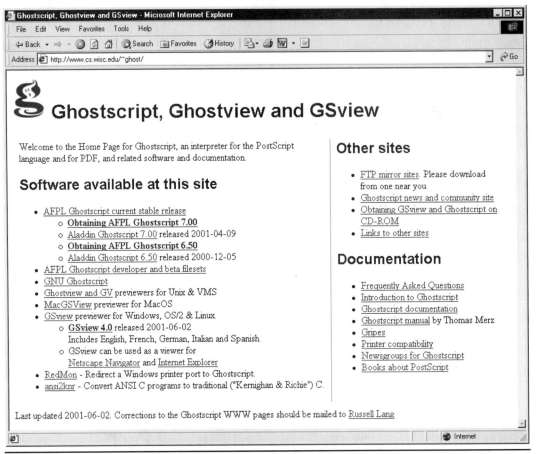

Figure 18.22   You can download Ghostscript to provide PostScript support to non-PostScript printers.

USE IT   To use an ECP or EPP, you must have the following:

- Your parallel port must be ECP or EPP.

- You must have a device (such as a printer) that supports an ECP or EPP connection.

- You must have an IEEE 1284–compliant cable.

- You must have ECP or EPP device drivers for your operating system.

If you meet these four criteria, you can enable parallel port attributes within the CMOS settings, as discussed in Chapter 7. Next, within Windows, perform these steps to ensure that your printer is using the ECP or EPP:

1. Select Start | Settings | Printer. Windows will open the Printers folder.

2. Within the Printers folder, right-click the printer you want to configure. Windows will display a pop-up menu.

3. Within the pop-up menu, select Properties. Windows will display the printer's Properties dialog box.

4. Within the Properties dialog box, click the Details tab. Windows will display the Details sheet.

5. Within the Details sheet, select the ECP or EPP port you desire from the Print To The Following Port pull-down list.

6. Click OK to close the Properties dialog box and to put your changes into effect.

Improving Performance of the Print Jobs You Spool

USE IT As you have learned, Windows spools the jobs you print to a file on the disk. If your system has multiple disks available, you should direct Windows to spool your jobs to your fastest disk. By default, Windows spools files to the path specified in the TEMP environment entry (which, unless you specify otherwise, points to the Windows/Temp folder). To change the path, you can place a SET command in your CONFIG.SYS file. Users normally place such entries within the AUTOEXEC.BAT file, however, you can issue SET commands from within either AUTOEXEC.BAT or CONFIG.SYS. By placing the command within CONFIG.SYS, the change will work under Windows 2000 as well. The following SET command directs Windows to use a directory on drive D to create temporary files (such as spooled files):

```
SET TEMP=D:\TEMP
```

After you make your change to CONFIG.SYS, you must restart your system for the change to take effect.

▶ NOTE

If the disk to which you are spooling your printer output is low on disk space, your applications may not be able to immediately spool the job and then return to perform additional processing. If your print jobs appear to slow down, check you disk to make sure you have sufficient disk space available. Many graphics artists print very large files that can often consume 100MB or more of disk space. Before you print large files, make sure your disk has available space to hold the files.

When you print a job, Windows lets you send the job to disk using one of two formats: raw or enhanced meta file (EMF). If your printer lets you select the EMF format for spooling, you will improve your printer performance. To select the EMF data format, perform these steps:

1. Select Start | Settings | Printer. Windows, in turn, will open the Printers folder.

2. Within the Printers folder, right-click the printer you want to configure. Windows will display a pop-up menu.

3. Within the pop-up menu, select Properties. Windows will display the printer's Properties dialog box.

4. Within the Properties dialog box, click the Details tab. Windows will display the Details sheet.

5. Within the Details sheet, click Spool Settings. Windows will display the Spool Settings dialog box.

6. Within the Spool Settings dialog box, select EMF from the Spool Data Format pull-down list and then click OK.

7. Click OK to close the Properties dialog box and put your changes into effect.

▶ **NOTE**

Depending on your printer type, the Properties dialog box may contain several options you can use to fine-tune spooling settings, as well as other options that will improve your printer performance. Take time to examine the options the Properties dialog box provides.

Use a PCL Driver for Better Performance

Today, most laser printers support PCL and some (the more expensive printers) have a PostScript processor. If you purchase a printer that supports and installs the printer's device drivers, the installation will often install several different device drivers, one or more for PCL operations and one for PostScript operations. Normally, a printer can process a PCL document much faster than it can process a PostScript document (the generic nature of PostScript and its advanced capabilities simply take the processor longer to interpret). In a normal office environment, most of the documents you print will not require PostScript support. As such, by selecting a PCL-based driver as the default printer driver (as opposed to a PostScript) driver, you will improve your printer performance. When you must print a document that contains PostScript, you can use the Print dialog box to select the PostScript driver to print the document.

USE IT   To select a PCL printer as a default printer, perform these steps:

1. Select Start | Settings | Printers. Windows will display the Printers dialog box.

2. Within the Printers dialog box, click the printer icon of the printer you want to use as the default. Windows will highlight the icon.

3. Select File | Set as Default.

Index

INTERNATIONAL CONTACT INFORMATION

AUSTRALIA
McGraw-Hill Book Company Australia Pty. Ltd.
TEL +61-2-9417-9899
FAX +61-2-9417-5687
http://www.mcgraw-hill.com.au
books-it_sydney@mcgraw-hill.com

CANADA
McGraw-Hill Ryerson Ltd.
TEL +905-430-5000
FAX +905-430-5020
http://www.mcgrawhill.ca

GREECE, MIDDLE EAST,
NORTHERN AFRICA
McGraw-Hill Hellas
TEL +30-1-656-0990-3-4
FAX +30-1-654-5525

MEXICO (Also serving Latin America)
McGraw-Hill Interamericana Editores S.A. de C.V.
TEL +525-117-1583
FAX +525-117-1589
http://www.mcgraw-hill.com.mx
fernando_castellanos@mcgraw-hill.com

SINGAPORE (Serving Asia)
McGraw-Hill Book Company
TEL +65-863-1580
FAX +65-862-3354
http://www.mcgraw-hill.com.sg
mghasia@mcgraw-hill.com

SOUTH AFRICA
McGraw-Hill South Africa
TEL +27-11-622-7512
FAX +27-11-622-9045
robyn_swanepoel@mcgraw-hill.com

UNITED KINGDOM & EUROPE
(Excluding Southern Europe)
McGraw-Hill Education Europe
TEL +44-1-628-502500
FAX +44-1-628-770224
http://www.mcgraw-hill.co.uk
computing_neurope@mcgraw-hill.com

ALL OTHER INQUIRIES Contact:
Osborne/McGraw-Hill
TEL +1-510-549-6600
FAX +1-510-883-7600
http://www.osborne.com
omg_international@mcgraw-hill.com